L.F.

The Connecticut Wits

THE UNIVERSITY OF CHICAGO PRESS
CHICAGO, ILLINOIS

*

THE BAKER & TAYLOR COMPANY
NEW YORK

THE CAMBRIDGE UNIVERSITY PRESS
LONDON

The Connecticut Wits

BY LEON HOWARD

Northwestern University

THE UNIVERSITY OF CHICAGO PRESS

CHICAGO · ILLINOIS

*The publication of this volume has been aided
by a grant from Northwestern University*

To

RAY HEFFNER

(1902–1942)

PREFACE

THE "Connecticut Wits" are known, by name, to everyone interested in the history of American literature;
but, although they have been the subject of numerous
essays and each of the more important ones has been given a
full-length biography, no complete account of their literary activities has ever been rendered. This book, accordingly, under-
takes to fill a gap in American literary history by telling the
story of their careers as writers rather than as men of affairs,
from their common beginnings before the Revolution to their
extraordinarily different ends during the early years of the
nineteenth century. Its emphasis is entirely upon their writings,
with no more attention to biographical detail than is made
necessary by a recognition of the fact that the men who wrote
books, and not the books themselves, were affected by the great
variety of changing cultural influences which makes this period
in American literature more interesting and important than any
of the literature it actually produced.

The entire group, as it is commonly identified, is not represented here. For upon close inspection the original "Pleiades of
Connecticut," as one essayist called them, increased in number beyond the familiar seven until they began to appear as two
distinct galaxies. The members of the two sets of wits were related by blood, temperament, and geography and by certain
superficial resemblances in their writings. But they were separated by the disparity of background which always distinguishes
a pre-war generation from that which immediately follows, and
this disparity made it impossible to treat the two groups as one.

If circumstances warrant, the younger wits may be discussed
later in another, smaller volume or in a series of articles. This
study is concerned primarily with the four older writers—
Trumbull, Dwight, Humphreys, and Barlow—who attended
Yale College before the Revolution and were sufficiently mature
to grasp the opportunities offered by the first burst of national
expansion.

Their story is told as a story, for in no other way did it seem
possible to give the fairly complete survey required to place any
one work in its proper perspective. The method proved to have
some advantages, even in the course of preliminary investigations, when it gave an unexpected meaning and interest to some
writings that at first glance had seemed dull and insipid, hardly
worthy of consideration. But it has made adequate documentation an economic impossibility. Too many minor points have
had to be investigated, too many byways explored, and too
many possibilities balanced and weighed for notes that would
bear any reasonable proportion to the text. Yet, in comparison
with the real need for such notes, page references for quotations
generally identified and citations of sources for elementary facts
seemed a superfluous gesture. Consequently, I have omitted all
footnotes and have substituted "A Check List of the Writings of
Trumbull, Dwight, Humphreys, and Barlow," which identifies
all editions quoted, and some "Bibliographical Notes," which
amount to short essays on sources of information not otherwise
indicated in the text for each chapter. From the latter I also
omitted references to standard editions of familiar authors, to
earlier discussions of the Wits which had not been particularly
informative, and to titles mentioned in the text in such a way
that they could be readily and adequately identified by con-
sulting such a standard reference work as the *British Museum
Catalogue*. On the whole, it seemed less undesirable to display
a certain reprehensible air of omniscience than to disguise it by
bibliographical boondoggling or to attempt its justification by
the elaborate judiciousness which Chaucer or Milton would demand but which might become intolerable when used on Timothy Dwight.

But the authority which might be given to the text by better documentation is a minor matter, for the most discouraging term that I could hear applied to this book would be the adjective "definitive." Its organization was determined by the desire to survey the seventy-five books and numerous miscellaneous compositions of the Wits in a way that would enable someone else to approach any one of them with more intelligence than I could direct at the lot, and it was written in the hope that it might encourage a more intensive study of these and other writings of this period. It might not have been finished at all during the past few years had it not been sustained by the impatient conviction that American students in general—immature and mature—were recklessly throwing away an invaluable heritage of experience by their failure to pay an adequate, serious attention to their own literature. The past is too vital a reality to be conjured away by the affectation of indifference to all but "eternal" values—yet it can be distorted and made noxious by being interpreted without the breadth and subtlety of understanding that can be supplied by literature which has had its original wealth of human associations restored by the investigations of scholars. It has been demonstrated, I believe, that a man who thinks he can be Caesar while the Goths are overflowing the North must pay a heavy penalty for the narrowness of his historical understanding; but it has not yet been shown that others may pay in equally hard coin for their attempts to be Jeffersonian democrats or Hamiltonian federalists because they have a similarly narrow perception of what they are trying to be. The literature of the past—rehumanized in the classroom by teachers with historical imagination and sound scholarship— has a place in the present world which even its professional advocates are slow to define but toward which, I hope, this study of four minor writers is a contribution.

The study itself grew—in spite, somewhat, of my own wishes —out of a more general interest in the intellectual life and the literary pretensions of America during the late eighteenth and early nineteenth centuries; and it was undertaken as a sort of test bore through the complex intellectual strata which make the exploration of this period as difficult as it is necessary to the understanding of later cultural developments in the United States. At the outset the knowledge and kindness of Professor Max Farrand provided me with materials for getting acquainted with the period which saved me a great deal of blundering effort; and the unfailing friendship of Professor Louis B. Wright, throughout, has been a source of stimulation which I hardly dare to estimate. Through them I am indebted to the trustees of the Henry E. Huntington Library and Art Gallery for the International Research Fellowship, without which the necessary investigations, in the Huntington Library and elsewhere, could not have been carried out. The Huntington Library has also earned a debt of gratitude for its resources, for the courtesy and helpfulness of its staff, and for the associations provided by an institution which is apparently unique in the way it throws its visitors into close intellectual contact with other scholars whose interests are not restricted to any time, place, or field of learning.

The officers and staffs of other institutions have been equally co-operative; and I wish to express my particular indebtedness to the following: the Yale University Library, the Library of Harvard University, the Library of Congress, the New York and Detroit public libraries, the Connecticut Historical Society, the Newberry Library, and the libraries of the University of Chicago, the Garrett Biblical Institute, and Northwestern University. It is to some extent ungracious to select two of these for special comment, but the Library Committee of Yale University has been extraordinarily generous in allowing me to use rare materials, and the director and staff of the Library of Harvard University went to unusual trouble in obtaining permission for my use of certain materials there. Among the many individuals who have assisted me in various ways are Mr. S. L. M. Barlow, of New York City; Professor Alexander Cowie, of Wesleyan University; Professor Stanley Williams and Mr. Norman Holmes Pearson, of Yale University; Professor Merle Curti, of the University of Wisconsin; Professor Florence Edler de Roover, of MacMurray College for Women, and Mr. Raymond de Roover; Captain George M. Riser, of the United States Army; Mrs. Josephine Waters Bennett, of Hunter College; and Professor James A. Work, of Wayne University.

As the work neared completion I acquired further obligations to the Research Council and to Dean Thomas Moody Campbell, of the Graduate School of Northwestern University, for several grants which enabled me to complete the manuscript perhaps a year sooner than otherwise would have been possible. Mrs. Wilda Miessner Stuart gave me invaluable help, both in research assistance and by a careful and intelligent review of the manuscript; and Mrs. Anna McTeer provided additional help with the manuscript while typing the completed version. Finally, President Franklyn Bliss Snyder of Northwestern substantiated his known interest in literary scholarship by the gratifying and admirably practical method of finding, in these troubled times, funds to assist in the publication of the finished work.

To all of them I am grateful.

L. H.

Evanston, Illinois
November, 1942

TABLE OF CONTENTS

PART I. THE POINT OF DEPARTURE

CHAPTER   PAGE

I. Yale College, 1763–78 3

PART II. "THE FLOWERY ROAD TO FAME"

II. John Trumbull 37

III. Timothy Dwight 79

IV. David Humphreys 112

V. Joel Barlow 133

PART III. DEAD ENDS AND NEW DIRECTIONS

VI. The Wicked Wits 169

VII. The Voice from the Hill 206

PART IV. THE WAYS OF THE WORLD

VIII. The Honorable David Humphreys 241

IX. Citizen Joel Barlow 271

X. President Timothy Dwight 342

EPILOGUE: BLAZED TRAILS

Epilogue: Blazed Trails 405

CHECK LIST OF THE WRITINGS OF THE CONNECTICUT WITS

A Check List of the Writings of Trumbull, Dwight, Humphreys, and Barlow 413

BIBLIOGRAPHICAL NOTES

Bibliographical Notes 429

INDEX

Index 443

xiii

PART I

The Point of Departure

CHAPTER I

YALE COLLEGE, 1763-78

I

DURING the decade and a half from 1763 to 1778 Yale College placed its stamp upon four young men who exhibited the signs of their common learning proudly for a while and then, under the pressure of temperament and circumstance, moved in different directions toward entirely different ends. The oldest, John Trumbull (1750–1831), became a judge of the Connecticut Superior Court and of the Supreme Court of Errors before he died in the western frontier town of Detroit. Timothy Dwight (1752–1817) lived out the better part of his life in New Haven, a minister of the gospel and the great president of Yale who guided the college through its first steps toward university status. David Humphreys (1752–1818) concluded an honorable diplomatic career as minister to Spain before devoting himself to the improvement of New England agriculture and the establishment of one of the first model industrial villages in the United States. And the youngest, Joel Barlow (1754–1812), as a special minister to Napoleon, died on the retreat from Moscow after having retired from his active career of business and politics in France during the first years of the Republic.

These four men were also, with the somewhat incidental collaboration of Lemuel Hopkins (1750–1801), the original members of a literary group known to posterity as the "Connecticut Wits." The label is the result of the most occasional and least substantial of their activities and is no more apt than a description of Shakespeare as a "sonneteer"; for the greater part of

3

their literary work represents a serious attempt to grapple with the aesthetic, intellectual, and social problems of one of the most important periods in modern history. They failed to achieve the sort of literature which gives pleasure to successive generations of readers; but in spite of their failure—and perhaps, in part, because of it—they illuminate an age which produced a revolution in literary taste and in social institutions. The inability of Timothy Dwight to make a successful application of psychological theory to literary composition serves as a foil for Wordsworth's accomplishment with a different system; and someone may yet show that the revival of classical rhetoric, with its emphasis upon the "means of persuasion" and its preference for the "lively image" over generalized description, had a happier effect upon some other poet than it had upon David Humphreys. The conflict between John Trumbull's satiric talent and his social environment clearly emphasizes a relationship between literature and society which was unusually important during his generation in America. And the clash between legalistic and humanitarian thinking which Joel Barlow experienced suggests one of the reasons for the intellectual turmoil of the era. But the suggestive implications found in the writings of the Wits are of less importance than the writings themselves. Composed by men who ranged as far afield and stayed as close at home, both intellectually and physically, as any of their contemporaries, they reflect most of the influences that operated in the United States when it was finding its place in the world and forming itself as a nation.

The career of each of the Connecticut Wits is interesting in itself, for each took a course which was followed, less eventfully in most cases, by other representative Americans in the late eighteenth century. But no other four men so perfectly reflected the change from a colony to a nation by taking their departure from such a common point and reaching such different ends. They were all born in small villages in or on the border of Connecticut, and they were all prepared for college in the studies of Connecticut ministers. The annual college commencement offered to each of them his first sight of a world broader and more stimulating than any he had imagined before. The crowds of learned visitors and rabble that overflowed New Haven, the procession of scholars, the literary exercises by the Bachelors in the morning and the Masters in the afternoon, and the visiting, dancing, and fireworks in the evening made the occasion seem at least as important as election day and even more exciting. At such a time the hopeful young candidate for admission became aware of the importance placed upon higher education in the colony. If he cherished any secret hopes for literary distinction, he could also see his future public and see it almost whole, for the college commencements brought together the only groups in America, of any considerable size, who shared a common intellectual background and a common interest in literary pursuits. The ordinary young man in Colonial Connecticut who took his pen in hand and addressed himself to the Muses may have dreamed of a public in London or even in Philadelphia, but the only audience of which he could be practically sure consisted of small groups of Yale graduates, ranging in age from seventeen to seventy, who were scattered throughout the colony and formed the reading public of each locality. Yale was not merely, as one contemporary described it, a place "to slick up your person and fill up your brain." It was a highly specialized institution in which students acquired the conventional points of view and basic assumptions necessary for communication with a public that had little time and less desire for novelty in thought or literature.

Accordingly, however different these Connecticut writers may have become after the Revolution opened up the world to their activities, their differences are most significant against the background of Yale College as they found it from 1763 to 1778: the formal course of study, the conditions under which it was pursued, and the supplementary studies which these conditions evoked.

II

The physical appearance of the college symbolized its impressiveness to the members of the Freshman class who entered with John Trumbull in 1763. Old College Hall, the largest building, was one hundred and seventy feet long and twenty-two wide, and it towered three stories, dormer windows, and a cupola above College Street. It provided sleeping accommodations for sixty-six students, a kitchen, and a hall which was used for dining and for assemblies during the school year and—when the doors were left unbarred—for dancing at commencement time. Although it was old and wooden and its sky-colored paint was not fresh, it made a brave show in the evening when it was fully illuminated for the pleasure of the annual visitors. Connecticut Hall, overlooking the town jail, was newer and all brick, a hundred feet long and three stories high, with dormer windows like those of the Old College. But the most elegant building of all was the newest—the brick Chapel, forty by fifty feet, with unfinished rooms for a library and museum on the second floor. It was not yet complete, but it had been dedicated during the preceding June and the auditorium authorized for use during the fall term; and plans were under way for finishing, by subscription, the steeple and for adding a spire that would rise a hundred and twenty-five feet above the ground. Except for the completion of the Chapel, Yale was practically unchanged in appearance when Joel Barlow graduated in 1778. The college block remained partly occupied by a number of unpretentious, miscellaneous smaller buildings; there was a continued demand for a decent fence around it; and the grounds revealed at each new commencement a bare, dusty need for the shade trees that were later to make them famous.

The curriculum was as dusty and, for the lower classes, as bare as the campus. Freshmen were advised by President Thomas Clap to study principally the tongues, arithmetic, and algebra; but the recitations were devoted almost entirely to the "tongues"—the Latin of Cicero's orations and of Virgil's *Aeneid* and, after a preliminary survey of Bishop Wetenhall's *Graecae grammaticae*, the Greek of the New Testament. Horace was the regular course of study for Sophomores, and further writings by Cicero for Juniors, although additional Latin authors might be introduced if the class made sufficiently rapid progress. On the other hand, a slow class might have one year's assignment carried over into the next and the college course reduced to the very minimum. It was customary to spend three entire years translating the New Testament from Greek into Latin; and even the candidates for Berkeley scholarships, who read the *Iliad* and were encouraged to read selected dialogues of Lucian, were provided with parallel Greek and Latin texts for the purpose. With most students the construing of classical authors appears to have gone slowly and inefficiently, for one of the ablest of Yale's eighteenth-century graduates reported his mortification, five years after taking his degree, at finding himself unable to read a line of Horace or to remember the Greek alphabet. Hebrew was also a theoretical part of the undergraduate course, but no attempt was made to teach it.

Progress in mathematics was an individual matter. The poorest students required instruction in some of the elementary branches of arithmetic, and all of them needed the elements of algebra and geometry before being introduced to natural philosophy in their Junior year. John Trumbull was unusual. Having passed his entrance examinations at the age of seven, he had completed the linguistic study of the first two years and had read Homer in Greek before entering. Accordingly, he was able to follow the president's advice to study mathematics; and he concentrated on algebra, geometry, and astronomy, probably under the direction of Tutor Richard Woodhull, who had been called to Yale a few months before because of his proficiency in those subjects. Woodhull, however, was dismissed in November, 1764, for his oversimplification of the doctrine of justifying faith and his criticism of established institutions; and Trumbull's further scientific study was left to the occasional direction of President Clap or of Naphtali Daggett, professor of divinity and pastor of the small College Church, who shared the president's interest in mathematical and scientific knowledge. All students learned the elements of natural science from Benjamin Martin's *Philosophical Grammar*, which, though compiled in 1735, remained a popular textbook in England and France as well as in America until near the end of the century. The *Grammar* consisted of an introduction to somatology, cosmology,

aerology, and geology, "treated in the familiar way of dialogue"
in order to facilitate recitation; and everything in it was guaranteed "easy to be understood" by the "youth of both sexes."
Yet for all this superficiality the atmosphere at Yale was sympathetic to mathematics and the sciences, and the president's
lectures before the student body often dealt with scientific
studies. Eventually, in 1770, a professorship of mathematics
and natural philosophy was established, and formal scientific
lectures became a regular part of the college exercises.

Although Sophomores may possibly have studied logic from
Isaac Watts's text, the only other classroom instruction certainly provided for the three lower classes was the Saturday recitations in divinity. Periodically the students recited the Westminster Confession of Faith, and between times the Freshmen
and Sophomores received religious nourishment from William
Ames's *Medulla theologiae*. Orthodoxy was conscientiously, if
sometimes ineffectually, drilled into them, and Yale went back
to the great period of Puritanism for texts uncorrupted by modern compromises with indifference or liberalism. Juniors were
allowed to turn from Dr. Ames to the *Compendium theologiae
Christianae* of Johannes Wollebius, who was especially recommended by the president as being "as good and sound as Dr.
Ames, and his Latin much more elegant." But students who
were still slowly parsing Tully may not have appreciated the
change.

If the Yale tutors allowed their students to dabble in the
shallows of learning during their first three years, the president
went to the other extreme and forced the Seniors far beyond
their depths. The final year of the college course was spent entirely in "metaphysical studies"—the philosophy of the mind,
theology, and moral philosophy. Locke's *Essay concerning Human Understanding* was the basic textbook, and the entire
Senior curriculum was bound together by reference to the epistemological system of the *Essay*. Of course, since Yale was, above
everything else, at the time an orthodox religious institution, a
more direct stress was placed upon historical revelation as a
source of knowledge than could be found in Locke; but there

was no tendency, within the curriculum, to question the empirical system. Students were encouraged to reason from God's Word and from experience, but intuitions were not formally recognized and the existence of internal "senses" was not admitted.

The careful consistency of philosophical theory may have been relaxed, however, in favor of the regenerate; for Jonathan Edwards' *Inquiry into the Freedom of the Will* was used as the text in theology, and the determined official approval of Edwards may have carried with it a tolerance of his insistence upon the preceptive powers of the moral sense after justification. Yet this point could hardly have been an important one. Yale, at this period, made no pretense at being a community of professed saints. Although the students were, on the whole, religious, they were allowed to attend either the Old or the New Light Congregational church in New Haven; and most of them kept their church membership at home, finding no occasion to invite the rigorous examination for admission to the strict college church. A large majority of them, in any case, found the fine points of Edwards' reasoning beyond their capacities and beneath their worry.

The Senior course most suited to the students' understanding, and the one most directly adapted to their needs, was that in moral philosophy. Yet, despite the compromise with the everyday world in this field of study, the old-fashioned notion remained that ethics was "mere paganism," and students were carefully warned that even the best ethical system fell short of the perfection upheld by religion. As a warning the Seniors were drilled in President Clap's own handbook, *An Essay on the Nature and Foundation of Moral Virtue*, which made three main points: first, that the nature and standard of moral virtue is a conformity to the "moral perfections" of God; second, that the obligation of man to such conformity arises, in one sense, from the divine nature of God which makes him the original and all-perfect standard, and, in another sense, from his declared will or law, emphasized by his sovereign power and authority; and, third, that divine revelation is the only means by which man can know God's perfections or the conformity of man's own dispositions and conduct. The definition of moral virtue, of course, was as old as Plato; and the exclusive reliance upon the Scriptures, as old as Protestantism. Both of these, President Clap evidently thought, might be easily accepted. The emphatic part of his treatise was the section devoted to the metaphysical nature of man's obligation. "Every rational Creature and moral Agent," he insisted, "is *obliged* to be perfect and conformed to God, in the highest and strongest Sense in which that Word *Obligation*, is ever used. And all those Obligations which arise from Self-Interest, Hope, Fear, Gratitude, &c. are but *low and faint*, in Comparison of this." He stoutly denounced those moralists who looked for the foundation of moral virtue and obligation in self-interest or self-love, benevolence, taste or some internal sense, reason, the moral fitness of things, or conformity to truth in the sense of facts and natural relationships.

Such a statement may have satisfied the orthodox conscience of President Clap and of his successor, Naphtali Daggett, but it was entirely too rarefied for the ordinary college student. Accordingly, the major part of the course was directed toward regulating the sinners rather than gratifying the saints; and the textbook adopted for that purpose was William Wollaston's *The Religion of Nature Delineated*, which could be understood, without too much mental strain, by the unregenerate majority. Wollaston had been criticized in Clap's *Essay* for his low definition of "moral virtue" as "conformity to truth"; but his book had, nevertheless, been selected as the best of the "many Treatises which contain good Rules of external Conduct." Whether Wollaston made a deep and lasting impression upon the minds of the students or whether his book was adopted because it so perfectly fitted the social environment of Connecticut cannot be determined. The alternative is, in any case, an entirely theoretical one; for parts of *The Religion of Nature*, at least, expressed in systematic form and so helped preserve an attitude of mind which was too deeply ingrained in Connecticut to be attributed to any single influence.

Indeed, Wollaston's system made a very proper study in a

colony which prided itself on the preservation of its steady habits. Although nominally a clergyman in the Church of England, the English moralist made no attempt to argue questions of formal theology but operated exclusively in the field of ethics left open by Edwards and dismissed arguments concerning human freedom with the succinct appeal to individual experience: "Up and try." His treatise was removed from the controversial realm of traditional doctrine by his definition of "religion" as simply "nothing else but an obligation to do . . . . what ought not to be omitted, and to *forbear* what ought not to be done." In other words, by the "religion of nature" or "natural religion" he meant ethics; and in insisting upon "conformity to truth" as his criterion of ethical action he defined "truth," in a catch phrase repeated over and over in the basic section of his essay, as "things as they are." By this he meant things in all their relationships: a man might be your enemy, but he was also a human being and a member of society; if you treated him simply as an enemy, your actions would not conform to the truth and thus would not be virtuous. The system made a well-informed, discriminating mind a prerequisite to ethical behavior; it encouraged a constant reference to "things as they are" and discouraged speculative innovations; and by its careful definition of "reason" as *reasoning*, it supported the Yale stand against heterodoxies that had already slipped into New England under the cover of loose terminology.

Wollaston's constant emphasis upon "matters of fact" and "things as they are" formed the basis of a practical philosophy so conservative that the ordinary well-bred Connecticut youth must have accepted it as the consummation of all proper ideas. For one thing, he taught the exact combination of independence of mind and deference to authority which was the peculiar (and, to outsiders, sometimes puzzling) characteristic of Connecticut democracy. The criterion of right reason and truth is private, he held:

One man can no more discern the objects of his own understanding, and their relations, by the faculties of another, than he can see with another man's eyes, or one ship can be guided by the helm of another. . . . . [But,] tho' I say men must judge for themselves, I do not say they must in all cases *act* according to their private and single judgments. In respect of such things as are private, and concern themselves *only*, or such as are left open and subject to every man's own sense, they may and ought; only preserving a due deference to them, who differ from them, and are known upon other occasions to have more knowledge and literature than themselves: but when a society is concerned, and hath determined any thing, it may be considered as one person, of which he, who dissents from the rest, is only a small particle; and then his judgment will be in a manner absorbed and drownd in that of the majority, or of them to whom the power of judging is intrusted.

Yale students, of course, were attending college in order to acquire the knowledge and literature that would command due deference from the mass and enable them to be intrusted with the power of judging. And Wollaston gave them grounds for a proper self-assurance when he declared that

he, whose faculties are intire and sound, and who by a proper exercise of his mind in scientific studies opens and enlarges its capacity, and renders his intellectuals active and penetrating; takes care to furnish himself with such leading truths, as may be useful to him, and of which he is assured in his own breast; and in treating any subject keeps them still in his eye, so that his discourse may be agreeable to them: I say, such a one is not in much danger of concluding falsely. He must either determine rightly, or soon find, that the subject lies out of his reach. However, he will be sensible that there are many things within his sphere, concerning which he may reason; and that there are truths to be found by the use of his faculties, in which he may securely acquiesce.

It would be difficult to find two statements that more accurately expressed the social philosophy and the theory of higher education that dominated Connecticut; and in another passage Wollaston expressed a simplified combination of attitude and idea which was to be echoed time and again by Yale graduates for two generations: "The reason why the *many* are so commonly in the wrong and so wretchedly misjudge things," he declared, is that "the generality of people are not sufficiently prepared, by a proper education, to find truth by reasoning."

On other subjects he was equally sound. His practical, matter-of-fact solution "Of the Obligations of imperfect Beings with respect to their power of acting" was thoroughly satisfactory to a generation wearied by theological controversy, especially perhaps to students who were reading Edwards on the will in order to satisfy the conscience of their president. Wollaston's representation of "Truths relating to the Deity" was acceptable enough, even though his proofs of these truths might be un-Calvinistic; the same might be said of his statement of "Truths belonging to the Private Man," which related to the immortality of the soul. On marriage and family relationships his doctrines were the boasted practice of Connecticut, and his theories of the nature of man and of society must have been altogether satisfactory—if not in their speculative content, certainly in the conclusions to which they led. One such conclusion, for example, was that a man in society should

consider *property* as founded not only in *nature*, but also in *law;* and men's *titles* to what they have, as strengthened by that, and even by his *own concession* and *covenants;* and therefore by *so much the more* inviolable and sacred: instead of taking such measures to do himself right, when he is molested, or injured, as his own prudence might suggest in a state of nature, to confine himself to *such ways* as are with his own consent markt out for him: and, in a word, to behave himself according to his *subordination* or place in the community, and to observe the laws.

These were among the last words read by a Yale undergraduate before he commenced Bachelor of Arts and set out to preserve the steady habits of Connecticut.

From this course of study, supplemented by the president's regular lectures on various subjects and by a supervised program of "disputations" or debates, a Yale Senior could receive a substantial intellectual training. He was offered a theology and a basic moral philosophy consistent with a clearly defined theory of knowledge and, in addition, a practical ethical scheme which could be adapted to his social environment without necessarily contradicting his fundamental beliefs. He did not have to take it, of course, for students had successfully revolted at the proposal of examinations before the end of the college course, and such was the "tenderness" of the final examination that the worst were usually able to "pass as smoothly and become as reverend as the best." Yet, if a boy possessed the faculty of strict self-discipline, he could be turned into a thoughtful man during his Senior year at Yale, even though he graduated—as Trumbull and Dwight did—at the age of seventeen.

III

Self-discipline was a necessary qualification, however, for the college was never in so confused a state as it was when the Connecticut Wits were resident undergraduates. President Clap was an obstinate and inflexible man. In the first years of his presidency he had been a strong opponent of the "enthusiasm" of the New Light converts in the Great Awakening and had gained, from a conservative legislature, a charter which made the college independent of all "visitation" from outside authority. As time went on, however, much of the enthusiasm disappeared among the New Light Congregationalists, leaving merely the orthodoxy of the old-time religion, while the Old Lights slipped into a new sort of halfway covenant between orthodoxy and social conformity. The president stood firm in his original principles, while his old enemies drifted toward him and his old friends veered away, with the result that by 1763 he found himself allied to a suspicious set of New Lights, in opposition to the embittered conservatives, and in the midst of a political squabble which echoed throughout the colony.

The period between the French war and the Revolution was, at best, one of ferment and change; and the president, denounced violently by his political enemies and distrusted by his friends, found himself without sufficient prestige to enforce the arbitrary discipline that was natural to him. Harsh laws against vice, extravagance in dress, and normal social activity antagonized the students. A rapidly decreasing student body, together with the lack of a subsidy from the general assembly, compelled a rise in tuition charges and made it impolitic to enforce the collection of fines assessable for absence from prayers and other collegiate actitivites. In addition, commons were poor, and students were developing the habit of dining in their rooms whenever possible, making a stolen chicken or homemade cheese the occasion for a celebration with wine or punch, followed by card-playing. After a supposed "poison plot" on April 14, 1764, and the following attempt by a student to have a "strong Physic" introduced for the second time into the food, the administration was forced to close the kitchen and brewhouse to everyone except the regular officers, waiters, cooks, and servants of the college.

Richard Woodhull, seconded by the other tutors, made an ingenious effort to curb the students' drinking by an appeal to patriotism in the autumn of 1764, getting a unanimous agreement among the scholars "not to Drink any foreign spirituous Liquors any more"; but Woodhull's good efforts were immediately brought to nothing by his dismissal in November for Sandemanian views. Tutor Ebenezer R. White was also dismissed for the same reason; and Jonathan Lyman, in Ezra Stiles's opinion one of the few "eminentissimi" tutors in the history of the college, resigned. Financial difficulties made it impossible to employ more than two tutors to take their places, and the offensive tests of orthodoxy required by the corporation made it difficult to get any good men. Punderson Anderson and Diodate Johnson, however, were finally brought into the office at the last minute, and the college limped through the year with about one hundred and twenty-five dissatisfied and demoralized students.

By the time the thirteen-year-old Timothy Dwight entered in the autumn of 1765 the college was approaching the worst of its evil days; and it was fortunate that Dwight, like Trumbull, had completed in advance the required course of study for the first two years. The merchant's son from Northampton broke his arm during the winter, was kept away from school by illness for several months during the spring and summer, and probably was sent home with the rest of the student body on July 1. But, at that, he did not miss much except some of the excitement. President Clap was attempting to instruct the eighteen Freshmen as well as the thirty-six Seniors, although he had little time to spend on them, and they were as dissatisfied with him as the middle classes were with their tutors. In February an organized attempt was made to force the president and tutors out of office. A paper, signed by the entire student body with two or three exceptions, was addressed to the corporation, bringing various complaints against the tutors, charging the president with being in his dotage, and accusing him of keeping them in ignorance of disciplinary laws, assessing ex post facto penalties, and refusing to publish an act granting appeals to the corporation "in respect to cases of serious discipline by the Faculty." While the paper was being delivered personally to the members of the governing body, disorders of various sorts increased until, by March 20, "all study was broken up" and there was a "general absence from prayers, especially in the upper classes." Tutors Anderson and Johnson resigned; and the corporation, meeting on April 22, two weeks before the spring vacation, dismissed the students. Professor Daggett was asked to act as tutor "as far as his circumstances will admit" until commencement; a list of six names for possible appointees was approved; and the alphabetical arrangement of future classes was voted in an effort to abolish the specific annoyances that grew out of the president's arbitrary "placing" of students according to social distinctions.

But conditions during the third term were even worse. President Clap had spent ten days riding about Connecticut in a vain attempt to find any competent man who would accept a position as tutor, and only about forty students returned to classes. Some of these were sent home by the president, who did not decide until the second day of the term to keep the college open. Although President Clap and Professor Daggett offered instruction to those who would attend classes, no attempt was made at discipline, and the friends of the college thought that it was "sinking into Contempt" and "ready to expire." The corporation met on the night of Monday, June 30, and continued meeting until Thursday afternoon. President Clap resigned, but the corporation prevailed upon him to remain in office through the fall commencement, since the students had already been dismissed for the remainder of the term. The Rev. Chauncy Whittelsey, a former member of the faculty, wrote to Ezra Stiles: "I am almost ready to weep: Alma Mater is truly in a deplorable Situation, and I fear will be ruined. . . . . ."

Trumbull's Senior year was one of drastic action in the college. The corporation met on September 10 and succeeded in appointing three capable tutors: Ebenezer Baldwin, Stephen

Mix Mitchell, and Job Lane. They had also been seeking a successor to President Clap; and, anxious not to jeopardize their independent control of the college by a refusal, they had attempted to determine the sentiments of various ministers who might competently fill the office. James Lockwood was finally offered the presidency, and the general assembly was petitioned for a grant of money to meet current expenses. Lockwood, upon consideration, refused the position; but the legislature began to take a sympathetic interest in college affairs, and a committee was appointed to investigate its needs and make recommendations. Although one member of the committee was sure that "the Reputation of the College was sunk," the group gave the institution "a most thorough Visitation," to which "their Reverences" of the corporation (who no longer had President Clap's aggressive leadership) "submitted, *Lamb like*," and made a report which was approved by the assembly. In recognition of the notoriously "slight Method of teaching the Classics" they required the college laws to be printed in English as well as in Latin; and they recommended that the existing system of fines be modified to "as few pecuniary mulcts" as possible, that the government of the college be "as near like paternal" as the circumstances would admit, and that the quarterly steward's bills should contain detailed disciplinary reports for the parents' information. In return, the assembly granted something over a hundred pounds for the current year and encouraged the expectation of annual grants. Professor Daggett was appointed president pro tempore at the October 22 meeting of the helpless corporation.

Professor Daggett was a well-meaning, clumsy man with no powers of discipline; but the new tutors, though young, were strong-minded and willing to take over the operation of the college. There were only about a hundred students in attendance, and some of that small number were expelled during the course of the year in a wholesome restoration of discipline. Others were reformed by good advice from men who meant business. Young Timothy Dwight, who was popular with the upper classmen and had been seduced into card-playing during his Freshman year, entered into that collegiate vice "with considerable ardour" when he returned to college as a Sophomore; but he was rescued by his cousin and tutor, Mitchell. Meanwhile the college was beginning to find itself. The new instructors were naturally unable to introduce any radical changes in the course of study, but they did attempt to make the work sounder and more satisfactory; and they encouraged an interest in belles-lettres, English composition, and oratory, which brought a new life into the college.

In September, 1767, Trumbull returned to New Haven as a Berkeley scholar and candidate for the Master's degree; Dwight, as a Junior, determined to settle down to a self-directed course of study far in advance of that regularly designed for his class; and David Humphreys entered as a fifteen-year-old Freshman from the parsonage at near-by Derby. The improved atmosphere was apparent from the beginning. The new arrangement of classes had gone into effect, and it was made clear that scholarship was the only road to distinction. After a few months of the new regime a member of Dwight's class wrote to Eleazar Wheelock: "There appears a laudable ambition to excel in knowledge. It is not he that has got the finest coat or largest ruffles that is esteemed here at present. As the class hence-forward are to be placed alphabetically, the students may expect marks of distinction put upon the best scholars and speakers." Dwight was the most remarkable illustration of this new ambition. Prayers began at 5:30 on winter mornings and at 4:30 in the summer, and he was getting up early enough to "qualify" himself to parse a hundred lines of Homer before these exercises began. Before the year was over this extra work by candlelight had caused an eyestrain that laid the foundation for the partial blindness which threatened him for the rest of his life; but, in the meantime, he had improved his handwriting to a copperplate quality and had begun a collection of church music. Spending fourteen hours a day "in close application to his studies" during his last two years as an undergraduate, he was settling down to the serious business of getting an education.

High standards of scholarship were not yet being forced upon the general run of undergraduates at Yale, but the admirable "passion" of emulation was being encouraged. The general assembly voted funds from an impost on rum to complete the library room in the new Chapel; and Ebenezer Baldwin, the youthful librarian and senior tutor, encouraged a more frequent use of the books. By the time Dwight was ready for his Bachelor's degree and Humphreys was ready for admission to the Junior class, the problems of discipline within the college were fairly well settled. The students were no longer given to overturning the president's "privy house" and breaking his windowpanes or to posting satirical letters in the college yard. President Daggett and the tutors were getting a better grip on their affairs, and political activities were beginning to provide a respectable outside means for the release of undergraduate energies. At the time of the Stamp Act the conservative corporation, anxious to play safe, had frowned on all revolutionary activity; and Joseph Lyman, of Trumbull's class, had been disciplined for an oration against Parliament. Opposition to the Townshend Acts, however, swept through the college. Dwight's class of 1769 voted to appear for their degrees in the homespun of their own country. Tutor Amos Botsford, a loyalist, probably looked coldly upon the resolution, and there were three or four dissenters among the twenty-six Seniors; but the class represented itself in the newspapers as unanimous. In spite of the fact that they had voted themselves more homespun than they could discover, the boys must have had an excited feeling of being in the midst of great events when they gathered for commencement and heard of the patriotic riots that had recently occurred in the town.

During the two years that followed, until Humphreys' graduation in 1771, there was further trouble over commons and some unpredictable confusion resulting from the accidental death of one of the tutors. But, on the whole, the college was reasonably quiet; and the new professorship of mathematics and natural philosophy (held by the Rev. Nehemiah Strong) improved the position of the faculty. Even the patriotic excitement died down until 1774. Trumbull and Dwight were appointed tutors in 1771, and they, with Joseph Howe, formed an unusually able group of instructors who kept the students occupied with their studies. For a while the spirit of education threatened to become dominant at Yale.

The threat had dissipated, however, by November, 1774, when Joel Barlow entered the Freshman class with a certificate of honorable release, as "a good Genius and Middling scholar," from Dartmouth. The preceding commencement program had included a public dialogue on "The Rights of America and the Unconstitutional Measures of the British Parliament," and by December some of the classes were voting to give up drinking tea until the duties were removed. Two months later a number of students were engaged in volunteer military training. The news of the Battle of Lexington, which arrived on Friday, April 21, so excited the undergraduates that all classes were broken up and the regular spring vacation began two weeks early. Soon after the opening of the new term an active British sympathizer in the Junior class was "advertised" on the dining-hall door for his references to "damned rebels," and his fellow-students publicly refused to associate with him. Shortly afterward, on June 28, the college patriotism reached its height when the undergraduate military company, led by Noah Webster playing on a flute, paraded before General Washington as he passed through New Haven on his way to take command of the American army at Cambridge. After a year of further drilling, which was subsidized by the citizens of New Haven, about a third of the graduating class went to war; and, when the prevalence of typhoid caused the dismissal of the lower classes before the end of the summer term, a number of undergraduates—including Joel Barlow—joined them. Whatever may have been Barlow's original intentions when he entered the Continental Army on Long Island, illness made him a summer patriot, and he returned safely to the college in the fall. The year, however, was more exciting than educational. The students were crowded four in a room because of the large enrolment and the recent razing of a section of the Old College; and it was difficult to obtain suffi-

cient food for the residents—who publicly complained, in a
broadside supposely written by Barlow, that they asked for
bread and were given beans. Classes were dismissed from December 10 to January 7, but with the opening of the new term
the food problem grew worse. The cost of board was raised;
yet by March 20 Colonel Jonathan Fitch, the college steward,
had already lost £100 on his year's agreement and was threatening to give up commons. Two days later President Daggett
gave the students an affecting speech in chapel, instructed them
to send for their horses, and announced that college would be
dismissed on the following Thursday. There was no immediate
expectation of assembling again in New Haven. Preparations
were being made to move the college library and philosophical
apparatus to a place of safety, and the scholars busied themselves with selling their possessions at half-price or less in an
effort to get rid of everything that could not be carried away in
saddlebags.

Adding to all this confusion was another student revolt
against the administration. Naphtali Daggett was never formally elected president of Yale, and he never took a strong
position of leadership within the college. The students had little
respect for him: they dreaded his sermons, referred to him frequently as "Tunker" and sometimes as "old damned Tunker,"
and treated him without reverence for his office or for his own
awkwardly well-meaning person. Of the able group of tutors
who had instructed the classes of 1771–74, Howe had left the
college, Trumbull had dissassociated himself from undergraduate affairs by becoming treasurer, and Dwight, who remained
in office, had become excessively ambitious. There is some evidence that the last, his head turned by the popular appreciation
of his real ability, gave his tacit encouragement to the revolt.
Barlow became deeply involved, with the result that, although
the various classes assembled in different places for another
year, he apparently spent only a month—or, at the very most,
nine weeks—in residence with the graduating class. He received
his degree and a place on the commencement program, for the
times did not favor an insistence upon academic standards; and

both the corporation and the new president (Ezra Stiles, who took up his duties in June, 1778, after Daggett's resignation during the preceding September) were anxious to smooth over their difficulties. But the Senior year, which ordinarily might mean so much in fixing the mental attitudes of Yale students, was for Barlow practically a total loss.

There had been some improvements in the curriculum between Humphreys' graduation in 1771 and Barlow's entrance in 1774. Instruction in mathematics had been formalized and greatly improved; the Sophomore course had been broadened by recitations from William Guthrie's *A New Geographical, Historical, and Commercial Grammar;* and an unemphatic gesture toward English composition had been made by the use, as textbooks, of Bishop Lowth's *English Grammar* and John Holmes's little catechism in rhyme, *The Art of Rhetorick Made Easy.* On the other hand, the study of divinity was simplified by the substitution of Thomas Vincent's handbook on the Shorter Catechism for the works of Wolleb and Ames. President Stiles also abandoned Edwards' *On the Will* as soon as he took office; but that act hardly affected Barlow, who missed most of the theological instruction anyway. It is difficult, in fact, to believe that Barlow got very much out of his formal college course at any time; and, with respect to the other Connecticut Wits, it seems possible to pay what undoubtedly would have been an acceptable tribute to most of their instructors by saying that the course of study did more to form their characters than to fill their minds. The dry, out-of-date curriculum at Yale, the poor morale within the institution, and the devitalizing effect of indifferent students upon classes conducted by the recitation method—such conditions made higher education, as planned by the college faculty, dull and unstimulating. The more alert and ambitious students were forced to seek release for their intellectual energies and satisfaction of their zeal for improvement outside the set program.

IV

The library was one means for going beyond the curriculum. Undergraduates were not allowed to browse in it at will; but the students of the sixties knew from President Clap's painfully made catalogue that, although the collection was by no means up to date, it contained many treasures. One shelf held the eleven volumes of Pope's Homer, Garth's *Dispensary* and his translation of Ovid, Gay's *Poems on Several Occasions, Hudibras,* and such more familiar books as *Paradise Lost, Paradise Regained,* and the Littlebury and Boyer translation of Fénelon's *Telemachus.* In addition, it held other, curious, volumes, placed at the very last in the order of reading recommended to students: *Don Quixote,* Addison's *Cato,* the plays of Otway, the tragedies of Nicholas Rowe, and the comedies of a man whom President Clap called "Wickerly." The *Spectator,* the *Guardian,* and the *Works* of Addison were probably the volumes most frequently recommended from this shelf, although the senior tutor who served as librarian might sometimes stimulate an extra interest in belles-lettres by offering his charges another edition of the *Spectator* which had been the gift of Sir Richard Steele himself. The shelf immediately below was probably even more exciting to a literary-minded student: On it could be found Dryden's Virgil, Juvenal, and *Fables;* Creech's Horace; Blackmore's *Creation;* and individual collections of poems by Denham, Cowley, Prior, Oldham, Waller, and Lord Lansdown. There were also the four volumes of Motte's *Miscellanies* of Swift and Pope, which also contained poems by Gay and Dr. Arbuthnot; a two-volume collection of poetic *Miscellanea* attributed to Pope by the catalogue; the *Tatler* in four volumes; Rowe's edition of Shakespeare; Steele's plays; and Hughes's six-volume edition of Spenser's *Works.* Various folio volumes of belles-lettres were also scattered about among the heavily "serious" books that made up the greater part of the library: the 1602 Chaucer, the 1616 *Works* of Ben Jonson, Montaigne's *Essays,* Blackmore's three epics and his paraphrase of the Book of Job, the works of Du Bartas, and Sir Thomas Browne's *Vulgar Errors.* Blackbourne's comprehensive folio edition of Bacon's *Opera omnia* had an impressive place on the shelves, and among the four books on American history was the great folio which was to captivate Joel Barlow: Sir Paul Rycault's translation of Garcilasso de la Vega's *The Royal Commentaries of Peru*. In addition, the collection included six octavo volumes of Ben Jonson's plays, Gay's *Fables*, *The Dunciad*, the essays of Sir William Temple, Shaftesbury's *Characteristics*, Dr. Watts's poems and hymns in separate volumes, as well as his *Miscellaneous Thoughts in Prose and Verse*, Fontinelle's *Dialogues of the Dead*, William Vaughan's *The Church Militant*, Governor Roger Wolcott's *Poetical Meditations*, and *The Turkish Spy* in eight volumes. Among the duplicate sets were copies of *Paradise Regained*, *Hudibras*, and the large paper edition of Hughes's Spenser; and for the idly curious were the *Athenian Mercury* for 1691 and the *Athenian Oracle* in three volumes and a supplement. Practically no additions had been made to the library since it was catalogued in 1743, but, at that, it was the best collection of modern literature in New England.

Neither the ordinary students nor the exceptional Connecticut Wits, however, became fully acquainted with it during their undergraduate years. The authority of "solid" learning was great; and even such studious lads as Trumbull and Dwight were induced (during the impressionable years before they graduated at seventeen) to spend their surplus intellectual energies improving themselves in languages and mathematics. The less studious, and more mature, Humphreys and Barlow had other diversions which were more pleasing and less expensive than reading books. For the Yale collection, unfortunately, formed a rental library; and, with charges running up to sixpence a folio volume, the fees for reading the books mentioned above would amount to considerably more than the cost of a year's tuition. This was prohibitive to thrifty, hard-pressed students who were sometimes known to economize by copying out their required textbooks by hand. A resident graduate student, however, who was subject to no tuition charges and could expect his second degree at the end of three years even though he engaged in no formal study, might make extensive use of the library. Trumbull, by his own report, did so; and he exhibited the results in the self-conscious erudition of his Master's oration in 1770. Dwight also remained in New Haven after graduation, but he was teaching in the Hopkins Grammar School for the first two years and was a Yale tutor thereafter and, accordingly, had less time for miscellaneous reading. Barlow spent almost two academic years in resident graduate study. Humphreys, alone among the Connecticut Wits, abandoned Yale entirely after taking his Bachelor's degree; and it is significant that his early work is almost entirely free from the influences of those books in the Yale library which so greatly affected Trumbull and, to a lesser degree, Dwight and Barlow.

Among the English poets not represented in the Yale library, Thomson and Gray, though much less admired, were almost as popular as Pope; and the fluent melancholy of Shenstone's *Elegies* held an inordinate attraction for young people. Students who were inclined to revolt against the old-fashioned curriculum at Yale, however, were acutely conscious of their own "modernity"; and Trumbull, at least, among them turned with some enthusiasm to the most spectacular of recent English poets— Charles Churchill, whose brilliant outburst of satire in the early sixties attracted more immediate attention than any other literary event during Trumbull's school days. Yet Churchill was too restricted and, at times, too gross in his subject matter to be wholly respectable or entirely admirable; and, although his style aroused the passion of emulation, his greatest influence may have been indirect: during the decade before *The Deserted Village* swept through America as the outstanding example of strictly contemporary vrese, Churchill's work seemed to prove the vitality and essential modernity of Swift and Pope. Thus his effect, in part, was to focus the attention of his admirers upon an earlier school, just as T. S. Eliot was later to stimulate, among the less self-reliant of his contemporaries, an excessive regard for the peculiarities of the school of Donne.

For these young Yale graduates did not move at ease among the English poets. The atmosphere in which they lived was academic and preceptorial, and they were culturally too inexperienced to trust whatever literary sensitivity they may have possessed. They wanted guides. And in no way did they give a better demonstration of their anxiety for guidance than in the

unanimity with which they turned to the most recent and superficially "modern" system of literary criticism—that of Lord
Kames, whose *Elements of Criticism* had appeared in 1762 and
had become so well known in New Haven that it was being advertised in "a new and cheap edition" by 1770. The attraction
which Kames held for Yale students with belletristic inclinations may be readily understood. His system combined the
charms of the novel and of the familiar. It was, in its elabora-
tion, different from anything they had seen before. Yet to students who had been introduced to literary criticism through
Addison his aesthetic conclusions appeared trustworthy, and to
boys thoroughly drilled in Wollaston his method of approach
seemed practical and sound.

Both Wollaston and Clap, of course, had warned their readers against the sort of "common sense" employed by Kames;
but the warnings had been directed against other moralists and
were too incidental to carry any weight in opposition to the
Scottish critic's impressive insistence upon "things as they are,"
rather than rules and theories, as the basis for literary criticism.
Kames explained his position in the Introduction to his book.
It was the author's intention, he declared, to apply to the fine
arts "some remarks and observations drawn from human nature, the true source of criticism"; and he described his plan as
an attempt "to ascend gradually to principles, from facts and
experiments, instead of beginning with the former, handled abstractly, and descending to the latter." In all this Kames was
in matter-of-fact conformity with the scientific bias which students acquired at Yale and in reasonable accord with their practical approach to ethical problems. He admitted, however, that
"though criticism be thus his only declared aim . . . . all along
he had it in view, to explain the nature of man, considered as a
sensitive being, capable of pleasure and pain." And as he
shuttled through his incidental explanation of "the nature of
man," he created a conceptual wedge so simple that it was
easily driven into the intellectual integrity of his New England
readers, whose minds were immediately stimulated but at the
same time exposed to a great many delusions. Kames's conclu-

sions concerning human nature were in no way difficult to understand: "Independent altogether of experience, men have a sense or conviction of a common nature or standard," he held; and, furthermore, "we have a conviction, that the common nature of man is invariable not less than universal: we conceive that it hath no relation to time nor to place; but that it will be the same hereafter as at present, and as it was in time past; the same among all nations and in all corners of the earth."

Young men who had been taught from childhood to admire the simple and steady habits of Connecticut already, perhaps, had a lurking conviction that the common nature of man was an invariable standard from which people in other times and places deviated only under the vicious influence of temporary "fashion"; and they may have been unconsciously relieved to find this conviction asserted without regard to the experience which neither they nor their teachers possessed. Furthermore, Kames's loose use of such technical terms as "common sense" and "taste" probably made them seem so familiar that many readers were readily able to forget Locke's *Essay* and accept the conclusion of the *Elements of Criticism:*

> Upon a sense common to the species, is erected a standard of taste, which without hesitation is apply'd to the taste of every individual. This standard, ascertaining what actions are right and what wrong, what proper what improper, hath enabled moralists to establish rules for our conduct from which no person is allowed to swerve. We have the same standard for ascertaining in all the fine arts, what is beautiful or ugly, high or low, proper or improper, proportioned or disproportioned. And here, as in morals, we justly condemn every taste that swerves from what is thus ascertained by the common standard.

In any case, Trumbull, Dwight, Barlow, and perhaps even Humphreys began their own literary careers under the guidance of this book.

The intellectual simplicity of Lord Kames was in perfect accord with an influential body of Connecticut opinion which, from outside, was beginning to attack the tough consistency of the Yale Senior curriculum. The conservative opposition to the so-called "New Divinity" was based in part upon a belief that many human minds were incapable of following accurately the fine points of theological reasoning. "Have you lately read

Mr. Edwards *on the Will*, and considered his Scheme?" Chauncy Whittelsey asked Ezra Stiles in June, 1768, adding:

It is recited at our College, and is, at present, very much the Standard of Orthodoxy, in these parts, and to the Westward; and I fear the Consequences, least Deism, if not Atheism should ensue. His Scheme, in proportion as it is admitted by any Mind, will, I think, unavoidably lessen the odiousness of Sin, in the view of the Mind; yea, if the Mind is not habitually virtuous before, will wholly destroy the Sinfullness of Sin. If his Scheme is received for true Orthodoxy, some, I fear, will become Deists from their dislike of what is said to be orthodox Christianity; others will become practical, if not speculate Atheists by substituting, in their minds, Fate instead of Deity, or necessity in the Room of an Intelligent Moral Governor.

Whittelsey reflected the resistless tendency of the eighteenth century to synthesize morality and theology into a single system; and he feared that young students of Edwards, in so far as they could follow his logic, or through a misinterpretation of his conclusions, would be led by this tendency into practical disregard for religion. While Edwards' "Book was regarded as a critical, metaphysical Treatise upon a dark, abstruse, unimportant Subject," he said, he "was little concerned about it." But the pastor of the First Church at New Haven believed that doctrinal controversy produced more heat than light, and he was antagonized by Edwards' insistence upon the "utmost importance" of his subject. For his own part, he implied a willingness to dismiss Edwards' refined notion of liberty as a "mystery" and so approach the practical problem of moral freedom through the injunction "Up and try!" Stiles later signified his acceptance of this attitude by his removal of the treatise from the list of textbooks as soon as he became president of the college in 1778; but, in the meantime, Yale students were signifying their own reaction against finespun reasoning by frequent arguments concerning the limitations of the human mind in regard to matters of theology.

Of all the new books coming into New Haven during the seventies, the one most in keeping with the current distrust of theological reasoning and the growing fear of extremes was James Beattie's *Essay on the Nature and Immutability of Truth*, first published in Edinburgh in 1770. A direct attack upon the

"sophistry and scepticism" of David Hume, it also criticized
Descartes, Locke, and Berkeley, stressed the limitations of human reason, and denounced school logic and metaphysics. Beattie based his argument upon the "common sense" of mankind
with which readers of Lord Kames were already familiar, and
so drove the wedge of loose thinking still further into the intellectual solidarity of Yale. The easy concept of a "common," internal sense proved an attractive one to young men who were
bored with John Locke and Jonathan Edwards and with too
much close reasoning. It reduced the demands made on their
youthful minds and their limited experience. It gave them the
courage of their ambitions. And, so, it played an important role
in directing their early intellectual activities.

Yale students in this period, however, were not encouraged to
spent all their time in their studies. The primary business of
the college was preparation for the learned professions, especially the ministry and the law; and a considerable emphasis
was placed upon public speaking. Formal supervised disputes
were held once or twice a week as a regular part of the college
exercises, and the best debaters were frequently given the privilege of demonstrating their talents publicly as a part of the
commencement exercises. Covering a wide range of subject matter, the debates undoubtedly stimulated an interest in new
ideas; but there are only occasional records to indicate how particular individuals may have been affected by these activities.
For example, Joel Barlow is reported to have "disputed inimita-
bly well," during the short term of his Senior year, upon the
question "Whether the Destruction of the Alexandrine Library,
and the Ignorance of the Middle Ages Caused by the Inunda-
tion of the Goths and Vandals, Were Events Unfortunate to
Literature." But there is no record of his arguments or even
of the side he defended. Only the reappearance of the general
question, treated somewhat elaborately, in a poem begun soon
after graduation enables one to guess that he took the optimistic negative side, and under the stimulus of this undergraduate
debate developed—out of the commonplaces of his time—a theory of progress which he regularly reaffirmed in his later life.

Other students may have had similar experiences, although no evidence remains; and it is observable that the more carefully prepared commencement orations of Trumbull and Dwight affected their other literary work during the years that followed.

The literary societies also encouraged activity on the platform rather than in the study. They alone at Yale encouraged an interest in the drama. President Clap's administration had in effect, and probably would have enforced, a legal fine against students of three shillings for acting in a play and one shilling for attending a performance. But by the second year of President Daggett's regime the societies were giving dramatic performances in secret meetings at private houses; and Timothy Dwight, as a Senior, was prevented only by accident from acting in *The Conscious Lovers*. During the Revolution theatrical exhibitions became open, despite the fact that the First Continental Congress had passed a resolution against such indulgences. On the afternoon of March 17, 1777, Barlow's society, the Brothers in Unity, celebrated its anniversary in the college Chapel with a public performance, before a large and splendid audience, of a tragedy, followed by Cumberland's *The West Indian*. Professor Strong was beginning to worry about the effect of such displays, "calculated only to warm the imagination"; and Jonathan Welles, a tutor in the old days under President Clap, confided in Ezra Stiles that the "College wants Regulation for they have left the more solid parts of learning and run into Plays and dramatic Exhibitions chiefly of the comic kind and turned College . . . . into Drury Lane." Trumbull as treasurer, Dwight as a tutor, and Barlow as a student all saw the literary societies take on a new and almost sprightly character in an effort to warm the imagination without regard to the solid parts of learning.

Stage performances, however, were given only at the anniversary meetings. The ordinary gatherings of the literary organizations were more conventional, and at least one of the Connecticut Wits acquired an enduring devotion to rhetoric as a result of his extracurricular training for the platform. The impulse toward industry and serious-mindedness which characterized Yale when David Humphreys entered in 1767 was reflected by the Freshmen. Since they were not admitted to the one literary society which existed at the time, they formed their own organization for training in oratory. Accordingly, with the encouragement of one of the tutors and the assistance of an older student, they met two evenings a week for study and practice. Each member pronounced "a speech about the length of a declamation"; and the others, "in the most friendly manner, without the last disrelish," criticized his performance. They purchased John Ward's *System of Oratory* for their "director" and at the close of each meeting read one of these Gresham College lectures, digested it, and made an effort to incorporate its recommendations in their next deliveries.

This intense, voluntary study of Ward was adopted as a means of practical training for the bar or the desk, but actually it served as a course in English composition. For less than half the lectures in Ward's two volumes dealt primarily with composition for oral delivery. A majority of them dealt with general matters of style, and some with such particular matters as the writing of epistles, dialogues, and history. The theories advanced were entirely classical, derived largely from Aristotle, Cicero, and Quintilian, supplemented by other Greek and Latin rhetoricians and only occasionally illustrated by references to such moderns as Erasmus, Milton, and Addison. From this system the students learned of the various passions to which the three types of discourse could appeal; the distinguishing marks of the low, sublime, and middle styles; and the sixteen internal and three external commonplaces by which a discourse could be arranged and through which the speaker could achieve copiousness. But particularly they learned of the three parts to "general elocution." "Elegance," which respected the purity and clearness of the language, and "composition," which regarded the turn and harmony of the periods, were treated with comparative brevity. Ten of the fifty-four lectures, however, were devoted to the subject of "dignity" and explained the various kinds of tropes and figures that played so great a part in the sublime and middle styles. The students may not have remem-

bered many of the four primary and eight secondary tropes that
Ward discussed or the thirty-seven different figures which he
named, defined, and illustrated; but those who had literary inclinations were evidently impressed with the possibilities of or-
namental writing in spite of Ward's frequent warnings against
the error of treating common subjects in "florid and pompous
language." It is more than a coincidence that the Linonian Society, which evidently was formed from this group during the
following year, was hailed as David Humphreys' particular
glory and that Humphreys' earliest ambitious verse was almost
wholly dominated by classical rhetoric.

V

The story of Yale, as it affected the Connecticut Wits during
their student days, is not a simple one. But one fact should be
clear: although the college was generally hailed as the "great
Nurse of learning," it did not play the same mother's part for
all its foster-children. Trumbull, Dwight, Humphreys, and Barlow all took the same educational path when they left their village homes for the opportunities of New Haven; and there they
all developed their literary ambitions and were inspired to follow what the first of them called "the flowery road to fame."
If the formal curriculum could have had its way with them,
they would have been turned out as nearly alike, intellectually,
as any four young men could be. But circumstances, as well as
temperamental differences, interfered. Trumbull and Dwight
were very young when they entered Yale, and they came to the
college in time to be thoroughly exposed to a systematic body
of conservative ideas. When conditions within the college forced
them to go outside the classroom for their real education, they
turned first to the conventional "solid" learning and then to
modern literature. Humphreys, slightly more mature and less
keen intellectually, was touched lightly by the solid learning,
turning instead to the superficial brilliance of the rhetoric and
failing to remain in residence for the profitable years of graduate study. Joel Barlow, old enough to be a soldier and a Sophomore at the same time, was graduated intellectually footloose.

Comparatively well exposed to the speculative tendencies of his period, he received little of the corrective offered by the Senior curriculum; and he attended Yale when even the younger undergraduates were more interested in events outside than those inside the college. Common associations and interests kept these four men fairly close together in their literary activities for a decade after 1778; but, when the pressure of chance and circumstance forced them in different directions, along less flowery roads to fame, these directions seem to have been determined, at least in part, by the different nurture they had received from their Alma Mater.

PART II

"The Flowery Road to Fame"

CHAPTER II

JOHN TRUMBULL

I

THE young Jack Trumbull who entered Yale in 1763 was already known to the learned citizens of Connecticut. Six years before, a few months after his seventh birthday, he had perched behind the Rev. John Trumbull's saddle and jogged from his native Westbury to New Haven, where he passed "a good Examination" for entrance in college, only to be returned home to await the greater maturity of thirteen years. His remarkable achievement had been, in part, the result of opportunity, for during the preceding year his father had taken time off from his sermons, horse-trading, and real estate dealings in order to prepare a young man for college, and the son had shared in the systematic study that became a part of the household routine. To a greater degree, however, this childish erudition was the result of a precocity which had exhibited itself even earlier: he had learned to read and had begun memorizing verses at the age of two, and by the time he was four he had read the Bible through and was composing original verse for himself.

He was not a healthy lad, and he perhaps had spent too much time in reading and dreaming—a "dupe of imagination," as he later recalled his childish self, who combined "the most extravagantly romantic feelings" with "an innate attention to the minutiae of criticism." In any case he was wise beyond his years, too well read to be overcome by the college course of study and too much apart from the crowd to fall into the usual thoughtless indiscretions and enthusiasms of his schoolfellows.

37

His literary talent both stimulated and provided an outlet for his feeling of superiority to his environment. While cultivating a slightly sardonic attitude toward the world about him, he also held to a youthful belief that genius could command its own reward; and, as he looked down his curving nose at the dulness of his associates, he apparently came to the conclusion that the reward would not be hard to get.

Yet he was not excessively ambitious. Socially he stood second in the class he entered, and he probably wanted nothing more from life than a place near the top in the stable little world of Connecticut. The world itself needed only a few minor improvements in order to be satisfactory enough. During his nine years at Yale, as student and teacher, he found many things to irritate him; but, when he finally struck out in his chosen profession before the bar, he showed little eagerness to join such colleagues as John Adams and other members of the Continental Congress in a violent revision of the foundations of their society. The Revolution left him cold. He took the patriotic stand proper for a Trumbull, of course; but he avoided service in the American army and spent the autumn that tried other men's souls enjoying a honeymoon with the former Sarah Hubbard of New Haven. The progress of the invading British forced him to change his residence twice during the war—from New Haven to Westbury and thence, in 1780, to Hartford. There he settled for the greater part of his life, devoting himself to a professional career that was occasionally disturbed by ill-health and enlivened by literature but was never in any way sacrificed to the art from which he had expected so much in his early youth.

II

Like that of most other young poets, Trumbull's early verse was fashioned by his reading. He is said to have begun writing before the age of five, and the single stanza which has been preserved from that early period shows that he began to lisp in the numbers of Dr. Isaac Watts, whose *Divine Songs for Children* he had memorized the year before. He had versified half the Psalms before he was nine and may have experimented with

the manners of other poets he read before entering college—
Milton, Thomson, Dryden, and Pope—although no records of
any such experiments remain. Later evidence, on the whole, indicates that, of these poets, Milton made the deepest and
most lasting impression upon his mind and Pope exercised the
most immediate charm over his style. The most interesting of
the surviving bits of his undergraduate verse are in Pope's
manner: some complimentary lines "From a Pastoral," apparently addressed to his brilliant young classmate, Joseph Lyman,
and an ironic "Introduction to a Satirical Poem." All such fragments, however, are entirely casual and show merely that Trumbull had a talented interest in writing which might quickly develop under the proper stimulation.

The stimulation seems to have come during the first months
of his graduate study, when he began to browse in the Yale library and turned up Motte's *Miscellanies* of Swift, Arbuthnot,
Pope, and Gay. The fourth volume, especially, contained poems
that were quite unlike the lyrics of Dr. Watts, and they seem to
have completely fascinated the young man of seventeen. Most
of them were in octosyllabic couplets, few were serious, and
many were characterized by a fluency and a flippant irreverence
for some of the conventionally serious things in life which appealed to Trumbull's nimble wits and his early feeling of superiority. Swift, in particular, did not take even poetry seriously;
and Trumbull's response to this attitude was immediate: he
took a suggestion contained in "The Progress of Poetry," combined it with the classical description of the Delphic oracle, and
produced his own vulgar account of "Poetic Inspiration," which
revealed for the first time his natural aptitude for satire and for
the octosyllabic couplet. Both the style and the attitude of the
Miscellanies continued to dominate Trumbull throughout the
remainder of the academic year. Although he apparently did
not write much poetry during that time, three of the four fragments that survive are in sardonic octosyllabics in which the
youthful Calvinist made scandalous remarks about the behavior of Adam and Eve, cited *Pilgrim's Progress* as an example
of unrestrained fancy in composition, and exhibited Swift's "hu-

morous biting way" in an irreverent comment on funeral orations. Trumbull, however, had not quit experimenting. He was
reading widely, and in the two volumes of Prior in the Yale library he discovered the meter for his short satiric poem "On the
Philanthropy of the Author of *Tristram Shandy*." He also tried
serious, elevated heroic couplets in an epitaph on Phineas White.
But his further reading gave him additional reasons for admiring
Swift: Prior, and possibly by this time Churchill, taught him a
greater appreciation of the Dean's fluency in the octosyllabic
couplet, and Samuel Butler's *Hudibras* emphasized the humorous possibilities of multiple rhymes, although Swift's own "innumerable" and "consume-a-Rabble" continued to represent an
ideal which the American poet did not approach until nearly
twenty years later. Accordingly, his most ambitious poem of
1769 was his "Epithalamium" on the marriage of his tutor,
Stephen Mix Mitchell, in August of that year—a poem supposedly burlesquing such "ancient Epithalamia" as Spenser's
on his marriage and Claudian's on Honorius and Maria but actually less reminiscent of its supposed models than of Swift's
"Cadenus and Vanessa." It circulated widely in manuscript and
proved so easily the most popular of Trumbull's early poems
that its success undoubtedly encouraged the author's natural
tendency toward clever, personal satire.

Before his "Epithalamium" achieved its modest but real success, however, Trumbull abandoned verse as a medium of expression and began to experiment with prose. Inevitably his
mind turned to the Addisonian essay. The attraction may have
been easy publication, for the newspapers of the late sixties
could never be sure of filling their columns with "domestic and
foreign advices" every week, and any American who could produce a weekly sheetful of thoughts for the benefit of his contemporaries was assured of a regular appearance before the public. Accordingly, Trumbull—assisted, if report may be trusted,
by the younger Timothy Dwight—began a series of essays
called "The Meddler" in the *Boston Chronicle* for September 4,
1769. The first paper was cautiously imitative. It proposed a
series of "moral, critical and poetical" essays "upon miscellane-

ous and mostly unconnected subjects," promised to avoid "party spirit and personal satire" as well as anything tending toward immorality, and described the club to which the author belonged. Thomas Freeman, John Manly, Esq., and the innocent clergyman were all types familiar to readers of Steele's description of the Spectator's club; and Jack Dapperwit, another member, was even identified as a descendant of Will Honeywood's friend Tom. Most of the ten numbers were more original than the first, but none of them reflected any great degree of individuality. They were sprightly, readable, and mildly amusing, fulfilling the rather colorless promises of the introductory number. The subjects of satire and the literary criticism which appeared in them anticipated the major themes of Trumbull's later work, but the style was affected and artificially flavored with allusions made familiar by the literature of Queen Anne's England rather than by personal experiences in Brother Jonathan's Connecticut. On the whole, the series might have been taken by an unsympathetic reader as proof of the observation made in the second number: "I believe that there are very few persons, who have not, at some part of their lives, been ambitious of shining in the character of Wits: but it happens unfortunately for most of them, that a good share of genius is necessary to attain it."

Trumbull's own "genius" was for more personalized satire than the prospectus for "The Meddler" permitted, and the essays may have been brought to an early conclusion because he was temperamentally incapable of carrying out the plan he had announced. On the other hand, the Whig-baiting *Chronicle* may not have seemed a wholly desirable medium of publication in the days of the Townshend Acts—especially since the local *Connecticut Journal and New-Haven Post-Boy* appeared willing to save the young author both trouble and postage by publishing his effusions. Whatever his reason or combination of reasons might have been, Trumbull brought "The Meddler" to an end on January 18, 1770, and introduced "The Correspondent" to a local public on February 23.

The new series was much more aggressive than the old. It

promised to be "rigorous against vice and folly," to encourage "merit and virtue," and to provide good advice. The first number made no proposal to avoid "personal satire" but, on the contrary, introduced a note of acerbity in reference to a recent contributor to the *Connecticut Journal* and, in general, was more direct and pointed than "The Meddler" had been. The second paper gave vigorous promise of an abundance of satire directed against Connecticut dignitaries. Under the pretense of describing "a curious set of manuscripts" that he had at his disposal when the fountain of his own wit was in danger of exhaustion, Trumbull mentioned a series of subjects upon which he planned to engage. Most of them were directed at controversial divinity and exaggerated emphasis upon "metaphysics." They included "A New System of Logic, or the Modern Art of Reasoning," "Creeds and Catechisms made and mended; by D. D. and Company," "The Art of Second Sight; shewing an easy and infallible method of discovering, by intuition, any person's character, principles, practices, state of body and soul, future happiness or misery, &c.," and "The Art of Quarrelling; being a curious and entertaining History of some late transactions." Others were to satirize ambition and the art of climbing, affectations in the practice of oratory, and the pious opposition to dancing. The titles suggest innocuous imitations of essays in the *Miscellanies;* but contemporary readers easily identified "D. D." as the Rev. Joseph Bellamy, newly a Doctor of Divinity from Aberdeen, whose arguments against the halfway covenant had raised a storm of controversy in 1769, and they recognized "The Art of Second Sight" as a proposed attack upon the followers of George Whitefield and of the New Light Congregationalists, who insisted upon assurance of salvation as a prerequisite to church membership. The others promised to be equally personal, undertaking a bold invasion of the sacred precincts of controversial divinity which could not be made in generalities. The barbed nature of the promised writings was made clear in the concluding sentences of the second essay:

I should be very sorry to draw a character that would hit nobody's likeness; and am desirous of the reader's assistance in making the application; with this direction only, that I would have him try it first on himself, and if he finds it does not suit him, he hath my free permission to apply it to his neighbours. I would also, for their own sakes, caution all those who find their own character drawn, to take as little notice of it as possible, and remember that although the arrow be shot at random, among the flock, yet the bird that flutters is certainly known to be wounded.

The irony and the aggressiveness of the beginning of "The Correspondent" promised something vigorous in the literary, non-political essay in America; but they did not promise an easy life for John Trumbull.

The first two numbers of "The Correspondent" may have created enough excitement to warn Trumbull of his danger and cause him to turn aside momentarily, in his third essay, with a mildly ironic defense of dulness as a means to happiness. But two weeks later he began his intensely satiric "New System of Logic" in a series of four papers. The whole system, he maintained, was erected upon two pillars:

1. That the common sense and reason of mankind is so weak and fallacious a guide that its dictates ought never to be regarded.
2. That nevertheless there is nothing so great that it can surpass, or so perplexing that it can entangle the understanding of a true metaphysician.

And he emphasized "the great enmity" that "hath in all ages subsisted between metaphysicks and Common Sense." The style of this and the three following papers seems to have been modeled on Swift, with Trumbull occasionally deviating from pure irony in such discussions as his comment on the way of a modern philosopher with the Gordian knots of reasoning:

Thus if they are caught in a dilemma, by arguments drawn from the natural world, they easily can elude the trap, by answering that there is no such thing as matter. Some very wise heads have lately projected to annihilate spirit in the same manner, and leave nothing but bare ideas to flutter up and down like atoms throughout the universe: which scheme I do hereby annex and tack on to this new system, as a refinement in metaphysicks, to which it would be difficult to find a parallel.

Certain "errors" in the modern world were pointed out, such as a belief that "a certain Dutch divine [William Ames, whose *Medulla* was the standard of orthodoxy at Yale] many years ago extracted the whole marrow of theology, and served it up in a small Latin treatise," and a notion that the pure gold of revela-

tion could pass current without the alloy of metaphysical interpretations. The author admitted "a gross deficiency as to technical terms and Latin phrases" in the science of divinity, in comparison with law and medicine; but he believed that the metaphysical writers had "invented a method, which though not
quite so grand, is attended with almost equal advantages"—
that of splitting words into so many definitions and meanings
that "the secrets of the science are as well concealed, as if you
cloathed them with the choicest Latin." He presented a sample
title-page for controversialists, which burlesqued recent publications by the Rev. Samuel Hopkins and Dr. Bellamy; represented "our controversial writers" as arguing that "Truth sometimes breeds contention; therefore whatever breeds contention
is Truth"; and concluded with the statement that he might have
illustrated every point from certain "famous writers" but that
he knew their modesty, wanted to avoid everything personal,
and so was "willing to leave them in the hiatus, which is no im-
proper emblem of that gulph of oblivion, towards which . . . .
both they and their writings are speedily hastening."

The Correspondent closed his career, for the time being, on
July 6 with a Swiftian "defense" of slavery, which was flippant
in some of its references to the Old Testament patriarchs but, on
the whole, much safer than the exercise of irony upon controversial divines. Dwight was probably consulted about the essays in this first series, but it is doubtful that he had any part
in the actual writing of them. At any rate, Trumbull was held
responsible for them all and, as a result, gained, at least in his
own opinion, a "set of Enemies" that cost him over a year of
quietude before he could get "pretty well" rid of them. He felt
that he had to fight his way through the world, and, from this
time on, the prospect of stirring up public antagonism gave him
pause. Yet his second experience as an essayist had been a vital
one. He had cultivated Swift's biting way in prose as well as in
verse and had discovered that he could not be both vigorous and
impersonal in satire of any sort. Furthermore, he had developed
a point of view with respect to the philosophical and religious
controversies of his age. His attitude was that of the easygoing

majority of educated men in Connecticut; but in expressing it
publicly he found himself in painful conflict with the most aggressive controversialists of the time. Since it suited his disposition neither to keep quiet nor to get into trouble, these essays really started him on that curious alternation of valor and
discretion which was to be characteristic of his literary career.

In June, 1770, after the fourth of the "New System of Logic"
essays, discretion was dominant. The foolhardy personal satire
of "The Correspondent" had antagonized the New Light ministry even more than the indiscreet octosyllabics of the "Epithalamium" had antagonized his former tutor. Trumbull, accordingly, began to cultivate a less irritating style and a more ingratiat-
ing subject matter. In verse he experimented with the heroic
couplets of Pope's Homer, translating the story of Orpheus and
Eurydice from the fourth book of Virgil's *Georgics* in preparation for an original poem on the "Prospect of the Future Glory
of America," which he was to deliver at the September commencement. Both poems proved too inflated for the subjects
they treated; and, although they represent the earliest verse
Trumbull preserved in his *Poetical Works*, he apparently found
the experiment unsatisfactory and made no serious attempt to
continue writing in that style. In prose also he turned away
from satire. The commencement poem was actually the peroration of an elaborate *Essay on the Use and Advantages of the Fine
Arts* which he delivered as his Master's oration; and the *Essay*
itself was so tactful and impersonal that it marked a full retreat from the Swiftian manner of "The Correspondent." Most
of it was merely a polite exhibition of the author's erudition in
English literature, but a few paragraphs are of unusual importance because they marked the introduction into Trumbull's
writings of a point of view and body of ideas that were soon to
dominate his mind and renew his valor.

The significant portion of the address is Trumbull's attack on
the Yale curriculum from a point of view which he made clear in
the second paragraph:

The knowledge of Languages, Mathematics, Metaphysics and philosophy,
undoubtedly deserve to engage the attention of the greatest Genius. . . . . But

when they are carried beyond a certain point; when they are of no advantage to the common purposes of life; when they are employed upon questions which human Reason can never with certainty determine, they degenerate into meer speculations of amusement, and become no farther valuable, than as they serve to enlarge the mind, clear the understanding, and entertain us in the hours of leisure from the important avocations of business.

His audience, who were fully aware of the conditions then existing at Yale, may have made a particular application of his words; and those who were aware that the speaker was also "the Correspondent" may have expected a sharp series of ironic local allusions from the platform. Trumbull, however, resisted any such impulse that might have come to him and followed up his statement with a judicious plea for a different sort of study—that of the fine arts and especially "polite literature," which he thought was "perhaps too much undervalued by the public, and neglected by the youth in our seminaries of science." His supporting arguments, as befitted his audience, were primarily moral. "Mankind in the present state," he pointed out, "are extremely liable to be led away by mean and sordid vices, to be attached to low enjoyments of sense, and thus degraded almost to a level with brute creation." Such a conception of man was a commonplace in Connecticut, where the church and state combined against inherent wickedness; but Trumbull's further words were, to his particular audience, neither commonplace nor orthodox:

As that increasing thirst for happiness, which is the universal spring of action, must have some object for its gratification; the Divine Being, to raise us above these low desires, hath implanted in our minds a taste for more pure and intellectual pleasures. These pleasures have their source in the fine Arts, and are more especially found in the elegant entertainments of polite Literature. They enoble the soul, purify the passions, and give the thoughts a better turn. They add dignity to our sentiments, delicacy and refinement to our manners. They set us above our meaner pursuits, and make us scorn those low enjoyments, which perhaps we once esteemed as the perfection of human felicity.

With these words the young graduate of Yale College, who had been trained in the self-abnegation of Clap's ethics, the predestinarianism of Edward's theology, and the empiricism of Locke's philosophy, stood before an audience with a similar intellectual background and advocated belletristic study on the grounds of self-interest, self-determinism, and innate aesthetic "taste." Furthermore, as proof of his argument he appealed to the common experience of "all persons of judgment" who had felt "an openness of heart and an elevation of mind" and had become "more sensible of the dignity of human nature" after "reading a fine Poem, viewing any masterly work of Genius, or hearing an harmonious concert of Music." Trumbull's inoffensive style and the discreet subordination of his ideas to his erudition, however, seem to have kept his hearers from becoming fully aware of the intellectual revolution that was beginning to take place at Yale.

Trumbull's part in the revolution was a direct result of his extracurricular reading, for the ideas in his Master's *Essay* were taken bodily from Lord Kames's *Elements of Criticism*. Kames had introduced his subject with a protest against "the common method of education; which, after some years spent in acquiring languages, hurries us, without the least preparatory discipline, into the most profound philosophy." He had insisted that "mathematical and metaphysical reasonings have no tendency to improve social intercourse: nor are they applicable to the common affairs of life." And in advocating the formal study of literature as "a great support to morality," he insisted that "the author of nature, by qualifying the human mind for a succession of enjoyments from the lowest to the highest, leads it by gentle steps from the most groveling corporeal pleasures, for which solely it is fitted in the beginning of life, to those refined and sublime pleasures that are suited to its maturity." Furthermore, he had specifically maintained that such progress was not "governed by unavoidable necessity" but by the desire for "happiness." Accordingly, he had been able to claim that

a just taste in the fine arts, by sweetening and harmonizing the temper, is a strong antidote to the turbulence of passion and violence of pursuit. Elegance of taste procures to a man so much enjoyment at home, or easily within reach, that in order to be occupied he is, in youth, under no temptation to precipitate into hunting, gaming, drinking; nor, in middle age, to deliver himself over to ambition; nor, in old age, to avarice.

In his constant appeals to a common, internal "sense" Kames provided Trumbull with the method of persuasion that he used on his audience, and he also supplied the young orator with the patriotic arguments he used in maintaining that "Learning and Glory walk hand and hand through the world." But the Scottish critic's most important contribution to the new intellectual climate of Yale was his identification of aesthetic and moral perceptions as the activities of an "internal sense" which was common to all men, immediate in its judgments and therefore independent of elaborate reasoning processes.

During the following year at Wethersfield the ideas which Trumbull had touched upon in his commencement oration continued to nag at his natural indolence. Like many respectable Americans of the time, he was extremely sensitive to the dangers of deism; and, as the "New System of Logic" essays had shown, he was afraid that the elaborate logic of theological controversy might cause a reaction, among plain thinkers, into skepticism. He re-read the *Elements of Criticism*, and as a result, produced "A Critical Dissertation on Descriptive Poetry"; but he seems to have been concerned primarily with the value of the common-sense philosophy as a support to orthodox religious beliefs. Accordingly, the chief product of his voluntary rustication was a series of "Speculative Essays," emphasizing the limitations of human reason, especially in matters of theology. Reasoning, he held, was valuable in connection with the affairs of common life; and it could usually, he tacitly agreed with Wollaston, determine the morality of one's own actions. Yet, when an exaggerated estimate was placed upon its ability to solve the mysteries of natural or moral philosophy, the result might be skepticism, philosophical idealism, systematic dogmatism, or any of the many varieties of religious infidelity. Trumbull's own opinion was plain:

> I think then we may with certainty conclude that Reason was never given us to be employed in framing metaphysical Systems and enquiring into those mysteries, which God has not seen fit clearly to reveal. Our mental capacity is as circumscribed as our Sight. With regard to things that lie so near, as to concern our own actions, we see with sufficient exactness, and by proper attention are in little danger of material error. But when we turn our eyes towards the heavens, our views are lost in the immensity of space. Here and there a bright Star appears amidst the darkness; others more distant are dimly seen; the remotest fade into the sky. We can neither discern their figures, measure their distances, or understand their nature.

Therefore, he decided that no "work would be of more advantage to the world, than an Essay on the limits of human Reason" and apparently set himself upon such an enterprise.

A number of Trumbull's European contemporaries had, in effect, the same notion; and only the fact that he directed his essays against the reasoning of Connecticut divines instead of the logic of David Hume prevents them from appearing clearly in the tradition to which they belong. The series—which exists only in rough, manuscript draft—represents an interesting attempt to unite all the intellectual impulses existing in Yale College during the sixties into a single coherent system. It reflects the distinction between God's perfect knowledge by genesis and man's imperfect way of knowing by analysis which is to be found in Ames's *Medulla*, the antagonism toward scientific dogmatism exhibited in Martin's *Philosophical Grammar*, and the popular indifference toward the problems which had seemed so important to Jonathan Edwards. Yet it also reflects the attitude Trumbull had begun to clarify under the influence of Lord Kames and reveals the method of attack used by most of the Scottish philosophers of the common-sense school. Trumbull, of course, was only twenty-one years old when the essays were written, and he had no disposition toward systematic thinking; but back of his philosophical gropings may be seen a coherence that had never before appeared in his work. He evidently realized that modern skepticism was the logical outgrowth of the epistemology of John Locke and so began his series with an attempt to find a weak point in Locke's empiricism. He agreed with his Scottish contemporaries in classifying the Berkeleian philosophy as "skeptical," and he also agreed with them in the respect with which he treated Locke and Berkeley while indicating his opposition to their theory of "ideas." Finally, he advanced his greatest objections to excessive logic by the Scottish method of reasoning from consequences. The *Elements of Criticism* alone could not have been responsible for such parallels, and Trumbull's other contacts with the Scottish philosophers are obscure—for there is no evidence that he had read, before composing the essays, James Beattie's *Essay on the Nature and*

Immutability of Truth; in Opposition to Sophistry and Scepticism,
which had appeared the year before in Edinburgh and offers the
closest parallel to Trumbull's method.

Although Trumbull attempted verse only occasionally during this period away from New Haven, most of the fragments
that have been preserved, except for a few parodies, were in
octosyllabics. He was gradually achieving an easy, natural
medium of poetic expression; but he distrusted it, for pieces "in
the Hudibrastic" had a tendency to become barbed, and Trumbull was weary of satire. In November, 1770, he marshaled his
arguments against such writing in a forceful letter to his undergraduate friend, David Humphreys, and two months later he
addressed an octosyllabic note to the same friend in which he
referred to his "dormant" muse. By the middle of the summer,
however, his satiric talent had been revived in order to close a
quarrel in which he had become involved "in vindication of
some young ladies, who were injured, as he believed, by malicious slanders." The consequent "Advice to Ladies of a Certain Age" resembled Swift's "The Journal of a Modern Lady"
in its unpleasant representation of autumnal gossips and the
viciousness of tea-table slander; but, in being addressed to a
couple of particular "remnants left of ancient time," it was both
sharper and less effective than Swift's more general satire. For
Trumbull, with all his attraction to Swift, did not share the
Dean's preference for individual men above mankind. In the
various trials of his genius in verse, as in prose, he was frequently led away from his general purpose by his dislike for specific
individuals: fools rushed in his head, and so, like Pope, he
wrote against them more than against their folly. Yet, when he
tried to imitate Pope—as he did in the fragmentary, undated
"Characters" in the manner of the *Moral Essays* and perhaps in
the unpublished (1771) "Epistle Addressed to Mr. I. J."—his
verse was colorless and ineffective. Soon after he left New
Haven, an anonymous and unduly enthusiastic admirer had addressed him as the "immortal Son of immortal Pope"; but, by
the time he returned in the autumn of 1771, he was probably
well aware that his proper medium for satiric expression was the

octosyllabic couplet of Swift rather than the heroic verse of
the *Dunciad*.

Except in this single, unpublished poem of "Advice," however, Trumbull resisted his satiric impulses, directing his major
poetic efforts in 1771 toward serious verse. Circumstances, as
well as discretion, governed his activity, for in May he had received news of the accidental drowning of his former roommate
and close friend, Buckingham St. John, who had been serving
as tutor at the college. The occasion, of course, demanded an
elegy, and Trumbull began one in blank verse which suggests,
by its morbid imagination, its Miltonic word order, and its
prosody, that the author had turned to Blair's "The Grave" for
proper guidance in his melancholy task. But neither the form
nor the manner of Blair proved adapted to his purpose and
talent. Accordingly, when the poem was published in the form
of a broadside—probably at the time of the college commencement—it appeared in the elegiac quatrains made popular by
Gray and Shenstone, with signs of particular indebtedness to
"An Elegy Written in a Country Church-Yard." *An Elegy, on
the Death of Mr. Buckingham St. John*, however, was more highly figurative than any similar work by Gray or Shenstone.
Trumbull may have been led astray by rhetorical theories concerning figures suited to express the passions, especially in the
elaborate prosopopoeia which introduced the "white-robed
shade" of St. John for the purpose of describing the vanity of
his youthful expectations and the circumstances of his death;
or he may have found a precedent for his ghostly figure in
Pope's "Elegy to the Memory of an Unfortunate Lady" or in
his varied reading from the classics. Whatever the particular
influences under which the poem was written, Trumbull seems,
for a while, to have devoted himself wholeheartedly to the melancholy muse and to have thoroughly saturated himself in
elegiac verse.

Such verse, indeed, was appropriate to his mood, especially
after he was appointed to St. John's position at Yale and given
his room to occupy. The feeling of youthful disappointment
which he had attributed to the "shade" of his friend was also

his own; and, although he did not become a permanent admirer of Shenstone's elegies, he seems to have adopted for a few months the English writer's fondness for a poetic type which could throw "its melancholy stole over pretty different objects" in a style "simple and diffuse, and flowing as a mourner's veil." Accordingly, in December, 1771, after brooding over the unavailing hopes of his friend St. John, his own disappointments in literature, and the failure of a student love affair to survive his departure for Wethersfield, he produced another elegy, "On the Vanity of Youthful Expectations." In it, more than in the elegy on St. John, he showed the influence of Gray in tone and phrasing, although he also revealed a recollection of "Il Penseroso" in his "Hence, gaudy Flattery" and his invocation to Sadness. While writing the poem, Trumbull was wandering, in his imagination at least, "o'er hallow'd ground" of a country churchyard; and his general theme was that he would have been happier had fate fixed the limits of his silent way in "life's sequester'd shade," so that he could never have turned aside to such scenes of "gilded pomp" as he had presumably dwelt in at Yale. Thus his poem was an affected but serious answer to Gray's, in which the young American regretted that "wild ambition" e'er had swelled his heart and led him away from "cheerful toils and rural sports." His first twenty-one years had been lived in vain.

At this time no observer could have prophesied the literary road which Trumbull was to take. His only published verse consisted of the patriotic conclusion to his commencement oration and the elegy on St. John. His published prose was limited to the oration and to two short series of essays, one of them lacking in color, the other in the sort of discretion which seemed requisite to literary survival in Connecticut. His most intimate friends were aware of his talent for verse satire and his considerable skill "in the Hudibrastic." Yet all their urgings that he attempt further work in a satiric vein seemed to have no effect: Trumbull had formally stated his arguments against satire to one of them, and he was giving every indication of a devotion to serious and even melancholy verse. But beneath the surface of appearances lay signs that Trumbull had accomplished a good deal during these few years of youthful effort. He had read and experimented enough to discover that his real spontaneous talent was for Swift's "way" in both prose and verse, and he had come to admire Swift's style more than that of any other writer. He did not yet know whether he was to be a writer primarily of verse or of prose, not was he quite sure that a man could write in Swift's manner and at the same time become a prosperous citizen of Connecticut. These doubts were later to affect seriously his literary career. Yet he had freed himself from other equally paralyzing doubts which affected his contemporaries. He had developed a point of view which enabled him to attack things that irritated him with an assured confidence in both his soundness and his modernity. And, in spite of all his good intentions, he was soon to be irritated. He might brood on the vanity of youthful expectations for a while, but it was not in his nature to envy for long the mute inglorious Miltons of a country hamlet, and he was not designed to spend his life in the valley of discretion. When he moved back to Yale College, he was returning to an environment to which he already had certain well-defined objections. Inevitably he was to express them.

III

In spite of his feeling of melancholy, Trumbull found his return to New Haven stimulating, for he entered upon the duties of tutor in the company of two other young men—Joseph Howe and Timothy Dwight—who shared his own interest in belles-lettres and were as anxious as he to improve the cultural atmosphere at Yale. Within a few months he was discussing with still another friend two projects that he had in mind. One was an outgrowth of the ideas he had developed in his "Speculative Essays"—a satiric attack upon deism and deistical writers in the general manner of Swift's *Tale of a Tub*. The other was a verse satire on dulness with particular reference to the method of education at Yale and the proceedings of the clergy. The first, he was inclined to feel, would attract attention and do good only if published in England; and he may have been diverted from it either by the unexpected difficulties of narrative prose or by the discovery, after an experimental attempt, of a temperamental inability to write sharply against any individual who was a complete stranger to him. The second proposal was obviously more attractive; but he described himself as being "a little afraid" to speak his mind freely on the subject, since he did not want to "make a new set of Enemies" after having "pretty well got rid of" those made by "The Correspondent." Nevertheless, he had written part of the poem by January, 1772, and was sending it around for his friends' opinions.

His friends, as usual, encouraged him to be valiant rather than discreet, and the first part of *The Progress of Dulness* was completed in time to make a "noise" at the 1772 commencement. It was Trumbull's most ambitious work up to date, and for it he seems to have reviewed most of the "Hudibrastic" poems he particularly admired: "The Progress of Poetry" (which he had already imitated), "Phyllis: Or the Progress of Love," "Cadenus and Vanessa," and others by Swift; "Alma: Or the Progress of the Mind" and various verse tales by Prior, whose "easy elegant humour and natural description" delighted the young tutor; and *The Duellist* and *The Ghost* by the more modern Churchill, whom Trumbull liked particularly for the "sprightliness and vivacity" of his imagination, the rapid flow of his thoughts, and his "bold and glowing" expression. Later Trumbull declared that in his own writing he had proposed the poems of Churchill and the "strong descriptive painting" of Swift as his models, having found it difficult to imitate Butler's peculiar kind of wit for more than a few lines at a time. His self-conscious awareness of his literary antecedents, however, did not mean that he was a mere imitator. From his unusually broad background of English verse he was able to select those qualities of expression which were best suited to his own talent and so produce a poem that was as individual as any other of its kind.

The first part of *The Progress of Dulness* included all the matters Trumbull had mentioned in his original reference to it:

"the rare adventures of Tom Brainless; shewing . . . . how he went to College, and what he learned there; how he took his Degree, and . . . . how afterwards he became a Great Man and wore a [clerical] wig." The author's subject, as he also declared in the Preface, was "the state of the times in regard to literature and religion," about which he had been "prompted to write by a hope that it might be of use to point out, in a clear, concise, and striking manner, those general errors, that hinder the advantages of education, and the growth of piety." The poem itself epitomized Trumbull's intellectual and literary development up to the time at which it was written. It represented the spontaneous emotional reaction of an exceptionally bright young man against collegiate dulness as he had experienced it as a student and as he was seeing it again as a tutor. It advocated the educational reforms which he had tentatively suggested in his Master's oration. It reflected the point of view and theory of human nature which he had developed under the influence of Lord Kames and had strengthened during his period of reading and meditation at Wethersfield. And it was composed in the style which Trumbull had found to be his most natural and spontaneous means of expression. No other American poem in the eighteenth century represented—in Trumbull's own phrase—a more perfect "tryal" of the author's "genius."

The major thesis of *The Progress of Dulness, Part I*, as Trumbull expressed it in the Preface, was simply a more aggressive expression of his earlier echo from the *Elements of Criticism*, "that the *meer* knowledge of ancient languages, of the abstruser parts of mathematics, and the dark researches of metaphysics, is of little advantage in any business or profession in life." The octosyllabics illustrated the thesis, directed it particularly toward the ministerial profession, for which the college course was primarily designed, and made a few practical suggestions for educational reform. The greatest fault of higher education, Trumbull clearly believed, was its failure to pay attention to the fine art of literature, and he advocated the introduction of modern literature and composition into the curriculum as a substitute for some of the study of ancient languages. He urged the

study of belles-lettres with the same moral arguments he had
borrowed from Lord Kames in his Master's *Essay*—because
every "nicer" and "nobler" art "mends" or "shows a passage
to" the heart—and he directly echoed the Scottish critic in such
lines as those objecting to the blind veneration of ancient writers and insisting upon an explanation of both their faults and
their beauties. His attacks upon logic and "metaphysics,"
mathematics, and the pedantry of classical studies frequently
offered close parallels to arguments that had only recently been
advanced in Scotland by Kames and Beattie; and, in general,
the educational satire in the poem, while certainly pertinent to
Yale, represented a reaction against conditions that were neither
wholly local nor limited to America.

The representation of the effect of such education, however,
was directed entirely against conditions in Connecticut; and,
although Trumbull curbed some of his impulses toward "humor" that he considered "a little too local," he certainly did not
exercise the caution which the "New System of Logic" essays
should have taught him. Tom Brainless, the hero of the poem,
became a minister who illustrated the author's opinion that "in
numberless instances throughout these colonies sufficient care
hath not been taken to exclude the ignorant and the irreligious
from the sacred desk"; and his career as a fairly common type
of clergyman gave the major point to much of the local satire.
Supplementing this theme was another which grew out of Trumbull's firm and frequently expressed belief that

the virulent controversies of the present day concerning religions, or in many
cases, meerly speculative opinions, savouring so highly of vanity and ostenta-
tion, and breathing a spirit so opposite to christian benevolence, have done
more to hurt the cause of religion, than all the malice, the ridicule, and the
folly of its enemies.

Trumbull, in effect, was attacking the majority of the Connecticut clergy either for being dullards or for tolerating dulness and
the minority for exercising their intellects to the disadvantage
of their religion. And, in addition, he was making a severe attack upon the beloved Alma Mater of the only readers he could
expect to have, offering, in the Preface, an invidious comparison

between their college and the one in a "neighboring province,"
which, of course, was Massachusetts. He had expected to publish the poem in Hartford, but actually it appeared in New Haven at the time of the annual commencement. The abandon-
ment of discretion had been complete, and Trumbull never rode
his Pegasus more valiantly than he did in the late summer of
1772.

Sensitive though the people of Connecticut were to any criticism of the established order, they might have passed over all of
Trumbull's strictures had he delivered them in a diffident manner and in a generalized language. But the poet, with his usual
emphasis upon the fool rather than his folly, could not be contented with a safe indefiniteness. His description of Tom's
licensing is typical:

> Mean while, from every distant seat
> At stated times the clergy meet.
> Our hero comes, his sermon reads,
> Explains the doctrine of his creeds,
> A licence gains to preach and pray,
> And makes his bow and goes his way.
>   What though his wits could ne'er dispense
> One page of grammar, or of sense;
> What though his learning be so slight,
> He scarcely knows to spell or write;
> What though his skull be cudgel-proof!
> He's orthodox, and that's enough.

This was less a fictitious account of an imaginary dullard than a
charge directed against every formal association of ministers
in Connecticut; and the impertinent young man who had just
passed his twenty-second birthday emphasized it with solemn
advice to his elders:

> Ye fathers of our church attend
> The serious counsels of a friend,
> Whose utmost wish, in nobler ways,
> Your sacred dignity to raise.
> Though blunt the style, the truths set down
> Ye can't deny—though some may frown.

Such lines invited more than frowns, however, for Trumbull
made his more sensitive readers uncomfortably aware that
many of his allusions were directed at specific individuals. If

he later felt it wise to sterilize a reference to controversial dialogues with a note that "writing in dialogue was then a fashionable mode among the controversial divines," it was because he was no longer concerned with the opinions of the Rev. Joseph Bellamy, at whose halfway-covenant dialogues the original allusion had been unmistakably directed. Trumbull's earliest readers recognized such allusions as easily as they could substitute "Bellamy" and "Hopkins" for the blanks in the lines on metaphysical quibbling in divinity; and, since by long-established habit "swains ceas'd to laugh aloud, when near" a minister, many good people in Connecticut were shocked by such irreverence and chose to be annoyed rather than amused.

The Progress of Dulness must have been a sharp appetizer for the annual gossip feast at New Haven. The first edition was soon exhausted, and Trumbull planned a second. In the meantime the authorship was an open secret, and violent attacks began to fall upon the young tutor. Nevertheless, he published a second edition of the first part by the end of the year; and a second part, *An Essay on the Life and Character of Dick Hairbrain*, appeared early in January, with a vituperative Preface dedicating the new work "To the Envious and Malicious Reader" who had condemned the first part and might be expected to deal in the same way with the second. In this Preface, Trumbull confessed that he had experienced the pleasure, on the first publication of his poem, of hearing the remarks made upon it by a cluster of the ill-natured fraternity "who might each of them have sate for the picture of *Tom Brainless*"; and he gave a report of their findings, which concluded with the discovery "that if indeed the world in one or two points was not quite so good, as they could wish it, yet things in the present state could never be altered for the better, and it was folly, or madness alone could propose it." For himself, Trumbull added:

Now to give you as much light as possible into this matter, I would assure you, the Author had very little hopes that the world would, in his day, arrive at the point of perfection, from which it is at present he knows not how many leagues distant; and his expectations are not very sanguine, that these pictures of the modern deffective manners will do much service. . . . . He is as much satisfied that the present year hath borne a sufficient number of fools to keep up the breed, as that there has been a tolerable crop produced every season, for these forty years past. But he thought, though perhaps the picture might not reclaim many, there could be no harm in trying his hand at the draught: In which, if the good people, who sate for the painting, have the ill hap to find themselves drawn with a wide mouth, a long nose, or a blear eye, he begs of them to get a little acquainted with their own faces, and see whether these be not their real defects of nature, before they begin to rail at the Painter, for the badness of their resemblance.

He attacked those who affirmed "the satire to be levelled at the clergy in general" as a "method of preventing the public from dragging to view those particular men, at whom it is, and ought to be, pointed"; and he especially threatened "those, *however dignified in station*," who railed at the poem in order "to gain favour with a particular party." His final emphasis on the particular nature of the satire was a "hint to two Persons, the haughtiest Dullard, and the most impertinent Coxcomb of this age; from whom he has already received numberless favours, and who by their future good conduct may stand a chance, at some fortunate period, to figure at the head of a Dedication to the first and second parts of the Progress of Dulness."

A clue on the title-page of the second part of the poem may have suggested to Trumbull's contemporary readers the identity of "the most impertinent Coxcomb of this age"; but, in spite of the apparent boldness of this personal satire and in spite of the aggressiveness of the Preface, the account of Dick Hairbrain carried on the battle with the poet's "enemies," mostly by jockeying them into a false position. Henceforth, if they kept up their earlier criticisms, they would have to denounce, as "an enemy to truth and learning" whose work was "both scurrilous in the sentiments and dirty in the style," an author who himself had strongly attacked a typical fop for idleness in study, French words and mannerisms, *double entendre* in speech derived from the Earl of Rochester and *Tristram Shandy*, and "free thought" borrowed from Hume, Bolingbroke, and Voltaire. If they accused him of writing a satire on Yale College, they were directing their charges against a satirist who had put himself on their side with the lines:

> Whoe'er at college points his sneer,
> Proves that himself learn'd nothing there.

And, if they represented him as meaning something more than he apparently said, they were misrepresenting an author whose style, in his most recent work, was chastely elegant, conventionally poetical, and free from the sinuous allusiveness that earlier had stung them to wrath. Such cleverness may now be recognized as evidence that Trumbull's valor was again giving way to discretion, but it did not impress his opponents in any such way. In their sensitiveness they had failed to understand the poet's exact attitude toward the clergy in the first part of *The Progress of Dulness*, and the same lack of penetration kept them from seeing how respectable he had made himself in the second; for, with all his elusiveness, Trumbull was following a coherent plan, and he kept up the appearance of a satire on college education, even though Dick Hairbrain was more like the conventional fop of English literature than a representative New Haven beau. Accordingly, as the attacks raged against him, he was altogether justified in feeling that his designs for the third part of his poem would "by many be ignorantly or wilfully misunderstood."

One of the more public attacks appears to have been directly responsible for a revival of "The Correspondent." Shortly after the second part of *The Progress of Dulness* was published, a letter appeared in the *Connecticut Journal and New-Haven Post-Boy* taking Trumbull to task for personal satire and for railing against metaphysics and asking specifically how far he imagined reason could be used in inquiries about religion. The question, of course, was one he had answered several times before; and his reply was of essay length, although he answered the particular query with a brief statement to the effect that reason "was given to assist us, in explaining the word of God, and not in going beyond it." In the next issue of the *Journal* for February 12, 1773, the Correspondent came back to life with a chip on his shoulder and an olive branch in his hand. The chip was revealed by a reminder to his readers that the first series had aroused a good deal of antagonism among "Persons of eminence" and by his reference to his reappearance "in this mild interval from the struggles of patriotism and self-interest." The olive branch was displayed in the otherwise innocuous character of the paper. Trumbull, however, could not remain peaceful; and, when the lack of contributions forced him to a new exercise of his wit, he began a series of papers on medical quackery—a sore subject in Connecticut during the latter part of the eighteenth century— which aroused a new set of "enemies." Accordingly, by the middle of June he found himself involved in another bitterly personal controversy.

By this time he seems to have become excessively sensitive; and, when he heard reports that his "enemies" were talking about him behind his back and threatening violence to his person, he became more pointed in his satire, explaining his position in "The Correspondent" for June 25:

> To expose vice by general animadversions, and not to brand characters by personal satire, was the principal design of these essays. The writer is sorry in this paper to be forced to deviate so much from his plan. He was ever averse to satire, that was merely personal. Every man, hath his faults, and infirmities, which to expose to the public, without just reason, whether by the pen of the Satirist, the tongue of the Slanderer, or the low buffoonery of the Mimic, is the mark of a mean and ungenerous mind, and is usually occasioned by a restless ambition of gaining the reputation of a Wit.

But, he added, satire was justified under three circumstances: preservation of one's self against personal injury, the protection of innocence against open malevolence or secret slander, and the defense of the public good against the vices of particular individuals. And the Correspondent, with a certain amount of self-righteousness, felt himself justified on all three grounds. At any rate, he threw himself into a satirical controversy with more vigor than he had shown in any of his essays on more general subjects. In the issue of the *Journal* for July 2 he anticipated a device later to be used in the *Anarchiad* by pretending to quote from "a very excellent antient allegorical production" which justified humor and satire on the grounds that they followed in the train of sense and genius, fancy and invention, in order to weed out the tares sown by folly and dulness, the children of chaos. Trumbull's "tares," however, though he claimed that they were the spirits of censoriousness, controversy, libertinism, and pride, were usually individuals; and his apparently generalized attacks were actually directed against particular persons. By a play on words and a subtle allusiveness, essays apparently against the drama and stage were pointed at a particular "enemy" (possibly the Universalist minister, John Murray) whom rumor had associated with the boards. Other essays on hypocrisy among the clergy were directed against a certain group of individuals (probably the growing school of New Light prophets at Stockbridge) who recognized themselves by signs other than the charges actually made against them. In August, Trumbull became so involved with his opponents that he was doubtless glad to see the college year draw to an end and release him from New Haven and the responsibility of continuing his series. Yet he did not retreat before the attacks made upon him. The irony of his "recantation" in the number for August 27 was as forceful as that in any previous essay:

> I have believed that folly and vice were the proper subject of ridicule, and that the public might receive benefit from a course of observations on life and manners.
> I have believed that in every profession the Quacks and Mountebanks were public nuisances.
> I have believed (contrary to the declared opinion of many among us) that the public Authority of this town ought not to be publicly insulted.
> I have believed that an illiterate blunderer, by obtaining a license to preach, would not become a proper representative of the Prophets and Apostles.
> I have believed that religion would receive little advantage from the virulent controversies and uncharitable censoriousness of parties.
> I have believed that the public would justify the writer, who returned tho' with severity, the personal violence of unprovoked slander.
> I have believed that the man, who published a falsehood, and afterwards suborned his accomplices to attest it, in whatever profession was unworthy of regard.
> I have believed that two and two make four, and that the sun shines at noonday.
> All which false and heretical opinions, which I have heretofore published to the world, I do now, at your instigation, renounce, abjure, and reject, and on this declaration of the Creed of my Unbelief, humbly desire you to restore me to your christian charity.

To all appearances it was the forthright expression of a high-spirited, fearless, candid man.

But appearances were not to be trusted. The seventh article of the creed was certainly a personal reference which, if not slanderous, could not be strictly justified; and other articles contained similar allusions, as the Correspondent's last will and testament indicated when it appeared a week later. Trumbull was changing sides too often during the summer of 1773 to be completely candid. Torn between a desire to stand up manfully to his opponents and a cautious unwillingness to commit himself to any position that aroused antagonism, he developed an extraordinary ingenuity in playing the role of a forthright but misunderstood man. When he satirized anti-British disturbances and received "some menaces of personal affront, in case public riots were any more hinted at," he "defied" his menacers with a satiric "stroke" at the pro-British celebration of the king's birthnight. Or, when his attacks on the New Divinity preachers drew fire, he "challenged" his opponents with the sort of horrified exclamations against clerical hypocrisy which the New Light ministers themselves liked to utter. He simply could not endure the inevitable results of the vigorous, justifiable satire of the first part of *The Progress of Dulness*. His satiric buzz and the bite of his ironic style remained superficially undiminished, but it had become the activity of a gadfly rather than an expression of righteous indignation.

In his parting literary gift to New Haven, published at the time of the 1773 commencement, after he had resigned his tutorship, Trumbull did not even play the role of a gadfly. The third part of *The Progress of Dulness* was satire so conventional that no one could misunderstand it or disapprove. The design of *The Progress of Coquetry, or the Adventures of Miss Harriet Simper*, he announced in the Preface, was to show that "all the foibles we discover in the Fair Sex arise principally from the neglect of their education, and the mistaken notions they imbibe in their early youth. This naturally introduced a description of these foibles, which I have endeavoured to laugh at with good humour, and to expose without malevolence." In all three parts of *The Progress of Dulness*, he added, he had been influenced principally by "a desire to promote the interests of learning and morality," judging that, unless he produced something "that might conduce to the service of mankind," he had spent "much time in the studies of the Muses in vain." And in the last paragraph of his Preface he explained that the particular service of *The Adventures of Miss Harriet Simper* was to "encourage and promote" female education, which had been "most neglected" in the "considerable advances" recently made by polite literature in America. The Preface also discussed other satires dealing with women; it condemned "general, undistinguishing satire," with particular reference to Juvenal, Pope (in the second of his *Moral Essays*), and Swift and recommended Young's fifth and sixth satires as the discriminating "reproofs and corrections of a friend." In spite of all this, as well as a discreet care to make Harriet frail in mind but not in body, Trumbull showed, in this part of his poem, clear signs of Swift's influence. But the satire was unmistakably confined to the coquette and the silly relatives who were responsible for her superficial education. The arguments were probably more moderate than those of the undergraduate debate on women's education held at the same commencement, and the poem was kept within entirely safe bounds, except for the minor danger involved in reviving Tom Brainless long enough for him to marry the frowzy Harriet (after she had been ignored by Dick), and so give the entire work a formal unity.

Trumbull's surplus energy during the period of his tutorship was almost entirely devoted to *The Progress of Dulness* and the supplementary "Correspondent." He attempted at some time during 1772 to carry out his scheme for a satire in the manner of *A Tale of a Tub*, evidently planning something more nearly like a novel than he had originally intended; but the one episode he completed attacked the New Light controversialists rather than the deists, and the further ideas he had for it were apparently absorbed by his series of essays. The four chapters which survive in manuscript represent the first sustained attempt at prose fiction in New England—and a completely mediocre talent for narrative prose. Dealing with an encounter between a philosophical traveler and a "Mathematical Metaphysician," they suggest the influence of *Rasselas* in structure and of *Gulliver's Travels* and *Tristram Shandy* in occasional details; but they are chiefly interesting because they reveal how constitutionally incapable Trumbull was of diverting his satiric impulses away from local conditions and personalities. Joseph Bellamy and Samuel Hopkins were the principal objects of his attack, with Stephen West, George Beckwith, Jacob Green, John Smalley, and Nathaniel Whitaker thrown in. All were New Divinity men whose argumentative publications were probably being displayed by Trumbull's own publishers at the time he was writing, and he had nothing to say of them that he did not say more skilfully, though less directly, in *The Progress of Dulness*. There is no evidence that he ever wrote the introductory chapters of his story or that he had any definite plans for its continuation beyond an encounter with a sort of "anatomical metaphysician," which he outlined in a brief postscript to the one completed episode.

The only other poems of these two years were occasional verse letters, most of them to his friend David Humphreys, who had taken Trumbull's place as a schoolteacher in Wethersfield. The first of these, written in the autumn of 1772, was a response to "a very humorous letter in ridicule of love." In it Trumbull expressed himself upon the inconstancy of women by a fable, "The Owl and the Sparrow." It revealed that, even while he was writing on the vanity of youthful expectations, the poet was thinking satirically about the subjects he was to attack in *The Progress of Dulness*. The verse also suggests that the posthumous collection of Gay's *Fables* and Edward Moore's collection of *Fables for Ladies* (especially the contributions by Henry Brooke) may have contributed to his octosyllabic style. Another letter to Humphreys, written in May, 1773, defended his satiric writing after Humphreys had become alarmed at his friend's ventures and had versified Trumbull's own arguments against satire. In the same year he addressed a fragmentary letter (modeled on Prior's "Epistle to Fleetwood Shepard, Esq.") "To a Lady on Returning Her Thimble," and in November he wrote a few scurrilous epigrammatic couplets "On the Marriage of Two Special Friends of the Author." On the twelfth of that month he was admitted to the bar by the New

Haven County Court and shortly afterward left for Boston, where he was to serve an apprenticeship in the office of John Adams until the autumn of the following year. His last poetic effort celebrated his departure: another octosyllabic letter to an anonymous friend, it announced that he had "turn'd philosopher, or so" and "Forsworn all wild poetic fancies" for visions of such "Sages learned in the law" as "the awful Coke," who was even then rising before him.

The departure to Boston brought an end to the second—and, on the whole, the most energetic—phase of Trumbull's literary career. Late in life he was to declare that his original genius was not for satire but that he had been forced into satiric writing by a disillusioned reaction to the reception of his more serious work. Actually, however, both his talent and his impulses were primarily satiric, and his reaction was from spontaneous irony and wit into artificial solemnity and forced seriousness. The progress of his satire on dulness from a vigorous pertinence to a circumspect innocuousness and the progressive irresponsibility of the Correspondent reveal one basic fact about Trumbull which all further evidence supports: he did not have the thick-skinned willingness to cause trouble that was necessary to a first-rate satirist in a land where his audience, his associates, and his subjects of attack all belonged to the same small class. Trumbull made full trial of his genius between the summer of 1772 and the autumn of 1773 and found it too great for his own good. The first part of *The Progress of Dulness* and the more vigorous essays in "The Correspondent" were remarkable literary achievements for any man of their author's age and experience. The difficulty was that the author was still a very young man, anxious to make his way in the world and really, in spite of his sharp pen, rather easygoing by disposition. When he found that he could not get along very far or very easily when he gave full rein to his satiric genius, he invariably checked and slowed down to a walk as quickly and as gracefully as possible. Among serious, plodding writers, however, he was indistinguishable from the crowd.

IV

If Trumbull left for Boston with a determination to avoid the indiscretions of satire, he had by no means abandoned poetry; and in his new environment he began a series of new experiments with serious—and even "sublime"—verse. The first sign of the wholly reformed Trumbull came as a solemn irregular "Ode to Sleep," which was probably written a few months after the last part of *The Progress of Dulness.* It was the most Miltonic of Trumbull's poems, containing many echoes of "L'Allegro" and "Il Penseroso" with rhyme patterns like those found in "Lycidas"; and it was also the most personal. In an allusion to his recent experiences in New Haven the poet invoked sleep as the "Balm of my wounds and softener of my woes" to lead him in his dreams to the heights of Parnassus or to the arms of his fiancée or, more seriously, in a "nobler flight" into "realms of the pure, ethereal mind" beyond the stars. How explicitly the original version revealed his own mental condition can no longer be determined. But after the death of Joseph Howe in 1775 he revised the conclusion by inserting a "tribute of affection" to his friend, in which he requested the shade of Howe to arm his "wayward weakness" against all assaults, raise his "low thoughts," and aid his "nobler wishes" against such raging passions and "vain allurements" as

> The pomp of learning and the boast of art,
> The glow, that fires in genius' boundless range,
> The pride, that wings the keen, satiric dart,
> And hails the triumph of revenge.

Furthermore, with a meekness strange to Trumbull, he asked that his friend's spirit teach him to realize "our humble station in this vale of woes," so that he might "to heavenly hopes alone aspire."

The poet was even then working on the first canto of *M'Fingal;* but, as an earnest of his continued interest in "nobler themes," he also produced another irregular ode, "The Prophecy of Balaam," in December, 1773. This versification of the parts of Numbers that foretold the beauty and order of Israel

and the future messianic kingdom was followed, in January, by
"The Destruction of Babylon" in heroic couplets, which the
author described as "an imitation of sundry passages in the
13th and 14th chapters of Isaiah, and the 18th of the Revelation
of St. John"—though, more strictly, he might have represented
it as a free paraphrase of the biblical passages in imitation of
Pope's *Messiah*. Both of these poems were probably written
under the direct influence of Timothy Dwight, whom Trumbull
had left in New Haven busily re-working parts of Joshua with
similar descriptive additions, and both may have owed something to Dwight's commencement oration on the poetry of the
Bible. Dwight's oration gave his friend little practical assistance, however, for Trumbull later believed that he would have
done better with the biblical paraphrase had he been acquainted
with Bishop Lowth's *De sacra poesi Hebraeorum*. On the whole,
he was not attracted by the results of his experiments with such
material; he believed that it required the genius of Pope "to express the bold images of oriental poetry in the style of modern
verse," and he later decided that neither he nor even William
Mason (who had written an ode "On the Fate of Tyranny"
based upon the same passages in Isaiah) had that genius.

The last of the poems written during Trumbull's attempt to
live down his youthful indiscretions and prepare for a career,
marriage, and the serious responsibilities of life was "An Elegy
on the Times." Composed in opposition to the Boston Port
Bill, it called upon the American people to resist, temperately,
oppression from abroad and assured them of a glorious future.
Although his conclusion was optimistic, the poet viewed contemporary social and political events with a melancholy inspired
by *The Deserted Village*. Britain was a "land in darkness and in
death," gradually being destroyed by "the powers of luxury and
pride"; and under the influence of British oppression the commercial beauty of Boston had faded very much as the loveliness
of sweet Auburn had disappeared. Appealing to the popular
American belief that Goldsmith's poem gave a true picture of
the mother-country, Trumbull also gave his readers a brief
glance at a poverty-stricken hamlet suggested by Auburn as a

warning of what might happen to them if they yielded their
economic privileges. He did not, however, allow the English
poet any authority concerning America, for he represented the
"wild Altama" of Goldsmith's fearsome American wilderness as
a river of gliding "silver waters"—hinting perhaps to the geo-
graphically minded reader of the London edition of his poem
that, if he had to emigrate, he would not find the colony of
Georgia nearly so "horrid" as it had been pictured. The melancholy stole of this elegy was the effect of British governmental
policy upon the ordinary people. Free from that, America would
be the "new-born empire" whose "ascendant hour" was already
approaching.

Trumbull was not able to maintain all this high seriousness,
however, even in Boston. Some young ladies who hissed an
oration at Harvard College provoked an epigram with the point
that woman's "earliest league was with the serpent"; and the
poet's removal from Boston to New Haven, in September, 1774,
was marked by a return to octosyllabic verse in a mildly satiric
fable addressed "To a Young Lady" who had asked that he
draw her character. In the meantime—if his own later report is
to be trusted—"he frequently employed his leisure hours in
writing essays on political subjects in the public gazettes."
If this employment represented anything more than secretarial
activity, however, its results were anonymous, for no original
prose contribution by Trumbull to the Revolutionary movement
has yet been identified.

His older friends, who had a correct estimate of his talents,
were anxious for him to become a verse satirist in the American
cause, but Trumbull was obdurate in his refusal to appear publicly in that role. Early in 1775 General Gage, the British governor of Massachusetts, declared martial law in Boston with a
high-sounding proclamation and shortly afterward damaged the
military dignity of Britain at Concord and Bunker Hill. Silas
Deane, who had encouraged his friend to publish *The Progress
of Dulness*, particularly urged Trumbull to "attempt a burlesque
on General Gage's victories"; but the poet, perhaps remembering the consequences of Deane's earlier advice, declined and, as

he supposed, dismissed the matter. Nevertheless, the suggestion
stuck in his mind; and, when the *Connecticut Courant* of July 17
published a satiric verse-parody of Gage's Proclamation, Trumbull was stirred to the point of sending to the same paper a rival,
and considerably better, burlesque of the same document.
Trumbull's *A New Proclamation!* appeared in two instalments,
of about fifty couplets each, in the issues of August 7 and 14, and
was reprinted as an eight-page pamphlet for sale at three pennies a copy.

The poem must have been sufficiently successful to have assured Trumbull that he might, at last, achieve popular acclaim
as a satirist, for he soon began to revise parts of it to fit into a
scheme for a running burlesque commentary on the progress of
the war. The Continental Congress had taken the momentous
step of making the army around Boston its own, and New
Haven was overflowing with patriotism during the autumn of
1775. But Trumbull was no enthusiastic revolutionist. His attitude toward the political controversies of the first year of the
Revolution was very much like his attitude toward the theological quarrels of a few years before—one of somewhat detached
superiority. He planned a poem which would enable him, as he
afterward confessed, "to describe every subject in the manner it
struck [his] own imagination"; and, although the imagination of
a Trumbull was naturally biased toward the Whig party, it did
not give way to the enthusiastic partisanship that affected
Philip Freneau, who had composed the first burlesque of Gage's
proclamation. Trumbull, though he later said that his poem
"was written merely with a political view," had something of
the same feeling about the warring political arguments that
Samuel Butler had held concerning the conflicting doctrines of
the English Puritans more than a century before; and he re-read
Butler's rambling commentary on the Presbyterians and Inde-
pendents while he meditated a similar work on the American
Whigs and Tories.

The design for this "Modern Epic Poem" was simple: the
poet introduced a protagonist for each side of the political argument who could make speeches before various audiences that

might supply or stimulate the necessary action; and he devised the "machinery" of second sight with the evident purpose of commenting upon succeeding events without disturbing the unity of action. The precedent set by *Hudibras* and his own talent for irony led Trumbull to make his "hero" a representative of the Tories whose name, M'Fingal, was probably chosen to suggest an ironic contrast between the comic manners of the modern epic and the refined simplicity so widely admired in the "ancient" Ossianic poem. M'Fingal himself is more recognizably a descendant of the good knight Hudibras, however, than of Macpherson's Fingal. An ambiguously "great" man with a militant disposition and a rusty sword, he had Sir Hudibras' love for tropes and figures, although as a very oracle he possessed the squire Ralph's mystical ability to penetrate into the nature of things. The Whig hero Honorius was a somewhat more dignified man than M'Fingal, although equally given to high-flown tropes in his public addresses. Neither was held up for public admiration, for Trumbull's wit was no respecter of persons, and he apparently had not given up a plan to satirize the affectations of orators which he had announced in "The Correspondent" five and a half years before.

The first instalment of *M'Fingal* opened with a town meeting of indecisive freemen who were listening to Honorius advocate the Whig side in the approaching struggle. Trope after trope fell from his lips until he had illustrated almost all the "nine faults" against which Yale students were warned in John Holmes's little handbook of rhetoric. The speaker's philosophy of history (as Trumbull himself implied in a note to the 1820 edition) was absurd, his rhetoric bad, and his facts inaccurate. Ten years later, in a letter to the Marquis de Chastellux, Trumbull was to claim that "with as much impartiality as possible" he had tried "to satirize the follies and extravagances" of his countrymen "as well as their enemies." Although this was not strictly true of the first instalment of his poem, he was certainly burlesquing political oratory on both sides; and his friend John Adams would have been shocked to know that later readers would suppose that he had sat as model for the pompous Whig champion. In comparison with M'Fingal's response, however, Honorius' speech was a fairly respectable, though bombastic, performance. For with M'Fingal, Trumbull turned from burlesque to pointed satire and used his irony as a scalpel for laying bare the tissue of false reasoning that he saw in the Tory arguments. Descending from the allegorical generalizations of the Whig orator to the particulars of M'Fingal's arguments, Trumbull represented with ironic clarity the attempt of the high-church clergy to justify parliamentary rule by the theory of the divine right of kings. He pointed out the absurdity of the claim that Gage's actions were designed to prevent civil war by having the squire place the blame upon the colonials who resisted the British troops:

> Since there's no war, each mortal knows,
> Where one side only gives the blows.

Gage's "victories" were burlesqued by quoting British prophecies of American cowardice and explaining how the king's officers came to be authorities upon running from action. General Gage himself was made comic by being held up to admiration in a naïve comparison with St. Peter's fish, Balaam's ass, the goose that saved Rome, an English bishop's cur, and the frogs and lice that plagued Pharaoh; and the excessive respect of the Tories for the English government was satirized by a comparison of the British ministry to Divine Providence. The most doubtful achievements of British troops in the Colonies were singled out for particular praise, and the power of the king's men to stir up the Indians and to frighten women and children was applauded. But the most direct satire came in Trumbull's citation of unworthy motives and disreputable grounds for the Tory behavior. In particular, he referred to Sir David Dalrymple and Dr. Johnson as authorities for the Tory belief that there was no such thing as love of country and

> That Self is still, in either faction,
> The only principle of action.

Nor was there any obligation to posterity. Thus Trumbull attributed to the Tories as a guiding principle of morality that self-interest which was the greatest evil attacked in the basic textbook of ethics studied by Yale undergraduates; and he had M'Fingal bring his address to a close with the summons "Awake to gladness then, ye Tories!" for the estates and titles that would soon be dispensed in America with a princely largess which would make even the squire himself a true knight.

Such was the original "first canto" of *M'Fingal*, which was printed in Philadelphia under the auspices of Silas Deane and sold by William and Thomas Bradford in January, 1776, at the London Coffee House, for perhaps a shilling. It was not a revolutionary poem. Trumbull gave his readers some witty paraphrases of Tory arguments with which to reassure themselves and some unusually quotable phrases, but he made no attempt to inflame them with patriotism in the manner of Freneau or Tom Paine. The poem was reissued in Philadelphia in 1776 and printed in London during the same year, but it was not widely popular; and after its initial flurry the patrons of the London Coffee House may have found it less stimulating than the glasses of flip they might buy for the same money. Trumbull himself, with the temperamental reversion of feeling that was characteristic of him, had exaggerated its defects and declared himself "heartily tired of it" even before its publication. Yet he had planned for its continuation: his adoption of *Hudibras* as a model, even to the extent of parodying Butler's poem in occasional passages, indicated that he thought of *M'Fingal* as a running commentary on events; the representation of the first part as "Canto I" promised as much; and the conclusion invited a sequel by setting the stage for further action on the village green. Either because he failed to receive the stimulus of a really popular success or because of his natural inability for sustained effort, however, he let the machinery of M'Fingal's second sight rust unused until the Revolution was over and his friends urged him to continue the poem as a piece of literature rather than as propaganda.

In the meantime Trumbull's mind had already turned toward belletristic activity, and after working on a series of essays in literary criticism in 1778–79 he was well prepared to change his

quondam political satire into "a burlesque poem which . . . .
Boileau would not have condemned, with those of Scarron and
Dassouci." In doing so, he made a number of revisions in the
part already published. He divided it into two cantos separated
by a dinner interval which interrupted the speaking and increased the illusion of action. He also added a twenty-two-line
conclusion to the new Canto I, an eighteen-line introduction to
Canto II, and seventy-eight lines of additional satire at the beginning of M'Fingal's speech after dinner. In these lines M'Fingal claimed the gratitude of colonists because they would not
have had the blessings of America had it not been for the actions
of King Charles and Archbishop Laud. Other favors from England included the generals sent over in 1755; the bishops and
priests offered, though not accepted; and the felons so generous-
ly transported to increase the American population. The least
the colonists could do in return, the squire argued, would be to
keep King George off the bankrupt list and provide support for
those "genuine sons of mother Britain," the bastards of an im-
poverished nobility. The new satire was more offensive than
that of the earlier version, and it may be that Trumbull thought
of it at the beginning of the war but was unwilling to put it down
in print as long as he himself remained a son of Britain who
might conceivably be taken to task for filial disobedience. Certainly, it was not the result of any end-of-the-war bitterness toward Great Britain, for the satire of the last two cantos was no
more intense, in its attitude toward the English and loyalists,
than the first had been. Leading Tories were still held up to
ridicule and the ineptitude of the British leaders ironically presented, but the scalpel that laid bare false logic was no longer
extensively used. M'Fingal, in fact, was no longer the fool that
he had appeared to be before the town meeting. Instead of indulging exclusively in absurdities, he launched into a forthright
attack on the mob, its noisy stupidity, its lawlessness, and its
low constituency and on the weakness of the Articles of Confederation. Furthermore, the most memorable lines spoken by the
squire in the third canto were those directed against the activities of radical patriots who had inflated the Continental cur-

rency. The "awful spectre" of paper money, propped by the crutches of "Regulation" and "Tender" and ironically marked with "The faith of all th' United States," was arbitrarily introduced into his vision, where it had no organic place, apparently as an expression of Trumbull's own sentiments. The Tory squire had become, in part at least, the spokesman for the conservative American patriot; and it is perhaps significant that, when the democrats, in 1801, satirized Trumbull himself as "M'Fingal," the sentiments which they attributed to the poet as evidence of his "aristocracy" were all taken from the speech of M'Fingal to the mob.

The new direction given to the literary form of the poem was as striking as that given to the satire, for *M'Fingal* became a mock epic in structure as well as in title. The third canto presented the necessary epic battle between the Tories and the Whigs, with the inevitable contest of champions—M'Fingal, of course, representing the Tories with his rusty sword, and the "stoutest wrestler of the green," armed with a spade, the Whigs. The ensuing duel was a professed burlesque of the single combats of Paris and Menelaus, Aeneas and Turnus, and Michael and Satan; but it was probably directly suggested by the fight between Hudibras and Whacum in the second part of Butler's poem, for there was a certain similarity of weapons, and the loser in each case was laid low by a blow to the same vulnerable spot. The tar-and-feathering of M'Fingal and the hoisting of the constable to the top of the liberty pole had no precedent in epic action, being a peculiar example of American manners; but the squire's power of second sight was used effectively in an imitation of Adam's vision of the future in *Paradise Lost*. M'Fingal, during his descent into the cellar (in itself somewhat reminiscent of Virgil), saw into the future by the help of Malcolm and gave his Tory followers an account of the progress of the war and the success of the Revolutionary forces, thereby leading up to the conclusion of the poem in which the squire escaped from the Whig raiding party and fled to the safety of Boston.

In addition to these general burlesques of epic action, Trumbull also added to his poem many more comic echoes of earlier writers, and he took great pains to point out such parallels even in the first section. In the 1775 edition of *M'Fingal* there were only four parallels to earlier poems indicated by the notes. In the last two cantos of the 1782 edition there were twelve. Joel Barlow, with Trumbull's encouragement, cited others in the edition of London, 1792; and the 1820 edition of the *Poetical Works* called attention to twelve in the first two cantos and nearly fifty in the last. There were also a great many allusions not formally noted, but their proportion is roughly indicated by those pointed out. Trumbull was much more conscious of the burlesque quality of his work in 1782 than he had been in 1775; and he was deliberately trying to emphasize the humorous effect of the parody especially introduced into the later version of the poem.

Trumbull made one attempt at serious patriotic verse during the Revolution when, in 1777, after the capture of General Burgoyne and his army, he wrote an ode on "The Genius of America," which he expanded somewhat after the Battle of Monmouth. But the poem was self-conscious and uninspired and, on the whole, the war seems to have had little effect upon his literary work. The revised version of *M'Fingal* was his most sustained poetic effort and, by the irony of circumstances, his most successful. Three rival printers in his home town published editions of the complete poem in 1782, but it was not designed to attract the sort of attention aroused by the more purposeful satire of *The Progress of Dulness;* and, even though it was not protected by copyright, no out-of-town edition appeared before 1785. In that year Noah Webster also began making it known to school children through selections printed in *A Grammatical Institute of the English Language.* As the dangers of mob rule began to threaten the country, however, the poem began to have a satiric pertinence which the author could hardly have expected when he wrote it. Newspapers began to discover in 1786 that the Tory squire's comments on irresponsible patriots represented neatly quotable expressions of the respectable attitude toward the followers of such people as Daniel

Shays. Two editions were published in Philadelphia during the year of the Second Constitutional Convention, and it was frequently quoted by the press during the debate over ratification. It reached its peak of popularity during the period of controversy between Federalist and Democrat and eventually became sufficiently well known to outlast the Federalist cause, which it inadvertently supported. Passing through the haze of patriotism in which a new American mythology developed, it came out with a halo of fancied historical associations. In comparison with the figures and tropes used by Fourth of July orators, the speech of Honorius lost its burlesque quality and began to sound like the plain sense of John Adams. *M'Fingal*, by the ex post facto legislation of public opinion, had become a Revolutionary poem.

V

· John Trumbull did not attempt alone any other major literary work. He wrote New Year's verses for the carrier of the *Connecticut Courant* in 1783 and for Elisha Babcock's *Freeman's Chronicle* in 1784. But, except for his work in collaboration, he had practically finished his literary career at the age of thirty-two, and he had not labored very hard at literature since his twenty-third birthday. All his experience had taught him that his genius was a narrow one, limited almost wholly to satire and burlesque and most effective when restricted in expression to the octosyllabic couplets of the greatly admired Jonathan Swift. No man could go on writing burlesque epics indefinitely, and Trumbull could not go on as a satirist. His failure to do so might be called lack of courage; but the real explanation lies deeper— in the absence of any fundamental desire, or motive, which would have provided the emotional drive for the full exploitation of his talent. He was sardonic, as only a man of exceptionally quick, well-informed intelligence can be; but he was also easygoing by disposition, fond of material comforts, and eager for recognition and approval. Whenever he yielded wholly to his satiric impulses and the sardonic promptings of his ready wit, he simply borrowed trouble which was as unnecessary as it was unwelcome. And it was pure trouble. There were no compensations. There was no circle in America into which he could escape for approval and praise after an onslaught upon the dullards. He had to live among his victims—and eventually expect them to be his legal clients and political supporters. Furthermore, he could not, by the practice of satire, gain any deep satisfaction for himself. In spite of his later, exaggerated memories of the mood which produced the elegy "On the Vanity of Youthful Expectations," he never experienced any real disappointment or profound hopelessness, and he was temperamentally so far from being able to understand his master, Swift, that he tried at the same time to "admire the force of his Genius" and "detest the sentiments of his heart." A different environment or a different disposition might have given a driving force to Trumbull's satiric genius; but, as he gradually increased his girth and his influence in Hartford, the semblance of original force faded away.

CHAPTER III

TIMOTHY DWIGHT

I

WHEN Timothy Dwight entered Yale in 1765 he was almost a match for Trumbull in youthful accomplishments. Had he stood for examination he probably could have been admitted to college at the age of eight; and when he did become a Freshman he had behind him five years of miscellaneous study culminating in a year with the Rev. Enoch Huntington, which had taken him through the classical readings of the Sophomore class. In all other respects, however, he was his distant cousin's complement. Robust in health and enthusiastic by temperament, he threw himself vigorously into college life, at first by participation in the youthful indiscretions of his schoolmates and later by an excessive zeal for study which permanently weakened his eyesight. His turn toward serious-mindedness came at the beginning of his Junior year, soon after his fifteenth birthday, and was accompanied by a general desire for self-improvement, which was satisfied in part by the acquisition of his copperplate style of handwriting, a collection of church music, and a sufficient skill in verse to attract the attention of the older Trumbull.

After his graduation Dwight continued his studies while teaching in the Hopkins Grammar School for two years before becoming a tutor in the college. By this time he had begun to fill out the large frame he had inherited from his father; and, despite the youth which caused the corporation to hesitate over his appointment, he soon developed the commanding presence and rich, mellow voice which made his reading and speaking a

delight to listeners and himself an object of extraordinary admiration to his students. Under the stimulus of his development he seems also to have come to the conclusion that he was
destined to become a great man, and he began to exercise the
rigid control over his life which his destiny required. Twelve
mouthfuls of food, he decided on one occasion, was the proper
dinner for a vigorous man who wanted to keep his mind clear
without wasting time on exercise; and, when the diet failed to
prove successful at the end of a six months' trial, he became a
vegetarian as well. The strength of character which enabled
him to hold to such principles might have proved fatal had not
his father come to New Haven and hauled him home to Northampton, where his mother nursed him through nineteen successive attacks of "bilious colic" and a sensible physician started
him on his lifelong regime of long walks and frequent trips on
horseback. When he was able to take up his duties again, in
the fall of 1774, he joined the strict College Church, which would
have been approved by his grandfather Edwards, started a new
class through the curriculum, and began to prepare for a legal
career.

Yet he remained an enthusiastic teacher, who instructed his
students in such extracurricular subjects as ancient history and
modern literary criticism and urged them into the unexpected
depths of Newton's *Principia*. This enthusiasm for learning
made him impatient with the interruption to his studies caused
by an inoculation for smallpox in 1775; and too quick a return
to them caused further damage to his eyes, leaving him with
the partial blindness from which he suffered periodically for the
rest of his life and requiring the thick horn-rimmed glasses that
became a distinctive feature of his appearance. But in spite of
this handicap he became more and more actively interested in
education, and as his hold upon the students increased in
strength he may even have developed a premature ambition to
become president of Yale. At any rate, when the office became
vacant in 1777 he was in a position to meet its major requirements: he had an excellent reputation as a teacher, he had given
up his legal studies in order to become a minister of the gospel,

and he had taken a wife. If he had any real expectations of the position, however, they were disappointed; and instead of returning to the college he became a chaplain in General Parsons' brigade in the Continental Army.

Dwight's patriotic service proved fortunate. His father, unwilling to violate an oath of allegiance to the British crown, had emigrated with two other sons to the Mississippi territory; and when news of his death was received in October, 1778, the eldest son was able to resign his commission and cast the protection of his war record over his mother, the ten younger children, and the two farms in Northampton. There he remained for nearly five years, carrying his responsibilities with such success that even his mother, according to report, came to look upon him more as a father than as a son. He ran the farms, filled vacant pulpits in neighboring towns, represented the county for two terms in the Massachusetts legislature, and conducted a successful school until he accepted a call to the pastorate at Greenfield, Connecticut, where he was ordained in November, 1783. He had not been freed from ambition, but he had developed a detachment and dignity far beyond his years. Although he acquired an unusual reputation for hospitality in his new home and kept the affectionate regard of many former students, even a younger brother who lived in the household was a little hesitant about referring to him by his first name.

II

There are no examples comparable to those in the Trumbull manuscripts of Dwight's early experiments in verse and prose, nor is there any evidence either in his disposition or in the reception of his early work that he might have become involved in so many difficulties before he settled upon his proper style. The translations from Horace which attracted Trumbull's attention during the younger poet's undergraduate days apparently have not survived, and the contributions he is supposed to have made to the newspapers during his years at Yale have not been identified. Dwight is reported to have assisted in the composition of "The Meddler," and the heroic couplets "On

Music" that were printed in the third number are, of several possible contributions, most probably his. He may also have had some hand in the first series of "The Correspondent," but, in any case, the early work that may be attributed to his pen is almost all ordinary and undistinctive.

The most striking newspaper contribution which presumptive evidence might credit to Dwight is a poem entitled "Mankind Pursuing Shadows: or False Notions of Happiness" that appeared in the *Connecticut Journal and New-Haven Post-Boy* for August 14, 1770. It was submitted by a friend of the author, who described it as a "production of a young Genius amongst ourselves" which was worthy of emulation by other young men. The false notions of happiness were those that influenced man's passions of hope and fear through his expectation of achieving bliss on earth, and the poem as a whole was an attempt to answer or contradict part of the fourth epistle of *An Essay on Man*. Mankind in pursuit of earthly happiness was compared, in a figure possibly suggested by Pope, to an idiot running to a hilltop in an effort to grasp the skies; and the burden of the American's answer to the English poet was contained in two couplets. The first—

> For happiness man's deathless nature cries,
> But needs a God to point out where it lies—

led to the advice given in the second:

> From earth, vain man, turn up thy wandering eyes,
> View God like virtue coming from the skies.

Imitative though the poem was in its echoes of *An Essay on Man* and its attempt to copy Pope's style in the heroic couplet, it was a significant illustration of the way an interest in belles-lettres was humanizing the Yale discipline, even when certain basic ideas remained unchanged. For Dwight, if he really was the "young Genius" who wrote the poem, was opposing President Clap's ethical system to Pope's notions "of the nature and state of man, with respect to happiness"; but in doing so he was also—under the influence of a poet whom he refused to follow—

placing a greater emphasis upon the importance of human happiness than Clap would ever have tolerated.

As soon as Dwight was appointed tutor, in the autumn of 1771, he began to think seriously of a literary career, and he immediately set up a more "elevated" version of Pope's heroic couplets as his own stylistic goal. Accordingly, for his first ambitious poem he chose *Windsor Forest* both as a model and as a point of departure, circulating the result, in manuscript, among his friends and their acquaintances for their "judgment of his poetical abilities." Claiming a less humble muse than Pope's and professing more ambitious strains than those of *Windsor Forest*, he began his poem with an echo of Pope's conclusion:

> From sylvan shades, cool bowers and fragrant gales,
> Green hills and murm'ring streams and flowery vales,
> My soul ascends of nobler themes to sing;
> AMERICA shall wake the sounding string.
> Accept, my native Land, these humble lays,
> This grateful song, a tribute to thy praise.

He prefaced the tribute, however, with a brief account of the Tatar invasion of Europe and a description of the Dark Ages, thus representing the discovery of America and its settlement by the English as the beginning of an era of light. After a short discussion of the effect of Charles II and Archbishop Laud on the settlement of New England, he mentioned the colonies of Penn and Oglethorpe, described the Indian uprisings, and treated the recent French war at some length. An allegorical figure of freedom foretold discord and war followed by peace, and the poem concluded with the usual prophecy of the future glory of America in science, art, morality, and religion until the coming of the millennium. Some of the prophetic couplets may have been added just before the work received its delayed publication, about ten years later, as *America: Or a Poem on the Settlement of the British Colonies; Addressed to the Friends of Freedom, and Their Country*. Most of it, however, was finished during the first months of Dwight's tutorship as a frankly experimental piece, in which, as Trumbull wrote Silas Deane, the nineteen-year-old poet designed "only a general view of America, by way

of tryal of his genius." Some readers of the manuscript failed
to become enthusiastic; but Trumbull, at least, believed that
there was "something original and sublime in his manner of
thinking and description" and was confident that "Mr. Dwight
is to be our American poet."

Dwight's lifelong habit of refusing to publish his poems at
the time they were written makes it impossible to give an accurate account of his experimental work, but he wrote at least
one surviving "Song" in 1771 which was the result of his early
interest in music. Beginning "Look, lovely maid, on yonder
flow'r," it followed the pattern of Herrick's "Gather ye rose-
buds while ye may" both in meter and in moral. He may also
have produced, during this early period, either or both of two
biblical paraphrases which were not published until 1786 and
1793. The first of these, *The Trial of Faith*, was a versification
of the first three chapters of the Book of Daniel, in which he
inflated the biblical narrative into the sublime style of the epic
by such means as translating the simple statement that Nebu-
chadnezzar's "spirit was troubled" into the figurative declaration that "deep convulsions shook his stormy mind." It was
either an extremely youthful effort or a remarkable example of
poetic backsliding; and, as a fragment, it looks like an early
indulgence in the popular practice of expanding the Scriptures
into heroic couplets after the fashion (among the poets Dwight
knew) of Cowley, Blackmore, Prior, Parnell, Pope, Young, and
Roger Wolcott. He was also acquainted with Du Bartas and,
of course, Milton; and under the latter's influence he attempted
an imaginative treatment of the story of Esther in blank verse,
parts of which were published in Elihu H. Smith's anthology,
American Poems, in 1793. Although this work also was probably never finished, it seems to have been an unsuccessful attempt to lighten the Miltonic style with a touch of sentiment
and to confine it to the historical narrative. There is no real
evidence concerning its date of composition, but Dwight implied in the Preface to *The Conquest of Canäan* that he had
thought of and perhaps experimented with Miltonic blank
verse, as well as the heroic couplet, as a narrative form early in

his career, and "The Message of Mordecai to Esther" may represent the result which determined him to adopt rhymed verse for his epic.

Whatever his literary experiments may have been during the first year of his tutorship, Dwight was unusually interested in the literary qualities of the Scriptures; and when he received his Master's degree in 1772 he delivered a commencement oration which was published as *A Dissertation on the History, Eloquence, and Poetry of the Bible*. As a self-conscious descendant of Jonathan Edwards and the nephew of the leading New Light minister in New Haven, he was acutely aware of his religious responsibilities and apparently hoped to combine his literary and religious interests in a single public exhibition. His subject was an original one, for neither he nor his audience had yet seen Bishop Lowth's *De sacra poesi Hebraeorum*, and his presentation was vigorous, especially when he found it necessary to defend the practices of Hebrew writers against the requirements of neoclassical rules:

> Unincumbered by Critical manacles, they gave their imaginations an unlimited range, called absent objects before the sight, gave life to the whole inanimate creation, and in every period, snatched the grace which is beyond the reach of art, and which, being the genuine offspring of elevated Genius, finds the shortest passage to the human soul. With all this license no writers have so few faulty passages. "But" says the Critic "they dont describe *exactly according to our rules*." True sir; and when you can convince me that *Homer* and *Virgil*, from whom you gather those rules, were sent into the world to give Laws to all other authors; when you can convince me that every beauty of fine writing is to be found, in its highest perfection, in their works, I will allow the beauties of the divine writers to be faults. 'Till that can be demonstrated, I must continue to admire the most shining instances of Genius, unparallel'd in force or sublimity.

Later in life, when Dwight felt obliged to defend the authenticity of the Bible against the attacks of skeptics, he placed an entirely different estimate on the quality of human "genius" that went into the composition of the Scriptures; but his youthful *Dissertation* formulated a critical point of view which had a permanent influence on his literary judgment. His strict adherence to a belief that the Bible could be all things to all men, when reconciled to his interest in literature, led him to a theoretical rejection of certain standards which was to affect curiously his own literary practices.

Yet for all his apparent independence Dwight was not standing absolutely alone against the critics. He undoubtedly shared his friend Trumbull's interest in Lord Kames's *Elements of Criticism* (which he was to use as a textbook in 1776, when he was permitted to give belletristic instruction to his students); and, if he declared his independence of neoclassic critics, he did so without violating any principle Lord Kames had laid down. Kames had taken the same attitude toward the rules, of course, and had placed a similar emphasis upon the desirability of stirring readers to a quick perception of beauty or sublimity in literature. He also had expressed an antagonism toward general descriptions and a preference for particulars with which Dwight wholly concurred. "Sensible that *General Descriptions* leave very faint traces on the memory," the latter wrote in a passage that might have been based on the *Elements of Criticism*, "the writers of Inspiration . . . . hurry on to events more particular, relations more minute," in an effort to kindle the passions and fire the imagination "to a pitch of enthusiasm" and so stir the human soul to receive "truths at once instructive, moral, and divine." Dwight found every "remarkable species" of poetry represented in the Bible except the dramatic—for he considered Job more nearly an epic than a drama—and he courageously defended its excellence, insisting, for example, that Pindar, Dryden, and Gray "must look up to" certain of the Psalms "with astonishment and despair." But, whether or not he was expressing his independent convictions concerning literary idols or literary critics, he seems to have derived at least part of his courage from the fact that he was not opposing so "modern" a critic as Lord Kames.

Dwight's *Dissertation* bore about the same relationship to his literary career that Trumbull's *Essay* bore to his: it foreshadowed the general theme of his most ambitious work and helped clarify, through a tentative expression, some of the attitudes that were determining the direction of his greater effort. Dwight's greater assurance, however, made the literary experiments of his youth more perfunctory, less significant, than Trumbull's. He never seemed to doubt his own abilities. None of his early experiments, accordingly, made him aware that his greatest danger was that of overreaching himself or gave him any indication that he had already begun to do so even before he quit experimenting.

III

Dwight's enormous self-confidence enabled him to plan and actually to begin his greatest literary effort before he had even tried to investigate the extent of his poetic talents. Soon after his nineteenth birthday, according to his own later testimony, he began an epic in which he apparently expected to combine all the good qualities of the two most popular modern epics— Milton's *Paradise Lost* and Fénelon's *The Adventures of Telemachus*—and include some innovations of his own. The example of Milton (whom Dwight considered the most "sublime" of all poets) encouraged him to avoid the patriotic subject with which he was experimenting and place his dependence upon the Bible for his subject matter; and Andrew Ramsay's "Discourse" on epic poetry which prefaced the Littlebury and Boyer translation of *Telemachus* gave him a definition of the genre which served as a general guide to his efforts. Some influence of his patriotic impulse, however, may be seen in his choice of Joshua's conquest of the Promised Land as his particular subject, for the New England habit of finding biblical precedents for later actions was so deeply ingrained that the wanderings of the Israelites had a peculiar emotional appeal to the descendants of the early Puritans.

But *The Conquest of Canäan* was not designed to be anything so simple as a versified biblical narrative presented with overtones of allusion to later events of a similar pattern. The definition of an epic to which Dwight apparently subscribed called for more than a heroic narrative in elevated style: it was "A Fable related by a Poet, in order to raise the Admiration, and inspire the Love of Virtue, by representing to us the Action of a Hero favour'd by Heaven, who brings about a great Enter-

prize, notwithstanding the Obstacles he meets in his way."
Therefore, as Ramsay pointed out, there were three things of
major consideration in an epic: "the Action, the Moral, and the
Poesy." Historical accuracy was subordinate to the moral purpose of the fable; and, in drawing the material for his "action"
from the Book of Joshua, Dwight took full advantage of his
poetic license to revise and invent. With an unexpected deference to the rules he condemned in his master's *Dissertation*, he
achieved unity of place by arranging that the entire conquest
take place in the neighborhood of Ai; and he gave unity to the
action by making Jabin, the Canaanite hero, comparable in
stature to Joshua, by condensing the campaign of many weeks
into the continuous activity of a few days, and by rearranging
the chronology in order that the victory at Gibeon might become the catastrophe of the poem and represent the final conquest of Canaan. He also took other liberties with his original,
especially with respect to the characters, leaving out most of
those who appeared in the Bible and inventing as many more
to take their places. Joshua, Caleb, and Eleazar, of course, were
important figures in the historical account of the Exodus and
the conquest; and the story of Achan, as Dwight told it, was
taken directly from the Book of Joshua. But Hezron, Zimri,
and Hanniel were barely mentioned in the Bible, with no hint
of the important roles Dwight allotted them. Of the heathen
leaders, only Jabin, Piram, Japhia, and a few others were mentioned by name in the Scriptures; and none was given any particular place in the narrative. Most of the others were products of pure invention. Ardan and Tadmore, the dissatisfied
Israelites, did not appear in the original story, nor did Irad, the
young hero whom the children of Israel expected to become a
second Joshua. The giants, Johab and Zedeck, and the other
mighty heroes of the Canaanites, all the Gibeonites, and all the
women characters were drawn from the poet's imagination.
The result was an apparent disregard for biblical authority
which greatly disturbed even so sympathetic a reviewer as William Cowper but, at the same time, a variety of characterization which none of Dwight's literary associates ever approached.

The entire action of *The Conquest of Canäan* possessed high moral significance; but Dwight was also aware that (in the language of the Introduction to *Telemachus*) "Virtue may be recommended both by Example and Instructions, either by the Manners or by the Precepts." Accordingly, although his poem abounded in Miltonic "high converse," full of precepts and instructions, he took particular care of the manners represented and called special attention to them in his own Preface:

> In the Manners, he has studied a medium between absolute barbarism and modern refinement. In the best characters, he has endeavoured to represent such manners, as are removed from the peculiarities of any age, or country, and might belong to the amiable and virtuous, of every age: such as are elevated without design, refined without ceremony, elegant without fashion, and agreeable, because they are ornamented with sincerity, dignity, and religion, not because they are polished by art and education. Of such manners, he hopes he may observe, without impropriety, that they possess the highest advantages for universal application.

Accordingly Joshua, "in peace, in war, the great all-moving soul," was represented as a God-fearing man of great wisdom and "calm endurance," "patient" and "serene," "Meek without meanness, noble without pride," faithful in friendship, ready to recognize merit in a foe, strong in his virtue, and domestic in his tastes.

> His form majestic, seem'd by God design'd
> The glorious mansion of so vast a mind:
> An awful grandeur in his countenance sate;
> Calm wisdom round him cast a solemn state.

In short, he was the finest type of leader, and a considerable improvement over the Old Testament Joshua. He could be terrible in his sudden wrath at treachery, as the unfortunate Ardan discovered; and,

> Tho' his feeling mind
> To crimes was gentle, and to misery kind,

he was just in his judgments. But he was never cruel. Instead of leading the Israelites in stoning and burning Achan and his family, he commanded Achan alone to die, committed him to the mercy of heaven, and with "Pity's eye pursued him to the grave." Dwight's Joshua could never have allowed his captains to put their feet upon the necks of the five kings of the Amorites, nor could he have killed them in cold blood and hanged their bodies. Instead, he was made to kill Piram and Japhia nobly in battle, in a fair fight. In other ways Joshua the epic hero was revealed as stern, just, and courageous, yet, at the same time, a kind, generous, and benevolent man of feeling. Other Israelites were formed according to the same ideal but to a lesser degree: Hezron, chief of Judah, was a truthful, honest man, strong and stubborn in virtue, benevolent, hospitable, and charitable, and simple and direct in manner; Aram was courageous and virtuous; Caleb was serene and vigorous in the ripeness of his years, calm in wisdom, sensible and persuasive in his speech; and Eleazar was contemplative, dignified, and holy in his great age. Such characteristics presumed sympathetic traits among the people who willingly submitted to these leaders, for, although the Israelites were ruled by God's elect, they were dominated by the persuasiveness of the leaders' virtues rather than by force. Nevertheless, the ideal manners of the Israelites required willing obedience to the elect and not to self-chosen demagogues: when "bold Ardan" dared to preach a democracy that would overthrow the established order, Joshua (without any biblical precedent) gave way to his single outburst of wrath, stepped from his place in the assembly, and drove his sword through "the culprit's" skull. Despite such primitive violence, however, Dwight was actually idealizing, in his "best characters," the sort of manners he thought he saw around him in New England—and Joshua, in particular, turned out to be so perfect a representation of the American ideal hero that later readers have persisted in confusing him with George Washington.

For the "Poesy" of *The Conquest of Canäan* Dwight "made use of Rhyme," either because he had experimented unsuccessfully with blank verse or "because," as he explained in the Preface, "he believed it would be more generally relished than blank verse, even amongst those who are esteemed persons of taste." The rhyme which he adopted was the heroic couplet of Pope's Homer; and, although Dwight apparently strove consciously for a greater animation in style than he found in his model, he seems to have paid little attention to the "harmony" of his numbers. For Dwight, like most of his contemporaries, was more concerned with the meaning than with the sound of his verse; and when he considered the subordinate sensory appeal of poetry he thought of achieving it through "imitation"—either by description or by the more "lively" method of using rhetorical figures. The young poet adopted the *Elements of Criticism* as his guidebook through the unfamiliar realm of poetry, beginning his epic "modestly" as Kames suggested and husbanding his "fire" until the readers' imaginations were supposedly well heated. He also subscribed to the Scottish critic's notion that the poet could appeal most readily and effectively to the visual sense. But neither of these critical commonplaces had the peculiar effect on Dwight's practice of poetry that was caused by the detailed advice given by Kames in his chapter on narration and description. Most of this advice was directed toward the single end of making the reader a spectator of the action by raising complete and "lively" images, by suppressing all useless incidents, and by representing things as they would naturally appear rather than as they might actually have been. Dwight, in a way that will be illustrated later, followed these suggestions with such meticulous care that Kames, had he read *The Conquest of Canäan*, could have obtained more illustrations of his precepts from the American epic than from the combined writings of Homer, Virgil, and Milton.

Dwight also had his own notions concerning poetry and apparently felt that the epic writers had unduly neglected physical nature as material for descriptions and a source for rhetorical figures. Accordingly, he was never content with a "rosy-fingered dawn" but usually described his sunrises and nightfalls rather fully and never as exactly the same. If the moon was high in the heavens on one evening, it was above the eastern hills on the next, and just rising on the evening afterward; and it gradually faded during the poem from its "clear, full beauty" until it shed only a "feeble twilight." Sometimes the morn was led "o'er misty hills" by the day star, and sometimes it burst into a cloudless blue sky. Other aspects and phenomena of na-

ture appeared in the poem; but Dwight made his greatest use
of nature in its grander, more sublime phases, with the result
that perhaps twoscore storms, figurative and real, roared
through the book and provoked a suggestion from Trumbull
that the author should have supplied his poem with a lightning
rod. Such excess was inevitable, however, and altogether in
keeping with Dwight's disposition. When he decided that an
idea was good, he usually pushed it to the limit of his own endurance. He had already, while an undergraduate, almost
ruined his eyesight by a self-established routine of excessive
study; and, while he was ruining his epic by an excessive devotion to critical precepts, he was also threatening his magnificent
physique by the rigid application of his curious theories of diet.

The Conquest of Canäan, however, was not based entirely
upon precepts. When Dwight ambitiously planned the poem
that was designed to be "the first of the kind, which has been
published in this country," he looked around with characteristic
thoroughness for the best examples he might follow. The modern composition of *The Adventures of Telemachus*, the continued
popularity of the works of Homer and Virgil, and the undoubted
greatness of *Paradise Lost* convinced him that an epic need not
appeal to a strictly "national interest"; and the simplicity of
manners which Lord Kames and others had found so praise-
worthy in Ossian may have encouraged him to believe that
primitive people need not behave like barbarians in order to be
convincing. But most of the influence that earlier examples had
upon his work was particular. All the machinery and many of
the structural and expository devices were Miltonic. The poem
opened with an invocation to the divine source of knowledge,
the action began with a parliamentary debate, and the narrative
occasionally paused for high converse in which the creation was
described, the history of the world summarized, the coming of
Christ prophesied, theology expounded, and the future envisioned—all of which was based upon Miltonic precedent as
firmly as was the machinery of angelic messengers or the Gib-
eonite hymn to the sun. The battle scenes, on the other hand,
were modeled on Pope's version of the *Iliad*. The Israelites and

the men of Canaan waved falchions in the air to make lightning play around their heads, threw their spears nimbly through the air or thrust with them in their hands, clashed their burnished, moonlike shields, darkened the skies with arrows, and threw huge stones at each other as they battled on the plain beneath the throngs watching from city walls. They might ride horseback between battles, but they fought only from low chariots; and, although there were some military improvements allowed in the form of mass tactics, steel armor, and trumpet signals, single combat with plenty of time for speechmaking was the rule, the heroes raging over the field in search of particular opponents whom they fought in spaces conveniently cleared by more insignificant warriors. In short, Dwight's poem was full of eighteenth-century Americans with Hebrew names who talked like Milton's angels and fought like prehistoric Greeks.

The original version of the masterpiece was finished sometime in 1775, and proposals for publishing it by subscription were made to the public on March 18, 1776. But the public was interested in other things. Accordingly, Dwight kept his manuscript in his private study, where it continued to grow by the spongelike process of absorbing new impressions made upon his emotions, very much as it had already absorbed the varied impressions made by his reading. The most important of these additions, as the author described them to Noah Webster, consisted of the third and fifth books and "a short passage or two in three of the others . . . . which were rather added, as the amusement of care and melancholy, than as necessary parts of the poem" in August, 1777. That month was the most trying, perhaps, in Dwight's life. Naphtali Daggett had announced his resignation on March 22, and Yale was to get a new president. Dwight, as senior tutor, had been given a special dispensation by the corporation to instruct the graduating class of 1777, thereby, in effect, taking over the educational duties of the president; and members of the class of 1778 were drawing up a petition requesting a continuation of the arrangement. Failing to appreciate in any way the vanity of his hopes, Dwight, with possible encouragement from one member of the corporation, apparently set his heart upon the college presidency. He had already qualified himself socially for the position by getting married during the previous March and by receiving his license to preach in June. He had little to do in August except wait for the September meeting of the corporation and avoid worry by writing verse.

Since the most perfect "amusement" of his "care and melancholy" appears to have been the contemplation of his own recent romance, the result was the introduction into *The Conquest of Canäan* of a long episode of romantic love in which Dwight added pathos to his epic and drew a picture of manners that would be especially instructive to young people. Irad, the hero of the episode, was a youth of twenty, rashly anxious for fame but at the same time gentle in love and affection for his parents. Pure religion, of the sort which neither "broods upon the surly brow" nor "walks on frozen joints," warmed "his manly brow." All the virgins in the Israelite camp felt "the conscious blush" when he approached; and, as he noticed them, "new, strange tremors through his bosom thrill'd." Selima, the heroine, was eighteen, "an Irad of a softer mould." She was tall, graceful, fair, and affectionate; "her voice was melody"; and "no vile cosmetic stain'd her lovely face," which was marked, instead, by "health's inimitable die." Already "her quick fancy, self-inspir'd to move" had "attun'd her feelings to romantic love"— the "spotless flame" that also secretly affected him. When finally he overcame his modesty sufficiently to confess his feelings, they developed their spiritual intimacy by taking long walks on which they discussed the attractions of nature, the evils of war, God's plans for the human race, and the fate of one of Selima's friends who was following the pattern of a chivalric romance through another episode in the poem. Neither the epic action nor the state of the author's own emotions, however, permitted poetic justice to be done to the idyllic couple. Irad, after a short career on the battlefield in which he proved himself the precursor of David and gave promise of becoming "a new Joshua," was unfairly slain by "some base hand unseen," leaving Selima to grieve for him.

Curious though this episode is as a revelation of Dwight's sentiment and possibly of his mental state at a critical moment in his career, it is most interesting as an illustration of how emotion could be strained through his rather pedantic, theory-ridden mind and so lose all force of reality in its expression. The young man would never have tried so hard to make himself a poet had he not possessed, to a considerable degree, the talent for verse-making which he occasionally revealed by a deft turn of expression. But he was too self-conscious to relax and let his talent have free play. He was acutely aware, of course, that an epic should be composed in the florid "sublime" and "middle" styles, never in the "low," for all his models illustrated that basic requirement and both Lord Kames and the more formal rhetoricians insisted upon it. Yet as time went on he should have become more at ease even in a style foreign to the natural pungency he displayed in conversation. Instead, however, he merely became aware of new theoretical possibilities of expression and so acquired an additional artificiality. In the course of writing *The Conquest of Canäan* Dwight composed approximately five thousand rather carefully considered heroic couplets; and, although he did manage to get much more poetic "fire" in the last book than he did in the first, the skill he developed reveals the lucubration of a schoolteacher rather than the ease of a poet.

Dwight had from the beginning intended *The Conquest of Canäan* to be a "sublime" poem and had evidently accepted the *Elements of Criticism* wholeheartedly as the best guide to the practice of his art. But, as he taught the principles of belles-lettres and literary composition to the Yale class of 1777 from Kames's book, he seems to have become more aware than ever before of the Scottish critic's psychological theories and of their pertinence to literary composition. The care with which he applied Kames's critical principles may be illustrated by a brief description from the Irad and Selima episode:

> In living green, the lawns at distance lay,
> Where snowy flocks mov'd round in vernal play;
> High tower'd the nodding groves; the cliffs sublime
> Left the low world, and dar'd th' assaults of time;

> Huge domes heav'd haughty to the morning fires,
> And the sun trembled round a thousand spires;
> All heaven was mild; and borne from subject vales,
> A cloud of fragrance cheer'd th' inchanting gales.

As a schoolteacher Dwight might have offered this passage to his students as a perfect illustration of theories they had just been studying. Conscious that "an elevated subject requires an elevated style" and that "a poet of any genius will not dress a high subject in low words," he had kept the diction florid; but within the limits of the diction he had made the "image" as "distinct" and "complete" as possible, allowing the reader to stand in "the very place" from which the scene was described and so behold it as "a real spectator" to whom the "appearance" of a thousand spires was more striking than the exact number that may have existed "in reality." Furthermore, the poet forced the mind's eye of his reader to follow the "course of nature" from the near to the far, the low to the high; and, realizing that "words are so far short of the eye in liveliness of impression that in a description the connection of objects ought to be carefully studied," he even held back the fragrance of the flowers in order that there might be no confusion between the senses of sight and smell until the complete visual image had been presented. He had missed almost none of Kames's recommendations concerning the proper way of appealing to the visual sense.

The fallacious psychology that lay back of this sort of descriptive writing may be found in *The Conquest of Canäan* from the beginning, but it appears to have become more completely dominant as Dwight's literary pedantry increased during the composition of the poem. An analysis of the critical ideas reflected in any given passage of verse represents, of course, guesswork at the best; and even the rigidly constructed images of *The Conquest of Canäan* do not reveal exactly when Dwight began to adopt—for purposes of composition, at least—Kames's other psychological theories of the "internal senses." By the time he wrote the passage quoted, however, he seems to have been fully aware of the possibility of constructing a description that would

appeal to the sense of the "sublime" as well as to the mind's
eye. The *Elements of Criticism* had emphasized the delightful
effect aroused "when elevation concurs with the course of nature," as it does in this case when the spectator raises his eyes
gradually up the mountains to the "heaven"; and this procedure
was supposed to appeal to "our sense of order" and also of "elevation." The similar procedure from "small to great"—sheep
on the lawns to the sun in the sky—was supposed to appeal to
the sense of "grandeur." And, in addition, a harmonious suggestion of sublime old age was introduced in reference to the
cliff. The eight lines, in fact, were as carefully calculated for
their effect on the inner sense of the sublime as for their effect
on the imaginative equivalent to the external sense of sight.

Although it should not be supposed, literally, that Dwight
had all these notions consciously in mind when he composed
these particular lines, the passage does epitomize and serve as a
convenient illustration for the sort of calculation that lay back
of *The Conquest of Canäan* as a whole. It was thoroughly characteristic of Timothy Dwight, who was later to become peculiarly celebrated for his habitual practice of "the art of method-
izing." What method lay behind the apparent madness of his
conglomerate epic is obscure, but there was at least a semblance
of one in his mind. During the course of the Revolution he
added a small but striking amount of new material that no ordinary theory of epic unity would have allowed him to introduce.
Yet he does not seem to have doubted the propriety of annexing
to the poem a considerable number of similes comparing the
biblical heroes with those who fell in the American war merely
in order "to indulge the Author's own emotions of regard to
the persons named in them." The most plausible explanation
for what would otherwise appear a completely uncharacteristic,
scatterbrained action is that Dwight, having rushed with youthful enthusiasm into the composition of an epic more eclectic
than *Telemachus*, found some justification of his plan in the
psychology of Lord Kames and was led by that justification
into an even more extraordinary eclecticism than he had shown
before. For one of the psychological rules laid down by Kames

was that "two pleasant emotions that are similar, readily unite when they are coexistent; and the pleasure felt in the union, is the sum of the two pleasures"; and he pointed out that such harmony of emotions might be called into existence by the perceptions of different senses. In another place, discussing the terms "grandeur" and "sublimity," he called attention to the "double signification" of words that were applied sometimes to qualities in objects and sometimes to the emotions aroused by these qualities, and he insisted particularly on the power of the mind to "abstract" all irrelevant emotions from the impression of sublimity that a certain object might make. Since the determining factor of Dwight's eclecticism seems to have been, in almost every case, his notion of the sublime or of something pleasantly like that, it is not impossible that he expected all his miscellaneous material—the "great" action, "elevated" manners, sublime descriptions, Homeric battles, profound discourses, patriotic sentiments, and everything else—to provoke emotions sufficiently alike to harmonize and so give his poem some sort of psychological unity. He never explained his procedure to the extent of developing an individual epic theory that he was willing to place before the public; but, if he had proceeded through the composition of *The Conquest of Canäan* without some possible explanation in the back of his mind, that action would have been both unique and completely out of character.

The only other published work that Dwight composed during his tutorship was *A Valedictory Address to the Young Gentlemen Who Commenced Bachelors of Arts at Yale-College, July 25, 1776.* As a commencement address, delivered at the private exercises on July 24, it was a stirring composition, full of general patriotism, optimistic visions of the future, and good advice for students who were going out into the professions. At the same time it was a cautious expression of revolutionary fervor, for the Declaration of Independence was to impel Dwight's father to leave the rebellious Colonies, and Dwight himself was at first unwilling to take a definite stand on the "great and important events" of the summer. He did, however, refer to the British

constitution as "an uncouth *Gothic* pile" and fill his address with
references to the rising glory of America. Evidences of the
world's constant progress, the westward course of empire, and
the prophecy of the millennium all led to the conclusion, he believed, that "here," in America, "the progress of temporal
things toward perfection will undoubtedly be finished. Here
human greatness will find a period." He did not expect his
hearers to witness the arrival of the millennium, but he called
upon them to regard themselves as men whose wishes, designs,
and labors were "not to be confined to the narrow bounds of the
present age"; and he felt that the great prospect should particularly inspire them to contribute to the advancement of science and avoid unprogressive "empiricism" in the practice of
their professions.

There was no inducement for Dwight to speak at the next
commencement. It was clear that Ezra Stiles was to be called
to the presidency, and Dwight resigned his tutorship and became a chaplain in the Revolutionary army. By leaving New
Haven he, like Trumbull, brought to an unsuccessful close the
most ambitious and energetic phase of his literary career. He
had not followed in his friend's footsteps to the extent of arousing antagonism by his verse, but he had notably failed to
arouse sufficient enthusiasm in a war-worried public to justify
the publication of his efforts. Verse, he had found, was not the
"flowery road to fame" that it was supposed to be. By the time
he at last was able to test the public reaction to his epic flight,
in the autumn of 1785, he himself had become doubtful of its
greatness. He used a couplet from Pope on the title-page:

> Fired, at first sight, with what the Muse imparts,
> In fearless youth we tempt the height of arts;

and he concluded his prefatory note with perhaps the most
apologetic statement he ever offered to the public:

That he wishes to please he frankly confesses. If he fails in the design, it
will be a satisfaction that he shall have injured no person but himself. As the
poem is uniformly friendly to delicacy, and virtue, he hopes his countrymen
will so far regard him with candour, as not to impute it to him as a fault,
that he has endeavoured to please them, and has thrown in his mite, for the
advancement of the refined arts, on this side of the Atlantic.

This oblique farewell to Calliope would have been rather pathetic had it not come from a young man whose chief fault was his determination to be great before he became merely good. *The Conquest of Canäan*—a "mite" nearly as long as *Paradise Lost*—was remarkable evidence of Dwight's energy and poetic determination, but it did little to develop whatever natural talent he may have possessed. He was too careful, too anxious to play safe, to allow himself a normal development; and he decided to be great in other fields before he really found what he was capable of achieving in literature.

IV

For over a year, from October, 1777, until he received news of his father's death in January, 1779, he followed the army as chaplain to General Parsons' brigade. His formal duties would have allowed him adequate leisure for composition, had he still remained ambitious for literary fame; but he seems to have contented himself with the preparation of his sermons, the instruction of uneducated soldiers, and the production of an occasional patriotic song. The one discourse from this period which he found worthy of preservation and later publication was *A Sermon, Preached at Stamford, in Connecticut, upon the General Thanksgiving, December 18th, 1777*. Neither very inspired nor very inspiring, it is interesting chiefly because it shows Dwight practicing the old New England custom of drawing parallels between the Americans and the Israelites—a custom which irritated him when the readers of *The Conquest of Canäan* practiced it and interpreted the poem as an allegory of the American war. Of the several "universally popular" songs he is supposed to have written, the only one which has survived is "Columbia, Columbia, to glory arise." It actually was sufficiently popular to have started echoes from a number of Dwight's contemporaries, for it paraphrased in fluent anapestic couplets the "rising glory" passages in his *Valedictory Address* and so was an easily remembered expression of the most overworked theme in eighteenth-century American verse.

Neither of these effusions had any significant relationship to

Dwight's later work. Up until this time he had been living the life of an academic recluse, reading the books that were pertinent to his own occupation as a schoolteacher or as a poet but showing no great interest in the world of contemporary ideas. After he accepted his father's position as head of the large household in Northampton, however, he began to settle into his permanent role as a commentator on modern fashions in ideas. The change in interest became apparent in *A Sermon, Preached at Northampton, on the Twenty-eighth of November, 1781: Occasioned by the Capture of the British Army, under the Command of Earl Cornwallis*. Energetic and vivid in style, the discourse was dominated by a spirited belief in "the tendency of human affairs, unless interrupted by extraordinary incidents, to be constantly progressive towards what may be termed natural perfection." Dwight cited specific evidence of this tendency as he saw it. Montesquieu and Beccaria (whose *Essay on Crimes and Punishments* was soon to appear serially in two Connecticut periodicals) represented progress in knowledge, and the American "convulsion" had been the result of inevitable political progress. Further evidence of this tendency might be found in the "increase of commercial intercourse," for "from this source," Dwight believed at the time,

is derived that expansion of mind peculiar to those who visit and converse with different nations; and who learn, by an acquaintance with the customs of others, to think with less prejudice and pride concerning their own. Hence springs a reciprocation of benefits; a general knowlege of wants, and the means of supplying them; and experimental acquaintance with the necessity, and amiableness of hospitality; and an universal enlargement of the habits of thinking, which effectually extirpates the homebred surliness of solitude. Hence naturally arise more rational ideas of civil policy; a milder administration of government; knowledge to discern and desires to enjoy, the usurped rights of men; and a general spirit of humanity; an universal civility of deportment, which, although due to man as man, have in most instances, been shamefully sacrificed at the shrine of superiority.

The optimistic spirit of the times for a while overwhelmed the man who only seven years before had been converted to the strict College Church and who had prepared himself for the ministry by devoting himself to the New Light theology of his grandfather under the directions of his grandfather's son, name-

sake, and disciple. Dwight's theory of progress was clearly teleological, of course, leading to a wholly orthodox millennium;
but it was not Calvinistic, and in its expression it was almost
identical with the "fantastic" theorizing Dwight was to denounce so vigorously some years later.

The optimism which dominated this sermon, however, was
not complete. It did not apply to England. "Within a few years
past," Dwight had discovered, "many principal persons of that
island have laborously imployed themselves in reducing wickedness to a system" by insisting that "selfishness" was "not only
a just spring of moral action, but the only possible spring." He
particularly attacked "Lord Chesterfield's scheme of education;
in which the great doctrine, I have mentioned, is made the basis
of the most winning, most deceitful, and most ruinous system
of evil, hitherto devised by the great adversary of men." The
Letters in which Chesterfield's scheme was set forth had been
advertised only a few months before in Hartford, and Dwight
may have been worried by their growing popularity in America. But it is more probable that he had already begun to cultivate his habit of using digests and secondary sources of information whenever possible and had seen in the same bookshop
Thomas Hunter's *Reflections Critical and Moral on the Letters of
the Late Earl of Chesterfield*. In any case his comments on Chesterfield form a rather neat summary of those made by Hunter.
Likewise, his attack upon the "crude incoherences of Voltaire"
as being more dangerous than the "subtle, refined sophistry of
Hume" may have been inspired by Hunter's attention to the
author of *The Reign of Louis XIV* and his special reference to
Voltaire's description of Calvinism as a "new pest, which has
laid waste the world." The antagonism roused in Dwight's
mind by Voltaire's writings (of which he evidently had the most
casual knowledge) and by the "dreams of universal redemp-
tion," which he contemptuously linked with them, proved much
more productive, as a permanent source of literary inspiration,
than the idea of progress that aroused his momentary enthusiasm.

His most immediate literary productions, however, were in

some way related to the critical reception given to *The Conquest of Canäan*. For in spite of the defenses set up in the brief, rather apologetic Preface to the youthful epic, *The Conquest of Canäan* was not well received when it appeared in the autumn of 1785; and Dwight, like many another poet before and since, anticipated its reception and began to brood on the subject of critics. The first result was a fable, written in September, 1785, entitled "The Critics." It was a vicious attack upon "the genuine curs of men" in octosyllabic couplets worthy of Trumbull, whose *M'Fingal* seems, by evidence of an occasional echo, to have been the model for the verse. The fable traced the origin of the critical tribe to a lot of curs whom Juno had caught yapping at a greyhound, transformed into human forms, and ordered:

> Whate'er adorns the ennobled mind,
> Sublime, inventive, and refin'd;
> With spleen, and spite, forever blame,
> And load with every dirty name.
> All things of noblest kind and use,
> To your own standard vile reduce,
> And all in wild confusion blend,
> Nor heed the *subject, scope,* or *end.*
> But chief, when *modest young beginners,*
> 'Gainst *critic laws,* by *nature* sinners,
> Peep out in verse, and dare to run,
> Thro' towns and villages your own,
> Hunt them, as when yon stranger dog
> Set all your growling crew agog;
> Till stunn'd, and scared, they hide from view,
> And leave the country clear for you.

Such an attack, of course, was beneath Dwight's dignity as a minister and an epic poet, and it was not published until nearly six years later. Yet as a private expression of spleen it did not provide sufficient release for the author's emotions. Accordingly, he began to read, carefully perhaps for the first time, the satiric verse of other poets. Pope's *Epistle to Dr. Arbuthnot* appears to have attracted an especially sympathetic interest; and the *Satires* generally, read under such circumstances, were sufficiently attractive to arouse the "passion of emulation." An occasion was ready at hand, for Dwight's younger friend, David

Humphreys, had addressed to him a verse letter on the occasion
of his departure for Europe the previous autumn. Dwight accordingly proceeded to compose his delayed answer in an "Epistle to Col. Humphreys," which imitated Pope's imitations of
Horace. The home-staying American was able to express his
general point of view in a single couplet—

> Of all the plagues, that rise in human shape,
> Good Heaven, preserve us from the travell'd Ape!

—for he apparently had the notion that many a good American
had dwindled into a "Fibble" as a result of European travel and
exposure to the manners of Lord Chesterfield, the ideas of Voltaire, and the subversive influences of "*acted* plays." Some of
the couplets were extraordinarily naïve for a man of Dwight's
age and position, such as those begging Humphreys to retain a
"great simplicity of soul":

> When round thy course temptations sweetly throng,
> When warbling sirens chant the luscious song.

But perhaps nothing better could be expected from a provincial
imagination that was being nourished by the pictures of London
society drawn by satiric poets. The "Epistle" in any case was
primarily a literary exercise, and it is less interesting as a revelation of what an educated and influential American may have
thought of London than as an indication of the way in which
Dwight's literary interests were developing.

Still, the suspicious antagonism toward English manners and
culture which Dwight had shown in his Northampton sermon
and his epistle to Humphreys probably had a determining effect upon his plan for a series of periodical essays for the *New-
Haven Gazette and the Connecticut Magazine*. "Addison owes his
principal reputation for fine writing to the Spectator, and Johnson derives his highest character from the Rambler," he held
in the first number of "The Friend" (for March 23, 1786), which
defended the diverse, familiar, and short prose sketch. He admitted that "many of the British collections of this kind possess
a high degree of merit, and will probably never be excelled, per-

haps never rivalled by any succeeding efforts." But American readers, he thought, could not derive the same pleasure and instruction that the readers in Queen Anne's age could from the *Spectator* because of the great difference in social conditions, many of Addison's apt illustrations from real life finding no application in the United States. "Yet from real life almost all valuable observations concerning the conduct of life are drawn," he insisted; "the human character, in its variegations, is a topic to the human eye literally boundless; and from it may be drawn sentiments, and methods of exhibiting them, ever new, various, pleasing, and important." Previous attempts at the familiar essay in America, he explained, possibly remembering "The Meddler," had failed because writers had drawn material from books and speculations rather than from life; for "such remarks, however ingenious, will rarely be interesting. .... Essayists will ever find themselves disappointed in the reception, with which their remarks on human life meet, unless they are drawn from life. Men must have seen the original, before they will be much pleased with the copy." Thus his own efforts in this field were to be original in material if not in manner. "Every age, every country, every stage in the progress of society" provided new matter for the essayist; particularly, "The present state of society, in this part of America, is replete with topics of this nature. The entire novelty of our circumstances is too manifest to require illustration." Accordingly, Dwight was to be "the Friend" to each reader and "to the whole human race"; and he promised that it would "be his aim to present the public with new topics, or new modes of considering them, and especially to exhibit a new series of sentiments, suited to the present state of society in this country." For he felt that, unless he was deceived, "this field, although a most interesting one to Americans, has been hitherto .... almost wholly unoccupied."

For the following week Dwight presented an autobiographical sketch of "James Littlejohn, Esq.," author of "the Friend," a retiring, nature-loving American, who was characterized by a quaintness of character that proved descent from the *Spectator* and would have made him, had he flourished on the other side

of the Atlantic, a reputed ancestor of the later Elia. Born in
1748, and so four years older than his creator, he had owed as
much as other children to "the standing-stool, and the go-cart"
and had been distinguished as a child only by early signs of
"wanting common sense" and by an abundance of refined sentiment which caused birdnesting to give him "the highest sensations of pain." His unwillingness to swear and the general peculiarity of his conduct gained him "many titles of distinction;
and Littlejohn was, in different mouths, a strange boy—a youth
of no life—a coward—and a simpleton." But,

in the meantime I was not without my pleasures. Every production of nature
gave me peculiar satisfaction; and every occurrence of happiness expanded my
bosom with joy. The cheerful, the beautiful, the solemn, and the sublime,
varied my sensations with a delightful series of agitation. In flowers, I traced
a pencil, to which I believed Titian was a dauber; and in many a human form,
an elegance of moulding, to which I convinced myself the author of the Venus
de Medicis was but a carver of radishes. A solemn dignity swelled all my feelings, beneath the wide wild grandeur of the rude, and lofty mountain. From
the summit of that mountain, I beheld with transport the majestic diversities
of infinite workmanship; and anticipated, with ecstatic vision, the period,
when a wish would waft me to a distant world, more easily than I beheld the
eagles sail from one summit to another.

As I was literally "good for nothing to work," my father sent me to a neighbouring College, to see if he could make anything of me. The original cast of
nature is irresistible. Amidst all my father's wishes, and my tutor's laborious
efforts, I was still Littlejohn. . . . . My fellow students loved and laughed at
me; some of them thought me a great genius, and some of them thought me a
blockhead: but all agreed that I was a strange creature.

After college he had attempted the art of healing, but his "extreme fears of doing harm" commonly prevented him "from
doing any good"; and when he received a competence at the
death of his father he retired to advise and assist his fellow-men.
Having reached the height of six feet, three inches, at the age
of fifteen, he was awkward as well as timid; and he thought that
such a person would ever be exposed to adventures, though he
anticipated that his would be more amusing to his companions
than to himself. Accordingly, Littlejohn set out to write down
his wisdom and observations, hoping to add to "the stock of
human knowledge" and with the further expectations "of furnishing the tea-table with a subject of convenient chit chat; of

assisting children in learning to read; of aiding the smoaker to light his pipe, and his wife to bake her gingerbread."

James Littlejohn was much more alive, as a character, than the *Spectator* had been; and if Dwight had kept him breathing throughout the entire series of fifteen papers he would have accomplished a coherent body of personal essays such as had never been seen in America. But Littlejohn was the product of a mood too occasional to sustain a character even in a series of essays. The underlying feeling of irritation which had appeared in the satires was still strong in Dwight, and, as a result, Littlejohn practically disappeared after writing his autobiography and was replaced by John Homely, a pretended contributor, who wrote in a "style and manner . . . . more replete with spirit" than Littlejohn's "mild disposition would have dictated." Homely's characterizing humor was resentment at the American "predilection for Britons." He hated the worship of European adventurers that he saw developing in his country, resented the arrogance and condescension of foreigners, and delighted in pointing out the humble origins of the English, Irish, and Continentals who had obtained positions of distinction in American community and political life. This last tendency involved "the Friend" in the sort of bitterly personal satire which had soured "The Correspondent" and may have had something to do with the curious appearance of the fifteenth and concluding number on October 4, 1787, nearly a year after the fourteenth. But in the meantime Homely had been allowed to give eloquent expression to Dwight's feelings about America and to underline the contrasting fears that had been growing in his mind since his optimistic sermon of 1781:

When I see ten thousand fetters of authority and system dissolved, as by the fairy touch of enchantment, and the mind, escaping from prison, beginning to prune its wings for elevated and daring adventures; I cannot but persuade myself that these mighty preparations of Providence are designed for advantageous changes in the affairs of men. I cannot but think arts, policy, science, and virtue, will begin to wear a brighter aspect, and claim a more extensive influence. Judge then of the mortification, I must experience, in seeing any event begin to overcast this delightful prospect, and threaten the return of all those prejudices, which, through a long and dismal continuance, have darkened the horizons of the eastern continent.

The fears, at the time Dwight published this on April 27, 1786, were rather vaguely founded upon a belief that "mere Europeanism" was beginning to count for more than ability in achieving "property, influence and reputation" in America. The author advanced some evidence in support of his belief, but to do so he had to strain so hard and go so far afield that the worries of John Homely give evidence less of Dwight's good sense than of the gradual decay of the optimistic spirit that filled him at the close of the war.

The reception of *The Conquest of Canäan* may have had something to do with its author's pessimistic view of the ability of homebred genius to achieve "reputation." The matter was still on his mind, and three numbers of "The Friend" dealt with literary criticism in a way that served indirectly to defend the epic. The first of these essays took the position that "among the prejudices which are entertained by the mind, none has a more powerful influence, than reverence for the opinions and practices of those who have lived before us." Writing of the "Aristotelian" rules, Dwight revealed an even greater impatience than Lord Kames had shown with "the blind veneration that is paid to the ancient classic writers":

This code of criticism has partly escaped the depredations of time, and is now a law less disputed, even by most persons of taste, than either of the two fundamental rules of moral rectitude. Had these three poets been moderns; had Milton written Paradise Lost, when the Iliad was written, and the best tragedies of Shakespeare been exhibited on the Athenian stage . . . . how different a system would these events have produced; and how many rules would have been received, with the same implicit faith, with which every age has now swallowed their opposites. Many of Aristotle's present laws would then have been considered as the lunacies of a Zolius.

"Every original genius adds," he maintained, in one of the commonplaces of the late eighteenth century, "to the stock of critical ideas. . . . . Hence criticism will advance towards a higher perfection, as the varieties of the human mind open new views of poetical objects, and the peculiarity of genius furnish new springs and meanderings of delight." His objection to the critical rules derived from the ancients was that of Lord Kames— that they were, in effect, unscientific because they attempted to erect a single specimen into a class or a species. They did not, in the phrase so thoroughly drilled into the minds of Yale students, consider "things as they are." Dwight apparently had little hope for the overthrow of critical rules in Europe, but

in our own happy state of society, disjoined from the customs and systems of Europe, commencing a new system of science and politics, it is to be ardently hoped, that so much independence of mind will be assumed by us, as to induce us to shake off these rusty shackles, examine things on the plan of nature and evidence, and laugh at the grey-bearded decisions of doting authority.

The other two critical essays in the series were on the specific subject of "Taste." Although these may have been inspired in part by Hugh Blair's new *Lectures on Rhetoric and Belles-Lettres*, Dwight began the first with a quotation from Lord Kames's *Sketches of the History of Man* and gave a definition of taste based so clearly on Kames that at least the Table of Contents of the *Elements of Criticism* seems to have been open before him while he wrote. Primarily an attack upon New England election sermons, the essay nevertheless made a strong defense of the "faculty by which we discern . . . . instinctively, and clearly" such qualities as beauty, grandeur, and sublimity; and the perceptions of that faculty were specifically defended against the "pope-like authority of Custom" and the "blind reverence for that, which has been done, or esteemed, by our ancestors." The second and more literary of the essays on taste professed, in the manner of Kames, to examine the subject with reference to "principles of nature and experience"; and in it Dwight emphasized his general, though slightly qualified, critical agreement with Kames by declaring that "a disposition to receive pleasure from some or all" of the objects of the moral and physical world "is probably common to the whole race of man; but, like all other human characteristics, in different minds in very different degrees." The most interesting passage in the essay, however, is one elaborated from the definition of terms in the Appendix to the *Elements of Criticism*, probably after Dwight had meditated his own procedure in *The Conquest of Canäan:*

Invention is nothing but compounding the ideas which the mind has derived from observation, so as to form new images, or pictures, out of those materials. . . . . Compounding these ideas is the whole of what is intended by invention, and compounding the different ideas, impressed by the beauties of the natural and moral world, is the whole of what is called poetical invention or imagination. Few words will be necessary to shew how great advantages for inventing and imagining he will possess over all others, whose collection of such objects [of taste] is large, distinct, and strongly impressed. His pictures will all be strongly and clearly traced, and, being formed from a great variety of materials, will possess a corresponding variety; while, from the possession of an accurate standard for the comparing his own pictures, as well as those of others, he will almost necessarily assimilate them to nature and propriety.

Neither this passage nor the essays as a whole attempted a defense of *The Conquest of Canäan*. Dwight was too sensitive to the dignity of his position to attempt any such thing directly, although he later gave Noah Webster material for an attack upon adverse critics. But any reader who absorbed the critical system advocated by "The Friend" would, theoretically at least, view the epic more favorably than would an unenlightened reader. For "compounding the different ideas, impressed by the beauties [or, more strictly, the sublimities] of the natural and moral world," was almost the whole of the "poetical invention or imagination" in *The Conquest of Canäan;* and Dwight had evidently depended to some extent for the psychological unity of his poem upon the disposition "common to the whole race of man" to receive pleasure from these ideas. He was in no position, of course, to understand how bad Kames's psychology was or to admit how pedantic had been his use of it. Querulous though his private fable on critics might have been, a public complaint was impossible for him. But somewhere in the back of his mind, despite his rather apologetic feeling toward his youthful epic, there was an irritating, defensive suspicion that his poetic reputation had suffered from a stupid and un-American "reverence for that, which has been done, or esteemed, by our ancestors."

V

The antagonism toward authority, toward reverence for literary models, and toward the American "predilection for Britons" which Dwight expressed in "The Friend" did not last.

It was a temporary product of a dual emotional state—the buoyancy that came from having been on the winning side in a political and military contest with the forces of oppression and the irritations arising from a belief that his literary battle had been lost to the same forces. The irritation eventually exhausted itself, and the optimistic buoyancy was exhausted by the strength of other influences operating against it. By temperament Dwight was given to obeying reasoned precepts rather than impulse. By training he believed in "things as they are" rather than in tenuous speculations. By profession of faith he accepted the unoptimistic religious beliefs of Jonathan Edwards, and by the practice of his profession he defended them. And by observation he became aware, especially during the winter of 1786–87, that his country was somewhat less than perfect and that its imperfections were the result of neither a reverence for authority nor a predilection for Britons. Accordingly, he restrained his progress in the direction indicated by his writings after the Revolution: only his interest in verse satire as a literary form and his antagonism to freethinking and free salvation (which also found expression in the sixth number of "The Friend") remained as a strong influence upon his later work. In his youthful, most ambitious work Dwight had set up a factitious ideal of greatness as a standard; in his early maturity, when he had lapsed into merely occasional writing, he indulged in an emotional sincerity which not only makes these writings more agreeable to later readers but apparently released, also, a genuine talent that had not been able to raise its head above the heights of his early ambition. The curious and unfortunate paradox, however, is that when Dwight was most attractive in his emotional sincerity he was expressing emotions that were neither lasting nor wholly true to his character.

CHAPTER IV

DAVID HUMPHREYS

I

THE youthful David Humphreys is a more shadowy figure than either Trumbull or Dwight. He entered college in 1767 at the comparatively mature age of fifteen, after having been prepared by his father in the parsonage at Derby; and if he exhibited any of the precocity which characterized his two later friends it seems to have been neither encouraged nor recorded. Yet he was apparently a serious-minded lad, well fitted to profit by the "passion of emulation" which was dominant at Yale when he became a Freshman. Already showing prophetic signs of the tall, handsome, rather florid young man who graduated four years later, he was restive under the exaggerated subservience which upperclassmen enforced upon new students and unwilling to wait a year before making a "show" of himself before the undergraduate public. Accordingly, he became an energetic student of the reviving art of oratory and, if tradition may be trusted, one of the founders of the new Brothers in Unity literary organization, which set itself up as a rival of the old, established, and somewhat exclusive Linonian Society. He also tried his hand at verse and, like Dwight, attracted the attention of the older Jack Trumbull by his compositions. But he had no remarkable success with the more solid learning and consequently received no place of honor on the commencement program. Nor did resident graduate study offer any overwhelming attractions to him after he received his first degree. He succeeded Trumbull to the school in Wethersfield for two years and from there wrote occasional verse letters to his predecessor, so playing a distant, minor part in the brief flurry of the New Haven renaissance until he moved into a different environment by becoming tutor to Philipse Manor on the Hudson. His literary reputation became such that he was invited to deliver a graduate oration when he took his second degree in 1774, but his remarks on "Taste" apparently were not sufficiently exciting to warrant publication and have not been preserved.

Under the influence of the well-to-do manorial Philipses, Humphreys may have decided even by this time to be a gentleman first and a scholar afterward. The war offered him his opportunity. He left the service of his loyalist employers, refused the offer of a tutorship at Yale, and entered the army—beginning as an aide to General Parsons and later moving up through the staffs of Generals Putnam and Greene until he became a colonel under Washington. He devoted both his talent for personal address and his skill at versification to his rise; but his ambition was modified by a genuine patriotism and an inherent tendency toward hero-worship, and he was completely happy as a member of the Commander-in-Chief's official family. Such public duties as the presentation of the captured banners of Lord Cornwallis to the United States Congress and such private associates as the aristocratic foreigners who surrounded the General gave him a new vision of the world and left him forever estranged in spirit from rustic Connecticut. His devotion to Washington lasted beyond the war until—like Ernest of *The Great Stone Face*—he came to look like him; and Washington, in turn, was so impressed by his loyalty that he took the unusual course of exercising his political influence in a friend's behalf. Humphreys, as a result, became secretary to the commission for negotiating treaties of trade with Europe and between 1784 and 1786 developed his lasting taste for diplomatic life abroad. Neither the best efforts of his pen nor his most suggestive hints, however, prevented him from being recalled at the conclusion of his mission; and he returned unwillingly to Connecticut, where he served in the state legislature and as an officer of the frontier guard until the turn of events brought him again into a larger, and more splendid, sphere of action.

II

Humphreys eventually came to believe that he and Trumbull had formed their "taste together, and on the same models," and he flattered himself that "a certain similarity of genius, and congeniality of soul" had been the basis of their early friendship at Yale. His belief was founded in sentiment rather than in reality, however, for, even in the classical authors to which he referred, Humphreys was less well read than his older friend; and, if he was thinking only of their undergraduate courses in Cicero and Horace, he was greatly underestimating the extent of Trumbull's learning and literary interests. Most of Humphreys' graduate study was done at a distance from the Yale library, and his knowledge of English literature and criticism was much more limited than Trumbull's. During his Senior year in college Humphreys had apparently exchanged a number of verse letters with his friend, who was then in Wethersfield, and —if the octosyllabic letter published as "The Correspondent" for July 23, 1773, actually was his—this correspondence was continued at intervals for a number of years afterward. These exchanges, of course, were similar in form and presumably based on the same models; but there the similarity between the early work of the two men stopped. Humphreys, the hero-worshiper, may have written the couplets comparing Trumbull with Pope that appeared in the *Connecticut Journal* for November 30, 1770, in an effort to encourage the downcast satirist, from whom he had received so disillusioned a letter a few days before. If the little poem was really his, it was an early revelation of the most marked contrast between the two friends: Humphreys regularly practiced a dignified flattery of important people that was utterly foreign to Trumbull's sardonic tendency to look upon most men, no matter how important, as fools. One of the earliest of Humphreys' acknowledged poems, which has not been preserved, was apparently written to celebrate the "illustrious actions" of General Washington and sent, on July 8, 1776, to his aide, Colonel Samuel B. Webb, with a hint that it be called to the attention of the Commander-in-Chief. Humphreys modestly admitted that "it was the employment of only half an hour"; but he felt that the subject was "a noble one and he must be a stupid fellow, who couldn't say one clever thing upon it." The poem was not presented, but its author continued to think of using his verse in the practice of a sort of democratic court-craft, though he later became smoother in his address. The letter to Webb, however, is of unusual interest because it reveals that from the beginning Humphreys affected an extremely casual attitude toward his verse and apparently really believed that the choice of a subject was of more importance to a poet than the literary skill he exercised upon it.

Except for one verse letter to Trumbull, the early experimental work of Humphreys, like that of Dwight, either has been lost or has remained unidentified. The essay on "Taste" which he delivered when he received his Master's degree in 1774 might have indicated that he shared his friends' interest in Lord Kames; but there is no direct evidence bearing on the possibility, for the essay has not survived and there are no signs of the Scottish critic's influence on Humphreys' published works. The supposedly early poems printed for the first time in his *Miscellaneous Works* of 1804 were probably carefully revised before publication. For example, Humphreys, if his own notes may be trusted, was one of the first Americans to write in the sonnet form. Yet the first of his sonnets, addressed to his friends at Yale College upon his departure to join the army, indicates a transition from "inglorious ease" to "the din of battle" which was much more direct than the actual fact, and the poet would have needed an extraordinarily prophetic vision to have been inspired by "starry banners" before he bade goodbye to Yale. Though this and the two following sonnets, "On the Revolutionary War in America" and "On the Prospect of Peace, in 1783," may represent later revisions of earlier attempts, they were curious experiments, nevertheless, for they seem to reflect a direct structural influence from Spenser which was distinctly unusual in America at this time. Humphreys adopted the concluding Alexandrine of the Spenserian stanza and the linked rhymes of both the stanza and the sonnet, making a single change by in-

serting his fifth rhyme in the eleventh line. The application of
the form to public events may have been suggested by Milton's
poems, which were certainly in Humphreys' mind when he
echoed *Paradise Lost* twice in the first sonnet. But the final
effect was neither Spenserian nor Miltonic: Humphreys completely avoided what Trumbull called "the drawling style of old
Spenser," and he used a smoothness of diction and an excess of
rhetorical figures far removed from the sonnets of Milton. The
single change in the Spenserian rhyme scheme was also of considerable importance, because it actually meant that the last
ten lines formed two linked quintains (which Humphreys separated by a pause) and that the entire poem was thus divided into
three equally distinct parts. The fourth sonnet, "On Disbanding
the Army," kept the same movement with a less regular rhyme
scheme, and the poet did not adopt the conventional division between octave and sestet until nearly twenty years later.

The most important of Humphreys' early experimental poems
were done as a result of accidental circumstances. In December,
1779, he was accompanying General Putnam on his way to join
the army in winter quarters when the General was stricken with
a paralysis that removed him from active service. Since the attack occurred in the neighborhood of Hartford, Humphreys decided to make use of his unexpected leisure by visiting Connecticut friends, with whom he remained for several months,
pleading an "ill-state of health" that made it inadvisable for
him to join the army "during the inactive season of the year."
Much of his time during the first four months of 1780 was spent
in New Haven; and there, "being instigated by the Devil and a
certain Jere Wadsworth," he wrote and "consented to publish"
an ambitious poem addressed to the American armies. He was
also induced to "turn Scribbler" in a more general way and experiment with various types of verse; and he humorously explained to General Greene that the "mischief" had probably
been caused by "keeping ill Company, such as the before mentioned Col. Wadsworth, a certain Mr. Trumbull, a Mr. Dwight,
a Dr. Stiles and some other similar Characters of smaller noto-

riety"—among them Joel Barlow, for whom Humphreys developed a friendly admiration toward the end of the winter.

One of the first experimental pieces was an "Elegy on the Burning of Fairfield, in Connecticut," which, he wrote General Greene in April, "was suggested (not inspired according to poetic custom) by a view of the ruins of that once beautiful Town; and was written to indulge a pleasing kind of melancholy, and while away a vacant hour the other morning." In attempting the elegy, Humphreys adopted the conventional quatrain, but he took the comparatively animated Shenstone as his model rather than the quieter Gray. Like Shenstone, who said that in his descriptions he "fairly drew his picture from the spot," Humphreys claimed that his poem was written "on the spot where the town stood." He dated it 1779, in the year of the event; referred to the "smoking ruins" and warm ashes; and described the "scorch'd elms" with their "untimely" loss of foliage almost as though he had followed with a notebook on the heels of Governor Tryon's soldiers in their July raid. In other ways, however, he grossly exaggerated the exclamatory style and lively imagery that he had found in Shenstone's elegies. Humphreys was so solemn about his patriotism and the subject seemed to him so grave that he felt it entirely appropriate to call up "visionary shapes," "red in their wounds," before his readers in order to arouse their emotions—and it did not occur to him that the emotions aroused would not be proper ones. This tendency to overwork rhetorical figures technically "suited to move the Passions" was revealed again in an "Elegy on Lieutenant De Hart" which was probably written later in the same year. In this he was trying to imitate "A Pastoral Ballad," with which Shenstone was to charm so many young Americans into attempts at pathetic verse. But, even though he avoided the pastoral allusions that Dr. Johnson considered sickening, the swinging trimeter, the pathetic representation of the sister mourning for her brother, and the gory description of De Hart's death did not make a sympathetic combination. The attempt at a new sort of elegy was unsuccessful, but Humphreys—who, in one

poem or another, celebrated perhaps a score of heroic deaths
during the Revolution—continued to think death in battle one
of the noblest of subjects; and during the following year he wrote,
partially in verse, "An Epitaph" on Alexander Scammel, which
he reprinted in every edition of his collected works.

The company in New Haven during the first four months of
1780 was too good for Humphreys to remain altogether in the
"pleasing melancholy" of his elegiac mood, and it was natural
that he should turn back to the humorous, octosyllabic verse
letter of the days before the war. In "A Letter to a Young Lady
in Boston," which he dated from New Haven, in April, 1780, he
showed that he was capable of an unpretentious ease in light
verse that was amusing for its mocking allusiveness to literature
and its casual treatment of the affairs of everyday life. In it he
paid graceful compliments to his associates in literature—Trumbull, Dwight, and the newly discovered Barlow. But in this case
again he did not publish an accurate version of verses composed
on the date given, for he concluded the printed copy with an
announcement of the appointment to Washington's staff, which
was not offered him until the end of June and not even anticipated in April. It was probably during this vacation, too, that
he wrote "An Ode Addressed to Laura" in the six-line stanza
used several times by Shenstone for his odes and also made
familiar by various popular songs. He felt that "enough with
war my lay has rung"; but, by introducing such a line as "De-
volves thy beauteous hair" into a love poem, he revealed the
same sort of ungraceful pomposity shown in his later frequent
republication of "An Impromptu" acrostic, in Anacreontic
trochees, addressed to Martha Redwood, "who desired to have
some manuscript verses written by colonel Humphreys" to take
to Europe with her. Humphreys' most elaborate attempt at
light verse was "An Epithalamium," which was such a carefully
designed, extremely close parody of "Alexander's Feast" that
Dryden's poem was always printed parallel with it in order to
bring out the burlesque effect. A cruelly satiric description of
what was apparently a real wedding, it conceivably may have
been written when association with Trumbull freshened his

recollection of the occasion satirized by the latter in an epigram of 1773; but there is no real evidence for dating it at this time. There is no evidence, either, by which to date "The Shepherd: A Song" which Humphreys translated from the French. It may have been composed during or after his first trip abroad; but Humphreys was writing songs earlier, for, when President Stiles first admitted a flute in the Yale Chapel, on December 17, 1783, it accompanied a song by Humphreys which the Seniors sang to the tune of "Washington."

The most ambitious of the poems Humphreys attributed to the persuasions of "the Devil and a certain Jere Wadsworth," however, was the patriotic address composed during the early months of 1780. At that time the young officer probably was thinking seriously about his position. He had refused a tutorship at Yale in order to go with the army, and he had served honorably as an officer on the staffs of Generals Parsons and Putnam. The latter's illness left Humphreys unattached, free to take a vacation during the winter months and subject to the possibility that his rapid military advancement had come to a dead end. As he revisited familiar scenes in New Haven and renewed his friendships with many of his old college associates, it is not strange that his thoughts were led into belletristic channels and, with the achievements of Trumbull and Dwight before him, directed toward the possibilities of advancement through literature. But Humphreys was more practical than his friends. General Nathanael Greene, his active superior officer, was known to be interested in the arts, and it was possible that he might need an additional aide on his own staff. The instigation of the young poet's associates, the pressure of his military ambition, and the seriousness of his patriotism all combined to determine the nature of his first pretentious attempt at literary achievement. It would be a poem designed to encourage the men in the armies of the United States by appealing to their patriotism and by pointing out the beauties of the Ohio territory that had recently been promised them as a reward for their military services. Humphreys, for all his dabbling with verse up to that time, was not so familiar with literary theory as was his friend Trum-

bull or nearly so well acquainted with English literature. His
primary extracurricular interest in college had been oratory;
and, since the occasion seemed to invite a rhetorical exhibition,
his mind naturally turned to the verse oration as the medium for
his ambitious display of literary talent.

John Ward's *A System of Oratory* had played the same part in
Humphreys' education that the *Elements of Criticism* had played
in Trumbull's and Dwight's, and he remembered a surprising
number of the rhetorical devices that Ward had analyzed. Inevitably he adopted for his poem the highly figurative "middle"
or "florid" style, avoiding, on one hand, the unaffected natural-
ness of the "low" as being unsuited to the dignity of his message
and, on the other, the transport and ecstasy of the "sublime"
as being too elevated for the occasion. The work was called,
with conscious dignity, *A Poem Addressed to the Armies of the
United States of America*, and its three hundred and fifty lines
were designed to inspire the American troops "with perseverance
and fortitude, thro' every species of difficulty and danger, to
continue their exertions for the defense of their country, and
the preservation of its liberties." Cast in the general framework
of a "deliberative" oration, it began with a brief exordium in
which was incorporated a short narrative leading up to the
proposition:

> The past review; the future scene explore;
> And Heav'n's high King with grateful hearts adore!

In the technical "partition by enumeration" of this couplet the
first two elements represented the main divisions of the poem,
and the third stood for a prayer that served as a peroration for
the entire work. The main divisions consisted of two "demonstrative" discourses. The first praised the American troops and
their leaders and dispraised the British in a survey of the war up
to date; the second celebrated the prospect of peace in the Ohio
lands after the war; and the two were connected by a rather
elaborate turn in which the scene changed, Britain was represented as exhausted and involved with European foes, and
America was pictured as being left in comparative peace.

The content of the two internal discourses was as elaborately rhetorical as the structure of the entire poem. In the first the poet summarized the situation before proud Albion "frown'd on her sons, and bade them turn to slaves," introduced the beginning of hostilities by a simile of a storm in the Andes, and continued through a formal treatment of his topic according to the chronological method. The appointment of Washington as commander-in-chief of the American armies provided the occasion for an apostrophe to that "first of heroes," which was followed by a more general celebration of the endurance of the Americans, who suffered "fortune's worst extremes" while the British and Hessians were overrunning the country and defeating the patriot armies. A series of exclamations and interrogations were addressed to Britain on her cruelty to American prisoners, the last of which made a transition to the indignation excited in the Americans by such conduct and so led up to the acclamation of American successes at Trenton, Princeton, and "in northern fields." An apostrophe to the "heroes" in the armies, in the name of liberty, virtue, and honor, followed; and the first discourse concluded with an invocation to independence, in the fourth year of its existence, imploring that "auspicious pow'r" to shed its "stern influence o'er the western world" and inspire hearts to greater deeds with its "congenial flame." The second discourse was shorter and simpler than the first, for in it Humphreys appealed only to the single "passion" of hope. After pointing out signs of British weakness, he invoked "heav'n born peace" and drew a picture of the "regions of delight" to which the soldiers might emigrate and, their "task of glory done," "crown the toils of war, with rural ease." By an alternation of hypotyposis or lively imagery and generalized description he represented the country as beautiful, fragrant, mild, and fruitful, and he celebrated its various advantages: there were no large landholders in the country of these "midland seas"; no diseases of cattle or crops existed there; the "calm pleasures of domestic life" would be encouraged; and evenings would be prolonged by "festal sports" such as music and dancing, with no fears of "painted bands" of savages. In short, the new land was represented as a place where "golden years, anew, begin their reigns" with a finer race of people, greater cities, richer agriculture and commerce, and a flourishing of arts, science, and religion that would spread into all the unsettled regions of the world.

Humphreys apparently had taken to heart Ward's statement that "poets in all languages have a sort of peculiar dialect, and take greater liberties, not only in their figures, but also in their choice and disposition of words; so that what is a beauty in them, would often appear unnatural and affected in prose." And when *An Address to the Armies* appeared in print, early in 1780, he probably took a naïve pleasure in the stylistic dignity he had achieved by the technical means of many rhetorical figures. The poem also pleased more disinterested readers, and Humphreys made the most of it. In 1782 he revised and enlarged it, dating it in the sixth year of independence instead of the fourth, introducing several new heroes in addition to those mentioned in 1780, adding a list of further American victories, inserting a tribute to the French king, and, incidentally, making the praise of Washington slightly less fulsome and possibly more agreeable to the taste of the Commander-in-Chief, who had, by then, made the poet a member of his staff. Humphreys also added a delicate reference to himself in a twenty-line description of the banners captured at Yorktown, which he had presented, on behalf of the American army, to Congress. Although the poem did not have any great immediate popularity, it was highly successful in achieving the practical result that the author may have had in mind while composing it. Even before finishing the *Address*, Humphreys had brought himself to the more careful attention of General Greene by writing him in detail about this and his other literary work. Greene appointed the young man to his staff; but in the meantime the 1780 version of the poem had appeared from the press, and the author had used a copy for the purpose of remembering himself to the Commander-in-Chief. Though Washington would never have confused literary and military ability and Humphreys, of course, had excellent recommendations as an officer, there is some sig-

nificance in the fact that the poet was offered the position of
aide-de-camp to the General exactly a month after he had sent
him this token of his genius. Humphreys became a good staff
officer, one of the very few poets whose writings Washington
would read, and a great and persistent admirer of his superior.
The appointment was the most influential single event in his life;
and if its relationship to the appearance of the poem was merely
coincidence, the coincidence became a determining influence on
Humphreys' early literary career. Henceforth, as his revision of
An Address to the Armies after Yorktown suggests, his thoughts
turned productively to literature whenever he was threatened
with the loss of a job or needed to attract particular attention in
order to gain preferment.

There was no real need for Humphreys to endure the cost and
trouble of republishing his poem at the end of the war, however,
for Washington was taking the extraordinary step of bringing
his influence to bear on Congress in behalf of his aide, who by
this time was anxious to broaden himself by a trip to Europe.
Washington's hesitant suggestion that he be made secretary of
foreign affairs was not approved, but another more definite proposal that he be appointed "Official Secretary to an Embassy
abroad" was followed, and Humphreys was made secretary to
the commission for forming commercial treaties in Europe. Accordingly, he set sail for Europe on July 15, 1784, with letters of
introduction from Washington which bore witness to his "excellent heart, good natural and acquired abilities and sterling integrity—to which may be added sobriety and an obliging disposition."

The voyage gave occasion for the last poem that may be attributed to the experimental stage of his career. "An Epistle to
Dr. Dwight," written "on board the Courier de l'Europe, July
30, 1784," attempted, in heroic couplets, some casual descriptions like those in "A Letter to a Young Lady in Boston." But
the occasion was either too important or the medium of expression too dignified to allow the easy informality the author had
achieved in octosyllabics. Humphreys may have elevated and
"improved" this poem also in a later revision before publica-

tion, for Dwight had not been honored with his Princeton doc-
torate when the letter was written, and there is no way to tell
whether the poet made any changes in the text when he introduced his friend's new title into the address. In any case, the
matter is of no great importance. Humphreys practiced the art
of incidental verse in a manner that befitted a gentleman rather
than with the seriousness of a poet; and his one extended, elaborate effort had apparently been designed less as a trial of his
literary genius than as a trial of his professional luck. Verse rhetoric had served him well, and verse rhetoric was to be tried
again. It was a normal product of his early training and, by
demonstration, was the proper sort of verse to write if one wanted to appeal to the proper people.

III

When Humphreys arrived in Paris with such excellent intro-
ductions, he found that certain circles offered a warm welcome
to a handsome American hero who was also a patriotic man of
letters. Reports of his *Address to the Armies* had been circulated,
and, as he wrote Washington, some of his new acquaintances
"solicited for copies in such a manner as to make publication of
it necessary." Accordingly, during the summer he issued an elegant edition of the revised version—including the dignified, but
rather elaborate, allusions to himself—and presented copies to
his aristocratic friends. It was published in London during the
same year, where it was also delivered as a public reading; and
in 1786 it was reprinted in Paris by the Marquis de Chastellux,
who introduced it with a flattering letter to the author and
made a prose translation which was printed as a parallel text for
the benefit of French readers. None of Humphreys' literary
friends had been complimented by such attention, and the American public was impressed. Mathew Carey, back in New York,
chose the poem as one of the first selections of original American
literature to be reprinted in his *American Museum*. Even
though his popular acclaim was delayed and not too spontaneous, Humphreys was the first of the Connecticut Wits to be
wholly pleased by the reception of his most ambitious work.

In the meantime Humphreys was going through another of those curiously productive periods when the welfare of his country made immediate demands upon his poetic talents just as he was approaching a change in occupation. The commission which he served was to expire in the spring of 1786, and the indifference of Congress to his services was threatening his immediate recall to America. By November, 1785, he was commenting to Washington on two subjects: the American need for negotiations looking toward a settlement of affairs with the Barbary powers and the necessity for giving "the lye" to damaging reports about America that were being circulated from England. Arriving in London early in December, he became "fully appraised" of these newspaper stories that were promoting "a belief throughout the Continent that the United States are on the brink of perdition." He straightway proceeded to give them the lie and serve his country by writing—in his "leisure hours," of course—a poem "addressed to the Citizens of the United States calculated to show their superior advantages for happiness over all the rest of mankind, whether considered in a physical, moral, or political point of view." He also considered the Barbary situation and suggested the way in which it should be handled. By Christmas Eve he had composed over a thousand lines and was able to write John Jay, the American foreign secretary (whom he had never met), that the poem was "in the press" and that he might expect to receive a copy soon. He also took occasion to mention in the same letter that unless Congress should find further use for his services in Europe he would embark for America during the following April. Jay, however, refused to take the hint.

But *A Poem, on the Happiness of America: Addressed to the Citizens of the United States* appeared anyway and, as if to compensate for its failure to have any immediate effect on its author's career, had a quick popular success. The London edition was reprinted in Hartford during the same year and by Mathew Carey in the following spring. In it Humphreys repeated the formula he had used so effectively in *An Address to the Armies*. He was further removed from his academic environment than he had been when he composed the earlier work, and, as a consequence, the later poem was freer from the prescribed rules of rhetoric. Yet it followed the earlier pattern of two formal discourses within a single oratorical frame. The exordium was clearly defined; and, although the narrative and proposition were less specifically presented, the peroration was distinct. The latter represented the dawn of a new golden age in America, made an appeal—

> Then wake, Columbians! fav'rites of the skies
> Awake to glory and to rapture rise!

—and prophesied improvements from age to age, until an enlightened people should "in open ocean quench the torch of wars," unite mankind into "one firm union," "unbar the gates of commerce," and "build the gen'ral peace on freedom's broadest base."

Within the general frame the two particular orations were also clearly defined. The first was a rather rambling discourse on the subject indicated by the title of the poem. The happiness of America was celebrated under six different heads: the virtuous origin of the nation, the simple joys of a free and agricultural people, the admirable domestic life found in America, the "middle stage" of American society, the genius of its people, and the admirable situation of the United States for naval development and the growth of commerce. In addition there were various digressions, most of them personal. The praise of Washington, included under the first head, provoked the author to a summary of his own relationship with the General and a reference to the voyage across the Atlantic and his duties in Europe. The discussion of winter amusements, in the second topic, produced a digression concerning the war and a survey of the author's military career under Parsons, Putnam, Greene, and Washington. The praise of domestic life inspired the poet to a coy expression of regret at his own bachelorhood. And the admission that America, in being a new, middle-class nation, lacked the remains of feudal splendor, produced the declaration that Humphreys had derived the inspiration for his own "rising song" from the "untrodden scenes" of nature rather than from more fashionable sources. A further digression between the last two topics called for a treaty of commerce between America and Great Britain— which was Humphreys' own particular business at the time he was writing the poem.

The sentiments in the celebration of America were those of Humphreys' earlier poem, but more clearly expressed and elaborately presented. The manifest destiny of the United States, for example, had become firmly rooted in moral grounds:

> All former empires rose, the work of guilt,
> On conquest, blood, or usurpation built,
> But we, taught wisdom by their woes and crimes,
> Fraught with their lore and born to better times:
> Our constitutions form'd on freedom's base,
> Which all the blessings of all lands embrace,
> Embrace humanity's extended cause—
> A world our empire, for a world our laws.

And the "philanthropic band" of Columbia's sons, "not lur'd to blood by domination's lust," were to carry the "torch of science" to all parts of the world with the spread of the fishing and whaling industries and commercial enterprises. Social ideals were also more accurately defined than in the conventionally pastoral joys foretold for the settlers of the Ohio country in the earlier poem. The enjoyments of each season were indicated, and, particularly, a long Thomsonian winter piece described the contentment of the American farmer with his "independent lot" of peace and plenty. American domestic life was praised, on one hand, for the "equal honour" allowed the fair sex in choosing a mate and, on the other, for the unwillingness of women to "wrest his bold prerogatives from man" by taking an active part in public affairs or even appearing very frequently outside the home. The "middle stage" of society and the "equal fortunes" in America would lead to an unprecedented increase in population where

> The eye no view of waning cities meets,
> Of mould'ring domes, of narrow, fetid streets:
> Of grey-hair'd wretches who ne'er own'd a shed,
> And beggars dying for the want of bread.

The poet revealed a similar turn from the general to the specific in his treatment of individual Americans: Washington was still held up for emulation as a "hero," of course, but he was also praised for his activity in developing waterways toward the west; and Adams, Franklin, and especially Jefferson were selected for particular attention as friends of humankind upon whose "high task" the author's "humbler toils" attended. Barlow was singled out as the "Bard, in conscious genius bold," who was most fired by vast ideas and the worth of American leaders; but Humphreys was forced to look toward the future for real progress in the arts and so invoked the genius of the Western World to inspire other poets, painters, sculptors, architects, and musicians "'till reason supercede the force of arms" and bring about a new world.

Through all this demonstrative discourse there was a "deliberative" thread, for the poem was professedly addressed to the citizens of the United States and consciously written to convince the British that America was not nearly so bad as she was represented in the newspapers. It was only in the second half of the poem, however, that Humphreys used the true deliberative discourse in an attempt to rouse the American people against the Algerines. He made his transition from a discussion of marine activities and commerce:

> 'Tis thus our youth thro' various climes afar
> From toils of peace obtain the nerves of war;

and straightway released all the rhetorical figures of speech that were supposed to appeal to the passions. The transition itself was an aposiopesis, and it was followed by nearly two hundred lines of exclamations and questions rapidly succeeding one another and rarely interrupted except by equally striking figures. Barlow, Dwight, and Trumbull were apostrophized to rouse their country with heroic songs; and Humphreys exclaimed over his own inability to do his feelings justice and invoked assistance:

> For me, tho' growing with conceptions warm,
> I find no equal words to give them form:
> Pent in my breast the mad'ning tempest raves,
> Like prison'd fires in Etna's burning caves:

For me why will no thund'ring numbers roll?
Why niggard language do'st thou balk my soul?
Come thou sweet feeling of another's woe
That mak'st the heart to melt, the eye to flow!
Come thou keen feeling, liveliest sense of wrong!
Aid indignation and inspire my song!

An exclamatory hypotyposis summoned a harrowing scene of the Americans in slavery, and the poet called down "great maledictions of eternal wrath" in an anathema upon the monsters who were responsible for such scenes. The Columbians were exhorted to arms in case the "force of reason" failed to have an effect upon the Algerines, for:

Revenge! revenge! the voice of nature cries—
Awake to glory and to vengeance rise!
To arms! to arms! ye bold indignant bands!
'Tis Heav'n inspires, 'tis God himself commands.

An apostrophe to the tribute-paying European powers taunted them with the question whether "self-interest or dastard fear" governed their policy; Americans were implored to stand firm, "the sword and olive-branch in either hand," against an enemy that, after all, was less powerful than the Britain so recently withstood; and a prayer was addressed to God to make his "red right arm of vengeance bare" as he led forth American forces to "crush the sons of pride." After the prayer the poet pictured the entire procedure of raising an army and constructing a navy in preparation for the war, presented an extended hypotyposis of the battle, and, making a transition from the sublime to the middle style by means of a simile, concluded the discourse with a contrast between the utter ruin of Algiers and a happy America after the war.

Whatever pertinence the Algerine section of this poem may have had to the author's career, it had no real place beside a demonstrative discourse on the happiness of America; and Humphreys' own recognition of its irrelevance is demonstrated by the fact that he later printed it separately, with some additions and revisions, as *A Poem on the Future Glory of the United States*. There may have been, indeed, a considerable amount of patchwork in the original poem. If Humphreys' allusions to its composition can be taken at face value, he wrote it at the rate of over fifty lines a day when he was also busy with diplomatic and some social duties; but it contains internal evidence of labored imitation which hardly suggests such fluent, continuous composition. For the elaborate rhetorical character of the poem does not conceal the fact that in some passages he was playing variations upon English models as he had in "An Epithalamium." The long winter piece, in spite of its rhyme, was in the manner of Thomson; and his invocation to and description of wedded love owed a good deal to Milton's lines on the same subject in the fourth book of *Paradise Lost*. These passages are sufficiently different from the momentary echoes of Pope, Gray, and Milton that had appeared in *An Address to the Armies* to suggest that Humphreys had been reading other poets with some care and perhaps had been amusing himself with verse exercises that he later incorporated in his own poem.

But the author of *A Poem on the Happiness of America* was still more strongly influenced by the precepts of formal rhetoric than by the examples of English poetry, and in the "copious and florid wisdom" which formed the usual substance of his verse he held to an ideal of rhetorical correctness that had been established in his mind by John Ward's *System of Oratory*—even though Ward's specific words may have slipped from his mind long before. His language avoided everything that was "uncouth, or disagreeable to its genius" and so was "pure" according to Ward's definition of the term; and he made no excessive use of his poetic license for unusual order in composition. His rhymes were always perfect and his couplets invariably regular, closed in form, with the caesura usually following either the fourth or the fifth syllable. Humphreys wrote in 1803 that "every poet who aspires to celebrity, strives to approach the perfection of Pope in the sweetness of his versification"; but in these earlier poems his ideal was less the "sweetness" of the English poet than an absolute regularity, which the American may have considered "correct" but which he certainly did not derive from a careful study of his professed master. This excessive regularity made his verse artificial and stiff, and its stiffness and artificiality were emphasized by the author's attempt at dignity. In following Ward's recommendation to choose language "suited to the nature and importance of the subjects" treated, Humphreys fell into the error of taste that trapped so many of his patriotic contemporaries. His belief that the American Revolution was to usher in a new golden age heightened every subject he touched, so that his poems were crowded to the bursting-point with figures and tropes which, to him, gave dignity to the style but, to later readers, seem unnatural and strained. Even his sympathetic English critics, however, thought them natural in an American at that time. Humphreys did not anticipate that the failure of a new golden age to come into being would place the nature and importance of his subjects in a different perspective. And he was neither sufficiently well read nor sensitive enough to perceive signs of the revolution of taste that was to transfer the association of dignity from the "middle" and "sublime," or "florid," styles to the "low," or "natural." Plain, correct, and dignified according to the best standards of his limited education, he set out to be a gentleman first and a man of letters on the side; and the success of his first ambitious work established him in a role that he never tried to give up.

IV

When Humphreys returned to the United States in the late spring of 1786 he had no reason for being disillusioned about the particular sort of poetry he had chosen to write. He was, however, disillusioned about the effectiveness of even the best poetry as a means to preferment—especially after he had visited his native Derby and compared the attentions of his fellow-townsmen with those of the French nobility. There he discovered, as he wrote his brother John after leaving, "that a poet like a Prophet is not without honor except *in his own country,*" and he responded to the discovery with a petulance that he never displayed before his superiors. After informing his brother

that he would return for the Yale commencement and so be with
him in September, he added:

and I have no objection to its being known by my friends who are freemen of
your town, that I shall be on the spot and if they should think proper to ap-
point me one of their representatives I will serve them as such—indeed you
may show this letter where you think you can do it with discretion and propriety.—Probably this journey to the Eastward may decide me whether I
shall in future consider myself a citizen of my native State or not. I have
several projects, some one of which I am confident will succeed.

But most of the letter was rather smug. For one of his projects
—which he had broached before his return to America—was a
history of the war written from Washington's own papers and
with Washington's advice and supervision, and he was even
then domesticated at Mount Vernon for that purpose. Neither
this project nor another to translate De Chastellux's travels
"succeeded." The latter was anticipated, and the former possibly was delayed beyond the crucial moment by the action of the
citizens of Derby—who surely did not see Humphreys' letter—
in electing him to the state assembly and so bringing him back
to Connecticut for a winter that involved him in literary activity of an entirely different sort. The only publication that
resulted from his study of Washington's papers was a series of
letters and documents, "The Conduct of General Washington,
Respecting the Confinement of Capt. Asgill, Placed in Its True
Point of Light," which appeared in the *New Haven Gazette* for
November 6, 1786, and was widely reprinted in other periodicals.
Humphreys was destined to turn biographer and historian within a short time and make his contribution to the new American
mythology. But it was a new project, growing out of a different
set of circumstances. When he ventured into politics for a brief
interlude, he inadvertently abandoned his most promising
materials to John Marshall and his greatest creative opportunity to Parson Weems.

CHAPTER V

JOEL BARLOW

I

ALTHOUGH there were no great social distinctions in eighteenth-century Connecticut, Joel Barlow came from an environment different from that of his later literary associates. The Redding farmhouse in which he was born in 1754 did not reveal the foreshadowing of New England Brahminism that might have been seen in the homes of Trumbull, Dwight, and Humphreys; and Joel was not bred to the routine of grammar school, college, and one of the learned professions. Yet, when he exhibited a youthful aptitude for "literature" which seemed to justify the sacrifices necessary for his higher education, he received the customary preparation, first from the local minister who discovered his talents and later, by an economical bargain, in Moor's Indian School at Hanover, New Hampshire. The necessity for proving his talents before cultivating them delayed his entrance to college until he had reached the age at which Trumbull and Dwight were taking their second degrees, but even at that he was recognized at Dartmouth as no more than a "middling scholar." After a few months as a Freshman, however, he excused himself from waiting on tables in the Hanover college and, on the plea of finding it more economical to attend college nearer home, transferred to Yale. Actually, the step was the first of his many gambles of security against the possibility of improvement, for he financed the venture with his small, recently acquired patrimony and entered upon an entirely new, more sparkling mode of life.

The "sober, regular, and good Behavior" which had so recommended him to Eleazar Wheelock would, in any case, have been out of place in Yale College from 1774 to 1778. The rising tide of patriotism made Barlow a soldier during the long vacation following his Sophomore year; and after his return to classes he was diverted from his studies by the vivacious social life encouraged by less patriotic students, who doubled the graduate enrolment while escaping military duty by a pretense of study. He also took a lead in the popular sports of nagging President Daggett and pestering the corporation. But New Haven society provided his most important sphere of activity at the time; and the tall, awkward youth with farmer's hands eventually acquired a remarkable ease at the tea table, facility at badinage, and skill at turning out a graceful bread-and-butter note in rhyme. His greatest academic achievement was also in the extracurricular field of verse-making; for, although he proved a recalcitrant Senior, spending only a few weeks at college, he was honored with a place on the commencement program and his poem was praised even by the tutor under whom he had refused to study. By this time he seems to have been convinced that literature was the best available path toward a satisfactory "interest" in the world, and after being disappointed in his hopes for a tutorship he displayed a curious belief that he could find a private patron in the land of steady habits. Such a notion would have been completely fantastic had it not been for the encouragement of friends, through whom, after two years of alternating hope and despondency, he obtained an appointment as chaplain in the army with the understanding that his major efforts would be devoted to poetic composition.

Beneath a certain superficial frivolity Barlow was dominated by a deep sincerity which he revealed clearly in a long series of intimate letters to Ruth Baldwin after they were secretly married in January, 1781. Yet for the years immediately following the war, at least, he was preoccupied with miscellaneous activities and economic expedients made necessary by his marriage and the long delay before the rewards of literary fame could be even tested. After the army was disbanded, he settled in Hartford, where he was successively an editor and publisher, a storekeeper, and a lawyer. He became modestly interested in local politics and slightly more interested in land speculation, but by the time he approached his middle thirties he was still not established in any profession and still unaffected by the conservatism of his native state. Longer than any of the Connecticut Wits he remained unsettled and undetermined, confidently awaiting the new vistas that were to open when he reached the first major stage on "the flowery road to fame."

II

Although Barlow's poetic talents were first discovered by the village minister in Redding, the only extant evidence of his youthful bent is a product of his Sophomore year in college. The poem has not been preserved, but a prose summary of its contents and a single surviving line indicate that it was a humorous work in heroic verse which derived its comic effect from the presentation of the homely events of college life against a background of mythological epic machinery. If the student poet derived this method from the descriptions and narratives in the *Miscellanies* volume of Swift and Pope that had been so useful to Trumbull, he did not remain under its influence for long. After his period of military service and patriotic excitement, when his class had settled in Glastonbury and he had leisure again for verse, he turned away from the Queen Anne wits and toward a different and more serious type of poetry. The ode addressed "To a Friend at Cambridge," dated July 5, 1777, was probably composed under the influence of the second book of Isaac Watts's *Horae lyricae* and even directly suggested by "The Complaint." But Barlow may also have been reading the English metaphysical poets of the seventeenth century, deriving from them suggestions for such a stanza as

> Bodies are massy and compact,
> The nearer join'd the more attract,
>   And parting faint and die;
> But the blest union of the soul,
> Can grasp th' equator and the pole,
>   And each its native sky.

The rough draft of another lyric, written at the same time and beginning "Go Rose my Chloe's bosom grace," reveals a fairly clear debt to seventeenth-century verse, for both the conceit and the phrasing of the first stanza seem to have been taken from Carew's "Ask me no more where Jove bestows"—though it is difficult to see where Barlow could have run across Carew at that time.

No other poems of Barlow's undergraduate days have been preserved; but, when he was appointed class poet on July 10, 1778, for the commencement exercises less than two weeks later, he was known as the author of a considerable amount of verse and probably already had a long poem, suitable for exhibition, under way. He read *The Prospect of Peace* on July 23, and it was published soon afterward. Like Trumbull's earlier commencement poem at the conclusion of his *Essay on the Use and Advantages of the Fine Arts*, and Dwight's *America*, both of which he had possibly read, it was a vision poem in heroic couplets. But Barlow avoided his friends' imitation of Thomson's figure of Liberty in a solemn grove and, instead, attempted to call up direct images of the rising glory of America and of her progress in science, art, and religion. In prophesying the growth of poetry in the new nation, he saw "Pride and Coquetry and Dulness" already falling before Trumbull's satire; and he paid a similar tribute to Dwight in a reference to the "unborn Joshuas" that would "rise in future song." Barlow brought his poem to a close with a hint of the civilizing of the western country through pure religion and with an account of the beginning of the millennium in America. He believed that

> Earth's blood-stain'd empires, with their Guide the Sun
> From orient climes their gradual progress run;
> And circling far, reach every western shore,
> 'Til earth-born empires rise and fall no more.

After the thousand years of peace that were to spread from the American shores, the "Church elect" would triumphantly survive the conflagration. *The Prospect of Peace* was another of the many American poems that opened with the trouble with England and closed with the Day of Judgment after the continent

had been settled and the course of empire could no longer westward take its way. They were all full of the idea of progress,
but it was a rather tenuous idea, born of the union of Bishop
Berkeley's famous poem and the Revelation of St. John the
Divine, and it flourished only in the hothouse atmosphere of
optimistic patriotism.

The Prospect of Peace was, on the whole, a successful first trial
of Barlow's literary talent. His old tutor, Joseph Buckminster,
wrote him from Portsmouth, New Hampshire, that everybody
who had seen it spoke "very highly of it," and he advised Barlow to "encourage and cultivate" his "turn for poetry." Whether Barlow needed Buckminster's advice or not, he determined to
remain in New Haven, where he found a number of friends—
including the sparkling and intelligent Elizabeth Whitman—
who stimulated his interest in writing verse. He was probably
the author of the local newsboy's address to his customers for
January 1, 1779, in the popular anapestic ballad meter, which
was printed as a small broadside and traded by the carrier to his
patrons for as many pennies as he could get. This light survey
of the political situation, however, was done to order; and Barlow's own mood at the time was more accurately reflected in the
unfinished poem in heroic couplets that he planned to address to
Dr. Benjamin Young Prime, a New Haven physician and poet
whom the younger man seems to have adopted as a patron.
Barlow was in a melancholy state. His patrimony was gone, and
he feared that while "daily toils but purchase daily bread" and
"a small school" was confining his "lessening views" the "young
muse must close her silent wing." If health, genius, and fortune
should smile on him, however, he promised:

> From darkling sense I'd soar on wing sublime
> Rove Nature thro and skip the bounds of time;

and, in particular:

> This new-born Empire should my voice employ
> The Muse's transport and the Patriot's joy.

By this time Barlow was convinced that he wanted a literary
career. Buckminster advised him to enter the ministry if he

wanted to indulge his poetic genius and warned him that a Pope
or a Milton might starve in America if he looked for support to
the few people capable of relishing literature. Barlow, however,
was more determined, and he wrote Noah Webster a short while
after receiving their former tutor's advice:

> You and I are not the first men in the world that have broke loose from
> college without friends and without fortune to puff us into public notice. Let
> us show the world a few more examples of men standing upon their own merit,
> and rising in spite of opposition. . . . . We are now citizens of the world, in
> pursuit of different interests, no longer in circumstances of warming the soul
> and refining the sensibility by those nameless incidents that attend the col-
> lege connection. . . . . Literary accomplishments will not be so much noticed
> till some time after the settlement of Peace and the people are more refined.
> More blustering characters must bear the sway at present, and the hardy
> veteran must retire from the field before the philosopher can retire to the
> closet.

Accordingly he was at a loss for a career—since he refused to
take Buckminster's advice to turn clergyman—and for an immediate means of support.

Yet he continued to experiment actively with various sorts of
poetry. For a while Shenstone was the dominant influence upon
him. Elizabeth Whitman wrote that the English poet's elegies
had aroused "a spirit of emulation" in the American, and this
spirit was reflected in a poem addressed "To Mr. Abraham
Baldwin" in the early spring of 1779. In these quatrains Barlow
echoed Shenstone's second elegy as he cast the melancholy stole
of a belief that "Want is the Wreath that crowns the Laureat's
Bays" over this trial effort. The poem also contained reminiscences of Gray in its theme: even though a poet left his homely
toils, quit the dull crowd, and sought the heights of fame, he
could never, in America, gain the applause of the world or of
listening senates. Shenstone, however, was more fully in the
poet's mind, for he imitated "A Pastoral Ballad" in two stanzas
addressed to Elizabeth Whitman and, possibly at about this
time, echoed "An Elegy to the Winds" in the lines on the death
of his brother Samuel that he later incorporated in *The Vision of
Columbus*. While Barlow was engaged in these informal imitations, he was also looking around for a more ambitious subject
for a long poem. Buckminster was advising him to go to "Sacred

History" for a subject and recommended Joseph, Cain and Abel, and Daniel. The poet had perhaps already considered the latter subject in connection with a poem on Cyrus the Great, for which he had drawn up a prose outline and written over a hundred lines in heroic couplets, depending for his material upon the *Cyropaedia* of Xenophon and the Old Testament. This poem, as he planned it, would have been an epic in the general manner of *The Conquest of Canäan*, of which he had certainly heard in some detail, with all the additions of epic action and speechmaking, visions of futurity, and romantic episodes that characterized Dwight's poem. Barlow did not hold to this plan, nor, despite his expansive attempt to versify the meeting of Jacob and Rachel, did he seriously consider the other subjects suggested by his former tutor. His mind was becoming more definitely fixed upon "this new-born Empire" of America as a proper subject for an epic.

By April, 1779, he apparently had tentatively decided upon an American epic with Columbus as his hero. The opening couplets he composed for this version indicate that he planned a thoroughly conventional epic treatment until he realized that his hero's personal adventures were neither sufficiently exciting for a "great" epic action nor sufficiently heroic to dominate the story of "this new-born Empire," which, according to epic plan, he would have had to present by means of visions and subordinate episodes. While Barlow was meditating such problems of construction, Dwight, whom he still held in high admiration, offered him a temporary position as usher in his school at Northampton and advice on his literary project. Accordingly, the would-be poet spent the summer in Massachusetts and, in August, produced

a plan for a poem on the subject of America at large, designed to exhibit the importance of this country in every point of view as the noblest and most elevated part of the earth, and reserved to be [the] last and greatest theatre for the improvement of mankind in every article in which they are capable of improvement.

The vision, which would have been incidental in an epic, had become the main subject for treatment; and he had decided positively that "the poem will be rather of the philosophic than epic kind." How much reading Barlow had done in anticipation of his work and how much Dwight contributed to the plan cannot be determined. The commonplaces which both poets had dealt with in earlier patriotic poems appear clearly in the outline, and it is evident that the two men had talked over the optimistic expectations from commerce that Dwight was to reveal in a sermon published two years later. Barlow's plans for the philosophical sections of the poem, however, were by no means clear or coherent; and, in fact, the most practical part of the outline was the geographical and historical section taken over from William Robertson's *The History of America*.

During this period when Barlow was experimenting with plans for his ambitious, philosophical work, he was full of rhymes and constantly engaged in writing incidental or occasional poetry which, if not strictly experimental, nevertheless showed that he was not yet ready to devote his entire energies to the composition of his masterpiece. Even his letters and casual notes frequently contained verses. When Humphreys met him first in the spring of 1780 he wrote General Greene that Barlow was "so far gone in Poetry that there is no hope of reclaiming, and making him attentive to anything else." The visiting officer was so greatly impressed with the younger man's plans and abilities that he decided "Great nature form'd her loftiest poet" in Barlow and joined with various others in an effort to find a patron who would give him employment which would enable him to pursue his original work. Barlow himself was thinking of going to Virginia, probably as a private tutor, but Humphreys and Abraham Baldwin were optimistic about the possibility of an appointment as chaplain in the army. After some investigation Barlow himself was convinced that such an occupation was both desirable and feasible. With secret assurances of an appointment he offered himself for admission to full communion in the College Church on July 2, 1780, was admitted on August 6, and eight days later passed a reputable examination and was licensed to preach by a special association of New Haven ministers, some of whom were irritatingly suspicious of the new convert's motives. His new position, however, offered him for the first time sufficient leisure for serious composition and a salary adequate for his needs.

Barlow had almost finished the first book of his philosophical poem before he entered the army, and he was able to complete it, as a sample of his abilities, while writing his first sermons. Most of his friends were convinced of his genius. On October 17, 1780, he dined at the right hand of General Washington and promised Humphreys that he might have the first book and the general plan of the poem to read at headquarters. There was also some talk of printing his recent sermon on "The Treasons of Arnold and the Glory of America"; but he was determined that "talk shall be all that shall be done about it." "For," he confided in a letter to Ruth Baldwin, "tho it would be a sweet mortification to my Reverend fathers the Association to see their heretic son gain such applause, yet I have no ambition of appearing to the world in the character of a *declaimer*." Army life was pleasant, and, for the first time, his prospects seemed good—so good, in fact, that he rested on them for the time being and, on January 26, gambled on them with a secret marriage to Ruth.

For a while he was able to "make the swiftest progress" on his poem, but the winter was by no means so successful as he had anticipated. In all, he managed to compose only about seven hundred lines and on occasions became completely despondent. Yet he still enjoyed trying his hand at incidental verse, for he celebrated his recovery from sickness in camp, during the summer of 1781, with a song addressed to Ruth, written to the "Tune of the Raptures" and beginning "Cease, Fidelia, cease complaining." And, whatever his accomplishments may have been, his reputation was growing impressively. Yale gave him an unusually important place on the program for a commencement at which an exceptionally able body of graduates appeared for their second degrees. Barlow preached the sermon in chapel before the exercises, took part in one of the commencement disputes, and delivered a poem on the afternoon the degrees were awarded. He was also, when he no longer wanted the office, elected tutor. The new poem, called "The Genius of

Literature" on the program and published simply as *A Poem,
Spoken at the Public Commencement in New-Haven; September 12,
1781*, resembled the one of three years before in its heroic couplets prophesying the future glory of America. But, in spite of
the fact that Barlow could not avoid, for a second time, the figure in a gloomy grove which was one of the distinguishing marks
of the patriotic-vision poem, the later work was more original
than *The Prospect of Peace*. The poet, in looking forward to the
ultimate effect of progress in the arts, science, and literature in
America, had begun to wonder about the actual means by which
mankind would be brought to a more perfect state; and instead
of concluding his new prophecy with a description of the millennium, he represented literature as arousing benevolence by its
emphasis upon "virtues and loves and heavenly themes" and so
eventually turning the thoughts of men into religious channels.
Possibly because of the inactive state of the author's inspiration
at the time, the poem was closely related to *The Vision of Columbus;* and Barlow, after some hesitation about publishing it at all,
agreed to make it public only as a trial "specimen" of the "larger work." Some of its lines were borrowed from the completed
first book, and many more were later incorporated in the
seventh and ninth books of the longer poem. As a commencement poem it received applause which Barlow took as an encouraging sign of literary success; but, if he accepted the applause as evidence of his genius as a philosophical poet, the sign
was unfortunate. For in its more philosophical portions the
poem reflected a curious wavering between the strictly teleological idea of progress which Dwight was to express in his
Northampton sermon two months later and the more self-reliant
theory of human improvement which Barlow, like Trumbull on
a similar occasion, had derived from the psychology of Lord
Kames. Had the commencement poem received the severe criticism it deserved, its author might have been able to take sufficient thought to clear up the obscurities and incoherences that
have prevented his major work from receiving serious consideration as the philosophical poem it was supposed to be.

But Barlow was not receiving serious criticism. His literary reputation was uncritically high throughout the army, and it was appropriate that he should be called upon to deliver an ode when a group of officers gathered to celebrate the fourth anniversary of Burgoyne's defeat. The occasion was made particularly happy by the expectation of another important British surrender in Virginia, and Barlow made the most of it in an elaborate lyrical outburst describing the circumstances of the earlier victory and anticipating the next. Based roughly on "Alexander's Feast" in form, imitating Dryden's simplified rhyme scheme for the irregular ode, and following Dryden's scheme exactly in the concluding grand chorus, the poem was Barlow's most ambitious attempt at the lyric. The metrical arrangement was original, and these hasty and unpolished verses possessed a rapidity of movement and variety of effect not found in any of the poet's other work. Barlow never achieved spontaneity or freshness of imagery in his verse, but he did have a lyric ease and lightness that was being disciplined by his serious ambition. He visited Trumbull in Hartford during the spring of 1782, became more friendly with the older poet than he had ever been before, and probably while there demonstrated his facility again in some humorous octosyllabics written in imitation of *M'Fingal*. The imitation was only an exercise developing a conceit used twice in the "Epithalamium" and adopted again for the opening of the second canto in the revised version of the mock epic. Barlow began with a reference to the sun who "never stops for stormy weather" and continued through seventy-four lines that contained other echoes of *M'Fingal* without having any importance except as a demonstration that he could adopt Trumbull's manner with an ease and felicity equal to Humphreys' and greater than Timothy Dwight could capture. He adopted the same style again a few months later in a comic advertisement for a lost mare, but he did not cultivate it in any of his early verse written for publication.

For Barlow, gay as he frequently was in company, was completely serious about his literary reputation; and, in spite of his praises for Trumbull, he knew that Connecticut had looked coldly upon the poet who attempted to usher the comic muse into respectable company. The public had a way of ignoring the quality of the verse and questioning the poet's sentiments and attitudes. Religion, patriotism, and death were the three subjects that guaranteed unquestionable solemnity of attitude and nobility of sentiment, and the poem Barlow was most willing "to brag of" by the end of 1781 was *An Elegy on the Late Honorable Titus Hosmer, Esq.*, which he had recently completed. Judge Hosmer had been the poet's most active patron before his death in 1780, and the elegy was one of Barlow's most ambitious early works. In it he paid a graceful though perhaps exaggerated tribute to Hosmer's patronage, and he displayed an unusual boldness of imagination; but the poem as a whole was uneven, thin, and artificial. Again he consulted literary precedent rather than his own emotions, sometimes inflating a single line from Gray into a verbose stanza and frequently revealing that "An Elegy Written in a Country Churchyard" was in the back of his mind, even though he avoided clear verbal echoes. This was the last of Barlow's experimental poems of this sort. He had determined to stake his literary fortunes on a philosophical poem in heroic couplets, and he did not spend enough time on his minor poems to cultivate his talent for another type of verse. His early experiments were almost as varied as Trumbull's, but they were much less exhaustive; and when he brought them to an end it seems to have been because he thought he had found the main chance rather than the only possible way for the further development of his talents.

III

After delivering his military ode on the anniversary of Burgoyne's defeat, Barlow was in high spirits and full of determination to finish his long poem during the winter. He apparently completed his elegy on Hosmer during the fall; and on December 3 he settled down to enthusiastic, rapid composition of *The Vision of Columbus*. While staying with his brother in West Redding during the following two months, he averaged about two hundred lines a week in addition to writing and preaching several sermons. Then, after a three-week vacation spent visiting his wife, discussing the possibilities for publishing his elegy, and preaching a six-dollar sermon in the Yale Chapel, he succeeded in tripling his rate of composition for the period of a month, producing twenty-four hundred lines in thirty-two days, despite interruptions caused by the discovery of his secret marriage, the necessity of a visit to Hartford, and the annoyance of a cold. He evidently planned to write about sixteen hundred additional lines, and by April, 1782, he considered his poem two books short of completion. Actually, he did make some additions during the following spring and summer, and just before publishing the poem he brought his survey of American cultural achievements up to date. But otherwise he seems to have completed his work by simplifying his plan. Except for the first book, which was finished before the autumn of 1780, and about seven hundred lines written in the course of the following winter, *The Vision of Columbus* was entirely composed in two spurts of activity that lasted no longer than three months altogether. The result was, by Barlow's admission, "very imperfect" and received a considerable amount of revision. There were also a number of additions, but these were balanced by excisions with sufficient nicety to leave the published poem almost the exact length of the work he had finished by March 16, 1782.

When a half-educated young man is encouraged by an uncritical approval of his trial efforts to compose his first ambitious work at the rate of two to six hundred lines a week, the result is inevitable—especially if the work pretends to be a "philosophical poem." *The Vision of Columbus* is so thin in substance and fluid in style that the reader finds its philosophical content elusive to the point of obscurity. Barlow himself seems to have been most interested in the narrative and descriptive portions of his work. Only after some reluctance had he given up the idea of writing an epic, and the models to which he continued to look for guidance were all epic in style. He knew Homer, at least through Pope's translucent glass; he had studied the *Aeneid* in the original; and, like most other literate Americans, he was reasonably familiar with *Paradise Lost*. But when he settled upon a subject that would not lend itself to the sort of treatment suggested by these great models he was forced to look elsewhere for suggestions. None of the modern epics of discovery and exploration was available to him; but he had been able to obtain, at an early stage in his planning, a copy of Voltaire's critical and historical *Essay on Epic Poetry*, which gave him a secondhand knowledge of the more recent heroic poems to which he occasionally referred. Voltaire had called particular attention to Camoëns' the *Lusiad* as a new species of the epic in which the action was based on the discovery of a new country by the aid of navigation. The importance placed upon this Portuguese poem may have encouraged the young American in his own enterprise, for the discovery of America by Columbus was, of course, much more important in its consequences and hence more worthy of celebration than Vasco da Gama's discovery of the eastern sea route to India. The example of Camoëns, however, at the most merely encouraged him. Although Barlow declared himself "sensible" that "the extensive and sublime objects opened to our view in a work which celebrates the discovery of one part of the globe, may well be thought worthy of the contemplations of a writer, who endeavours to trace the consequences of a similar event in another," he was not able, even by sending to Europe, to obtain a copy of the *Lusiad* before he had finished his own work and so had not been tempted to imitate any of its curious "sublimities."

Another chapter in Voltaire's *Essay* which particularly excited Barlow's curiosity and proved the most profitable of all in its suggestions was the account given of the *Araucana* of Don Alonzo de Ercilla, which had not been translated into English and was not available in America even in Hayley's summary. Yet this poem, as it was described by the French critic, opened to Barlow's mind "a new field of Poetry, rich with uncommon ornaments"; and it undoubtedly inspired him to devote a considerable part of his own poem to South America and its original inhabitants. Voltaire had also commented upon the organization of the *Araucana*, which began with a description of the geography of Chile and a representation of the manners and customs of its people, saying that such an introduction was made necessary by the strangeness of the material, although otherwise it would be insupportable. Barlow, knowing the ignorance of his own countrymen concerning their geography and history, probably welcomed such a precedent for an introductory survey, as well as the critic's unwilling justification for it. At any rate, he felt that a preliminary book of geographical description was practically necessary and so included it, offering it for inspection as a sample of his genius with confidence that his own judgment was supported by one of the best-known modern critics.

Voltaire's discussion of the *Henriade* in the "Conclusion" to his *Essay* may also have encouraged Barlow's patriotic plan by its insistence that the genius of the modern age favored real rather than fabulous heroes and battles and was interested only in those fictions that represented truths. But the only modern epic, other than the *Araucana*, which had any measurable influence on the structure of *The Vision of Columbus* was *Paradise Lost*. The "machinery" which Barlow described in his original plan as "simple" and, he hoped, "natural" was borrowed directly from Milton. The relationship between Columbus and his angelic mentor was that of Adam and Raphael, the "high converse" in which they engaged was based upon Miltonic precedent, and some incidental passages in the poem, such as the Incan hymn to the sun, were imitations of passages in *Paradise Lost*. Milton may also have supplied the model for the rather general, grand effects which Barlow apparently attempted in his North American battle scenes, for he seems to have made little effort to represent warfare through the particular details of heroic conflict which were characteristic of Homer and considered so sublime by Timothy Dwight. The influence of *Paradise Lost* was pervasive in *The Vision of Columbus*, since it and the less admired *Paradise Regained* were the only two modern epics that Barlow knew at first hand which solved some of the peculiar difficulties of the "philosophical poem" with epic leanings.

The design of *The Vision of Columbus*, however, did not lend itself to patterns set by earlier poems, and the form of Barlow's work was frequently determined by his materials and the non-literary sources from which they were derived. The first three books of his original plan corresponded rather closely in structure with the sections of Robertson's *History of America* on which they were based. But, as the poet began to look more closely into the "uncommon ornaments" of poetry offered by the Indian civilization of South America, he became captivated by new material to such an extent that he revised his outline and increased the hemispheric part of his work by an entire book in order to interpolate an episode "in epic form" dealing with the Incan hero Manco Capac. Various friends apparently were suggesting episodic stories to Barlow during the spring planning of 1780, but the book which finally caught his fancy and directed his purpose was one of the very few works in the Yale library on the subject of American history—Garcilasso de la Vega's *The Royal Commentaries of Peru* in the London, 1688, folio edition of the English translation made by Sir Paul Rycault. This volume, written by a man of Incan blood who had listened in childhood to the stories of his race, was full of detailed information about the history of the Incas and particularly about Manco Capac, the great founder of the Peruvian dynasty. Furthermore, it was a sympathetic volume: Garcilasso emphasized the humanitarianism of his ancestors, their benevolent conquests, and the agricultural society which they established; and either he or the translator had interpolated hints that the Incan empire was one of the greatest achievements ever dictated exclusively by "the laws of Nature and Reason." Thus Barlow found the suggestion for the major episode in his poem—an episode designed to suggest a contrast between the best that unassisted nature could do for civilization in America and the achievement of the English colonists who operated in the light of revelation. The poet's desire to throw "the episode into an epic form," however, caused him to make some changes in Garcilasso's bare narrative. He followed the original story of Manco Capac, as it had been approved by Robertson, fairly closely, and constructed his epic action mostly about the young prince Rocha. Rocha, the sec-

ond Inca and son of Manco Capac, had lived a quiet and comparatively uneventful life, but the sixth Inca had borne the
same name and, as a child accompanying his father on cam-
paigns and as a youthful leader in his own right, had been one of
the most active and interesting Incan conquerors. Barlow, using
the identity of names as an excuse and the resulting confusion of
some Spanish historians as a precedent, telescoped his history
and created a story unified in time and eventful in action by
attributing to the first Rocha the deeds of the second. But
even this combination did not provide adequate military action
for an epic (for the Incan conquests frequently resulted from
wars of nerves rather than from doubtful battle), and Barlow
may have borrowed, as a contemporary biographer suggested,
further details from Marmontel's *The Incas: or the Destruction
of the Empire of Peru*, particularly the business of an eclipse
during a battle which is not to be found in Garcilasso's account
of the Inca conquests.

In the other historical portions of *The Vision of Columbus*
Barlow, like his master, Robertson, was concerned with a "view
of the progress of society," and, as a poet, he was even less concerned than Robertson with a detailed, factual treatment of the
past. The enormous amount of material that he attempted to
cover led him away from Robertson toward the more summary
methods of historical writing represented by Lord Kames's
Sketches of the History of Man and Voltaire's *Essay on the Manners and Spirit of Nations*, both of which he may have known.
And, although Barlow showed no great admiration for "the dif-
fusive writings of Voltaire," he would have agreed that the aim
of history was "not to collect an enormous multitude of facts . . . .
but to select the principal ones, and such as are the best established, and at the same time the best suited to direct the
reader in his inquiries, and to enable him to distinguish the ex-
tinction, the revival, and the progress of the human understanding." Thus he might have justified his scheme, and the
practical limitations of the poetic form may have forced him into an even more summary use of material. Accordingly, the sections of *The Vision of Columbus* surveying European events can-

not be traced to any particular source, although he undoubtedly supplemented Robertson with some of the histories and historical dictionaries available to him. The books dealing with the recent history of the North American colonies, of course, were largely based upon Barlow's own firsthand knowledge, newspaper material, and common report.

But in the episode dealing with the pre-Columbian history of Peru, Barlow used a source which was colorful, detailed, and full of "curiosities"; and the interesting thing about that section of the poem is that almost none of the curious, detailed color struck the poet's imagination with sufficient force to work itself into the verse. Barlow wanted to represent, in the political and religious systems of the Incas, a remarkable achievement for "the unenlightened efforts of human wisdom"; and that single purpose dominated the entire episode with its colorless intellectuality. His attempts at epic decoration by the representation of action and the use of figures are cold and abstract, even in comparison with the epic verse of Timothy Dwight; and, if he made any conscious efforts to conjure up the "ideal presence," they were, on the whole, futile. This apparent failure to avoid the dangers of an excessively generalized style, while it may be attributed in part to the author's desire to do too much, is especially remarkable because Barlow, even more surely than Dwight, was writing with Lord Kames's *Elements of Criticism* at his elbow. When he left his copy with Ruth soon after their marriage, he wrote back promptly urging her to "read Kaims thoroly and soon, partly because I want the book"; and the instructions which followed make it clear that he was referring to the critical work. Consequently, unless his wife proved remarkably less obliging during their first month of married life than she ever was afterward, he had the Scottish critic at hand for consultation during the period when he was laboring most seriously with his work, composing only seven hundred lines during an entire winter, while cultivating the style in which he later proved himself so fluent. Some of the descriptions in *The Vision of Columbus* follow the principles laid down by Kames, but the poem is in no way comparable to *The Conquest of Canäan*

in its meticulous obedience to critical theory. Barlow, of
course, had none of Dwight's pedantry, and for that reason, perhaps, he reflected Kames's literary influence less clearly in his
descriptive style than in his avoidance of some of the structural
pitfalls against which the critic warned epic and narrative poets.

Barlow may have owed a more positive debt to the ideas of
Lord Kames in certain sections of the last two, more abstractly
philosophical, books of his poem, although these books, as a
whole, represented a vision of progress of which the Scottish
critic would never have approved. The curious union between
a complacent belief in the westward course of empire and an
orthodox belief in the biblical millennium gave the minds of
many Americans, especially New Englanders, a bias toward any
general theories of progress that might explain the improvements they themselves had witnessed in the Colonies. Furthermore, the Revolution provided an emotional impulse in the
same direction, for the Americans had been enabled to justify
their independence and carry on their struggle only by a conviction that the future would somehow be better than the past.
Even among the orthodox Calvinists, who had looked closely
into the prophecies and had come to believe that the fifth vial
of Revelation had been poured out, there was a good deal of
cheerfulness about the intervening time before the millennial
period dawned—perhaps in the year two thousand. The era of
miracles had passed, they argued, so why should not the world
be expected to move toward its eventual state of peace and
happiness according to the same progressive plan God followed
in the creation? In such an atmosphere—which affected even
so hardheaded a man as Timothy Dwight—there was no need
for a man of Barlow's hopeful temperament to get his idea of
progress from any sources more distant than the histories he had
read and the popular beliefs of his own friends and countrymen.

Nor is there any evidence that the poet had read, before writing *The Vision of Columbus*, any of the French perfectionists who
became the inspirers of his later thoughts. The idea of progress
which is implied throughout his poem and made explicit in the
last two books was entirely teleological, completely free from

the notions of self-determination toward which he seemed to have been groping in his commencement poem. Man's "progressive paths" had been determined by "the counsels of the unchanging Mind"—not by his own efforts. Yet "the unconscious steps of human kind" were represented as being led along no mysterious roads, for "Heaven's extended plan" provided, among other things, for the eventual construction of the Erie, Suez, and Panama canals, a great improvement in medical science, the elimination of the study of foreign languages in schools, and a league of nations. The vision stopped short of the peace and happiness of the millennial period; but, even if it was confined to the "deeds and blessings" of humankind, it was still represented as a survey of God's intention rather than of man's aspiration.

This extremely passive idea of progress was paralleled by an equally passive optimism which was much more characteristic of the "whatever is, is right" men of good eighteenth-century cheer than it was of the men who looked as shrewdly as Barlow did into the possibilities for future improvements. The poet found much that was bad in human history but nothing that failed to contribute to a good end; and, in taking this attitude, he stood in clear disagreement with the historians who supplied evidence for the "progressive plan" he described. It is possible that Barlow evolved this optimistic attitude toward history from the practical necessity of denying, in an undergraduate debate, that the destruction of the Alexandrine library and the ignorance of Europe after the barbarian invasions were events unfortunate to literature. In any case he took the attitude in his poem that without "bickering tribes" in the past the greater part of the world would have remained an unpeopled waste in which the foundations for progress could never be laid. He agreed with Lord Kames that differences in human languages originated with the Tower of Babel; but, instead of agreeing further that the event was a misfortune hindering progress, he looked upon it as one of the essential, necessary conditions of the divine plan. This attitude could not have come from Robertson or Voltaire, any more than it could have been derived from Kames or the other historians Barlow had read. It is rather closely parallel to the attitude taken by Turgot in his early lectures before the Sorbonne, and the parallel is emphasized by occasional illustrative details. The probability is, however, that it was a product of the poet's own environment and his ordinary reading—of the popular but nebulous belief in progress which was so widely current in America and so common, with qualifications, among the historians; of the facile optimism of Pope's *Essay on Man* and perhaps other writings of the same school; and of the relics of Calvinistic predestination, to which Barlow and most of Connecticut were at least paying lip service. This section of *The Vision of Columbus* is a remarkable one, because in it the author anticipated some of the most ambitious goals for later human efforts, without at any time implying that human effort was necessary for their attainment.

One reason for the indeterminate character of Barlow's philosophical attitude was that he considered his point of view original and, as he later confessed, "first ventured upon these ideas, in the course of the Poem, with all the timidity of youth." When he found that his "general ideas, respecting the future progress and final perfection of human society" were "supported by those of so respectable a Character as Dr. Price," he determined "to risk a serious illustration of the sentiment in prose." Accordingly, he introduced a long note in which he clarified some of the obscurities of his poem:

It seems necessary that the arrangement of events in civilizing the world should be in the following order. *First*, all parts of it must be considerably peopled; *second*, the different nations must be known to each other; and *third*, their imaginary wants must be increased, in order to inspire a passion for commerce.

The world, he believed, was in the second stage, and the third was soon to arrive "as a necessary consequence of the two former." He continued to look upon the general plan as a predetermined one, however, for

the spirit of commerce is happily calculated by the Author of wisdom to open an amicable intercourse between all countries, to soften the horrors of war, to enlarge the field of science and speculation, and to assimilate the manners, feelings and languages of all nations. This leading principle, in its remoter consequences, will produce a thousand advantages in favour of government and legislation, give Patriotism the air of Philanthropy, induce all men to regard each other as brethren and friends, eradicate all kinds of literary, religious and political superstition, prepare the minds of all mankind for the rational reception of moral and religious truth, and finally evince that such a system of Providence, as appears in the unfolding of these events, is the best possible system to produce the happiness of creatures.

Some of these notions had already been expressed in his poem; some were borrowed directly from Price's *Observations on the Importance of the American Revolution, and The Means of Making It a Benefit to the World;* and all of them, in so far as they imply that well-informed men will always choose the good, are based upon the same un-Calvinistic conception of human nature that enabled Price to maintain that "principles rooted in human nature will resist" any doctrines with an "avowed and direct" tendency toward immorality.

Barlow had already developed such a conception of human nature in a section of the eighth book of *The Vision of Columbus* which, of all the philosophical portions, is the most interesting, because it contradicts the superficial Calvinism of the entire work, because it represents a continuation of the Yale revolt against Locke that had been revealed by Trumbull's *Speculative Essays* of more than a decade before, and also because it was one of the earliest of the many American attempts to answer Pope's *Essay on Man.* For, if Barlow believed with Pope that "whatever is, is right," he also believed that Pope had not engaged upon "the proper study of mankind" with sufficient nicety to be wholly accurate. The American poet's own theory of the nature of man was developed in the "high converse" which followed a question put by Columbus after the angel had given him his first summary of the "progressive plan": "How shall truths like these to man be given?" Or, as he paraphrased it in a more complex form that demanded both a theological and an epistemological answer: "What connecting chain . . . . Links earth to heaven, and mortal with divine?" The theological answer given by the angel, though wordy in its evolution, was succinct in its essence: "The attracting force of universal love." This much was so thoroughly orthodox that there is no perceptible

difference in the theological views of Columbus' angel and of the
one who expounded the binding force of "Love's mighty chain"
to Joshua during his vision in the tenth book of *The Conquest
of Canäan*. The epistemological answer, however, was much
less casual and more elaborately given, for it required a rather
comprehensive exposition of the nature of man and an attack on
a still popular philosophical system.

The exposition began with clear echoes from Pope, first, in its
reference to

> The passions wild, that sway the changing mind,
> The reasoning powers, her watchful guide design'd,

and, second, in its thesis concerning the "ruling passion":

> Of human passions, one above the rest,
> Fear, love, or envy, rules in every breast;
> And, while it varies with the changing clime,
> Now stoops to earth, now lifts the soul sublime,
> Forms local creeds of superstitious lore,
> Creates the God, and bids the world adore.

But between these two passages Barlow inserted his criticism
of Pope's optimistic attitude toward both the passions and
reason:

> Each, unrestrain'd, alike subvert the plan,
> Mislead the judgment and betray the man.
> Hence raging zeal, or sceptic scorn prevails,
> And arms decide the faith, where wisdom fails.

And he expanded these couplets into an extensive warning
against both irrational "superstition" and too great a dependence upon the "reasoning powers," which control the
"passions" yet are equally dangerous in their tendency to
"shroud in deeper glooms the mental ray." On one hand, he
claimed, the "proud sage," placing excessive dependence upon
human reason, doubts the perfection and wisdom of God because of plagues, earthquakes, wars, and other physical and
moral evils in the world and comes at last to the conclusion that
there is

> No love, no wisdom, no consistent plan
> No God in heaven, nor future life in man!

On the other hand, disappointed with this materialistic conclusion (the denial of any "form beyond what human sense perceives") because it left him still curious concerning the nature and powers of his own mind, he makes a new start with "conscious thought" as the point of departure for his "reasoning force." In that way he discovers "the active soul"; but, since he postulates no relationship between thought and substance, he concludes that perceptions merely deceive the reason and material substances exist only in name. Thus:

> All matter, mind, sense, knowledge, pleasure, pain,
> Seem the wild phantoms of the vulgar brain;

while

> Reason, collected sits above the scheme,
> Proves God and nature but an idle dream,
> In one great learned doubt invelops all,
> And whelms its own existence in the fall.

Human reason, as Barlow was representing it, had definite limitations, and, pushed beyond these limitations, it would produce a Voltaire or a David Hume.

The first attack on the materialistic conclusion of the reasoning process may have been derived from suggestions contained in Pope's own attack on intellectual pride and from what Barlow had heard of Voltaire; but the second, which represents the "proud sage" as taking "conscious thought" as his starting-point and arriving at a thoroughgoing idealistic skepticism, is so curious that it may provide a clue to the meaning behind the whole, rather obscure, discourse. The conclusions are those of Hume; but Hume, of course, did not begin his system of reasoning simply from "conscious thought," and the description does not fit any other actual philosopher. It does, however, form an accurate epitome of the history of skepticism from Descartes to Hume as given in James Beattie's *Essay on the Nature and Immutability of Truth*, with which Barlow was also in close accord in his general insistence upon the limitations of human reason and in such particulars as his incidental expressions of contempt for philosophical jargon and formal "schools." Beattie's book had been advertised in Connecticut well before Barlow began to

plan his poem and hence was available to him; but there is no
direct evidence as to whether he based his own beliefs upon the
Scottish work or evolved his system independently, as Trumbull may have done in his *Speculative Essays*, in reaction against
fine-spun reasoning and from a point of view absorbed from
Lord Kames.

In any case the Scottish philosophy of common sense plays a
key part in the epistemological answer given to Columbus'
question. The "wide extremes" of philosophical error into
which man is led by his intellectual pride and of the superstition
induced by his passions might both be avoided, according to
Barlow's system, by the acceptance of "Science" (in Beattie's
sense of "well-informed thought") as a guide toward the eternal
goal of truth. With such a guide,

> First, his own powers the man, with care, descries,
> What nature gives, and various art supplies;
> Rejects the ties of controversial rules,
> The pride of names, the prejudice of schools;
> The sure foundation lays, on which to rise,
> To look thro' earth and meditate the skies;
> And finds some general laws in every breast,
> Where ethics, faith, and politics may rest.

In a careful estimate of his own powers man would see that
"Sense" was the "great source of knowledge," the chief of human powers, which secured but did not exalt the race. "Reason"
would be seen as the power of enlightenment and refinement
which distinguished man from beast, increased knowledge, restrained the fancy and the passions, and enabled men to make
judgments, comparisons, and laws. Neither, however, could rise
above mundane things: they could "raise no thought of spirit,
or of God." Thus the answer to the question concerning the way
to know or the "connecting chain" between God and man could
not be discovered within the bounds of the epistemological system of John Locke. Neither sensory perception nor the power
of reason could disclose the connection between earth and
heaven. The idea of God was "not taught by nature nor acquired by art"; and, similarly, the idea of a mediator or "recon-
ciling plan," though widely "diffused thro' all mankind" and

all religions, "rose not from earth, or force of human mind." Nor
did it reach man by the only orthodox method of revelation
through the Scriptures, for the idea of God, Barlow specifically
declared again, had been caught at different times by many
nations. "Thro' every age the conscious mind perceives" conceptions of God and of spiritual beings, he said; and in a sum-
marizing passage he described these fundamental religious perceptions as the "few fair truths, to common feeling plain," that
apparently satisfied man's search for those

> general laws in every breast,
> Where ethics, faith, and politics may rest.

He was not quite willing to use so technical and controversial a
phrase as "the common sense of mankind"; but his meaning
seems reasonably clear, and his reference to God as the "great
moral Sense" around which all human "sense" revolves may reveal an indebtedness even in terminology to the Scottish
philosophers.

The Vision of Columbus was neither a profound nor an entirely
coherent "philosophical poem." But it was a safe one. Barlow
called upon the greater part of literate Connecticut, at one
time or another, for advice; and his work was read by a dozen or
more of his friends and acquaintances without giving offense to
any. Accordingly, he set about the tedious and trying job of
getting subscribers and arranging the publication of his book
with "good and extensive" prospects based upon recommendations from readers of the manuscript. He went to Philadelphia
in the autumn of 1782 in order to promote the work, carrying
with him no fewer than fifteen letters of introduction to various
gentlemen of importance, all of whom were interested in his
poem; and he sent subscription papers to practically all the
northern and middle Colonies and to France and England. His
reception in Philadelphia was "flattering beyond . . . . expectations"; and, in particular, he found that he had good prospects of satisfying his "old romantic wishes" that even his wife
"used to laugh at"—a desire to dedicate his work, with permission, to "His Most Christian Majesty, Louis the Sixteenth,

King of France and Navarre." By the end of 1786, when the
poem finally went to press, the king had given his permission and
subscribed for twenty-five copies, Washington (who never got
around to reading it) subscribed for twenty, and Lafayette
(who did) subscribed for ten. Barlow's most loyal support,
however, came from the army. The original list of subscribers
included, in addition to Washington and Lafayette, the names of
twelve generals, three major generals, thirty-three colonels,
seventeen majors, and fifty-two captains; and, since they averaged nearly three copies apiece, over one-fourth of the subscribed copies went into the upper ranks of the army and to
their friends. It was their greatest exhibition of patriotism since
the siege at Yorktown; and with the Continental Army so
strongly behind him Barlow grossed over fifteen hundred dollars
on the edition and became probably the first of the Connecticut
Wits to receive financial reward for his literary efforts. The
poem was published on May 14, 1787, an English edition appeared in October, and in the same month proposals were announced for a second edition, which appeared during the following spring. In both England and America the poem received
notices that were complimentary, although they fell considerably short of enthusiasm. Barlow may have been disappointed,
but he could not have been bitter. The second American edition,
however, did not have any great number of subscribers; and
when Mathew Carey suggested reprinting it in 1788, Barlow,
afraid of losing money on his own project, offered him unbound
copies of the second edition instead. The reception of *The Vision
of Columbus*, although on the whole favorable, offered no practical inducement for Barlow to devote his entire time to literature.

IV

From the time Barlow completed the major part of his work
on *The Vision of Columbus* in the spring of 1783 until the poem
was published four years later he was searching, in various ways,
for his proper place in the world. His plans had always been
"large," but they were still indefinite. As an author he engaged

in the active attempt to promote a copyright law which his classmate Noah Webster was pressing in the spring of 1783, and he also helped promote the first part of Webster's *Grammatical Institute*. But he had not yet settled upon a profession, for his career as a chaplain was coming to a close with the disbanding of the army and he had no intention of remaining in the ministry. For a while he contemplated the possibility of practicing law in Charleston, following the southward footsteps of so many other Yale graduates of the time, and in the spring of 1784 he thought of going into the business of printing and bookselling in Baltimore. Elisha Babcock, a printer from Springfield, Massachusetts, finally settled his problems for him during the summer by agreeing to a partnership in Hartford, which would publish a newspaper, sell books and stationery, and engage in whatever miscellaneous printing Barlow's literary connections would provide. Accordingly, the poet formally became a newspaper editor with the appearance of the first issue of the *American Mercury* on July 12, 1784.

As editor, Barlow probably composed the fluent anapestic address of the newsboy to his customers for January 1, 1785, and he may even have written the casual octosyllabic broadside for the following year after he had become disassociated with the paper. But he had little time for occasional verse. The greatest asset he had brought into the partnership and perhaps the determining cause for his remaining in Hartford was an authorization from the General Association of Connecticut to revise Dr. Isaac Watts's version of the Psalms in order to remove the allusions to Great Britain and the king and so to make them more adaptable to singing in the United States. He also planned to make "some slighter corrections in point of elegance, where the rules of grammar, established since the time of Doctor Watts, have made it necessary"; and he agreed to versify the dozen psalms Watts had not already "imitated" and to add a collection of hymns. While he was engaged in this project, an old friend and fellow-poet, Dr. Lemuel Hopkins of Litchfield, was living with him, and the two friends collaborated on the work, possibly with the further assistance of John Trumbull. Only six

of the psalms needed extensive revisions for national reasons,
but the poets made a considerable number of incidental changes
throughout the collection. The whole was inspected and approved early in January by a committee of ministers appointed
for that purpose, and the volume was published on March 21,
1785, with a separate edition of the new psalms and hymns in
August. The revisions were perhaps excessive, but the whole received general approval and praise except for the natural objections to a change from habitual usage—and some of these
may have been unjust metrical criticisms resulting from the
fact that Barlow was sympathetic enough with Webster's
theories of pronunciation to spell out a few of the words Watts
habitually abbreviated. The exact authorship of the various revisions and even of the completely new versions cannot be determined, but Barlow apparently did the eighty-eighth and the
one hundred and thirty-seventh paraphrases and had the general editorial responsibility for the lot. His editorial responsibilities, indeed, kept him fully occupied during the early part of
1785, for he not only had his newspaper and the Psalms on his
hands but during the same time published the third part of
Webster's *Grammatical Institute* (which contained some sections
of the still unprinted *Vision of Columbus*) and supervised *The
Conquest of Canäan* in its journey through the press.

The firm of Barlow and Babcock was dissolved by mutual consent in the autumn of 1785, Babcock keeping the printing business while Barlow opened a store for the purpose of disposing of
their stock of books, adding enough general merchandise to
make the enterprise justifiable. He also decided to follow his
earlier plan of practicing law, and throughout the winter that
followed he read in preparation for his entrance to the bar and
probably continued to debate with his friends the sort of philosophical questions that Noah Webster had recorded as topics
for discussion during the preceding January. He had little to do
except collect subscribers for his poem and tend his small shop,
and during this leisurely period of reading and meditation his
mind began to turn along new paths. Over five years earlier
he had made a half-humorous declaration of an attitude that

became more and more serious as he grew older: "I am determined to love mankind if they kill me." He also had been
greatly impressed by Dr. Richard Price's belief in the essential
goodness of man and in the practical possibilities for human
improvement, for he had already published extracts from
Price's *Observations* in the *American Mercury* and was soon to
publish the footnote to *The Vision of Columbus* in which he declared his intellectual kinship with the English clergyman. But,
as he began his serious study of Blackstone's *Commentaries on
the Laws of England* and such other works as Montesquieu's
The Spirit of Laws and Burlamaqui's *The Principles of Natural
and Politic Law* (both of which he had on the shelves of his bookshop), he may have begun to wonder about the real possibility
of any large improvement in mankind. Such questions were
being debated among the open-minded citizens of Hartford in
1785; and, although most of them may have been highly skeptical of such a possibility, not only was there room for a difference
of opinion, but differences of opinion were probably encouraged
for the sake of the debate.

The crux of the problem lay in the concept of human nature
and fundamental natural law which had been taken so thoroughly for granted during the Revolutionary period that such people
as Barlow, who read the pamphlets of Thomas Paine and the
Declaration of Independence in college, had never even thought
of it critically. It had dominated Barlow's political thinking,
and, under a different guise, it dominated the most thoughtful
part of *The Vision of Columbus*. But, however attractive the
doctrine of absolute law based on the immutable aspects of
human nature may have been as a justification for revolt
against human oppression, it had nothing at all to recommend
it to men who wanted to improve humanity and hence, in effect,
revolt against themselves. The difficulty seems to have become
clear to Barlow as he consulted his various legal authorities and
found them affirming the immutability and the fundamental
character of natural law. When God "created man," wrote
William Blackstone, "and endued him with freewill to conduct
himself in all parts of life, he laid down certain immutable laws

of human nature, whereby that freewill is in some degree regulated and restrained, and gave him also the faculty of reason to discover the purport of those laws." Burlamaqui was in agreement: "natural laws are immutable, and admit of no dispensation." And Montesquieu, although less explicit and more in accord with the vaguer notions Barlow had expressed in his poem, gave a similar importance to natural law and did not, even by implication, quarrel with the other authorities' point of view. Was mankind's trouble, the poet began to wonder, the result of what Blackstone called "the frailty, the imperfection, and the blindness of human reason," as he said it was in his poem? Or was it the result of a mistaken belief in the sort of "natural laws" which Montesquieu had discussed and illustrated by reference to "the law which by imprinting on our minds the idea of a Creator, inclines us to him"? Barlow had accepted this theory of innate knowledge in *The Vision of Columbus;* but, as he began to see it more clearly and dogmatically set forth and had time to think about it, he began to have doubts.

The doubts were not sufficient to cause him to engage in the tedious job of revising a poem which had already met wide approval in manuscript, nor were they wholly solved until many years afterward. But they were strong enough to cause the expression of an entirely different point of view on so formal an occasion as his examination for admission to the bar in April, 1786. He apparently had just been reading Beccaria's *Essay on Crimes and Punishments*, which was also for sale in his shop, and the views of the Italian reformer emphasized the poet's own humanitarianism, thus giving a bias to the dissertation he wrote for the occasion, as well as supplying substance for his observations. The humanitarian impulse revealed in the essay, however, was of less importance at the moment than its effect in causing Barlow flatly to contradict the beliefs of his legal authorities and the notions that he himself had hitherto taken for granted. "The laws of Nature applied to any particular species of Beings are supposed to be absolutely unchangeable so long as that species of Beings continue in existence," he declared in a statement that would have been accepted by Blackstone, Bur-

lamaqui, and Montesquieu no less than by the Scottish philosophers. But, he continued: "This I conceive to be a mistake, and
that it has given rise to many unjust conclusions when applied
to human actions, and received as the foundation of human institutions." Accordingly, his humanitarian attack upon cruel
punishments and undesirable distinctions based on custom and
common law led to a conclusion that the "supposed difference
between a state of nature and a state of society is a trivial metaphysical distinction without any foundation in reason and com-
monsense." Many people, of course, had maintained the same
thing in opposition to reforms advocated on the grounds of
"natural rights." It is remarkable in Barlow, however, because
it marks a departure from the passive idea of progress in *The
Vision of Columbus:* his unpublished dissertation of 1786 reveals
his first determined steps along an intellectual path which
eventually would lead to the advocacy of a large "renovation of
society" for the sake of its beneficial effects upon human nature.
If Beccaria was right in his observation that "the passions and
vices of one age are the foundation of morality of the following,"
the existence of an inherent moral sense was, at best, doubtful;
and the first step toward the substitution of humanitarian
sentiments for these "passions and vices" as a foundation of
morality would have to be a denial of this legalistic conception
of immutable natural law. The eloquent humanitarianism of
Beccaria's essay bore witness to his belief that the substitution
was possible; and Barlow, sympathizing with that humanitarianism, contemplating it in immediate contrast with a colder
legality, saw the necessity of the denial. Three years before he
went to France he was beginning to look toward the perfectibility of man.

V

When Barlow's interest was diverted to a new line of literary
activity in the autumn of 1786, he was still awaiting the public
judgment upon his most ambitious work His career had followed the usual pattern of experiment, major endeavor, and reaction into merely incidental and miscellaneous activity; but in

his case there had been no disillusionment with literature. He was still optimistic in his expectations, and he was continuing to receive flattering recognition from the public—some of it in anticipation of the reputation he was expected to achieve by the publication of his poem. When he was elected to the Common Council of Hartford in March, he was being recognized, with Trumbull, as one of the responsible citizens of the town; but, when the Society of Cincinnati, later in the year, voted that he deliver the annual Fourth of July oration for 1787, they were consciously choosing the author of *The Vision of Columbus*. Except for some secret grumbling by Ezra Stiles at his revision of the Psalms and the prominence of his name on the title-page, he had aroused little antagonism by his writing, and he suffered none of the wounded pride that affected several of his friends. More important, perhaps, he had not yet been put on the defensive intellectually. Not having been drilled thoroughly in the theoretical importance of "things as they are" while at Yale, he also had never been forced to consider the practical importance of "things as they are" in the outside world. He liked to indulge in what he called "romantic wishes"; and, although he had suffered the usual discouragements of a young man trying to lift himself by his own bootstraps, wishful thinking still formed an important part of his intellectual activity. He had found no reason, by the middle of 1786, to feel dissatisfied with the quality of his verse, but he had begun to feel that he lived in a closed intellectual world—a world of arbitrary restrictions which needed only to be thrown away in order to enable a man to look beyond the horizon. His later development was to be that of a dreamer and thinker rather than that of a poet.

PART III

Dead Ends and New Directions

CHAPTER VI

THE WICKED WITS

I

DURING the years that followed the Revolution the
United States faced the problem of restoring trade and
commerce with neither the advantages nor the dis-
advantages of membership in the British Empire. Massachusetts, Rhode Island, and, to a considerable extent, New York
were looking across the ocean for prosperity; but Connecticut,
although lacking a good seaport, had an excellent river highway
to the interior, and the town of Hartford, on the edge of the
upper valley, soon became the flourishing commercial center of
the state. Trumbull had moved there as early as 1780, Barlow
had taken a house in his neighborhood during the winter of
1782–83, and Lemuel Hopkins and his wife had arrived in 1784,
making their residence with the Barlows until they were able to
set up their own establishment. By the autumn of 1786 all three
poets were substantial citizens. Trumbull was a successful, well-
established lawyer with good connections and some prospects, if
health and energy permitted, of a political future. Barlow, less
successfully established in a profession, nevertheless was also a
member of the Common Council and a person of some importance in the town. Hopkins had built up a professional reputation that made him so nearly Connecticut's leading physician
that he had been specially called from Hartford to attend the
aged and beloved Governor Jonathan Trumbull in his last illness. They had known one another for a long time; Hopkins had
probably been one of the contributors to "The Correspondent,"
and they had all collaborated after a fashion upon Barlow's edi-

tion of Dr. Watts's *Psalms*. But their literary productivity had become very casual. One had been fairly well disillusioned concerning the prospect of achieving fame and fortune through literature; another was still waiting to test the results of his efforts; and the third, Hopkins, had never been stirred by any great literary ambition.

Hopkins, as a matter of fact, lacked the first requisite to practical literary ambition, for he was wholly skeptical concerning the patriotic optimism which most American poets seemed to accept as a necessary ingredient in successful composition. "My best compliments to Trumbull and Barlow," he had written Oliver Wolcott shortly before he moved to Hartford:

Tell them that I am glad we have some poets who have not liv'd long enough to see all the variety of folly and perversness the humane is capable of: for I hope posterity will judge of a century or two to come by their poetic prophecies provided no historian should think it worth his while to write a word about it.

Yet he was an exceptionally generous man, tolerant of his friends' faults; and, if he had a brusque, eccentric manner to match his ungainly figure and bright staring eyes, his sharp tongue could lay bare pretensions with an efficiency that even Trumbull had to admire. He had not attended Yale, but his professional achievements and his knowledge of the classics had been recognized by an honorary Master's degree in 1784. And he had demonstrated his individual talent for versification in the *Connecticut Courant* for November 7, 1785, by "A new and certain CURE for CANCERS! In an EPITAPH on a Patient Who Died of a Pimple in the Hands of an Infallible Doctor." From its beginning—

Here lies a fool flat on his back,
The victim of a Cancer Quack—

to its moralizing conclusion—

Go, readers, gentle, eke and simple,
If you have wart, or corn, or pimple;
To quack infallible apply;
Here's room enough for you to lie.
His skill triumphant still prevails,
For *Death's* a cure that never fails—

the poem announced, in almost every line, the appearance of a new writer whose rough, nervous wit was as stimulating in its matter-of-fact purpose as it was unpretentious of the "higher" literary aims of more ambitious men.

Such wit on the subject of medical quacks had aroused a host of vehement "enemies" when Trumbull tried it before the Revolution, but in the Hartford of 1785 it was almost completely lost amid the post-war concern for more gross and violent stimulants. The town may have been small enough to have a characteristic smell of new lumber, molasses, and old Jamaica, but it was frequented by men who had moved far abroad and were alert to everything that was happening in the new country which had just burst its colonial bounds. Colonel Jeremiah Wadsworth—the "certain Jere" who had assisted the devil to inspire David Humphreys in New Haven nearly seven years before—was perhaps the leading host in the town; and, although he was still appreciative of literature, he was more concerned with the possibilities of making a fortune. The breadth of his interests, which ranged from poetry to politics, from land speculation to manufacturing, was the measure of Hartford. Some of its inhabitants and their numerous visitors occasionally got together in the evening to discuss philosophical and literary subjects, but they spent so much of their time talking of more "practical" matters that stronger-minded poets than the Connecticut Wits would have found their attention diverted from abstractions to immediate concerns.

Two topics of immediate concern played an important part in the origin of a new, co-operative literary venture by Trumbull, Barlow, Hopkins, and their regular visitor, David Humphreys: the disposal of the public lands and the growing influence of the debtor classes upon the government of neighboring states. The first, in all its complicated ramifications, provided the original motive for the satiric enterprise which formally introduced the Connecticut poets to the world as "wits"; the second provided a secondary motive and an excuse for their activities. As their work became more self-consciously literary and their wit began to form a burlesque epic, they found additional, more patriotic excuses for writing; but the beginning was neither patriotic nor entirely excusable.

II

The first of the land controversies which involved the Hartford poets and had some effect upon their writing grew out of the conflicting claims of Connecticut and Pennsylvania to the territory including the Wyoming Valley. This section of what is now Pennsylvania had been developed by the Susquehanna Company of New England interests and settled largely by Connecticut families. Doubtful titles, however, had caused a good deal of trouble. In 1782 a court of arbitration meeting in Trenton had awarded the section to Pennsylvania without settling the matter permanently, for the court's decision led to the "Pennymite and Yankee war" in 1784, when state authorities tried to enforce the award; and subsequent appeals to Congress to review the decision met with no response. The Susquehanna Company, meeting in Hartford in July, 1785, had voted to support its claims before Congress and, in the meantime, to offer inducements to "able-bodied and effective" men who would settle in the territory and protect the company's interests by force of arms. The company also induced Colonel Ethan Allen to interest himself in the business, apparently with some notion that if events justified it he might play the same role in the amputation of Wyoming Valley from Pennsylvania that he had played in removing Vermont from New York. Allen, after seeing his *Reason: The Only Oracle of Man* through the press, visited the settlers in April, 1786, paraded in full regimentals for the encouragement of the Yankees, promised to bring in a lot of Green Mountain Boys, and put the Pennsylvanians in a high state of excitement. On May 17 he was in Hartford to attend another meeting of the company and apparently to encourage its defiance of court, Congress, and the state of Pennsylvania; for in December, 1786, the organization of proprietors met and threw its full weight into an effort to protect its interests—an effort which, incidentally, turned out to be in vain.

The affair must have caused a large amount of talk in Hart-

ford during the summer of 1786, when the numerous citizens interested were throwing straws in the political wind and planning
the course of action they would adopt in the December meeting.
In any case it affected the local poets in two ways. First, it
roused Dr. Lemuel Hopkins to an outburst of disapproval. The
Green Mountain colonel's book offended every standard of
sense, orthodoxy, and rhetoric to which he subscribed; and the
demagogy represented by Allen was more than could be stom-
ached by a man who had seen the public incited before and had
observed that, on such occasions, a certain text "grin'd horrible
a ghastly smile" at him: "wo unto thee, oh land, when thy king
is a fool." Accordingly, he burst forth in the *American Mercury*
for July 27 with a satiric denunciation of "the seer of Anti-
christ," who a few months before had descended

> To feed new mobs with Hell-born manna
> In Gentile lands of Susquehanna,

with "one hand . . . . clench'd to batter noses, While t'other
scrawls 'gainst Paul and Moses." Individual and independent
though Hopkins was, however, he could hardly have realized the
complexities of the Susquehanna affair. For the event which
provoked his denunciation involved at least one of his fellow-
poets in land speculation and eventually led to Hopkins' own
service as a literary cat's-paw for some of the very people who
had sent Allen into Pennsylvania.

This second, indirect effect of the Susquehanna affair upon
the activity of the poets was accomplished through the medium
of Joel Barlow, who was interested in the affairs of the company
and who served as secretary pro tem at the December meeting
and afterward as one of the board of commissioners appointed
to investigate the company's chances and act accordingly. The
federal Congress had already attempted to compromise with
Connecticut's land claims by guaranteeing the state's title to
the Western Reserve; and, as a consequence, many of the speculators—including Barlow—turned their attention to the possibilities of opening the country on the banks of Lake Erie. Plans
for the disposal of the Western Reserve were still undetermined;

but it was generally understood that, whereas the United States was expecting to sell its western lands at the basic price of one dollar an acre, Connecticut was to undertake a quicker disposal at half that price. Details, however, remained to be settled, and in the summer of 1786 two schemes were under discussion. The first called for the sale of unlocated lands, with both state and Continental securities accepted at par in payment. The second proposed that the sale be made by townships, with the acceptance of Connecticut paper alone at par. The difference between the two plans was momentous. One encouraged a rapid sale and favored the large companies which could survey and locate the most desirable holdings; it also meant that the state would be paid in Continental obligations, which it could use to pay off a share of the national indebtedness that admittedly could not be paid by the current methods of taxation. The other looked toward the retirement of the state debt and the ignoring of national obligations. The second plan also meant a positive first step toward disunion, although the fact may not have been at first widely appreciated.

The particular difference between the two proposals which excited the citizens of Connecticut, however, was less momentous. The first favored the officers and men of the Revolutionary army who held commutation certificates—the most depreciated form of Continental securities—and who might be expected to profit more than the holders of Connecticut paper by the acceptance of their securities at face value. The second gave the advantage to the state militia and in effect excluded the members of the Continental Army from participation in the speculative profits of their patriotism. Since Connecticut had paid its own militia longer than any of the other warring colonies, the amount of state paper in circulation was large, and the division of economic interests within the state was correspondingly acute. Yet it cannot be really determined to what extent differences of opinion concerning the disposal of the Ohio lands were affected by financial self-interest and to what extent they were caused by an appreciation of the larger implications of the two plans. The men who had acquired a more or less national

point of view through associations in the Continental service
stood to make a profit through the sort of land sale that would
promote national unity, whereas the neighborhood-minded militia would find it profitable to repudiate national obligations.
Patriotic vision, temperamental disposition, and economic self-
interest were inextricably confused from the very beginning to
such an extent that even the people concerned could not have
given an accurate account of their primary motives. The dissension did not continue long enough to become really serious, for it
was relieved, on the one hand, by the tendency of the Connecticut legislature toward the satisfaction of state interests
and, on the other, by the formation of the Ohio Company with
good prospects for obtaining fifty-cent land from Congress. But
in the meantime the land-conscious citizens were divided into
two camps that eyed each other with mutual suspicion; and differences growing out of a temporary condition were to be sustained on other grounds.

Such was the situation during the summer when notices appeared in the Connecticut newspapers requesting a full attendance of the Society of the Cincinnati at the regular September
meeting. The organization was composed of officers in the regular army of the Revolution; its members held quantities of commutation certificates; and a decision had been reached, in the
first triennial meeting in 1784, that the state chapters would act
together in exerting pressure upon Congress for an early grant
of western lands. The Cincinnati were suspected because of
their unity of interests and also because their original provision
for a hereditary membership was taken by many people as an
indication that they were trying to establish an order of nobility. Accordingly, the hint of an important meeting at this
particular moment aroused suspicion among some of the land-
conscious officers and men of the militia, as well as among citizens who had no military connection. Judge William Williams
of Lebanon, the serious-minded, public-spirited son-in-law of
the late Governor Trumbull, brooded over the situation and
prepared an address in which he outlined the two plans for disposing of the lands and strongly supported the second. He sent

a copy to Joseph Hopkins, of Waterbury, inclosed in a private letter that hinted at his fears of the Cincinnati and suggested the publication of the address before the regular county meetings of Freemen, which were scheduled for the same day as the meeting of the Society. The letter, however, was opened in transit, copied, and withheld from Hopkins until a few days before the scheduled meeting.

Judge Williams, who was in the embarrassing position of trying to prevent the uncertain actions of an organization in which his brother-in-law, Colonel John Trumbull, the painter, was secretary and an active member, had begged that his name be kept "impenetrably concealed"; but on October 9 the letter was published in the *Connecticut Courant*, in Hartford, followed by a burlesque version in octosyllabic couplets signed "William Wimble," in a thin disguise of the real author's name. The parody represented the letter-writer as comically self-important, mildly peccant, and suspicious of others from a consciousness of his own political chicanery. It also cast similar aspersions upon the recipient, whose identity was revealed by an allusion to the "copper-coining mint" that Joseph Hopkins had been operating in Waterbury up to the preceding June. The poem seems to have had no important purpose. Though it would inevitably sting so self-conscious a man as Williams and embarrass him in his personal relationships, it was probably no more than a slightly malicious warning for him to mind his own business—for he had guessed completely wrong concerning the reason for the special call to the Cincinnati. As a literary exercise it was clever and smooth, but notable primarily for its success in rhyming "to the rabble" and "impenetrable" and so copying, if not really rivaling, the "innumerable" and "consume-a-Rabble" standard of multiple rhyme which Swift had set for the octosyllabic couplet.

The *New Haven Gazette and the Connecticut Magazine* immediately copied the letter and the parody, and, as innocuous as the latter was, it seems to have put ideas in the head of Josiah Meigs, the editor, who had been running a series of "Observations on the Present Situation and Future Prospects of This and

the United States" under the signature of "Lycurgus." The
series of ironical essays had pointed out the dangers of a federal
government that had no power, made use of "Anarchus" in a
pretended attack upon Washington and the late Governor
Trumbull, and expressed an ironic preference for a poverty-
stricken country over a prosperous one. The stand taken by
Williams with regard to the Western Reserve was clearly opposed to the Federalist position supported by Meigs, and the
Gazette quickly set out to destroy the political reputations of
both Williams and the sympathetic Hopkins, who was nick-
named "Joseph Copper" in an effort to associate him with the
idea of a depreciating currency—for Hopkins' coins had already
begun to be held at less than face value. Accordingly, the next
issue of the paper carried an alleged "answer" to Williams' letter, supposedly by Hopkins, and another burlesque in octosyllabics. The parody of the second letter—which Williams insisted was itself a forgery—was both less clever and more vicious
than the poem of the previous week. It represented the author
as a politician and a rogue whose cynical philosophy might be
expressed briefly:

> However the public's torn and tatter'd,
> The people must be coax'd and flatter'd—
> Their interest, sir, and ours, require it—
> We'll ride this hobby till we tire it:
> You know I've labor'd in this vineyard,
> And led our chosen like a swine herd.

His confidant, by implication, was no better; and it was hinted
that he would not be returned to the assembly after the spring
session. The new poem had the air of a premeditated, purposeful attack; and, although lower in quality than the first, it contained one insidious phrase in "Copper's" defiance of "all the
wicked wits" who had attacked him.

The first poem, which had given Williams the name "William
Wimble," had done so with the purpose of associating him with
the Will Wimble of the Spectator and so branding him as a
trifler. The second, in making him—with Hopkins—a type of
demagogue, was attacking him by associating his political ac-

tivity with the mob rule that was beginning to fill the newspapers with dispatches from Massachusetts. For several years
there had been sporadic outbursts of mob activity in the rural
sections of New England, where the farmers were suffering from
a post-war depression and the lack of currency; and by the late
summer of 1786 the situation had grown critical. The state legislature of Massachusetts had adjourned without providing a
hoped-for relief, with the result that popular conventions had
been held in the western part of the state to demand unsecured
paper currency and the restraint of legal actions against the
debtors. As the autumn sessions of the courts of common pleas
approached, with the usual crowded calendars of suits and the
prospect of numerous imprisonments for debt, the people who
had previously been excited by the Rev. Samuel Ely, of Hampshire County, rose as mobs and, on August 29, prevented the
sitting of the court at Northampton. A week later the courts at
Worcester were also closed by a mob. On September 12, Job
Shattuck led another outbreak that closed the scheduled session
of the court at Concord. Luke Day and Daniel Shays were the
leaders of the western uprisings, and late in September they led
their followers on Springfield in an effort to close the supreme
judicial court from which they might receive indictments for
their earlier activities. The militia was ordered out, and the
court sat for three days but was forced to adjourn on September
28 without having transacted any business. By this time reports of the uprising were beginning to pour into the Connecticut newspapers, emphasizing the fears caused by earlier reports
of the New Hampshire outbreak under Moses French; and when
the "Joseph Copper" letter was published on October 23 the
implication of demagogy and of an association with depreciating
currency was a serious political charge

In the meantime, while the first news of the Massachusetts
insurrections was appearing in the papers, Humphreys was in
Hartford on a visit, between the September meeting of the Cincinnati and the October meeting of the general assembly, both
of which he attended in New Haven. He was already viewing
the situation with alarm in his "Mount Vernon: An Ode,"

which he published in the *Courant* for October 9, and he doubtless found his sentiments shared by most of his friends and associates. Dr. Hopkins had forcefully expressed his opinion of
men whose fists were "clench'd to batter noses"; and a rising
young lawyer like Barlow, no matter how he may have felt
about Colonel Allen's activities in Pennsylvania, must have
looked askance at the closing of courts so near by and the mobs'
violent objections to the legal profession. At this time Barlow's
efforts were frankly devoted to attaining "an interest," and he
had not yet firmly established his humanitarian convictions.
Accordingly, though he had opposed imprisonment for debt in
his dissertation submitted for admission to the bar, he probably
convinced himself that the law should be obeyed until it was
changed—especially when he realized that his classmates, Noah
Webster, Oliver Wolcott, Jr., and Josiah Meigs, and such prized
friends as Dr. Hopkins, Trumbull, Humphreys, and Colonel
Wadsworth were strongly of that opinion. There had never been
any doubt concerning Trumbull's feeling about the checked-
shirt-and-leather-apron men, even when he had been a patriotic
poet writing about patriotic mobs, and *M'Fingal* had already
been quoted in a Massachusetts newspaper against the insurrectionists.

It may have been while Humphreys was in Hartford that he
discussed with his friends the possibility of some continuous
satire directed against the conditions that threatened the American experiment in republican government. Colonel Wadsworth
had been in England while a group of poets were causing much
excitement with "The Rolliad" in the *Morning Herald* for 1784;
and Humphreys had visited London while the same satire was
still popular in book form and while sequels to it, by the same
group of wits, were appearing periodically. Other members of
the group may also have seen the publications, which professed
to be criticisms of an ancient epic that foretold contemporary
political developments, and Trumbull had already used the device of an ancient prophetic manuscript for purposes of satire in
"The Correspondent." Dr. Hopkins had expressed, three years
before, a sardonic conviction that the optimistic glimpses into

the future presented by his friends in their commencement poems were altogether at variance with the real prospects; and he was doubtless ready to help them correct their youthful mistakes. Thus the minds of a group of accomplished versifiers were prepared for the idea of a satire based upon the "discovery" of an ancient prophetic manuscript; and, if Noah Webster had been riding his hobbyhorse of antique fortifications on the banks of the Muskingum during his June visits to Hartford, the location of the discovery had already been fixed in the Ohio country, in which some members of the group were actively interested at the time.

No single person need necessarily have been responsible, but somehow out of this ferment there arose a scheme for a series of satiric papers on American antiquities—critical observations on the *Anarchiad: A Poem on the Restoration of Chaos and Substantial Night*, with extensive quotations from its twenty-four books. There was no novelty to Trumbull, Humphreys, and Barlow in the situation of "the prophetic bard," who seemed "to have taken for the point of vision one of the lofty mountains of America, and to have caused, by his magic invocations, the years of futurity to pass before him." But there was novelty in a vision of the rising glory of America that began "with unfolding the beautifying scenes when those plagues to society, law and justice, shall be done away with; when every one shall be independent of his neighbor; and when every rogue shall literally do what is right in his own eyes." The poets, who were still comparatively young men, were not profoundly disturbed; but the facile optimism of their earlier years had been displaced either by disillusionment or by less passive ideas of progress, and they began to affect pessimism in a literary effort to counteract the influences leading toward a social revolution unanticipated during the civil war against England.

If Humphreys took a fully matured proposal for the *American Antiquities* to New Haven when he and Wadsworth left to attend the general assembly, Josiah Meigs undoubtedly gave him enthusiastic encouragement; for the Lycurgus papers had been exhausted the preceding April and he had found no similar series that would take their place as featured satires directed against federal impotency, extreme democracy, state debt, and paper money. The first number appeared in the *New Haven Gazette* for October 26. It outlined the plan for the series by describing the supposed discovery and gave a brief sample of the *Anarchiad* in the form of heroic couplets presenting a vision of Massachusetts. The mobs of Day, Shays, and Shattuck had risen, the court had fallen as the frightened official ran to cover, and the constitution of Chaos had been restored as the "newborn state" was overwhelmed in the gulf of darkness. A week later the second number appeared with "a fragment of the speech which the old Anarch makes to Beelzebub, for the purpose of persuading him to come over and help his faithful friends in our Macedonia, since his affairs were in so thriving a posture in Massachusetts and Rhode Island." Like the Joseph Copper letter in the *Courant*, this was marked by bitter personal satire, with more than a dozen offensive allusions to individuals in less than twice as many couplets. Williams and Hopkins appeared again as "Wimble" and "Copper"; General James Wadsworth, of Durham, the state's leading advocate of a loose confederacy, was introduced under the name of "Wronghead"; Samuel Ely was referred to as "Froth, the sep'rate," glowing "with pop'lar rage"; Thomas Goodman, of New Hartford, was mentioned with him as a type of dotard from the lawless north; old Dr. Benjamin Gale, of Killingworth, received a sneering allusion; and a number of others were mentioned under aliases that can perhaps no longer be penetrated. They were all fairly prominent citizens of Connecticut—with the exception, perhaps, of Leonard Chester, who was satirized as "Laz'rus"—and all were identified as "Anarchists" by their opposition to the requisitions of Congress for the settlement of the national debt.

It was nearly two months before another number of *American Antiquities* appeared, but this issue had made it clear that a coordinated political attack was being organized by a group of men who made high-spirited references to themselves as "the wicked wits." Growing out of such a complexity of motives, the satires cannot be unmistakably attributed to particular authors.

Unsympathetic contemporary opinion, as expressed by an anonymous poet in the *Courant* for November 20, held that it was "*Hudy's* great rival" (John Trumbull) who was "thrumming his lute." Humphreys wrote Washington, on November 16, that he, Trumbull, and Barlow were the authors of the papers. And a persistent tradition, beginning soon after the last of the group died, has insisted that Lemuel Hopkins was a prime mover in the business. Judge Williams, who was deeply hurt by the whole affair, publicly expressed the conviction, in October, that the Cincinnati were back of the attack upon him and that General Samuel H. Parsons, president of the Connecticut Society, had taken the lead in "employing a poet" to burlesque a letter dishonorably obtained. Parsons immediately denied the accusation with an irate honesty which the Wits soon indorsed by promoting and ridiculing a public quarrel between the two men. The Cincinnati were perhaps unofficially back of the William Wimble burlesque. They had been unjustly accused of scheming for preferential treatment in the Western Reserve (their special request for a full attendance having been made for entirely different reasons), and they had been subjected to so much criticism that they were highly sensitive; but the most likely instigator was Colonel Jeremiah Wadsworth, vice-president of the Society, who was intimate with the entire body of Hartford versifiers. The poet was probably Trumbull. He was Wadsworth's close friend and a sort of unofficial adviser to the inner circles of the Cincinnati, and the original poem has all the stylistic marks of such burlesques as his "Epithalamium" and *M'Fingal*. Trumbull could hardly have written the Joseph Copper burlesque, however, unless he had suddenly lost the smoothness and facility that had characterized his use of the octosyllabic couplet during the previous seventeen years. Barlow, who was soon to become a shareholder in the Ohio Company and so had financial interests at stake, may have done it, either of his own accord or at the instigation of Meigs. The first number of *American Antiquities* was undoubtedly planned and probably written in conference by the authors mentioned by Humphreys—himself, Trumbull, and Barlow. The second could not have been prepared under such circumstances because the authors were separated by half the state. They may have followed the procedure adopted for the later *Echo* of sending the manuscript around, when the authors were separated, for emendations and additions. The first paragraph of the prose criticism and some parts of the verse reveal a quality of phrasing that was characteristic of Hopkins alone among the members of the group, and the probability is that it was begun by Barlow and Hopkins working in collaboration, passed through Trumbull's hands, and was sent to Humphreys for final improvements and publication. Humphreys, who had spent only a few days in Hartford since Hopkins had moved there, could have had only a bare acquaintance with him and probably was unconscious of the physician's contribution. The intimacy of Trumbull, Barlow, and Hopkins was such that the latter was sure to have had a part in any literary activity that interested the other two and fitted his satiric temper; but the informal collaboration of a "friendly club" including Humphreys was physically impossible. In any event the activities of the wits became so complex that even their best friends were soon uncertain about what was going on; and, though Humphreys remained, perhaps, the guiding spirit of the *American Antiquities*, his associates became engaged in a high-spirited quizzing too subtle for his participation and too much like lèse majesté for his approval.

This new development at first had no serious political purpose and apparently was the result of the temptation provided by an exchange of public letters between Williams and General Parsons. Late in October Williams had sent a brief note to the *Connecticut Journal and New-Haven Post-Boy* explaining the circumstances of the earlier letter, accusing General Parsons of being responsible for the burlesque, and insisting that the alleged reply from Hopkins had been a forgery. The *Gazette* reprinted this communication on November 2 with an aggressive reply from Parsons, in which he denied his responsibility for any of the actions of which he was accused. A week later, David Smith, one of the carriers of the letter, who had been charged with providing the Cincinnati with a copy, wrote in his own defense; and the same issue of the *Gazette* carried corrections by Williams designed to place the true contents of his first letter before the public. The tone of Parsons' letter and the agitation of Williams were an open invitation to the Wits, who undoubtedly were aware of the General's innocence; and they published, on the first page of the *Gazette* for November 23, another octosyllabic burlesque signed "Trustless Fox," with a postscript to the effect that it might have been signed "great General P—rs—ns" were the other name not more suited to his "unbooted" character. The same issue also contained an ironic prose defense of Williams, signed "Benevolence, Jr.," which professed to support him against "the *wicked wits* and snarling critics" who had inconsistently tried to represent him as both a knave and a fool. The tenor of the "defense" was to show that Williams was the latter, though the author refused to venture his own opinion of the appropriateness of the nickname; and it concluded on a note of sympathy "that an honest man should be a little disturbed, when so many wicked and malicious heads should be jumbled in HOTCHPOT to deprive him of his good character and office."

Benevolence, Jr., closed with a political hint which was fully developed when the Wits returned to the attack in the *Gazette* for December 14 in an ironically fatherly letter by "Benevolence, Sr." The supposition that Williams would lose his place in the next election was emphasized; and the author advanced the opinion, with ironic regretfulness, that "nothing could have been more opportunely, more happily, and more effectually calculated, than your essay, to fix indelibly the nickname 'William Wimble' upon Mr. Williams, and to exclude him from a seat in the upper house." Every implication contained in the letter by Benevolence, Jr., was made clear by the supposed father's attempt to warn him against "the *wicked* wits who are already sufficiently formidable to some of the grave pillars of our state." The letter concluded with a veiled hint that Benevolence, Jr., was the disliked "Laz'rus" of the *Anarchiad* and so gave a starting-point for "Anonimous," who contributed another letter, in the December 21 issue of the *Gazette*, addressed to Benevolence, Jr., or "Grey Goose the Younger." This letter developed the theme that "as Don Quixote had his *Sancho Panca*, Hudibras his Ralpho and M'Fingal his Constable, so hath William Wimble been accompanied to combat by his trusty squire Benevolence Jun." Anonimous was somewhat ironic about General Parsons; but his main effort was directed toward representing Williams as both a fool and a knave, for he not only associated him with the burlesque heroes of literature but accused him, in a bit of verse later included in the eighth number of *American Antiquities*, of leaguing with Joe Copper for the purpose of buying votes.

While the wicked Wits were carrying on at Hartford—probably under the direction of Trumbull, who had been well trained in this sort of darting, ingenious attack—Humphreys was active in other things. He had been appointed by the assembly on October 20 to raise a regiment of Connecticut militia for defense against a possible Indian uprising along the border, and he was busy making plans for recruiting and carrying out his legislative duties. He also took occasion to place his name before the public in a literary way. He arranged the series of documents which he published with an introduction, in the *Gazette* for November 16, as "The Conduct of General Washington, Respecting the Confinement of Capt. Asgill, Placed in Its True Point of Light"; and he also reprinted in the same issue his "Mount Vernon: An Ode," which had been originally published in the *Courant* five weeks before. Although the ode was pessimistic about existing conditions, it concluded with an optimistic belief that Providence would not leave "imperfectly achiev'd" the task begun in America. The *Gazette* for November 9 and December 7 also carried extracts from *A Poem on the Happiness of America*. The latter selection was accompanied by an introductory note in which the editors explained that it was printed in an effort "to put their Readers in better temper with respect to themselves, their neighbours, the community at large, and their fellow creatures in general"; and the reprinting of these pieces—which was almost certainly done with Humphreys' approval—would seem to indicate that the poet might be using his old optimism to cover his retreat from satiric activity. The concluding sentence of the editor's note approved the activities of the Wits, however, in a declaration that it was an effort "not less worthy of patriotic genius" to demonstrate to one's fellow-citizens "that the perverse disposition which induces them to spurn at greater privileges and blessings than are bestowed on any other nation, is madness to themselves, injustice to posterity, and the blackest ingratitude to heaven." Meigs had no intention of talking his prize satirist out of making new contributions.

Humphreys himself, as he indicated in his letters to Washington, was too firmly convinced that the antifederal and paper-money men were all demagogues and evil characters to give up his role as savior of his country. By the latter part of December he had rounded up the wicked Wits of Hartford and brought them back into the marked-out path of *American Antiquities*. The third number appeared in the *Gazette* for December 28, fulfilling the promise made in each of the earlier issues to present a selection from the epic episode dealing with Rhode Island. The paper-money party had come into power in that state during the spring elections, choosing John Collins as governor and Daniel Owen as lieutenant-governor, and their large issue of paper had immediately been subject to an enormous depreciation. An enforcing act had been passed requiring that the new currency be accepted at face value and providing that debts might be paid—if the creditor refused the legal tender—by depositing the requisite amount with the local court and advertising the fact in the newspapers. The neighboring states were full of such stories as that of the Connecticut man who inadvertently drove a load of wood over the Rhode Island line and was forced to sell it for worthless paper. The enforcing act had already been brought before the state court, and, though it had been vigorously supported by Henry Goodwin, a Newport attorney, it had been declared unconstitutional in September. But in spite of this legal doubt cast on the efficacy of paper money in Rhode Island and the fact that a paper-money proposal had already been easily defeated in the Connecticut legislature, the satirists launched a bitter personal attack upon Collins, Owen, and

Goodwin (who was charged with writing the governor's speeches) and upon the Sodom-like "Island" of unrighteous rogues. "For it will scarcely be denied, in any part of the United States," they explained, "that paper money, in an unfunded and depreciating condition, is happily calculated to introduce the long expected scenes of misrule, dishonesty, and perdition."

When the time came around for the annual New Year's verses for the carriers of the Hartford papers, the local Wits took a holiday from the purposeful satire which Humphreys was fathering. Their masterpiece was the two-poem broadside for the *Connecticut Courant*. The first poem was a burlesque "Eclogue," consisting mostly of a dialogue between Ira Jones and Tertius Dunning, carriers of the *Courant* and the *Mercury*. The two boys professed to have received their respective verses from "a Bard sublime," who was given to rhymed compliments and from "the wittiest Bard in Town"; Tertius claimed only that he sang the news dealt out to man by Jove's own Mercury, and Ira that he was inspired by "the Politics of these intriguing Days." Both took liberties with the Connecticut poets. Tertius begged:

> Inspire me, Phoebus! in my Wimble's praise,
> With Humphreys' strains, and Barlow's moving lays;
> No more his Plots reveal'd should he deplore,
> And wicked Wits should versify no more;

while Ira wished:

> Oh, in our Poet's Corner could I write
> As Trumbull witty, and sublime as Dwight;
> Copper should brighten in the polish'd strain,
> And trustless Foxes seek their Holes again.

They glanced at the Rhode Island paper money, the New York impost, and the Massachusetts mobs; and, when they were stopped by the printer, they had begun to query each other about the authors of the *Anarchiad* and about how a republican government might exist without power. The poem was a good-humored piece of nonsense and was immediately ridiculed in the accompanying "The News-Boy's Apology for the Foregoing Verses. Written by Himself." In the "Apology" Ira complained that he had given one of the poets five shillings for the "con-

founded Eclogue" and had been able to get neither his money
back nor another poem. He had protested that he had never
talked in such a way to Tertius and, that point of view having
made no impression on the poet, had objected to the political
allusions:

> So I told him flat and plain I thought 'twas quite improper,
> To say any thing in New-Year's Verses about Wimble and Joe Copper;
> And besides it was not politic, for all these Jokes so tickle us,
> It made them Folks important instead of being ridiculous,
> And when you keep pelting at 'em, and trying to be so witty,
> Their Friends will stick to 'em like sheep-ticks and vote for 'em out
>   of pity.
> And I told him as to Shaise and all his Fraternity,
> I didn't care if they got in a Snow-Drift and stay'd there to all Eternity.
> And as to Paper Money, now Cash they say so scarce is,
> I don't care a farthing about it, if they won't tender it to me for my
>   Verses.
> For my Master-Printers and I, satisfied with our Conditions,
> Don't mean to torment ourselves by turning great Politicians,
> We are all true-born Yankies, to our Country firm and hearty,
> And join none of your Factions, but print for every Party.

That argument did not work, either, and though Ira concluded
by talking "to him out of the Decalogue" the only satisfaction
he could get was that the poet had the money and he "must take
the Eclogue." Accordingly, he could only apologize and suggest
that he be paid double because of all his difficulties.

The comic "Eclogue" and the "Apology" (which was modeled
after Swift's poetic representation of Mrs. Harris' petition "To
Their Excellencies the Lord Justices of Ireland") were reprinted
in the *Gazette* for January 11; and two weeks later the same
paper published the New Year's verses from the *Mercury*, introduced by a note from the *Massachusetts Centinel*, which claimed
that "Pegassus is not perhaps back'd by better Horseman from
any part of the Union, than he is by those from the State of
Connecticut." The "poetic Horsemanship" used to illustrate
the claim consisted of octosyllabics based on the conceit of a
chain of being extending from Jove's great toe to the earth; but,
in spite of the insistence attributed to the carrier in the "Eclogue" that he sang only the news, the poem contained a light
political satire more pointed than anything found in earlier

Mercury verses for the New Year. In the meantime, other self-elected "wits" were trying to join in the chorus of verse. The *Gazette* for January 18 contained an announcement that the editors had recently "received a piece entitled American Antiquities No. 3" but that it was "evidently a spurious production" and so had not been printed, because "when any one assumes to write under a particular title, we think he ought not to be interfered with." Some verse "Advice to the Wits and Poets" adapted to "the Latitude and Longitude of Connecticut" appeared a week later, urging the Wits to let Wimble, Wronghead, and Copper alone and direct their attentions toward "the Spectator" who had undertaken to defend the actions of the legislature against the sensitive federalism of "Cato." A professed admirer of the *American Antiquities* offered "The Soliloquy of the Spectator" in satiric blank verse, for February 1, from a manuscript of tragedies recently discovered in Kentucky. A "Female Patriot" took her pen in hand two weeks later to speak while Anarch slept. The *Courant*, also, accepted contributions from outside the circle of "wicked wits"; and even the issue of February 26, which omitted all advertisements because the paper was so full of insurrection news, found room for "A Song" beginning "Come, come my bold boxers, 'tis Liberty calls," satirizing the "Tag, Rag, and Bobtail" mobs.

The inner circle of Wits, however, kept to their regular plan and on January 11 published their most ambitious selection from the *Anarchiad* in the form of preliminary speeches by Anarch and Hesper before their epic battle. Anarch contrasted the gold-respecting, patriotic British to the paper-money hypocrites in America; found evidence of his existing reign in the boldness of Shays and the insurrectionists, the Barbary corsairs, and the border Indians; and saw the "ghost of empire" stalking "without a head" in America. He also found encouragement in the retirement of Washington and the recent death of Greene, though he professed to fear that the time would come when there would be a reaction from mobs to monarchy. Hesper, in his turn, attacked Aedanus Burke for his pamphlet against the Cincinnati, prophesied a bad end for Shays, and

called on new Greenes and Washingtons to rise. The selection
broke off as they rushed to combat, but the paper closed with a
note of optimism in a "conjecture that the combat ended with
some disadvantage to old Anarch." There was, in fact, reason
for the optimism, for the newspapers had already reported the
successful outcome of Colonel Hichborn's campaign against the
Middlesex mob and the capture of Shattuck, Parker, and Page;
and the suppression of the insurrection in Vermont had been
announced. When Humphreys' "The Genius of America: A
Song" appeared as a supplementary manuscript to the *Anarchiad* for the fifth number of *American Antiquities*, on January
25, 1787, the author could only call for peace without venturing
a prophecy of the outcome, which he still felt to be concealed in
"shades of night." Yet on that very day General Lincoln met
and permanently dispersed Shay's mob, bringing the insurrection to an end as far as the Wits were concerned, except for an
aftermath of dispatches and the February tour of Humphreys'
Connecticut regiments through the scenes of January excitement.

By February the Wits were convinced of the necessity of a
formal attempt at a stronger federal union; and, with the dying-
out of the excitement over regulators in the west and paper
money in the east, they were free from emotional compulsion to
slash out at their neighbors and so could direct their satire toward some constructive end. Their first campaign was to destroy the political influence of General James Wadsworth,
leader of the anti-Federalist forces in the Upper House, whom
they had already introduced into their papers as "Wronghead."
On February 22 they presented his soliloquy, representing him
as railing against Congress, courts, legal powers, trade, great
men, and lawyers in *"cant pretense of Liberty"*; enjoying the
salaries of his many offices; selfishly scheming for the destruction of the Union in order to preserve his own position; and
fearing the military forces authorized to "awe each mob, and
execute the laws." Anarch, invoked by his fears, warned him
that the greatest threat against him came not from force but
from the free appeal to reason and that his plans would never

succeed until reading and writing were practically eliminated, the press restrained, and the Wits hanged. On March 15 they returned to the attack even more directly and unmistakably. Wadsworth was presiding justice of the New Haven County Court of Common Pleas, a delegate to the Continental Congress, member of the Executive Council of Connecticut, comptroller of the state, and registrar or town clerk of Durham, as well as a former major general of the militia. They taunted him with being a "milleped of office" drawing a salary for every position, accused him of cowardice at the time of Tryon's first invasion of the state, denounced him for opposing the requisitions of Congress and the state and impost taxes recommended by the federal body, charged him with trying to protect the state from commerce by isolating it from the others, and laughed at him for joining with Wimble to save the people from the fancied machinations of the Cincinnati. And in conclusion they wished that he might "in *brighter* reagions *burn*" as a "*glowing* seraph" after death.

The Wits were also after their original butt, Judge Williams. While in Hartford during February, recruiting his regiment of militia for service on the border, Humphreys took time to write a fable on "The Monkey Who Shaved Himself and His Friends," which was "Addressed to the Hon. William Wimble" and published in the *Courant* for February 26. According to the story, the monkey (who represented Williams) was wonderful at imitating his master, a York barber (presumably Governor George Clinton, against whom Federalist activity was being organized); and, after frightening his friends by his efforts to shave them, he lathered himself and—in a couplet contributed by Trumbull:

> Drew razor swift as he could pull it,
> And cut, from ear to ear, his gullet.

The renewal of the attack on Williams was stimulated by a continuation of his quarrel with General Parsons, with whom Humphreys was closely associated as an active member of the Cincinnati. During the unusually cold month of December,

Williams had adjourned the Windham County Court and had immediately been charged with being under the influence of the Massachusetts mobs. He had defended himself in the *New London Gazette* by a letter which was reprinted in the *Courant* for January 1. Parsons had published satiric comments on his defense three weeks later, and on February 19 Williams lost patience and responded with a severe personal attack upon Parsons. Humphreys' poem was designed to suppress Williams by making him lose confidence in his literary ability, and the "Moral" of his fable was specific:

> Who cannot write, yet handle pens,
> Are apt to hurt themselves and friends.
> Though others use them well, yet fools
> Should never meddle with edge tools.

As the spring elections approached, however, it became apparent that Williams had hurt himself little, if at all, by his communications to the papers, and there were whispers of plans to make him lieutenant-governor instead of Oliver Wolcott. The Wits, accordingly, set out to hang him, bury him, and pronounce "An Elegy on a Patriot" over his grave. The ballad elegy, which was supposedly taken from an ancient Ohio newspaper, appeared as the eighth number of *American Antiquities* on March 22; and on April 3, General Parsons published in the *Courant* a bad-humored prose attack on Williams. But neither served its purpose. In the May elections Williams received the third highest vote for membership on the governor's council; and within a year, as a member of the convention for considering the new federal constitution, he surprised his enemies by voting for its ratification. Hopkins, also included in the attack, was re-elected to office and eventually gave his approval to the plan of union. And James Hillhouse, who was satirized as the "Sachem of Muskingum," was chosen delegate to the Continental Congress, though he refused to attend. Humphreys had sent some of the *American Antiquities* to Washington with the comment that "pointed ridicule is found to be of more efficacy than serious argumentation"; and he informed his chief, in a letter of March 24, that the Connecticut assembly was under the influence of a few "miserable, narrow minded and . . . . wicked Politicians." But he was wrong in each observation. The Wits accomplished no measurable results by their satire; and in several cases they failed to estimate correctly the men they were opposing, with the result that they spent a good part of their energy denouncing enemies who existed solely in their imagination.

It may be that most of them had no really serious political purpose anyway; for, instead of pushing their attacks upon Connecticut politicians up to the eve of the May elections, they turned their eyes to New York. Stephen Mix Mitchell, a delegate to the federal Congress, had written Jeremiah Wadsworth in January that "the Anarchiad, book 23d is read here, with much pleasure and obtains applause"; he had added that it was "judged to be a meritorious performance." The authors, who were having the satisfaction of finding the papers generally "reprinted in more papers and read with greater avidity than any other performances," were particularly pleased with their new audience. Accordingly, they prepared another selection from the twenty-third book for the benefit of their New York admirers and published it on April 5. Representing the soliloquy of Anarch after having been vanquished by Hesper, and the consolations of his mother Night, this ninth number emphasized New York's rejection of Congress' request for a federal impost and satirized the antifederal leaders in that state. Governor Clinton was attacked as an "illustrious changeling," who had begun to "court the low crowd"; Samuel Jones was satirized for his personal appearance, for his legal activities within the British lines during the Revolution, and for his antifederal leadership in the state legislature; and another of Clinton's followers was represented as "blind Belisarius," full of fantastic fears of congressional power. All these satiric portraits were personal and offensive, though the characters were perhaps sufficiently concealed to be recognized only by the initiate. But the Wits were most brutal and clearly outspoken in their attack upon Abraham Yates, author of some of the "Rough-Hewer" essays and New York delegate to the Congress, who was considered by some members the man of least understanding in the federal

body because of his constant and undeviating opposition to anything that looked toward a closer union. This selection of the
Anarchiad was undoubtedly composed for the amusement of
those members of Congress who were already fixed in their
political beliefs rather than for the purpose of influencing the
public. But young Alexander Hamilton was credited by name
with a brilliant speech in the New York legislature favoring the
impost; and his failure to carry his point was explained by satiric
reference to the "band of mutes," who, according to a New York
wit, had strangled the measure by voting against it without
making any attempt to answer Hamilton. The theme of the entire piece was that, though Anarch had been vanquished by
Hesper, mother Night still had dreams of establishing her realm
with the assistance of the new leaders that were springing up in
New York.

The tenth number of *American Antiquities*, published on May
24, was not satiric at all. The constitutional convention had
just begun its meetings in Philadelphia, and Hesper, in the concluding book of the *Anarchiad*, was represented as addressing
the assembled sages in the interest of union. The heroes who
had fallen on the battlefields of the Revolution were celebrated,
the dangers of faction and of irresponsible rule were pointed out,
and the patriotism of the federal leaders was praised. Anti-Fed-
eralists were warned that disorder would inevitably lead to
monarchy; and the point was made that a loose confederation of
states, forming a restless government by factious crowds, going
from one extreme to another, would be just as bad. The sons of
freedom who had settled in America, however, did not have to
choose necessarily between license and despotism. They had resigned enough of their power and natural rights to form social
leagues, and from ancient habit they obeyed the local powers.
But their establishments had not taught them reverence for a
general government, nor had it given them an interest in the
federal welfare. The point at issue, therefore, was not the fundamental principle of union but the practical expedients of standing against foreign foes, regulating finance, and controlling
trade. Yet action was necessary, for the country had reached

the point where it would have to take seriously the warning "Ye
Live United, or Divided Die!"

The concluding numbers of the *American Antiquities* made an
anticlimax. Publishing their observations on August 16 and
September 13, while the constitutional convention was meeting in Philadelphia, the Wits had nothing further to say in the
interest of union and no ideas to contribute toward the solution
of practical problems. Instead, they went back to the seventeenth book of the *Anarchiad* in order to represent "the land of
annihilation" and "the region of pre-existent spirits," in which
the politicians satirized in the earlier numbers and the writers
critical of America and American institutions passed in review.
The Abbé Raynal, the Count de Buffon, and the Abbé de Pau
were denounced for their derogatory comments on American
genius and the American climate and soil; Dr. Robertson was
satirized for echoing their opinions; and Robert Morris was
intemperately condemned as a worshiper of Mammon because
he had publicly indorsed Raynal's statement concerning the
absence of literary genius in America. Aedanus Burke was again
attacked for his pamphlet against the Cincinnati, Demeunier for
borrowing an account from him for the *Encyclopédie méthodique*,
and Mirabeau and Linguet for their writings against the society.
Significantly, however, Jefferson was not mentioned. Humphreys thought and had informed Washington that the foreign
minister and not Burke was the source of the article against the
Cincinnati in the *Encylopédie*, but it may have been that he felt
it wise to refrain from satirizing a man from whom he might expect further employment in a public capacity. The last group
to pass in satiric review were the imaginative writers on American history and politics—the Abbé Mably, Target, D'Auberteul, and even the Rev. Samuel Peters, "the fag-end man of
M'Fingal," who had published his libelous history of Connecticut from the safety of London five years before. Such satire at
that time, however, was rather pointless, and the Wits seem to
have engaged in it only because they hated to give up a series of
literary productions that had been so spontaneously popular.
It was not until February 21, 1788, that they brought the series

to a definite close, allowing Anarch to bury all his followers and
issue an "Edict of Penance."

When the Philadelphia convention presented a definite plan
of union in the form of a constitution, the Wits had nothing to
say. As a group they kept completely silent during the controversy over its adoption. The New Year's verse of the Hartford
Courant for 1788 dealt with "The Forc'd Alliance" in the form of
"A Dialogue" between two patriots, Wronghead (General
James Wadsworth) and Lamb (John Lamb, collector of customs
at New York), in which the Constitution was discussed. The
author—probably Lemuel Hopkins—considered the approval a
foregone conclusion and had Wronghead regret that Connecticut could not be surrounded by a wall of brass which would protect the blue laws, the rude living conditions, and the "equal
poverty" of the old days of dependence upon the "hard-bound
soil." Lamb, for his part, praised the imperial position of New
York, with a state impost forcing tribute from the sister-states;
expressed confidence in the efforts of Clinton, Jones, and Yates
to protect the state against outside influences; and found encouragement in the "trite objections" to the Constitution made by
Gerry, Mason, Lee, and other "scribblers." Thus opposition to
the new plan of union was branded as the result of ignorant conservatism and contemptible self-interest; but there was no concerted action even to influence the Connecticut convention
which was to meet in January. Humphreys, whose ambition
had probably kept the Wits together as a more or less unified
group, had gone to spend the winter with Washington at
Mount Vernon; and even before he left he had turned his mind
to the idea of gaining fame through the medium of the drama.
The literary possibilities of the *Anarchiad* had been exhausted
just as it had begun to have some large political significance.

The Wits themselves had applied the term "hotchpot" to
their activities, and they perhaps could have selected no better.
The motives that lay back of their writings were certainly complex and varied. Barlow and possibly Trumbull had some speculative interest in the disposal of western lands; and Humphreys, as a former army officer, may also have retained com-

mutation certificates that gave him some concern in the matter. Trumbull and Hopkins both had a deeply rooted antagonism to mobs and the irrational activities of the crowd. Humphreys and Barlow were members of the Society of Cincinnati, Trumbull had been closely associated with the organization since its first general meeting, and all were sensitive to the criticism—much of it unfair—to which the Society had been subjected. Trumbull and Barlow were lawyers at a time when the people were closing courts, disrupting legal procedure, and promising violence to lawyers; and naturally they saw their livelihood threatened. None of them owned any considerable amount of real property, the economic welfare of those who resided in Hartford was dependent upon the growth of manufacturing and trade, and all were peculiarly vulnerable to the dangers of paper money. They were men of better education, wider experience, and broader vision than the average citizen; and their friends—particularly Humphreys'—were men whose horizons extended far beyond Connecticut. In addition, Hopkins and Trumbull were high-spirited men with a peculiar talent for satiric writing and an unquestioning belief that the rod was proper to a fool's back; Humphreys had a solemn conviction that he should benefit his country with his pen as well as with his sword; and Barlow was sufficiently adjustable, high-spirited, and ambitious to keep on good terms with them all. Living in a land of steady habits from which the wilder spirits had already emigrated, a state which had remained unaffected by the new fashions for constitutions and so had kept the lower classes safely disenfranchised, the Wits had to look beyond their borders for political bugbears or else create them out of their own imaginations. Accordingly, they had never been welded into a close group by the heat of any real passion of fear or belief. They were held together by literary success and the accidental similarity of their wayward impulses; and, when they lost the stimulation of their first objects of satire and worked their literary design up to a climax, the political job which remained to be done had no great appeal for them, even though they had finally achieved some unity of belief and purpose.

The superiority of their literary ambitions over their political
inspiration was revealed by the growing plan of their burlesque
in comparison with the continued "hotchpot" of their satire.
The design of the *American Antiquities* was suggested by the
Rolliad papers; but the poets attempted humorous effects by
calling to their readers' minds, by allusion and parody, more
familiar poetry than that written by the *Rolliad* group. At first,
though the authors suggested that they might show, in a future
essay, that Homer, Virgil, and Milton had borrowed "many of
their capital beauties" from the *Anarchiad*, they contented
themselves entirely with a parody of Pope. The subtitle describing their work as "A Poem on the Restoration of Chaos and
Substantial Night" was, of course, suggested by the *Dunciad;*
and a considerable section of the first two numbers was nothing
more than a re-wording of the vision in the third book of Pope's
poem. The picture of Rhode Island in the third number probably owed something to the English poet's representation of
England in the same vision, but the borrowing was less definite;
and in the fourth number the *Essay on Man* was also called upon
for a contribution. In addition, Humphreys had paid his own
Poem on the Happiness of America the tribute of parody in the
second number. It was not until the poets had reached Number
VI that they began to give their selections a definite place in the
epic from which they were supposedly quoting (though they had
previously used the Homeric and Miltonic councils of war and
lists of heroes); but with the citation of particular books they
also began to take on a more positive epic manner, and the
"dark world" invoked by Wronghead was that revealed by Sin
when she opened Hell-gate in the second book of *Paradise Lost.*
The next selection returned to the heroic games of an earlier
part of the imaginary epic, and again the poets drew on the
Dunciad for the opening lines. The soliloquy and consolation of
Anarch after having been vanquished by Hesper—a conventional bit of epic action—was based upon Milton; and the advice of Hesper to the assembled sages, supposedly taken from
the concluding book of the *Anarchiad*, was structurally characteristic of the moral epic from *Paradise Lost* to *The Vision of*

Columbus. When the poets tried to carry on their work after the climax of Hesper's address, they leaned heavily on literary precedent for their representation of the lower world, citing in their critical notes Homer, Virgil, Milton, "the Gothic bards," Tasso, Ossian, and Dante; and the poem concluded with an imitation of Pope's versification, in the *Messiah*, of the prophetic passages of Isaiah. Throughout there was a good deal of additional literary allusiveness (including one couplet borrowed from Churchill's *Rosciad*), echoes of Virgil, Homer, and even *The Conquest of Canäan.* Barlow and Humphreys frequently imitated their own serious works, perhaps both consciously and inadvertently; the selections contained a number of allusions to and verbal echoes of *M'Fingal;* and on one occasion, in the fourth number, Hopkins used phrases and ideas that he later developed into an independent poem. In general, the history of the *Anarchiad* was like that of *M'Fingal;* it began as a rather haphazard political satire, containing a large element of simple parody, and it grew into a literary burlesque to which the satire was subordinate, at least in the minds of the authors. As in the case of *M'Fingal*, too, the tradition of its political effectiveness seems to be mostly a myth.

The significance of the *American Antiquities* series lies in the fact that it illustrates how easily even such serious poets as Barlow and Humphreys could be diverted from their chosen "road to fame" into a superficial "hotchpot" of satire and how trivial and literary their interests remained in the face of momentous political changes. All four of the authors were comparatively young men, and men of some vision; naturally they were inclined to be impatient with such older conservatives as William Williams and James Wadsworth and to be sympathetic toward the experimental proposal for a closer union under a strong general government. Yet they were led by the example of the *Dunciad* to waste their energies with ineffectual attacks upon harmless individuals, condemning mobs and paper-money movements on grounds already discounted by the participants, and, in general, climbing on the bandwagon of public opinion instead of trying to lead it. As the issue of federalism gradually became clarified for them, they did take sides and try to be of some practical political use; but when the issue became acute they quit writing. It was not because they failed to appreciate the situation: Barlow, in a Fourth of July address before the Society of Cincinnati in 1787, devoted a large part of his speech to the constitutional convention and concluded:

Every possible encouragement for great and generous exertions, is now presented before us. Under the idea of a permanent and happy government, every point of view, in which the future situation of America can be placed, fills the mind with a peculiar dignity, and opens an unbounded field of thought. The natural resources of the country are inconceivably various and great; the enterprising genius of the people promises a most rapid improvement in all the arts that embelish human nature; the blessings of a rational government will invite emigrations from the rest of the world, and fill the empire with the worthiest and happiest of mankind; while the example of political wisdom and felicity here to be displayed will excite emulation through the kingdoms of the earth, and meliorate the conditions of the human race.

This sort of oratorical optimism and broad point of view—like the cheerful belief expressed in the same address that "the majority of a great people, on a subject which they understand, will never act wrong"—was much more characteristic of Barlow and of Humphreys than the irresponsible wit of the *American Antiquities*. But these two poets, who might have been expected to guide the series safely past trivialities, were hagridden by self-consciousness and awareness of precedents; and they seem never to have realized that a writer might adopt a literary form and then so completely lose himself in it that he could devote his entire energies to some serious purpose. As concerned as they were with literature, they were in an environment in which spontaneous energy expressed itself in other ways, and they never escaped from a basic assumption that poetry was not quite real—that polite literature, like polite behavior, was a cultivated affectation.

III

For two of the wicked Wits the Hartford episode was a halfway point in careers that were to take new directions toward more varied activities in a wider world. For the other two it was a dead end. Lemuel Hopkins, to whom verse was never more than a social activity or a relief from occasional irritation, continued to write in the peculiarly caustic vein that makes his work the most distinctive of the group. A new body of wits grew up: Theodore Dwight, the younger brother of Timothy, who was later to become a distinguished newspaper editor; Richard Alsop, a remarkably well-read young man from Middletown, who was talented enough to become a fine poet had he been willing to devote himself wholeheartedly to the art; Elihu H. Smith, a young physician from Litchfield with unusual literary ambitions, who was to die of yellow fever before he fully revealed his independence of mind; Mason W. Cogswell, another young physician, who was too modest about his literary ability to co-operate fully with the others, although he wrote copiously in secret; and Nathaniel Dwight, another of Timothy's younger brothers, who occasionally contributed bits to the collaborated efforts of the others. Hopkins joined them and guided their efforts. They began *The Echo*, which reversed the line of development of the *American Antiquities* by starting as literary burlesque in the *American Mercury* for August 8, 1791, turning to political and personal satire, and finally going to pieces in a "hotchpot" of New Year's verse and individual satires. The *Courant* offered a rival burlesque, "The Versifier" (probably by Cogswell), for a short while in 1793; but when *The Echo* became politically embarrassing to the democratic *Mercury*, the Federalist *Courant* took it over and perhaps made Elisha Babcock regret that he had ever encouraged such irritating young men.

Hopkins, who was always loyal to his friends no matter how he may have reprobated their opinions, spent some years in indifference but apparently wrote the New Year's verses for the *Mercury* in 1793 and 1794. As he became aroused by French machinations and the activities of southern politicians, however, he came to feel more at home in the *Courant*, into which he moved in January, 1795, followed by *The Echo* upon its next appearance in August. There he began, in 1796, "The Guillotina," an annual post-boy's satire as sharp as its name, which he continued until his death. His most important single work, however, was an attack upon medical quackery, aroused by the "metallic points to relieve pain," patented by Dr. Elisha Perkins in February, 1796. These "tractors," designed to cure disease by the "electrical fluid" of galvanism, marked the high point of charlatanism in Connecticut medical history; and, when a pamphlet of enthusiastic testimonials appeared in October, 1796, Hopkins responded with a long satiric "Patent Address" in the *Courant* for November 7. Full of medical terminology but as biting as anything Hopkins had ever written, it probably had a good deal to do with encouraging the members of the state medical society to expel Perkins at their next spring meeting. Hopkins himself, during this time, was acquiring distinction as a physician and teacher of medicine and laying the foundation for lasting fame as a rival of Benjamin Rush in his treatments of consumption. His sudden death of pneumonia, on April 14, 1801, brought a close to the career of one of the few literary men of the time whose reputation for good sense and forthrightness was such that it could earn from an editor of opposite political views one simple comment: "He was an honest man."

Trumbull was less active in literature than Hopkins. Although he retained his sardonic attitude toward the world, even describing Washington as "all-fragrant with the odour of incense" during the first year of his presidency, he kept such comments for the ears and eyes of his friends and restrained himself in public. Political ambitions may have influenced his discretion, for after serving as one of the city fathers of Hartford he was appointed county attorney in 1789 and elected to the state legislature in 1792. But he probably shared Hopkins' indifference to politics during the first term of Washington's administration and found little in the affairs of the nation that could whip his indolent spirit into expression. In any case the state of his health induced more melancholia than satire. Hopkins was worried about both the health and the spirits of his friend during the summer of 1792 but reported that he was "much better" the following year. Trumbull himself showed sufficient signs of recovery in May, 1793, to compose a virulent attack in verse upon

Pierrepont Edwards, which he perhaps recognized as the most vicious poem he had ever written and, consequently, did not publish. He was one of the managers of the lottery authorized for building the Hartford courthouse, in 1794, but he had to spend so much of his time traveling to various watering places for his health that he was despondent about his political prospects. Eventually, however, he recovered and in 1800 again went to the state legislature, from which he was elevated a year later into a judgeship on the superior bench. From that time on he "declined," as he said, "any interference in the politics of the state, and applied himself exclusively to the duties of his office—being of the opinion, that the character of a partizan and political writer was inconsistent with the station of a judge and destructive of the confidence of suitors in the impartiality of judiciary decisions." He was also made judge of the Supreme Court of Errors in 1808 and retained both offices until the spring of 1819, when the democrats finished taking over the state.

Unless Trumbull's character had changed greatly during these years, he must have had some difficulty in keeping his hand from the pen. His literary reputation had flourished during the nineties, when the Federalists found so many of the sentiments of M'Fingal useful to their own purposes; but the democrats had taken advantage of the situation by attributing to the author some of the most objectionable opinions of the Tory spokesman. Leonard Chester, in particular, took a belated revenge at his appearance in the *Anarchiad* by giving a cruel portrayal of Trumbull in *Federalism Triumphant in the Steady Habits of Connecticut Alone*, a political farce widely circulated by the democrats in 1802. In addition to representing Trumbull as M'Fingal himself in his more objectionable moments, Chester told a libelous story of an ingenious Federalist scheme to get the author into the legislature and thence on the bench: "Thode" Dwight had been sent around the country saying that Trumbull "had been in a state of intoxication for years" and was utterly worthless—which made the republicans heatedly insist that Trumbull's opinion drunk was better than Dwight's sober and so elect him. There was probably just enough truth in the sug-

gestion of the poet's interest in the bottle to drive Trumbull to a
fury. How the former "Correspondent" and author of the second part of *The Progress of Dulness* managed to remain quiet is a
mystery, but he apparently stayed out of the Connecticut controversy although he made occasional surreptitious contributions to the *New-England Palladium* in Boston. The only literary work attributed to him during his years on the bench was a
short *Biographical Sketch of Governor Trumbull*, published in
1809.

Yet Trumbull retained his interest in literature. He kept an
approving eye upon the satires of *The Echo* poets and may have
made occasional contributions to them. When the collection
was published as a volume in 1807 he was able to annotate his
copy and note the authorship of many individual pieces. He also kept up with the new poets of his time, making notes for
critical essays or expressing opinions concerning modern literature in letters to his friends. He had always been interested in
the art of poetry and particularly enthusiastic about the metrical variety Pope achieved within the bounds of the heroic couplet; and in a discussion of prosody for the second part of Noah
Webster's *Grammatical Institute of the English Language* he had
attempted to point out the possibilities of that measure. The
new writers who seemed to depend upon novelty rather than
craftsmanship for their effects had no charm for him. They
were "discordant" and "unnatural," given to "confusion,"
"rant," and "eccentricity." He had no use for the "lullaby of
Wordsworth's lyrical ballads" and none for Crabbe's *The
Borough* or for Southey's *Thalaba* or *The Curse of Kehama*. As
one who had been early taught by Lord Kames to prize the
complete visual image, he saw Crabbe and Wordsworth "bath-
ing in the muddy bottom of the streams of Helicon" and certainly would have found nothing more than pure confusion in
the association of ideas that led away from the actual scene in
"Tintern Abbey." Coleridge (and perhaps Southey as well)
wrote "as though a poetical Bedlam was about to be erected on
the summit of Parnassus." Thomas Moore, with a "poetic fire"
that was "mostly phosphoric," delighted in "gaudy" images,

painting similes when he should have been describing the object. Byron also failed to excel in description, specializing in passion and feeling "of the *worst* sort." As a moralist, Trumbull saw no excuse, in 1820, for "the voluptous licentiousness of T. Moore, the profligate buffonery of Peter Pindar, or the unprincipled spleen and misanthropy of Lord Byron." As an artist, he found fault, in 1814, with all blank verse—even that of the previously admired Milton. He did not approve, on any score, German ballads or Scottish imitations of them. Not one of the Connecticut Wits, as time went on, grew further out of touch with his age.

But Trumbull could not realize it. The substance of his irritability had produced a few poetic pearls, but most of it ultimately went into the shell that he built around himself for protection against the world. His friend Samuel G. Goodrich published his *Poetical Works* in two well-printed volumes in 1820 and lost a thousand dollars on the venture. The thousand dollars went to the poet as advance royalty, but he never fully believed that the sale of his works could barely pay the cost of printing and was never quite convinced that he had not been mistreated. He remained in Hartford until 1825, composing rather surprisingly mild and cheerful New Year's verse for the *Courant* in 1824, then joined his daughter in Detroit, where he lived the last six years of his life, dying on May 11, 1831, the longest lived of all the Wits, although he had been the first to give up the struggle for literary distinction.

CHAPTER VII

THE VOICE FROM THE HILL

I

TIMOTHY DWIGHT settled at Greenfield Hill in the autumn of 1783, not yet fully reconciled to having been crossed in his early ambitions. Ezra Stiles was convinced that he was the instigator of the sniping attacks on the administration of Yale College which were occasionally made through the public press; and Dwight's identifiable critical writings during the eighties show that when he let his mind dwell upon himself as an epic poet he became irritable about the public and sour on the world. He had shown no great eagerness to undertake the humdrum duties of pastoral care, but the unanimous call from the Greenfield congregation was flattering, the financial arrangements were more than satisfactory, and the location—a pleasant, prosperous rural community on the well-traveled road between New York and Boston—was as agreeable as any he could have found. The new situation, by enabling him to exercise his benevolence upon his parishioners and his intellect upon numerous guests from the outside world, brought out and matured a kindly, generous element in his character which had hitherto been so overshadowed by his ambition that it had hardly come within the public view. For a while, however, there was a severe internal struggle between the man who thought the world needed castigation and the one who thought it a comfortable place in which to live and work. This conflict between two distinct aspects of Dwight's personality was clearly defined in the differences between "John Homely" and "James Littlejohn" in "The Friend," and it may also be seen in other writings composed before these phases became reconciled in the great Doctor Dwight who, in the spring of 1795, became president of Yale.

Perhaps the most important factor contributing to the formation of Dwight's personality during these years was his undoubted success at Greenfield. When he arrived there, he found himself pastor of a halfway covenant congregation which had been touched by Arminianism; and he felt that one of his major duties was to herd his charges safely into the fold of his own New Light orthodoxy. This he accomplished successfully and without dissension by setting an example of earnestness and good will while systematizing his own theological beliefs and delivering the system in a series of sermons, which, with revisions and additions, he later used for the formal religious instructions of Yale undergraduates. He also built and operated an academy which pioneered in higher education for women and eventually proved an annoying rival to Yale in its ability to attract both students and visitors to the public exhibitions. He became noted for his hospitality to respectable travelers along the coast, who soon learned that they could expect a splendid view of Long Island Sound, good entertainment, and a vigorous exchange of observations and opinions whenever they could manage to stop over at the parsonage on the hill. And, as he became famous as a host, an educator, and a preacher, he found himself attaining a position of steadily increasing importance in Connecticut. Former students began to return to him for advice, and dignitaries of both the church and the state began to listen to him with respect. He also found time to operate a farm, contribute to the newspapers, and write poetry. His years were busy; and, with little opportunity for overreaching himself as he had done in his youth, almost everything he undertook was successful.

The greater part of his intellectual energy during this period was, of course, devoted to the preparation of sermons. Between two and three hundred of these were later published, but the published versions do not accurately represent his ideas or opinions on matters of general interest at the time they were preached. The condition of his eyesight was such that he was

forced to limit his written composition to outline notes and
fill them in with illustrative and expository comment, which
probably varied with each delivery until the sermons were
finally written out in full from ten to twenty years later. Accordingly, his literary career at Greenfield Hill can be followed
only through a group of miscellaneous pieces (some already considered in connection with the publication of *The Conquest of
Canäan*), two volumes of verse, and a small number of sermons
that were immediately made public in manuscript or in print.
Yet in these writings Dwight spoke in all the voices that were
characteristic of him at that period—the rasping tone of a man
ready to pick a quarrel with an indifferent world, the contented
tone of one who knew and loved the land in which he lived, and,
finally, the blended, vigorous, and assured tone appropriate to a
man whose physical voice could "enter into the soul like the
middle notes of an organ."

II

During his first three or four years at Greenfield Hill, Dwight
seems to have had little time for literary composition other than
that provoked by emotions associated with the publication of
his epic. He had little contact with his friends in Hartford;
and, although he probably followed their exhibitions of "wit"
with sympathetic interest, he remained silent during the winter
of 1786–87 concerning the various events that were agitating
the state. Yet he was beginning to brood about the times. In
his brief communication concerning the Gothic Gospel which he
sent to the *New Haven Gazette* for March 1, 1787, he took occasion to moralize over the "selfishness and infidelity of the present
times"; and, as he read the newspaper dispatches and his friends'
satires and talked with the many visitors who passed through
his home, he eventually worked himself up to a state of considerable excitement. The *Gazette* for April 12 published his
speculations concerning the judgment of history upon the
United States. After approving the war, history, he thought,
would continue:

"A most honourable peace was established—All nations courted them—Their rank amongst the nations, their liberties and privileges, the temper and conduct shown through the mighty struggle, appeared to place them in a point of elevation for future progress, in glory and happiness, unknown to any nation before them upon the face of the earth.

But soon, very soon, by those freaks of human nature which are very common, though unaccountable, all their bright prospects were overcast, and their rising glory tarnished. The danger over and past, all the little selfish passions, with all their baleful influence, rushed in upon them at once, and with so much the greater force the more they had been restrained before. From hence arose amongst themselves (for they had no foreign controul) disunited councils and opposing measures, ingratitude to their benefactors, injustice, cruelty and oppression, contempt of government and laws human and divine, disaffection, distrust and jealousy, with a numberless train of follies and vices, and, at length the flames of a civil war were kindled, and"—what follows let future historians record. What they will record depends upon ourselves, the present living, active generations, whether respecting our nation and ourselves, the title of *virtuous sons of liberty in America* shall be handed down to future time as a perpetual mark of distinguishing honour and praise, or as a stigma of everlasting shame and reproach.

The immediate result of this excitement was published in the *American Museum* for June, 1787: a serious, poetic "Address of the Genius of Columbia, to the Members of the Continental Convention," who were meeting in Philadelphia for the purpose of forming a new constitution for the United States. The poem emphasized the physical greatness of America, pointed out the providential timeliness of its settlement after the Reformation had brought an age of bigotry to an end, and held up for emulation the example of political unity and unselfishness set by Colonial leaders during the Revolution. Furthermore, it undertook to give concrete advice concerning the proper organization of the new government:

> O'er state concerns, let every state preside;
> Its private tax controul; its justice guide;
> Religion aid, the morals to secure;
> And bid each private right thro' time endure.
> Columbia's interests public sway demand,
> Her commerce, impost, unlocated land;
> Her war, her peace, her military power;
> Treaties to seal with every distant shore;
> To bid contending states their discord cease;
> To send thro' all the calumet of peace;
> Science to wing thro' every noble flight;
> And lift desponding genius into light.

The delegates, however, probably did not find the advice very useful. The powers recommended for the general government were those generally agreed upon by everybody who advocated a stable national existence; the rights assigned to the states were somewhat indefinite but, by implication, extreme; and the problem of promoting the general welfare was left hopelessly vague. The poet was an extremely cautious Federalist. He wanted the assembled sages to "entwine" the "federal bands," but he had no notion that a perfect system could spring, full armed, from the human mind:

> Slow, by degrees, politic systems rise;
> Age still refines them, and experience tries.
> This, this alone consolidates, improves;
> Their sinews strengthens; their defects removes;
> Gives that consistence time alone can give;
> Habituates men by law and right to live.

Accordingly, he advised the convention to "learn, cautious, what to alter, where to mend"; and, for his own part, he suggested no innovations that had not already been generally accepted as necessary changes in the Articles of Confederation.

Even in the days when Dwight was a Yale tutor and a young reformer, his reforms had been directed toward a greater emphasis upon "things as they are" instead of speculative theories; and the "Address" to the Continental Convention merely applied to politics the same attitude of mind that had earlier been exercised upon the Yale curriculum and upon epic poetry. He would make improvements that experience had shown to be necessary, but he would not attempt to anticipate the teaching of experience or give way to any "enthusiasm" for change; for human nature was too untrustworthy to be gratuitously freed from the strict control of steady habits. Apparently with the idea of entering more specifically into national political controversy, he conducted a tentative revival of "The Friend" in the *Gazette* for October 4, 1787, which touched upon political personalities as far away as Pennsylvania and Georgia. He quickly thought better of the impulse, however; and, even though his first essay provoked an immediate response from

Philadelphia, he fell silent. The occasion tempted him, but before he left Northampton he had decided against any further direct participation in politics; and he was able to abide by that decision, despite other occasional temptations, until the "un-American" party of Thomas Jefferson began to offer a real threat to his security.

Political satire, in any case, could hardly have had more than a momentary attraction for Dwight at this time. He was by no means free from the feeling that the world needed castigation and that he was the man to give it, and he had only recently developed an interest in satiric verse and a desire to practice that form of the poetic art. The popular success of his Hartford friends may also have stimulated an ambition to appear before the public in the character of a wit. But, if their fame challenged his abilities, it deterred him from following in their footsteps. They had pre-empted the field of political satire in verse, and the minister at Greenfield could not afford to risk being called an imitator of the "wicked wits." Furthermore, Dwight was much less concerned at the time with the subtleties of political differences than with the doctrines of theology. Having renounced a political career in favor of the ministry, he had also committed himself to the belief that the Kingdom of God was the only proper foundation for a republic of men. "The same principles, which support or destroy Christianity," he wrote, "alike support or destroy political order and government"; and he apparently assumed that mob rule, paper money, and luxurious living could not flourish in an atmosphere of pure religion. But religion in New England was no longer pure. He was gradually reforming the beliefs of his own congregation; but heresy had become a commonplace among congregations taught by graduates of Harvard, and fantastic doctrines of all sorts were being preached to the common people by self-elected itinerant ministers who roamed the country. The boldness of the forces of evil had only recently been exemplified by the appearance in Vermont of a damnable book which stirred Dwight to a communication, printed in Mathew Carey's *American Museum* for October, 1787, "On the Doctrine of Chance, Containing Re-

marks on Ethan Allen's Oracles of Reason." Dwight may also
have been the author of articles in the same journal for July and
September, 1788, attacking widespread indulgence in spirituous
liquors, horseracing, cockfighting, Sunday amusements, and
similar immoralities. But in the meantime he had written a long
poem which attempted to go beneath the superficial political
concerns of his friends and strike at the root of all evil—infidelity.

The Triumph of Infidelity, printed anonymously "in the
world" in the year 1788, was, like the Anarchiad, an ironic narrative in heroic verse with "the prince of darkness" as its hero,
although, as the enemy of God rather than government, he took
the name of Satan rather than Anarch. The design of the two
satires was different: Dwight could not, of course, repeat the
device of a newly discovered ancient epic, translated with prose
commentaries by the discoverer. He presented, instead, a
straight narrative of the progress of infidelity from its state at
the beginning of the Christian era down to its condition in contemporary America and particularly in New England. For his
prose commentary he used explanatory footnotes and editorial
notes, usually satiric, by "Scriblerus." In other respects, however, the two poems were so much alike that the second seems to
have been inspired by the success of the first. Like the production of the wits, Dwight's poem depended upon parody and
literary allusiveness for many of its supposedly humorous effects,
making the same extensive use of Pope's works that the Anarchiad had made. Both poems were characterized by the same
exaggerated harshness of satire upon comparatively innocuous
contemporaries. And both were misnamed in an excess of irony.
The Anarchiad was not, strictly speaking, "a poem on the restoration of Chaos and substantial Night," for the account of the
land of annihilation came in the early books, and the epic closed
on a note of optimism; and in The Triumph of Infidelity, for all
its contemporary satire, eighteenth-century America was represented as giving no encouragement to Satan, who was shown, at
the close, fleeing in confusion rather than advancing in triumph.

In his historical survey Dwight made an extraordinarily bold

use of irony in allowing Satan to express his opinions of the
Apostles, apparently because he had even then developed the
ingenious idea—which he was later to use so often, in contrast
to the attitude he had adopted in his commencement oration on
the poetry of the Bible—that an emphasis upon the low origin
of the men helped demonstrate the divine origin of their Gospels.
Having no similar justification, the poet could use little irony
in speaking of the Protestant reformers of the sixteenth century.
The greatest part of the historical satire was directed against
the Roman Catholic church (which he described as the "First,
fairest offspring even of Satan's mind") and the age of modern
philosophy, ushered in "under the auspicious influences of
Charles II, and his contemporaries." The work itself was dedicated to Voltaire in an ironic letter addressed to him as though
he were still alive, and Hume and Voltaire were singled out for
particular satire within the poem. The attack was harsh, outspoken, and humorless; for, even if Dwight had possessed the
humor of his friend Trumbull, he spent some time in his poem
condemning the idea—popularized by Shaftesbury and accepted even by Lord Kames—that ridicule was a test of truth,
and, accordingly, he could not have used that method of attack
in his own work. The progress of modern infidelity was traced,
in England, through deism; and Lord Herbert of Cherbury,
Bolingbroke, Toland, Tindal, Collins, Chubb, Morgan, and
Woolston were condemned by name. A glance around the world
provoked the poet to a digression satirizing the Chinese (which
showed, according to Ezra Stiles, that Dwight "knew only some
ignorant second hand accounts of Chinese History" and that he
was "profoundly ignorant in the Chinese Literature"), a satiric
reference to Jacob Boehme, and rather elaborate attacks upon
the doctrines of Socinus and upon the theology and materialistic
philosophy of Priestley. Dwight's criticism was in no case profound: he could damn four deists in five iambic feet; but he had
almost no firsthand knowledge of their writings, for his opinions
and his information both came from John Leland's *A View of
the Principal Deistical Writers.*

When the poet turned to America he found himself in difficulties: he could call to mind only one materialist and one deist. He knew that Isaac Ledyard had published a little *Essay on Matter* in Philadelphia four years before, and he was acquainted with Ethan Allen's *Reason: The Only Oracle of Man.* Despite the fact that the poem on the *triumph* of infidelity was drawing toward a close, Satan was forced to confess that he had found his "chief bane" in "that moral Newton, and that second Paul" of New England—Jonathan Edwards, the poet's grandfather and the theologian to whom all such New Divinity men as Dwight looked back. Consequently, the prince of darkness had to look for some new means for plunging America "in the gulph of sin," and the poet had to find some other object of satire. Had the pastor of Greenfield Hill been more concerned with the general currents of ideas in America and less with controversial divinity, perhaps he could have found more objects of attack in his own country comparable to those he had satirized in England. But he was considerably involved in the theological quarrels that were still going on in Connecticut fifteen years after Trumbull—with some assistance from Dwight himself—had attempted to satirize them out of existence in "The Correspondent."

Ezra Stiles, who had little sympathy with such controversies, had observed and reported on these quarrels in his diary for August 10, 1787. "The New Divinity Gentlemen are getting into Confusion and running into different sentiments," he wrote in commenting upon their doctrinal differences:

It has been the Ton to direct Students in divinity these 30 years past or a Generation to read the Bible, President Edwards, Dr. Bellamy and Mr. Hopkins Writings—and this was a pretty good Sufficiency of Reading. Now the younger Class, but yet in full vigor suppose they see further than these Oracles, and are disposed to become Oracles themselves and wish to write Theology and have their own Books come into Vogue. The very New Divinity Gentlemen . . . . all want to be Luthers.

Dwight was one of the would-be Luthers among the "very New Divinity Gentlemen" mentioned specifically by President Stiles, and he had moved naturally into that position from his earlier satiric attitude. He had received advice in his theological studies from his uncle, the second Jonathan Edwards, who had studied with Dr. Bellamy and had been, since 1769, pastor of the White Haven Church in New Haven. Edwards was only seven years older than Dwight, and their connection remained close while the former was growing more and more stubborn in his New Divinity opinions. Hardly a member of his church and congregation shared his sentiments, in the unsympathetic opinion of Ezra Stiles; but by February, 1789, Edwards had reached the point where he would publicly impeach Dr. Ebenezer Beardsley, an eminent New Haven physician, for a belief in universal salvation; and he would have no communion with the First Church of New Haven because he looked upon Dr. James Dana, its new pastor, as a heretic. Dwight himself had been quoted, in the fall of 1787, as having said that he "had as lieve communicate with all the Devils in Hell as with that corrupt Church" in his native town of Northampton.

In the light of such strong feelings among the strict Calvinists toward the halfway covenant men, there may be some doubt as to whether Dwight originally intended to satirize deism and materialism in *The Triumph of Infidelity* and turned to heterodox Calvinists only for lack of better material or whether he planned a New Divinity satire from the beginning and wrote the first three-fifths of the poem merely as an introduction. The probability is that Dwight did want to be a Luther who would purify New England Protestantism but that he wrote the historical part of his poem not only as an introduction but also for the aggrandizement of his particular subject, in order that readers might share his own opinion of its importance. At any rate, in the last part of his poem he turned quickly from American infidelity to differences among New Englanders who professed Christianity and even Calvinism.

The chief object of the poet's attack, the man against whom almost half of the contemporary satire was directed, was Dr. Charles Chauncy, pastor of the First Church of Boston, who was old enough to have engaged in controversy with the first Jonathan Edwards at the beginning of the New Light movement. Chauncy represented the antithesis of the conservative theology and radical manners of the New Lights; and by 1768 he had evolved a system of doctrine that greatly shocked the strict Calvinists as it was gradually revealed in a series of publications after the Revolution. The climax of this series came when he dared to publish, in 1784, *The Mystery Hid from Ages, or the Salvation of All Men*, in which he advanced the belief—in arguments supported by textual criticism of the Greek Testament—that punishment after death was for disciplinary purposes and that all men, after they had received the wages of sin, would be saved. Jonathan Edwards began to prepare an elaborate answer to Chauncy's arguments, and Dwight attacked them savagely in his poem. Such doctrines, he charged, were the product of Satan's appeal to Chauncy's "love of system," his "lust of fame," sophistry, avariciousness, conceit, perversity, sinfulness, and dishonesty. He attributed them to the influence of Origen and Tillotson, attacked the method of textual criticism which he himself used regularly in his sermons, and (despite the fact that Chauncy had died long before the poem went to press) sneered that "palsied age has dimm'd his mental sight." Dwight's justification of the severity of his attack was that "False friends may stab, when foes must fly the field"; and he demonstrated his point by comparing the influence of the Congregationalist, Chauncy, with the ineffectuality of the avowed Universalist, John Murray (then preaching at Gloucester), whose ideas and personal history were satirized, though the man himself was dismissed as having the will but not the means for mischief.

The poet denounced the moral effect of the belief in universal salvation, as advanced by Chauncy, in a satire upon various individuals who might conceivably be encouraged in their evil ways by that belief. Fifteen years afterward an attempt was made to embarrass Dwight by identifying these individuals with some of his new political associates. Condemning the "spirit of the bigot, with all the fulminating vengeance of a Sovereign Pontiff," shown in the poem, the later commentator declared:

In emptying his quiver, the arrows were for the most part traced to the intended victims. Tho' they were a shower, and some of the most envenomed were hurled from the darkest ambush and with the deepest circumspection, yet few of them eluded public cognizance so as that their mortal aim was not by one means or another well ascertained. Some were known by their *whizzing*, such incidents of character being marked as could not be mistaken. Others were known by the subsequent *whisperings* of the Author and his bosom-friends. But in sundry places *blanks* are left in the original to be filled up at the pleasure of the reader—*magical names* are used to be construed and applied as wisdom teacheth. In several instances the Rev. marksman so far comes out of the ambush as to set down the *initial letters* of gentlemen's names, supplying the rest with dashes and stars, and forming the metre so as to accord with the pronunciation of the names.

But the identifications were rather far fetched and untrustworthy. And when the poet turned away from his attack upon the doctrine of universal salvation to more general satire, he dealt in blanks and magical names so discreetly and so entirely that only the echoes of a few whisperings and whizzings remain to prove that he had particular persons rather than character types in mind when he wrote. No hint has survived concerning the possible identity of the epicure and the "lecher" whom the poet condemned. But there were contemporary whispers that "Hypocrisy, in sober brown" represented either the Rev. Joseph Lyman of Hatfield (Dwight's predecessor in the tutorship at Yale) or the Rev. Benjamin Trumbull of North Haven. Such "whizzing" as may still be heard suggests the latter, for, though there was no theological quarrel between such leading New Divinity men as Trumbull and Dwight, they were supposed to have been at odds at the time over some ecclesiastical plans, and Trumbull had the reputation of preaching with a countenance "expressive of the lament of Jeremiah." The village character of the "smooth Divine" was reported to have been a satire upon the Rev. Dr. James Dana, then of Wallingford, a leader among the Old Divinity men, who had written against the theology of the elder Jonathan Edwards and was considered a "heretic" by the younger Jonathan. The description of the same type "plac'd in some great town" was supposed to be directed against the Rev. Dr. John Henry Livingston, the popular Dutch Reformed clergyman of New York. Whispers have failed to keep alive "the infidel of modern breed," and the dead man described next was a mystery even to contemporary readers. "Demas"

was a magic name generally understood, however, as representing the "amiable Dr. Beardsley," whom Edwards "impeached"
the following year in a New Divinity quarrel between the minister and congregation of the White Haven Church; and the sinful "Euclio" of "rank appetites, and passions fraught with fire"
was identified by very clear "whizzing" as the poet's own uncle,
in whose home he had been married, Pierrepont Edwards.

Though Edwards continued to be a favorite subject of gossip
among Connecticut scandalmongers, these were all respectable
men; and Dwight himself became intimate with most of those
who lived to see the poet established in the presidency of Yale
and more interested in politics than in New Divinity doctrines.
His authorship was well known, and the poem survived to embarrass him. Even at the time, the poem aroused antagonism
among readers who were not personally touched by it. Ezra
Stiles, whose unfriendliness toward Dwight may have been
counterbalanced in part by his willingness to believe every
scandalous story about John Murray, read it carefully and observed in his diary for August 15, 1788:

> His Poem is filled with a Degree of ill Nature, Acrimony and Malevolence,
> which ought never to enter into the mind of a Christian, and especially of a
> Christian Minister. Candor, Fairness and Honor ought to have shone thro' so
> good a Piece of poetical Composition. He has overshot the Mark, and hurt
> the Cause which he meant to defend.

Noah Webster did not even allow it an honest character as a
poem. Although he had already written a defense of Dwight as
a poet for the July issue of his *American Magazine*, he added, in
the same number, a review of *The Triumph of Infidelity*, which
accused the author of plagiarism from Pope and harshness of
versification in the lines that were not borrowed. Webster
was as severe as Stiles about the imperiousness of the dogmatism and the lack of liberality in the poem. "A man who can
group together such men as Shaftsbury, Priestly, Chauncey
and Allen," he wrote, "and stigmatize these and many of the
first philosophers promiscuously as fools and knaves, can hardly
be a candidate for that heaven of love and benevolence which
the scripture informs us is prepared for good men."

There was much justice in such criticisms, but there was also some acrimony: President Stiles was resentful of the fact that students were being taken from Yale for the academy at Greenfield Hill, and he believed that Dwight had participated in the anonymous attacks that had recently been made upon the college administration. Webster, for his part, may have felt that Dwight was double-crossing him by agreeing to contribute to Mathew Carey's rival magazine, the *American Museum*. And they both, in some ways, misunderstood *The Triumph of Infidelity*. Dwight echoed Dryden and Humphreys as well as Pope in his verse, and the "Scriblerus" notes were supposed to suggest to his readers Swift, Arbuthnot, and other Queen Anne wits. This was not plagiarism. It was the same sort of allusiveness that the *Anarchiad* group had depended upon so heavily for literary effect; and Dwight differed from them only in that he did not have the critical mechanism that allowed them to hint at some of their more obvious borrowings. The poet undoubtedly expected his readers to participate in the game of verbal tag which he was playing with English literature and to be amused by it. He also expected them to recognize the fact that he was writing formal satire and that in dealing with individuals his purpose was to present a caricature rather than to draw a true picture. He looked upon Pope's *Satires*, the *Dunciad*, and *Moral Essays* as the proper models for modern satiric verse, and, contrary to his usual procedure, he made no attempt to improve upon his models except to give his particular subject a broad historical background. Accordingly, it took very little acrimony to make such unsympathetic readers as Stiles and Webster see ill-nature and malevolence where there may have been only literary imitation.

Yet, despite the fact that some of the seemingly malign qualities of Dwight's poem yield to explanation, *The Triumph of Infidelity* was not in any sense a good-natured satire. During the decade preceding its composition the author had accumulated a good deal of spleen, which he finally poured out in heavily imitative verse. His feelings of self-righteousness were deeper than those of the Hartford poets, and, with such feelings, he was not able to achieve the lighter touch of the Wits. Furthermore, the clergyman had always believed that any appeal, to be effective, must be made to the "heart" as well as to the "head"; and in practicing the art of persuasion he often allowed himself to appear overly violent—sometimes even hysterical—in his treatment of opposition in matters of vital importance. Even after he had attained his highest ambition and rarely yielded to feelings of personal spleen, this rhetorical quality remained a part of his style and greatly affected his public reputation. The voice of "John Homely" was almost always raised above that of "James Littlejohn" in his public utterances, but in none was it more strident, more rasping, than in the undiscriminating satire and the injudicious "wit" of *The Triumph of Infidelity*.

III

Dwight himself apparently did not find full satisfaction for his poetic impulses in the composition of *The Triumph of Infidelity*, for before he finished his satire he undertook and largely completed another, and longer, poem which was dominated by the quietly contented tone of "James Littlejohn." *Greenfield Hill* was wholly unpretentious in its origins. Dwight had kept up the practice prescribed to him in his youth of taking long walks in the afternoon or early evening, and he liked to amuse himself by composing verses that he dictated to an amanuensis upon his return home. As a born "methodizer," however, he was incapable of carrying out even so casual an amusement without a formal plan; and he adopted the sort of literary exercise that William Mason had made popular in his "Museus: A Monody in Memory of Mr. Pope" and Isaac Hawkins Browne in "The Pipe of Tobacco"—an imitation of a considerable number of English poets in a work unified by a single theme. The tendency of his thoughts to wander to "the face of nature" with a frequency he sometimes found bothersome made the theme inevitable: he united his exercises by directing them toward the composition of a topographical hill poem of the sort that was then becoming so popular in England.

Eventually, however, he discovered that a formal imitation of English poets was too mechanical a task for his inclinations; and, although he published the work with a certain amount of residue evidence of his original purpose, he did not sustain it throughout any part of the poem. Thus the greater part of *Greenfield Hill* represented for the first time in print a Dwight who was more interested in his subject than in his reputation, more natural than affected.

For Dwight loved America, especially New England, which was almost the only part of the country he knew. The superficial, unjust reports of European travelers in the United States had begun to irritate him by the time he began *Greenfield Hill* in 1787, and the stories told by David Humphreys of the calumnies that inspired *A Poem on the Happiness of America* appear to have had an important part in arousing his impulsive desire to celebrate his own locality, which he believed more interesting in its appearance, inhabitants, history, and future prospects than such well-poetized English scenes as Cooper's Hill and Windsor Forest. His ingrained didacticism caused him to print his poem with an avowal that his aim was "to contribute to the innocent amusement of his countrymen, and to their improvement in manners, and in economical, political, and moral sentiments"; and the poem itself reveals Dwight's opinions and beliefs on many subjects better than almost any of his other works. He gave advice on the subjects mentioned in his Preface, but the underlying theme was always a deep-seated satisfaction with his "much-lov'd native land"—"the happiest realm . . . . the all-searching sun beholds."

> Oh, would some faithful, wise, laborious mind,
> Develop all thy springs of bliss to man;
> Soon would politic visions fleet away,
> Before awakening truth! Utopias then,
> Ancient and new, high fraught with fairy good,
> Would catch no more the heart. Philosophy
> Would bow to common-sense; and man, from facts,
> And real life, politic wisdom learn.

The old, theoretical belief in "things as they are" had received a new emphasis by Dwight's emotional satisfaction over his

temporary escape from ambition and his situation in Greenfield; and the fact had influenced his conception of poetry,
diverting him from the artificial theory of invention he had expressed in "The Friend" and making him think of poetry primarily as an "instrument" for setting the "truth" of things as they
are in "a strong and affecting light."

The truths which Dwight set about celebrating in his poem
were the beauty of the prospect from Greenfield Hill, the admirable quality of Connecticut institutions, and the romance of
local history. The view from his own residence on the top of the
hill, with the forests and mountains on one side, Long Island
Sound stretching out on the other, and the farms and meadows
near by, was described with an accuracy of observation and a
sensuousness of appreciation which pierced through the Thomsonian turgidity of his verse and showed how good a nature poet
he might have become had his mind been less pedantic and had
he accordingly been free in his youth to write as he felt rather
than in the manner considered proper by Lord Kames. But his
most vigorous expressions of appreciation, stimulated by "the
American predilection for Britons" which he had attacked in
"The Friend," were for American society and institutions:

> For here, in truth,
> Not in pretence, man is esteem'd as man.
> Not here how rich, of what peculiar blood,
> Or office high; but of what genuine worth,
> What talents bright and useful, what good deeds,
> What piety to God, what love to man,
> The question is. To this an answer fair
> The general heart secures.

Consequently he urged his countrymen to revere their native
land:

> Look not to Europe, for examples just
> Of order, manners, customs, doctrines, laws,
> Of happiness, or virtue. Cast around
> The eye of searching reason, and declare
> What Europe proffers, but a patchwork sway;
> The garment Gothic, worn to fritter'd shreds,
> And eked from every loom of following times.

Only in America could be found "The noblest institutions, man
has seen, Since time his reign began": small farms descending

from generation to generation without entail; equal rights; liberty under law; education for "the mass of man"; society that followed "the golden mean" between poverty and luxury; and, above all, pure religion. These were the things, he believed, that made America different from a Europe which was suffering from the corrupt "Gothic" origin of its social garment.

The second part of the poem—"The Flourishing Village"— represented an attempt to place the difference between America and Europe in a "strong and affecting light" by drawing a picture of Connecticut's "Fair Verna" which offered a sharp contrast to Britain's "Sweet Auburn." This was the most imitative of all the sections of *Greenfield Hill*, for Dwight not only admired *The Deserted Village* as the finest pastoral ever written but he apparently echoed Goldsmith's verse in a number of cases in order to emphasize the fact that he was comparing the social effects of American and British institutions. He was not, however, uncritical. The very fact that he praised America as a place "Where one extended class embraces all" made him especially indignant in his attack upon slavery as "The uncur'd gangrene of the reasoning mind." Even when he fell completely into a James Littlejohn mood, while contemplating the country schools, he showed a real, if tolerant, awareness of the shortcomings of a typical schoolmaster:

> Some half-grown sprigs of learning grac'd his brow:
> Little he knew, though much he wish'd to know,
> Inchanted hung o'er Virgil's honey'd lay,
> And smiled, to see desipient Horace play;
> Glean'd scraps of Greek; and, curious, trac'd afar,
> Through Pope's clear glass, the bright Maeonian star.
> Yet oft his students at his wisdom star'd,
> For many a student to his side repair'd,
> Surpriz'd, they heard him Dilworth's knots untie,
> And tell, what lands beyond the Atlantic lie.
>
>   Many his faults; his virtues small, and few;
> Some little good he did, or strove to do;
> Laborious still, he taught the early mind,
> And urg'd to manners meek, and thoughts refin'd;
> Truth he impress'd, and every virtue prais'd;
> While infant eyes, in wondering silence, gaz'd.

But, on the whole, America was good. To Dwight, at this time, even the frontier was an admirable place where "Young Freedom wantons" in the "cheaper fields" of a western world designed by Heaven in its entirety as an "example bright, to renovate mankind."

The contrast Dwight drew between America and Europe was partly the result of an excessive dependence upon such works as Pope's *Satires* and Goldsmith's *The Deserted Village* as sources of information. But to an even greater extent it may have been affected by a curious, but not uncommon, sort of imaginative shyness that impelled him to a long, affectionate contemplation of familiar things and to a distrustful, rather hasty glance at distant and unfamiliar objects. For Dwight, like many other people who pride themselves on their hardheaded realistic emphasis upon "things as they are," showed a noticeable unwillingness to examine carefully anything—no matter how real—that lay beyond the range of his habitual observation. The representation of Europe which he had made in his "Epistle to Col. Humphreys" and paraphrased in the first part of *Greenfield Hill* was not the product of realistic observation, even at second hand. It was merely the excited reaction of an imagination so timid that it fell into gaucherie before it became at home in its field of operation. His comparison between Europe and America, of course, was false; but more important than the naïveté of his comparison was the general attitude into which he was forced by this temperamental peculiarity and by a social philosophy that was closely related to it. For Dwight's advice to his countrymen—

> Change, but change alone,
> By wise improvement of thy blessings rare—

recommended a procedure not materially different from that he had scornfully attributed to the Europeans—that of eking out the social garment from "every loom of following times." Since the results of slow improvement in the two continents so greatly differed in his view, the cause must necessarily be attributed to a difference in the original fabrics. And Dwight, again unwilling to look closely at distant objects, merely assumed a great difference between the "Gothic" origins of European civilization and the "rock of truth" on which American institutions were based, casually advised his readers to "think whence" their "weal arose," and let the matter go with a hopeful assurance that "From the same springs it still shall ceaseless rise." His attitude reflected the same sort of wishful thinking directed toward the past that Barlow was beginning to reflect while looking toward the future. Americans of Dwight's temperament were soon to quit expressing themselves in literature, and consequently his sort of wishful thinking is less well understood than Barlow's. But the two men represent rival brands of intellectual nebulosity that Americans have been forced to choose between in politics ever since.

There was nothing nebulous, however, in the specific advice Dwight offered his parishioners either in his proper role as a clergyman or in the adopted role of a plain farmer who had succeeded to the mantle of Poor Richard. As a pastor he avoided strictly theological matters, stressed the importance of human life in relation to eternity alone, and described the strait and narrow way in contrast to the wide and downward path. Be guided by the Bible and be good to your fellow-man were the two great commandments in his gospel, which emphasized the necessity for faith and constant effort even while promising, in true Calvinistic fashion, nothing more than the possibility of "Hope." As a later Poor Richard—or, more exactly, Father Abraham— he preached the way to competence rather than the way to wealth, recommending industry and thrift but at the same time insisting that "The Labourer's worthy of his hire" and should "Use freely, and *with pleasure* use" the best produce of his fields instead of sending it to market for less admirable people. Dwight's aphoristic advice, however, was superior to Franklin's, for he had a greater respect for the common people and a more genuine appreciation of their problems. Some of his commonplace advice concerning industry and thrift was specific and detailed, and he supplemented it with further concrete recommendations concerning the conservation and improvement of farm property and the education of children, until the sixth part of *Greenfield Hill* became a practical octosyllabic handbook of enlightened agricultural methods and parental behavior.

Dwight revealed his Calvinistic theory of human nature more clearly in his discussion of methods of child-rearing than in his religious instruction and, in doing so, showed how far apart he stood from the sanguine notions Barlow was beginning to develop at about the same time:

> By reason's power alone,
> From guilt, no heart was ever won.
> Decent, not good, may reason make him;
> By reason, crimes will ne'er forsake him.
> As weeds, self-sown, demand no toil,
> But flourish in their native soil,
> Root deep, grow high, with vigour bloom,
> And send forth poison, for perfume;
> So faults, inborn, spontaneous rise,
> And daily wax in strength, and size,
> Ripen, with neither toil, nor care,
> And choke each germ of virtue there.
> Virtues, like plants of nobler kind,
> Transferred from regions more refin'd,
> The gardener's careful hand must sow;
> His culturing hand must bid them grow;
> Rains gently shower; skies softly shine,
> And blessings fall, from realms divine.
>   Much time, and pain, and toil, and care,
> Must virtue's habits plant, and rear:
> *Habits alone thro' life endure,*
> *Habits alone your child secure.*

Such a belief in the inherent badness of the human disposition and the possibility of improvement only through the careful cultivation of good habits was also at variance with the theory of moral improvement through the cultivation of taste, toward which Dwight had at least leaned in his youth and had not yet fully rejected. The twelve years spent on Greenfield Hill were, in fact, years of considerable philosophical wavering. His insistence, as he expressed it in another line of advice, that "*Habits alone yield good below*" was not in accord with his belief in the real efficacy of putting truth in "a strong and affecting light"; and his Calvinist conception of the "heart by nature prone to sin" was frequently counterbalanced by the assumption of some common, internal sense of "taste" or relish for good. He recognized the lack of harmony in his thought and in the concluding section of his poem, "The Vision," looked forward to the time when "Moral science" would explain

> How taste, mysterious, in the Heavenly plan,
> Improves, adorns, and elevates, the man.

In the meantime he accepted the mystery and as convenience suited was either a strict Calvinist or a hesitant follower of the Scottish philosophers in his view of human nature. Seriously questioned, Dwight unquestionably would have affirmed the former position and excused evidences of the latter on the grounds of poetic license; but the latter, whether formally heeded or not, had the greater influence over both his writing and his actions.

One reason for not taking "The Farmer's Advice to the Villagers" as a well-rounded expression of Dwight's own opinions is that the poet who, in advising parents how to deal with their children, said *"All wond'rous stories bid them shun"* had devoted the preceding two sections of his poem to wondrous stories celebrating the history of his neighborhood. The first of these, "The Burning of Fairfield," was a patriotic, anti-war, historical narrative of the type common in America after the Revolution. Written soon after the event for people who witnessed it, the account was characterized more by verbal decoration than by the quality of wide-eyed wonder which made the narrative part of "The Destruction of the Pequods" the most agreeably unusual of Dwight's poems. Drawn from Neal's *History of New England* and Morse's *American Geography*, the account naturally praises the actions of Captains Mason and Stoughton, but its most interesting characteristic is less the inevitable historical bias than the poet's emphasis upon the "romantic" possibilities of his subject—such "wond'rous" elements as the attraction of spirits by magic rites:

> The woodland rumbled; murmur'd deep each stream;
> Shrill sung the leaves; all ether sigh'd profound;
> Pale tufts of purple topp'd the silver flame,
> And many-color'd Forms on evening breezes came.

> Thin, twilight Forms; attir'd in changing sheen
> Of plumes, high-tinctur'd in the western ray;
> Bending, they peep'd the fleecy folds between,
> Their wings light-rustling in the breath of May.
> Soft-hovering round the fire, in mystic play,
> They snuff'd the incense, wav'd in clouds afar,
> Then, silent, floated toward the setting day:
> Eve redden'd each fine form, each misty car;
> And through them faintly gleam'd, at times, the
>   Western star.

Dwight had allowed himself a similar indulgence of fancy in the nightmarish, though realistic, description of "the house of Sloth"; but in repeating the indulgence here—especially as part of a tale he professed to have heard in childhood—he was not writing in the same character in which he advised his readers to keep such stories from their own children.

But Dwight was torn between his lifelong habit of carrying his principles to their logical conclusion and his desire to make American history appear as interesting and as productive of poetry as that of Greece and Rome. He did not deceive himself with a belief that he was successful, however, and so he concluded his poem in the customary manner with "The Vision, or Prospect of the Future Happiness of America" as it was revealed by an allegorical figure. The "Splendour of Europe," he maintained in the "Argument" for this section, was already "excelled by the Happiness of America"; and as he looked into the future he could see no brighter prospects for his country than

> One free elective sway;
> One blood, one kindred, reach from sea to sea;
> One language spread; one tide of manners run;
> One scheme of science, and of morals one;
> And, GOD's own Word the structure, and the base,
> One faith extend, one worship, and one praise.

And such a sight, he believed, would strike other nations with rapture and enable "peace and freedom" to "re-illume mankind." Other poets might be beginning to dream of the perfectibility of mankind, but Dwight had escaped from any tendency toward these "lunar dreams" and clarified his own idea of progress by a vision of the whole world getting more and more like Connecticut.

Greenfield Hill was published in 1794; and, in spite of Dwight's failure to take any great pains with its revision, it serves as the best memorial to his poetic talents. The evidences of imitation that he did not bother to remove show that he intended to adopt the manner of Thomson's *Seasons* for the first part, Goldsmith's *The Deserted Village* for the second, and Beattie's *The Minstrel* for the fourth. The heroic couplets of Pope were probably models for the verse in the concluding section, for the author's notes indicate that he still had both the *Satires* and Pope's own model, Horace, in mind while writing it. There are also a number of echoes of Pope in the second part and at least one imitation of Virgil's *Georgics* in the first. The other three sections are in octosyllabics less easy to identify, although the fifth part is frequently Miltonic in its cadences, the third suggestive of Dyer in its descriptive passages, and the sixth reminiscent of Gay's *Fables*. But Dwight's notes also showed a consciousness of Edward Moore's octosyllabics, and he was so widely acquainted with that sort of verse, having recently tried his own hand at fables, that he probably had no single poet in mind when he wrote these sections. Yet *Greenfield Hill* is not really an imitative poem except in occasional introductory lines and in those passages which deliberately alluded to Goldsmith and Pope in order to emphasize the contrast between English and American life. The Thomsonian blank verse of the first part often disappears in favor of a quieter, more direct style which reminds the reader of Cowper, although it most probably was Dwight's own; and the Spenserian stanzas of the fourth are frequently more colorful and imaginative than Beattie's or even Thomson's. The imitative plan of the work gave Dwight an opportunity to try his skill with various kinds of English narrative and descriptive verse, and the results indicate that the most unfortunate decision he made during his literary career was the arbitrary determination to make use of rhyme in his first ambitious work because "he believed it would be more generally relished than blank verse, even amongst those who are esteemed persons of taste." By the time *Greenfield Hill* appeared, however, his poetic career was practically over, and, even when he turned back to one of these newly cultivated verse forms by writing the first part of his debate between "Genius and Common Sense" in Spenserian stanzas, it was only to leave the poem unpublished and perhaps permanently lost.

IV

The only other verse Dwight was to compose during his residence in Greenfield consisted of such occasional poems as "A Hymn," beginning "Hail child of light, returning Spring," written for the public exhibition of scholars on May 2, 1788, and "The Seasons Moralized," another song in the same octosyllabic couplets, which may have been inspired by a desire to improve on a similar poem by Philip Freneau. The condition of the world was becoming so grave that it demanded consideration in reasoned, serious prose rather than in flowery rhyme. If Dwight's idea of progress was that of a world growing more and more like Connecticut, then it was retrogression everywhere that he saw when he looked abroad—and even the slowly changing land of steady habits was beginning to creep in the wrong direction. The selfishness of Lord Chesterfield was no longer a symbol of European decadence but a sign of the times. The social and economic movements his friends had attacked in the *Anarchiad* indicated one sort of threat to America which the Constitution had repressed but not entirely abolished, and the theological liberalism he himself had condemned in *The Triumph of Infidelity* indicated another. The ideal of competence—the golden mean between poverty and wealth—celebrated in *Greenfield Hill* was being endangered in Connecticut no less than in the rest of the United States by the passion for land speculation that overcame some of the most respectable characters in the country. The habits which alone yielded good below were in danger of being destroyed by selfish men who ignored the great "truth" of things as they are and strove to have things as they wanted them to be.

Dwight was not yet seriously concerned with political matters,

and neither he nor his intellectual associates showed any signs
of being frightened by the early stages of the French Revolution.
He was still ready to match laws against popular uprisings
in America, and moral suasion against excessive self-interest.
His own social philosophy had grown out of a dispositional bias,
a conservative environment, and his early ethical training. His
Calvinism, kept in a separate compartment of his mind, had
nothing to do with its origin. But, whenever he found occasion
to avoid tacit assumptions and give a clear exposition of his beliefs concerning human nature, he adopted, as *Greenfield Hill*
shows, the Calvinistic point of view. He revealed his own
opinion of the intellectual conflict in the world around him in
two couplets whch represented an attitude as permanent as
their optimism was temporary:

> For soon, no more to philosophic whims,
> To cloud-built theories, and lunar dreams,
> But to firm facts, shall human faith be given,
> The proofs of Reason, and the voice of *Heaven*.

There were, of course, many "firm facts" of one sort or another, but the most important of them were the voice of Heaven
as it was heard exclusively through the Bible and the rational
demonstrations to be drawn from it. To a New Light theologian
such as Dwight, Calvinistic tenets were the basic deductions
made by reason from the Scriptures; and if these tenets contributed nothing to the development of his social theories, they
served as an anchor of stability when the theories were threatened by a whirlwind of contrary doctrines.

Anchors of stability were a primary need in the world,
Dwight apparently thought when he did not allow himself a
poetic license for optimism, and he set about forging them in
the only sermons published during his pastorate at Greenfield
Hill. The earliest of these, *The Dignity and Excellence of the
Gospel*, although it was not actually printed until it had been
delivered a second time in 1812, circulated widely in manuscript after it was preached in 1785 and pleased William Cowper
"almost more than any" sermon he had "either seen or heard."
In it, as the title indicates, Dwight began his efforts to hammer

out the first of his anchors—a renewed appreciation of the *excellence*, the eminent goodness, of the Bible. The sermon was delivered at the ordination of a neighboring minister, and Dwight attempted to gain assistance in his efforts by means of a passage of advice concerning the purpose of preaching:

> To prove the truth of a Scriptural doctrine is, however, but one, and that, often, the least necessary, and the least laborous object of preaching. To illustrate the nature of the doctrine, and the manner in which it is true, and to impress its importance on the minds of those who hear, are always objects of high moment; and often demand the chief attention of the preacher.

Most of the sermon, however, was devoted to the development of Dwight's own theme by methods which ranged from the conventional one of calling the roll of great men who believed in the Bible to a more unusual emphasis upon the extra delights of "taste" growing from the contemplation of the universe as an expression of the Infinite Mind rather than as a "lifeless mass." Dwight had also begun to discover that a man who takes the defensive on certain fundamental issues is obliged to recall a good many opinions expressed when the fundamentals were taken for granted, and the first of his old notions to disappear was that of the literary genius of biblical writers, which he had defended so vigorously in his Master's *Dissertation* of 1772. Since the eminent goodness of the Scriptures was more impressive as pure revelation from on high, the human authors lost the "elevated Genius" that had been attributed to them: the Jews, unlike the Greeks and Romans, he pointed out, "were never distinguished for learning, or science" and accordingly could not have produced so superior a work alone. Dwight was convinced that the advancement of religion was so important to political and social stability that, as he expressed it in *Virtuous Rulers a National Blessing*, an election sermon of 1791, "in forming an idea of its influence, the most romantic imagination will easily fall short of the truth." Consequently, he returned to the subject of the eminent goodness of the gospel in *A Discourse on the Genuineness and Authenticity of the New Testament*, which he delivered before the general association of Connecticut ministers in 1793 and expanded for publication during the following year. Drawn largely from Nathaniel Lardner's *The Credibility of the Gospel History*, the substance of the sermon is of less interest than the subject, although in it Dwight again pointed out that it was not necessary to think of the Gospel writers as being any more than plain, ordinary men without the attainments of "superiour genius."

The second anchor of stability that Dwight attempted to forge in these sermons was a more complete and perfect respect for tradition. His admiration for the Connecticut way as it had been established in some vaguely defined manner by the forefathers became more inclusive, less discriminating. The custom of preaching election sermons, which he had denounced in "The Friend" as a blind perpetuation of ancestral bad taste, became wholly admirable by the time he was called upon for a discourse on election day in the spring of 1791. He completely reversed his earlier opinion in his opening sentences:

When our ancestors instituted the solemnities of this day, they gave the world a fair exhibition of their wisdom and piety. The election of the great officers of a state is an event highly important, and solemn, and ought to be regarded with solemn emotions. To inspire such emotions, they justly determined, nothing would more effectually conduce, than the union of the Legislature in the public reverential acknowledgement of the presence, and agency, of Him, "whose throne is prepared in the heavens, and whose kingdom ruleth over all."

To some extent he may have been influenced by the fact that he instead of someone else had been invited to deliver the sermon, but, on the whole, his words represented a sincere change of opinion. In his growing concern for stability he developed an increasing respect for prolonged experience as a test of value: the word "experimental" began to appear in his vocabulary with increasing frequency, and he had decided that the election sermon was the result of the fact that his ancestors had been "experimentally convinced" of the desirability of religious influences on public occasions.

In his attack upon election sermons in "The Friend" Dwight had thrown into clear conflict the "pope-like authority of Custom" and the perceptions of the internal sense of taste; and when he turned with greater respect to the authority of custom in his 1791 election sermon this conflict still remained clear in his mind. Accordingly, the next of his old notions to disappear under the pressure of new circumstances was the conception of an internal common sense. "Sometimes," he told the Connecticut legislature with reference to the meaning of "true honour," "it is asserted to be an instinctive and exquisite sensibility to right and wrong, to that which is noble or debased; by which the mind is irresistibly, or at least very forcibly, led to pursue that, which is right and noble, and to shun that which is wrong or debased." But that opinion, he added, "is fairly presumed to be chimerical; no satisfactory evidence having been hitherto offered, of the existence of such a principle." He returned to the same denial of the internal sense in his next published sermon, *A Discourse on the Genuineness and Authenticity of the New Testament*, deliberately bleaching the term "common-sense" of its technical connotations by defining it as a "degree of understanding" and distinguishing between it and "the usual senses of men." In *The True Means of Establishing Public Happiness*, a sermon delivered before the Connecticut Society of the Cincinnati in July, 1795, he was even more specific in eliminating all anti-Lockean technical significances from the term. His terminology had nothing in common with that of the Scottish philosophers when he wrote:

There is in the human mind a faculty, called Common-sense, which though never in high estimation among Philosophers, seems to have originated, and executed, almost all the plans of human business which have proved to be of any use. The reason is obvious. Employed in forming near and evident deductions from facts, and in closely observing facts for that purpose, contended with moderate advances, and cautious innovations, its step, though slow, has been sure; a real approximation to the end in view.

"Common-sense" was too good and too useful a term for Dwight to throw away, but in keeping it he redefined it to mean "cautious reasoning" rather than "intuitive perception."

The sermon before the Cincinnati is of unusual importance because it was preached two months after the death of Ezra Stiles, when Dwight knew that he was to be the next president of Yale and was probably in the process of settling upon the textbooks from which he would teach the Seniors the philosophy of the mind, moral philosophy, and rhetoric. He put the seal upon his reaction against the Scottish philosophers by selecting William Paley's *The Principles of Moral and Political Philosophy*, with its reasoned conclusion questioning the existence of an internal sense:

> Upon the whole, it seems to me, either that there are no such instincts as compose what is called the moral sense, or that they are not now to be distinguished from prejudices and habits; on which account they cannot be depended upon in moral reasoning: I mean, that it is no safe way of arguing, to assume certain principles as so many dictates, impulses, and instincts of nature, and then draw conclusions from these, as to the rectitude or wrongness of actions, independent of the tendency of such actions, or any other consideration whatever.

Dwight also determined to maintain the intellectual consistency of the Yale curriculum by retaining Locke's *Essay concerning the Human Understanding* as the basic textbook in the philosophy of the mind; and he anticipated this decision in his sermon. "Almost all real knowledge, and all practical knowledge," he declared, "is derived either from Experience, or from Revelation." The qualifying "almost all" which he applied to "real" knowledge undoubtedly was introduced to provide an epistemological niche for the intuitions admitted by Locke and the uncommon "moral sense" affirmed by his grandfather Edwards, not for the common sense of the Scottish philosophers. After twenty-six years of cautious dalliance with the intuitional will-o'-the-wisp, Dwight had returned to the intellectual position in which Naphtali Daggett had tried to fix him during his Senior year at Yale.

It was under the influence of a desire for stability so powerful that it forced him to discard some of the cherished notions of twenty-five years that Dwight formed the political philosophy which influenced greatly his later observations and writings. He expressed it in his sermon on *The True Means of Establishing Public Happiness*. His point of approach was the very simple one that if "happiness" is "extended through a century, it is mathematically proved to be a hundred times the value, which it would possess, if extended only through a year." He continued, in consequence:

A free government has always, and justly, been supposed to be a primary source of national happiness. To form such a government has been found sufficiently easy; but to render it durable has ever been considered as a problem of very difficult solution. Yet in its durability plainly consists almost all the value of such a government. Hence most of the political knowledge and labour of freemen has been employed, and exhausted, in endeavouring to give stability to their respective political systems. Hence have arisen the numerous checks, balances, and divisions of power and influence, found in our own political constitutions, and in those of several other nations. In other nations, these means have been generally insufficient to accomplish the end. Whether they will issue more happily in our own is uncertain. In several instances, we seem to have approached the verge of dissolution; but we have providentially withdrawn, before the season of safety was passed.

Since the wisdom of depending upon checks and balances had not been experimentally proved, a more trustworthy method should be adopted for the purpose:

The primary mean of originating and establishing happiness, in free communities is, I imagine, the formation of good personal character in their citizens. Good citizens must of course constitute a happier community than bad ones, and must better understand the nature and causes of their happiness. They may safely be governed by a milder policy, and cannot but be better judges of the desirableness of such policy. More the children of reason, and less the slaves of appetite and passion, they will naturally be more satisfied with real happiness, and less allured, by that, which, however shewy, is unsubstantial; will need fewer restrictions, and be more contented under such as are necessary; will prize more highly such liberty, as is suited to the condition of man, and proportionally disregard that, which is Utopian.

Too much emphasis, he had come to believe, had been put upon liberty as an end of government and too little upon the virtues of piety, benevolence, and temperance:

Liberty has often been the price of lives scarcely numerable, and of property exceeding calculation. Yet Liberty is a possession of less importance than Virtue. Had half the efforts been made to promote virtue, which have been made to extend war and slaughter, virtue would now, probably, constitute the prevailing human character. But Virtue, though the first good of man, has least engaged his attention. . . . . The formation and establishment of knowledge and virtue in the citizens of a Community is the first business of Legislation, and will more easily and more effectually establish order, and secure liberty, than all the checks, balances, and penalties, which have been devised by man. With the Legislature this business should begin; and with reference to it most, if not all, their important measures ought to be concerted.

He had taken for his text a prophetic passage from Isaiah: "And wisdom and knowledge shall be the stability of thy times"; and he had preached that rulers should strive for stability by promoting the wisdom that automatically accompanies virtue and by encouraging the knowledge derived from experience and revelation. He had denied intuition, and he condemned speculation:

> Theories are generally mere dreams, which ought to be placed on the same level with the professed fictions of poets, and to be written in verse, and not in sober prose. Tho' dignified with pompous title of Philosophy, they have usually, after amusing the world, a little time, gone down the stream of contempt into the ocean of oblivion. They cannot be practical, because they cannot be true; and hence, being of no use, except to please the imagination, they are of course neglected and forgotten.

Dwight had settled into a permanent social and political philosophy.

V

The defense of revelation, steady habits, and an unspeculative political philosophy which Dwight began in these sermons became the primary mission of his literary life. The ambition revealed in *The Conquest of Canäan*, the strident aggressiveness in *The Triumph of Infidelity*, settled into a firm purposefulness. Henceforth Dwight was to devote his pen and voice to the preservation of the civilization he had idealized in *Greenfield Hill*. "James Littlejohn" acquired "John Homely's" vigor, renounced dilettantism, and began to take an active part in the world. When the ideal civilization seemed to be too dramatically threatened by the combined forces of infidelity and democracy, the strident tones were to be heard again; and the quietly humorous tones of Littlejohn were often to be caught by students in the classroom. But Dwight's public literary tone was usually, for the rest of his life, a blend of the two, strong without stridency, mellow without affectation—in literature as in life, like the "middle notes of an organ."

With the acquisition of this new tone, Dwight gave his literary career a new direction. He discovered that verse-making and belletristic fame were of less importance, to him, than plain prose and an attentive audience; and he was not to try his hand again at poetry until the close of the second war with England had relieved some of the tension that had existed in the American atmosphere for two decades. The discovery was a fortunate one, for he was too much a "methodizer" to develop a style that would appeal to a public that loved Goldsmith and Cowper, and he was too ambitious in his designs and too hurried in his execution of them to become a decent craftsman. He had to have a practical purpose in view and an actual audience before him in order to exercise his native good sense upon his pedantry and ambition. He also discovered that his proper audience was to be found in the congregations of the righteous and among people who were interested in the land and institutions of New England. Henceforth he was to neglect the nebulous "literary" public and direct his writings toward the sort of people he knew.

PART IV

The Ways of the World

CHAPTER VIII

THE HONORABLE DAVID HUMPHREYS

〰〰〰〰〰〰〰〰〰〰〰〰

I

COLLABORATION with Humphreys apparently had been a trial for the three more nimble-witted members of the *Anarchiad* group. Trumbull expressed their general attitude toward him, in 1789, in a letter to Oliver Wolcott concerning their friend's diplomatic prospects:

> The President has tried him on McGillivray first, and he did not suit the skull of the savage, but we cannot argue from the circumstance that he would not fit as easy as a full bottomed Wig upon the fat-headed, sot-headed, and crazy-headed Sovereigns of Europe. Tell him this story for his comfort, and to encourage his hopes of speedy employment—A King being angry with an Ambassador, asked him whether his Master had no wise men at his Court, and was therefore obliged to send him a fool? Sire, said the other, my Master has many *wise men* about his court, but he conceived *me* the most proper Ambassador to your Majesty. Upon this principle, I am in daily expectation of hearing that he is appointed Minister Plenipo to George, Louis or the Stadtholder. For is not his name *Numps?*

Trumbull proved a fair prophet. In August, 1790, Humphreys was appointed special secret agent to Europe with instructions to look into the difficulties between England and Spain and the prospect of encouraging friendly relations with Portugal. During the following year he was made resident minister to Portugal and in 1793 sole commissioner for Algerian affairs. In June, 1796, he became minister plenipotentiary to Spain; and during the term of his service, which lasted until Jefferson became president in 1801, he married Ann Frances Bulkeley, the daughter of a well-to-do English banker and merchant in Lisbon. Although Jefferson, as secretary of state, had found him a source

of annoyance and Barlow, as his diplomatic collaborator in the
Algerian negotiations, had decided that he had "too much beef
in his head" to do anything but keep a secret, Humphreys did
fit the court at Madrid "as easy as a full bottomed Wig." He
was a popular minister, who loved the formality of the court and
had a high appreciation of the social opportunity for associating
with the nobility. When he returned to America, in the spring
of 1802, neither he nor his wife looked forward with much satisfaction to the prospect of a New England farm which lay before
them, and accordingly they took up their residence in Boston,
where they remained—except for one trip abroad—until Humphreys' death on February 21, 1818.

The latter years of Humphreys' life, however, were closely
associated with Connecticut. During his visits in Hartford he
had been interested in the woolen mill organized by his friend
Jeremiah Wadsworth, and his interest may have been further
stimulated by the fact that the cloth it supplied for Washington's inaugural suit proved to be—in the President's opinion—
not quite of the first quality. The fault, as everyone knew, lay
in the poor quality of American wool, and Humphreys seized
the opportunity offered to him by his position in the Spanish
court to improve the resources of his country by importing a
large flock of merino sheep when he returned home. The flock
greatly improved the local breed in Connecticut and led, in 1806,
to the establishment of the former ambassador's own woolen
mill, near Derby in the industrial village of Humphreysville,
which manufactured numerous varieties of cloth and soon added
papermaking to its activities. Staffed mostly by unpaid ap-
prentice boys, some of them orphans from the city of New York,
and by women at wages of fifty cents to a dollar a week, it
proved a highly profitable enterprise, especially during the days
of the embargo; and it developed into a paternalistic community which served as a model for later industrial villages.
The proprietor became an active promoter of improvements in
industry and agriculture, a strong supporter of scientific societies, and an unofficial adviser to the national government during
the War of 1812. His later life reached its climax on his sixty-

third birthday when, dressed in blue and buff with gold buttons and lace ruffles, he sat in the largest hall in Humphreysville, his plump hands folded and his pink face beaming, while his mill boys performed, for his particular benefit, one of his own comedies which in rough draft had been praised by the great William Gifford. He was a hero, a great gentleman, a public benefactor, and a man of letters. Few men in America could claim as much.

II

When Humphreys left Connecticut for Mount Vernon in the autumn of 1787, he was flushed with enthusiasm over the literary success of the Wits and determined to continue his own belletristic activity. Washington, in inviting him, had insisted that his time should be his own, and Humphreys still had two projects in mind. He had already spent some time at Mount Vernon examining records with the intention of writing historically about the Revolution, and before leaving France he had made a start at translating from the French. He was soon to become aware that he was being anticipated in the former project by David Ramsay, and he already knew that he had been forestalled in the particular translation he wanted to undertake; but both fields were broad enough to accommodate more than one genius, and they both continued to attract him.

Since he seemed to look upon Dr. Ramsay's proposal for his *History of the American Revolution* as news in November, 1788, there is no real evidence concerning the reason why he himself turned from his early plan for historical writing to biography or why, if he undertook the latter, he did not attempt the life of his friend and hero, George Washington. His actual subject seems to have been determined, in part at least, by accident. During his winter of activity as a Wit and a member of the Connecticut legislature he renewed his acquaintance with his former commander, General Israel Putnam, and under the influence of a new flow of reminiscences decided to do a sketch of the old warrior's life. He was also undoubtedly influenced by the satiric picture of the General in the Rev. Samuel Peters' *History of Connecticut* (which the Wits attacked in their *American*

Antiquities) and by a desire to restore his character by placing
him in a more favorable light. The plan for a memoir seems to
have been announced to his friends sometime during the winter;
but the decision to carry it out may not have been final until it
reached the ears of Putnam's physician, Dr. Albigence Waldo,
who had spent the preceding year collecting anecdotes of the
General and offered to forward them to Humphreys for his own
use. The anecdotes were colorful, and they fitted so perfectly
into the Plutarchian conception of biography which Humphreys
had in mind that they may have contributed as much to his decision to write the book as they did to the extraordinary popularity which the finished work enjoyed.

For Humphreys was not especially qualified to engage in
biography. He was so uninformed that, on the one hand, he
announced his attempt as "the first effort in biography, that
has been made on this continent" and, on the other, he showed
no awareness of even such famous English biographies as Johnson's *Lives of the Poets*. His point of view was clearly and rather
simply expressed:

> When we thus behold a person, from the humble walks of life, starting
> unnoticed in the career of fame, and, by an undeviating progress through a life
> of honor, arriving at the highest dignity in the state; curiosity is strongly
> excited, and philosophy loves to trace the path of glory from the cradle of
> obscurity to the summit of elevation.

Thus, as he declared in a prefatory letter addressed to Jeremiah
Wadsworth, his subject "could not be destitute of amusement
and instruction, and would possess the advantage of presenting
for imitation a respectable model of public and private virtues."
Accordingly, his purpose was moral, never critical or scholarly;
and it does not seem to have occurred to him that it might have
been desirable or necessary to check his facts by going to any
other source than the General himself, his own reminiscences
from his period of service as Putnam's aide de camp, and such
military records as he found at Mount Vernon that would illustrate points he had already made in his narrative. If documents
were available showing that Washington sometimes considered

Putnam stubborn and disobedient to orders, Humphreys would not be so indiscreet as to hinder his purpose by reflecting upon the character of a hero held up for emulation; and, if he had any notion that Major Robert Rogers' published *Journal* paralleled and frequently contradicted Putnam's own story, he was too loyal and too patriotic even to consider the word of a renegade Tory in connection with a hero's deeds.

The result was that Humphreys, to the detriment of his character as an accurate biographer, contributed more than any of his associates to the creation of an American patriotic mythology and came far nearer immortalizing a hero than Dwight and Barlow did in the poetic tributes imbedded in their epics. Israel Putnam creeping into a narrow, low cave with a rope around his legs, a torch in one hand and a gun in the other, and a ferocious wolf growling in front of him; Putnam leaving his plow in the furrow and riding off to war at the first news of Concord; Putnam plunging on horseback down artificial steps in the side of a mountain so precipitous that the British dragoons paused in consternation at the brink—these are the pictures of his hero which Humphreys fixed in the minds of millions of Americans who saw them in his book, in other biographies largely copied from it, or in extracts that received a prominent place in school readers for generations. Dr. Waldo rather than Humphreys may have been originally responsible for these stories; but, in any case, it was the uncritical hero-worshiper among the Connecticut Wits who put them in their final form and so reached the largest audience of any member of the group. Had Humphreys, with his unconscious ability to invoke the attraction of myths for the simple, gone on to make another study of Washington, the world might have had a narrative so remarkable that even Parson Weems's cherry tree would have been lost in the enchanted forest.

But, unfortunately perhaps, Humphreys' essential simplicity of mind was overlaid by a veneer of sophistication about which he was inordinately self-conscious; and he spent most of his literary effort at Mount Vernon upon a translation from the French:

> We now prepare—we strive to make your own,
> The classic wealth of France—too long unknown!
> This gold of Gaul coin'd in Columbia's mint,
> 'Tis yours to fix the current value in't.

Humphreys had not taken Dwight's advice to avoid "*acted* plays" while abroad, and the subject he chose for translation— after he had been anticipated in his plan to put the Marquis de Chastellux's travels into English—was Antoine Marin Le Mierre's *La Veuve du Malabar*. He evidently had discussed and may have begun the project before leaving Connecticut, for in an introductory letter to Trumbull he referred to their collaboration in composing the Prologue and Epilogue. Although the letter also mentioned "a certain similarity of genius, and congeniality of soul" between the two poets—a claim that Trumbull may have found embarrassing—the chances are that the serious Prologue, pointing out the superiority of America to a country in which custom is more powerful than reason, was, despite the advertisements, largely Humphreys' and the humorous Epilogue with its feminine rhymes, allusive wit, and light echoes of "The Rape of the Lock" was mostly Trumbull's. The greater part of the translation, however, was made at Mount Vernon, where Humphreys, occupying one of the small bedrooms with three younger relatives of the Washingtons, composed many of the lines of blank verse after a day in the saddle and occasionally roused his companions from their slumbers in order to get their critical opinions of his effort. The play, printed as *The Widow of Malabar, or The Tyranny of Custom,* dramatized the conflict between such Hindu customs as the burning of widows and the impulses of humanity and sensibility, generalized this conflict to some extent by references to cruel customs in other lands, and, even though called "a tragedy," represented humanity and sensibility as victorious. Back of it, as the Prologue and Epilogue made clear, was a patriotic effort to celebrate America by contrast with other countries; and the play seems to have had some public success when it was performed by the American Company in Philadelphia in May, 1790. Humphreys also printed in his *Miscellaneous Works* a "Prologue to the Translation of Athaliah; A Tragedy," by Racine, in which he advertised the "Gold of Gaul" in the quotation given above and revealed similar patriotic motives, made even more clear by his attempt to fix the moral in the Epilogue by emphasizing the value of political "concord."

Humphreys had been invited to deliver the annual address before the Connecticut Society of the Cincinnati in 1788, but he had been unable to attend the meeting and had sent *An Essay on the Life of the Honorable Major-General Israel Putnam* instead. Parts of it may have been read in the meeting, and the entire work was published by order of the Society in Hartford that October with a notice that "the genius, elegance, and ability of the author are too well known both in Europe and America to need a panegyric." He was also invited again to deliver an oration for the following anniversary meeting of July 9, 1789. In this address, published as "An Oration, on the Political Situation of the United States of America, in the Year 1789," Humphreys returned in prose to the sort of demonstrative discourse he had delivered in the first part of *A Poem on the Happiness of America*, celebrating his country's current situation under four formal heads:

[1] a few observations on the American Revolution: [2] on the necessity which afterwards appeared for establishing a general government of more energy than the original confederation: [3] on the nature of the government which has lately been carried into effect: [4] and on the national prosperity which we may reasonably expect will result from the faithful administration of that government.

As an exhibition by a would-be diplomat, the address was a rare display of talents; for not only did Humphreys keep a safe middle ground in praising the new form of government for its insurance against "a wanton levity of innovation on one hand, and an unalterable practice of error on the other," but with a practical orator's indifference to consistency he appealed to each member of his audience by momentarily adopting his individual point of view. Thus in one sentence he expressed

Dwight's dogmatic opinion that "a free government ought to be founded on the information and morals of the people" and in another adopted Barlow's growing liberal belief that "freedom of enquiry will produce liberality of conduct"; in one place he assumed that the vast undeveloped continent of America was evidence that God had some great plan in reserve for the improvement of the world, in another that "the great scenes of nature with which we are surrounded" would call into action an inherent "grandeur of soul." It is doubtful that he was aware to any great degree of the implications of all his fine phrases; but, deliberately or not, he did a remarkable job of putting the cart before the horse, getting the animal back in his traces, and repeating the process so rapidly that his audience was completely dazzled and even a later analyst cannot get from the orator's words any trustworthy evidence concerning his intellectual processes or beliefs.

The only other literary enterprise undertaken by Humphreys before his official trip abroad was the publication of his *Miscellaneous Works*. Mathew Carey had already brought out, in 1789, a small volume of *Poems by Col. David Humphreys, Late Aid-de-Camp to His Excellency General Washington*, which formed a cheaply printed second edition of the poems already published in the *American Museum*, with a few small additions. The author apparently thought that a more complete and better edition would be desirable, especially when he began to anticipate his second foreign appointment and remembered the service rendered by his *Address to the Armies* on his earlier mission. Accordingly, he gathered together the poems printed by Carey, added his exchange of verse letters with Dwight, his drama and the two prologues and epilogues, Dwight's "Columbia," the sketch of Putnam, and the Cincinnati address, and published them all with several new prefaces and complimentary letters and such favorable reviews of his work as he had on hand. The whole was dedicated to the Duke de la Rochefoucauld with the gentlemanly depreciation of his efforts which he had cultivated throughout his career: "In presenting for your amusement the trifles whch have been occasionally composed at my leisure

hours, I assume nothing beyond the negative merit of not having written any thing unfavorable to the interests of freedom,
humanity, and virtue." Of the new material, the only matter of
particular interest was a brief statement included in his "Preface to the Ninth Edition of the Poem on the Happiness of America" which passed unnoticed at the time. An explanation of
one of the "many circumstances" that "conspired to give facility to the execution of the task he had imposed upon himself"
in writing the poem, it lengthened the shadow of a notion expressed in the Cincinnati speech by suggesting that the great
scenes of nature in America called into action a more lively
poetic diction. "Our minds," he said with reference to himself
as a typical American, "imperceptibly impressed with the
novelty, beauty or sublimity of surrounding objects, gave energy to the language which expressed our sensations." Two
years later he again hovered around the same idea with a reference to "Columbian Bards .... to nature's guidance true";
but he never made it wholly clear, and he never let it affect his
own writing to the extent of causing him to renounce the florid
style in favor of the language of "humble and rustic life." The
passage referring to the lively figures of *A Poem on the Happiness of America* is of interest, however, because it calls attention
to the ease with which a poet can acquire a style under one set
of influences, practice it without strict regard to its origins, and
eventually attribute it to an entirely different cause. If the
atmosphere of psychological theory in the late eighteenth century was such that Humphreys showed even the slightest inclination to attribute the habitual use of hypotyposis to the im-
perceptible influence of nature upon the mind, it is not surprising that the Preface to *Lyrical Ballads* evolved by the end of the
decade.

III

During the first year of his ministry to Portugal, before he
had become involved in Algerian affairs, Humphreys had sufficient time on his hands to become homesick for his American
friends and literary associates. Accordingly, he composed, for

the benefit of his friend Trumbull, what he described in a letter
to Mrs. Nathanael Greene as "a tolerably humorous account" of
his peregrinations; "but," he added, "what was more in the
Character of one of your wicked wits, I never sent it. And now
ten to one, but that the wit is lost to all eternity." He also occupied his time in composing a sentimental comedy which he
admitted was "an excellent one" (although he did not finish it
until twenty-four years later) and another work which was completed immediately as *A Poem on Industry, Addressed to the
Citizens of the United States of America*. The latter he sent to
Washington in a letter dated July 23, 1792, with the request
that it be given to the president's secretary, Tobias Lear, for
publication. Humphreys accompanied it with the comment:

> As far as I can judge of my own heart, I conceived myself to have been
> animated by love of Country in writing the Poem. I own I have received
> pleasure in composing, however others may or may not in perusing it, for it is
> not for me to decide how I have succeeded in the execution. I have endeav-
> oured to polish the versification as highly as in anything I have before written.
> The conceptions are mostly the result of observation. And the sentiments, I
> know, are such as comport perfectly well with Patriotism and good morals. I
> wish never to write anything but what is friendly to the cause of Humanity.

The poem itself (which was eventually brought out by Mathew
Carey in October, 1794) was less rhetorical and pretentious
than any of the author's other long compositions. It made a
direct attempt to impress upon the minds of Americans that
"nothing is more essential to the Wealth and Prosperity of a
State, than *Industry*," in the sense of honest toil. Humphreys
made his attitude clear in the opening invocation:

> Tho' many a nation hate thy heavy yoke,
> Thee, *Industry!* a votary dares invoke:
> Inspire my song, my nation's earliest friend!
> Prompt, with kind aid, rude nature's works to mend,
> With all the arts of polish'd life to bless,
> And half thy ills, Humanity! redress.

Humphreys, like Dwight, believed strongly in the moral value
of work; and he attacked both slavery and current notions of
the noble savage on the grounds that one encouraged and the
other idealized sloth. His poem represented a combination of

motives: the desire to cultivate steady habits among his countrymen, sincere humanitarianism, and a rather paternal, special
interest in all the activities that had come under his personal
observation. Since Hamilton had not yet made his report on
manufactures in the United States, Humphreys was not yet
conscious of patriotic reasons for encouraging factories; but his
friends' woolen mill in Hartford stimulated him to say a few
words in favor of weaving. His New England breeding similarly
encouraged him to find humanitarian reasons for making maple
sugar: each productive bush meant a demand for fewer African
slaves in the cane fields of the West Indies. His belief in the
moral value of industry led him to approve child labor on the
plantation:

> Bid infant bands, with little fingers, cull
> The pendant pods of vegetable wool.

It also induced him to believe that the factory system, with its
employment of labor unfit for heavy work, was a humanitarian
enterprise:

> Teach little hands to ply mechanic toil,
> Cause failing age o'er easy tasks to smile;
> With gladness kindle rescu'd beauty's eye,
> And cheek with health's inimitable dye;
> So shall the young, the feeble find employ,
> And hearts, late nigh to perish, leap for joy!

Such lines might have been suspect fifteen years later when he
had begun to "Teach little hands to ply mechanic toil" for his
own profit; but, written nearly a decade before he learned that
he would not live his life out as a gentleman diplomat, they
show merely that when he did turn to child labor at Humphreysville he adopted his profit-making scheme with a clear conscience
and a conscious feeling of benevolence.

A Poem on Industry, as usual with Humphreys' literary works,
had a specific immediate purpose other than the general patriotic one which was openly avowed. The condition of the American prisoners among the Algerines was bad, the attitude of the
Barbary powers toward the United States was openly insulting,
and Humphreys had maintained since 1786 that his country

should take vigorous military action if the situation demanded it. Accordingly, part of the concluding section of the poem was devoted to urging the men who had defeated Britain on land to build a navy and fight Algiers on the sea:

> Now stronger motives kindle nobler rage,
> And rouse in Nature's cause the riper age;
> With added heat, each heart heroic warm,
> String the tough nerve, and brace the brawny arm.
> Let not that arm its pond'rous strength relax—
> Give me the music of the sounding axe—
> Let the keen adze the stubborn live-oak wound—
> And anvils shrill, with the stronger strokes resound,
> Give me the music, where the dock equips,
> With batt'ries black and strong, the battle-ships,
> To whose broad decks, the hast'ning crowds repair,
> And shouts, and drums, and cannon, rend the air.

He also had planned to include in his poem a rather elaborate description of Portugal; but, apparently feeling that it would lessen the patriotic effect of the whole, he omitted it from the published version and contented himself with a brief tribute to the country and to Prince Henry the Navigator, concluding with a strong—and apparently sincere—expression of love for his native land. Humphreys was sufficiently eager to do something about the Mediterranean problems to embarrass his government by writing an appeal to the people, which was published in several American newspapers, and he was eventually put in charge of the business. For once, however, his poetic appeal for action was part of an indiscretion. It earned only an official reprimand and neither forwarded nor was intended to forward his own career.

During the years of his ministry to Spain, from 1796 to 1801, Humphreys maintained his literary character by writing poems for the annual dinner arranged for American residents and visitors to Madrid on the Fourth of July. He was growing self-conscious over the facts that "no blossoms of wit could flourish amidst the sterility of official notes" and that he was confining his use of the English language almost exclusively to official notes and to occasional conversations with visitors. Accordingly, as he relaxed from the cares of diplomacy into the arms of the Muses, he turned with more attention than ever before to the great English poets for direction concerning the propriety of his behavior. If internal evidence may be trusted, his two major guides were Milton and Pope—the first for his "conceptions" and the second for his versification. For Humphreys demonstrated his own complete severance from modern streams of English poetry, in 1803, by a statement that his time was one "when, in the British dominions and the United States, every poet who aspires to celebrity, strives to approach the perfection of Pope in the sweetness of versification." The result of his segregation from other men of letters and of the emotional occasions for which his poems were written was that the two Fourth of July poems he kept and published were less pretentious than his earlier verse and more completely personal. The first of these, *A Poem on the Love of Country*, written for the 1799 celebration, illustrates the personal emotional quality that produced the lines:

> And oft in recollection sad, but dear
> I soothe long absence with a secret tear—
> Where'er I wander, or where'er I rest,
> The love of country warms my lab'ring breast;
> And as the flame within my bosom burns,
> Each trembling feeling tow'rds Columbia turns.
> 'Tis like the steel whose magnet-instinct guides
> O'er unknown oceans and bewild'ring tides,
> And though the lone bark, wrapp'd in darkness, roll,
> Still points its path and vibrates to the pole.

The entire poem of over four hundred couplets seems to have been deeply serious in its insistence that patriotism was not incompatible with philanthropy and the love of mankind and in its scorn for "affected sensibility" which destroys real feeling by "generalizing" it:

> I hate that new philosophy's strange plan,
> That teaches love for all things more than man;
> To love all mortals save our friends alone,
> To hold all countries dearer than our own;
> To take no int'rest in the present age,
> Rapt to th' unborn with philanthropic rage;
> To make the tutor'd eyes with tears o'er flow,
> More for fictitious than for real woe!

Humphreys' reaction against the *philosophes* was clear enough. It was also clear that the French army no longer represented to him "the forces of liberty" that it had represented a few years before, for he was not a good enough diplomat to refrain from denouncing "the Roman pride" that braved the world in order "To make for one free state all nations slaves." Part of his feeling undoubtedly came from an antagonism to Napoleon's military ventures—an attitude which, though expressed only by indirection, caused him to look back with enthusiasm upon the soldiers of the American Revolution and introduce into his poem a roll call of heroes almost comparable in length to Homer's catalogue of ships.

Of his two Fourth of July poems Humphreys said that one contained "a dissertation on, and the other an exemplification of, real Patriotism." The second, *A Poem on the Death of General Washington*, was another of Humphreys' attempts to "elevate the rising generation to emulate the exalted deeds of their fathers" through the influence of "the examples of illustrious men placed in action before them." Though undoubtedly an expression of deep and sincere feeling on the part of the man who had been aide de camp to the general and private secretary to the president, it was formal and even stilted in its expression of grief, illustrating perhaps better than any of the author's other works his contentions concerning the evil effects of disassociation from the habitual and natural use of his native language. He devoted most of the poem to a survey of Washington's life, career, and character, holding him up to emulation as a model in peace and war, especially in opposition to the great man of contemporary Europe. Humphreys again refused to attack Napoleon by name, yet the following lines were certainly italicized not because of their echoes from Gray but in order to call attention to a contrast which leaped into every reader's mind:

> Soon show'd our chief, retiring to his farms,
> *The pomp of pow'r for him display'd no charms:*
> He show'd *th' ambitious, who would mount a throne,*
> *Greatness is seated in the mind alone.*

The appointment of Joel Barlow as actual negotiator in the effort to free American seamen in Algiers had already been made necessary because Humphreys did not have the approval or support of the French government; and, if the minister to Spain made a habit of dropping such broad hints of disapprobation toward a friendly power, it is not surprising that one of Jefferson's early acts as president of the United States was to call him home.

Humphreys reached America in June, 1802, and, as usual, celebrated his change in fortune by the publication of a book. This time it was a second edition, revised and enlarged, of his *Miscellaneous Works*, which appeared two years after his return. The volume was the most pretentious work yet issued by one of the Connecticut poets. In addition to the general dedication to the Duke de la Rochefoucauld it contained special dedications of the poem on industry to "His Royal Highness the Prince Regent of Portugal" and the poem on the love of country to "his Majesty Louis, King of Etruria, Hereditary Prince of Parma, Infant of Spain"—the latter dedication being accompanied by a letter of acceptance. The list of approximately five hundred subscribers was headed by the King and Queen of Spain, the president of the United States, and other people of importance, and included large numbers of Spanish, Portuguese, and Swedish diplomats, members of the royal household in Spain, and officers in the American consular service. International diplomats did not do so well by Humphreys as the Continental Army had done by Barlow when he published *The Vision of Columbus;* but the list of subscribers was unusually distinguished, and Humphreys probably took as much pride in it as in any other dozen pages in his book. The volume also contained an engraved portrait of the author, a reproduction of the gold medal recently presented to him by the Massachusetts Society for Promoting Agriculture, and a considerable number of additional complimentary reviews, notices, and letters, including a series of friendly personal letters from Washington.

The new edition contained all Humphreys' works printed in

the 1790 volume with the exception of the text of *The Widow of Malabar* and the Prologue and Epilogue to *Athaliah*, but much of the reprinted material was extensively revised. Over two hundred of the concluding couplets were dropped from *A Poem on the Happiness of America* and reprinted with some changes and additions as "A Poem on the Future Glory of the United States"; this he accompanied by a statistical table of American growth from 1774 to 1799, in order to "shelter us in the future from such ridicule as one British reviewer attempted heretofore to throw on American writers for their propensity to poetical predictions." The amount of revision in this case, however, was less than might be expected, for Humphreys simply reprinted his earlier prophetic battle scenes as descriptions of actual fact and followed them by a long prose note justifying and urging the war with Tripoli. As he looked back over the years between the original composition of the poem and its revision he found occasion for optimism in the establishment of the Constitution and the binding force of the "triple cord" of balanced legislative, executive, and judicial powers. He was also able to retain his optimism concerning the future, despite the post-diplomatic violence of his opinions concerning the French Revolution:

> From disappointed hope, the baffled plan,
> That promis'd bliss with liberty to man;
> From tyrant force too long to be withstood,
> Corruption, terror, ruin, fire and blood;
> A Pow'r shall rise to bid the Discord cease,
> And join all nations in the leagues of Peace.

His optimism, however, was by no means clear-cut or definite in its meaning; for the poet, while retaining his earlier expressions of confidence in the power of commerce to unite mankind in leagues of mutual interest, seems to have had reference to religion as the "Pow'r" mentioned in these lines. There is no evidence that he dreamed of the political union which Barlow first prophesied in *The Vision of Columbus* and of which he was still dreaming during this period. Humphreys, as usual, was adopting a middle-of-the-way—or, perhaps more accurately, an indeterminate—position. He shared the conservative feeling that the Revolution represented an apocalyptic beastliness, but he did not have the provincial inability to view the situation without hysteria which characterized Timothy Dwight. Humphreys had a fair share of the dispositional quality which caused Dwight to fall into imaginative gaucherie when he contemplated distant events and strange ideas, but his wider experience shaded some of the black and white differences so apparent to his friend.

A Poem on Industry, which was reprinted as "A Poem on the Industry of the United States of America," was more extensively and meticulously revised than any of the other works in the book. Some of the revisions clarified earlier phrasing, some made the verse more regular than it had been before, and some, unfortunately, revealed how much less discriminating Humphreys had become in the use of his native language during the decade of residence abroad. The following lines from the poet's original invocation of "Industry" were, to be sure, not much to boast of:

> Hail, mighty Pow'r! whose vivifying breath
> Wakes vegetation on the barren heath;

But when they were changed to

> Thou, toil! that mak'st, where our young empire grows,
> The wilderness bloom beauteous as the rose,

they exhibited an indifference to cacophonies and clichés which was a possible, through by no means necessary, result of his infrequent use of English. The most important revisions in the poem, however, were the product of the different purpose toward which it was directed. Humphreys was no longer anxious to encourage an attack upon the Algerines, and he no longer had any reason to express admiration for Portugal. He was returning to New England, setting up a business in Connecticut, and settling down among old friends for the rest of his life. Accordingly, he removed the latter parts of the original poem and substituted extravagant praise for Connecticut as the "model of free states," the home of "inventive genius," "common-sense," "sober habits," middle-class manners and economy, Yale College, and Timothy Dwight. With his rather elaborate celebration of the geography of his paradise among the rocks, Humphreys approached the pattern of demonstrative oration much more nearly in this new section of the poem than he had in the descriptions of Portugal, which he suppressed from the first version; but he did not follow the classical formula for praising countries with sufficient accuracy to be charged with a deliberate return to the methods of his early verse. The concluding passages, in any case, were words of advice rather than praise. He no longer called for a navy but called instead for better doctors and more honest lawyers; and in the final lines he took the privilege of a "time-taught bard" and a military hero to advise the youth of the land:

> Ye junior patriots, listen! learn, my friends!
> How much your lot on industry depends:
> For God, a God of order, ne'er design'd,
> Equal conditions for the humankind.
> Equality of rights your bliss maintains,
> While law protects what honest labour gains.
> Your great exertions by restraint uncheck'd,
> Your gen'rous heat undamp'd by cold neglect;
> The wide career for freemen open lies,
> Where wealth, and pow'r, and honour yield the prize.
> Yet should dark discord's clouds your land o'ercast,
> Lost is your freedom and your empire past.
> Be union yours! To guard your union, heav'n
> The general government, in *trust*, has giv'n:
> Then, when ere long your fathers sleep in dust,
> Preserve, like vestal fire, that *sacred* TRUST!

The form of address, the reprobation of the Declaration of Independence, and the sanctification of the Constitution—these all reflect the complacency which Humphreys wore like a robe of state throughout his late career. He wore it naturally, for he had been a hero-worshiper from his youth; and, as his heroes receded into the past, they became the giants of the earth, and their lengthening institutional shadows grew until they covered the entire field of activity proper for "junior patriots" whose business was to listen and learn from their elders.

The other verse published for the first time in the 1804 volume consisted of twelve sonnets which the poet confessed to have found "upon lately looking over" his papers and to have published for their interest as representations of points of view peculiar to the times at which they were written. The first three, in a modified Spenserian form, were supposedly written during the early, experimental stage of his career; the others ranged in time from the prospect of peace in 1783 to the author's reception of the news of Washington's death. Of the latter, the eleventh, addressed to the prince of Brazil in 1797, was in the form of the first three, and the twelfth, on Washington, was a modified version of the Shakespearean sonnet. All the others represented a six-rhyme compromise between the Shakespearean and the Italian forms, with the concluding Alexandrine characteristic of the first three; they ranged in subject matter from elegiac, personal commentary, and observations "On Life" and "On the Immortality of the Soul" to "On a Night-Storm at Sea," inspired by actual experience, and "On the Murders Committed by the Jacobin Faction in the Early Period of the French Revolution." They cast little light on Humphreys' own opinions or points of view at particular times or upon the history of the sonnet form in America, for it seems highly probable that if they were "found" in 1802 they were carefully revised for publication, according to Humphreys' custom. One thing made clear by the second edition of the *Miscellaneous Works* is that the author did revise his work and did so dramatically—that is, by introducing into his poems new knowledge and later attitudes as though they had been there from the beginning.

When Humphreys removed his call for a United States navy from *A Poem on Industry* for its second edition, he did not change his mind about its desirability, even though the establishment of peace in 1802 had made the need less vital than it had apparently been a decade before. At any rate, he included in his works a prose treatise entitled "Thoughts on the Necessity of Maintaining a Navy in the United States of America," which consisted of an expansion of the rejected lines of the poem with some additions, such as the suggestion for "maritime conscription" or the raising in time of peace of a "naval militia" which would be able to man a war fleet in time of emergency. Probably written at some time during the nineties, it advocated

a navy because of the English example and because of the rav-
ages of French privateers and the Barbary corsairs, and it concluded with an affirmation of the freedom of the seas as a part
of the divine plan: "It is time the ocean should be made what
heaven intended it, an open highway for all mankind." By the
time he was preparing his book for publication, however, Humphreys was more immediately concerned with building up a
trained army in the United States as a guaranty against invasion. "General Washington," he reminded his countrymen, "had
few projects nearer to his heart, than that of providing a safe
and competent defense, in time of peace, for the security of the
country in time of war"; and Humphreys, asking "Who can
count on the stable enjoyment of peace, in the convulsed situation of Europe?" printed the "Considerations on the Means of
Improving the Public Defense" which he had addressed to
Governor Trumbull in September, 1803. The philosophical
theories that had justified the French Revolution had been overthrown by such actual events as the invasions of Holland,
Switzerland, and Italy, he held.

> Notwithstanding the vaunted perfectibility of human nature, we cannot
> conceal from ourselves, that the rage of domination still invents excuses for
> aggression. Lessons, on invasions of peaceable and distant States, are too dis-
> tinctly printed in characters of blood, not to be legible. . . . . Shall we, struck
> with judicial blindness not be able to read, for our own benefit, the book of
> their destinies? Or rests the day in darkness ere long to dawn on our own
> encrimsoned land, when we too, by want of military spirit and national union,
> shall become the vile vassals of insidious and powerful invaders, and be com-
> prehended in the ignominious list of those degraded States which have lost
> their independent rank among the nations of the earth?

His answer, as befitted a hero, was "No; never shall mortal eye
witness that sight"; but his considerations were to the effect
that it might be prevented only by drafting and training a
militia which would avoid, on the one hand, the danger of a
standing army and, on the other, the even greater danger of
"supineness."

By this time Humphreys was taking up his permanent role as
adviser to his countrymen on all sorts of subjects, and the prose
pamphlets printed in his *Miscellaneous Works* were by no means

limited to politics. At a hint from the Massachusetts Society for Promoting Agriculture he prepared, during the summer of 1802, a "Dissertation on the Breed of Spanish Sheep Called Merino," dealing with the procedure he had employed in importing them into the United States, the distinguishing characteristics of the breed, and the possibilities they offered for improving the agriculture, manufactures, and commerce of the country. He also printed "A Memorial of the Society of the Cincinnati in Connecticut," which he had assisted in drawing up as a request for an act of incorporation by the general assembly of the state, and he appended a copy of the brief speech he had delivered before the governor and council in support of the request. Their plea, which grew out of a desire to protect the funds of an organization that had become benevolent in purpose and was on the verge of changing membership as a result of the deaths among its founders, was rejected by the upper house of the legislature, with the consequence that Humphreys' only other publication of 1804 was *A Valedictory Discourse, Delivered before the Cincinnati of Connecticut, in Hartford, July 4th, 1804, at the Dissolution of the Society*. Much of the discourse, in its review of the history and purposes of the organization, was what might be expected; much, in its discussion of the "Civil Virtues—Moderation, Industry, Justice and Valour," was commonplace; but parts of it are of interest because they reveal the contradictions and difficulties in which Humphreys always became involved through his indeterminate stand on many of the new questions which were arising at the time. For example, he had the usual "respectable man's" appreciation of the frontier:

It has been apprehended that the rapid increase of wealth in a country like ours, where the citizens in the seaports, are animated by such a spirit of commercial enterprize, would produce refinements; that refinements would be attended with luxury and effeminancy; and that these would be followed by the loss of liberty. Were all parts of our *settlements* like our large towns, this might possibly be the case. But the vast quantity of land to be settled, its superiority in quality over most of that which has already been located, the facility of obtaining farms by persons in moderate circumstances, and their natural propensity to make such a permanent provision for their families, will doubtless continue Agriculture as the principal business, in United America, for many years. We need not fear that trade will gain an undue ascendancy in our affairs.

Yet he strongly opposed the opening of further frontier regions by means of the Louisiana Purchase. Part of his opposition was based on his antagonism to the "Land-Jobbers and Negro-Owners" who would profit at the expense of "the *sale* and *improvement* of our other unlocated districts" (in which he himself retained claims as late as 1813); but part grew out of an attitude he himself had satirized seventeen years before in the *Anarchiad*—the notion that a republic had positive geographical limitations—and part was based on his very reasons for appreciating the frontier—that it would "likewise thin the old settlements of inhabitants, by attracting settlers from them." He had reached the end of the intellectual path on which he had started at the beginning of his literary career, and the end was one of inconsistencies and incoherences. He was suffering the mentally—but, unfortunately, not vocally—paralyzing results of using his audience as his only point of reference in his written work, with no attempt to check his words against any central core of private beliefs. The process started when he adopted classical rhetoric—the art of persuasion—as his first literary guide, and it was encouraged by his habitual hero-worship and the conventional standards of second-rate diplomacy. Had his name not been "Numps," these influences might not have been so effective; but, granting a person not too bright to begin with, they produced a type which is all too common, although it rarely reveals itself so clearly in literature.

IV

Humphreys' return to America marked his last change in occupation, and his publications in 1804 marked his last public appearance as a man of letters for more than a decade. Yet he continued to maintain his gentlemanly interest in literature. When he took his homesick wife abroad in 1806–7, he also carried with him the manuscript of the "excellent" sentimental comedy on which he had been working in Portugal fifteen years before, and while in England he submitted it to the criticism of William Gifford. The author of the *Baviad* and the *Maeviad* found it sufficiently different from the popular drama of the time to justify an expression of "favorable sentiments" and to make specific suggestions for its improvement. Humphreys, however, seems to have found no inducement at the time for completing the work: the revisions suggested were perhaps too elaborate for him to undertake while traveling with a socially minded wife, and at home the Connecticut law providing a fifty-dollar fine for each appearance of a professional actor reflected an attitude that did not stimulate dramatic composition. Hence, despite Gifford's encouragement, the manuscript remained untouched until the winter of 1814, when plans for the grand celebration at Humphreysville called it forth from obscurity.

The Yankey in England, as it was finally acted (by amateurs) and published, was hardly a credit to Gifford's reputation as a critic, and the then powerful editor of the *Quarterly Review* may have found the author's fulsome prefatory letter an embarrassing claim for patronage. It is true that the critic's mind, like the author's, might have been "perfectly satisfied" with "the moral tendency of the whole"; and he may have been equally satisfied by the meticulous care with which Humphreys distinguished between the "gay" and the "serious" scenes in a sentimental comedy. But the main plot (which was finished while the play had still another act to go) was a poorly combined structure of stock situations, acted out by superficial, conventional characters—a French nobleman-adventurer, two schoolboy friends who had fought on different sides in the American Revolution and were reunited by the discovery that a long-lost son of one was in love with a long-lost daughter of the other, a wealthy but somewhat mysterious countess of questionable morality, and a respectable American woman who proved to be the long-lost wife of one character and the long-lost mother of another. The subplot was even slighter, but, historically at least, it is more interesting, for its hero, Newman, represented a conscious attempt to portray an American type. Humphreys insisted that he "should be represented as possessed of goodsense, with a little propensity to Yankey drollery. These dispositions should be accompanied by a faculty of judging charac-

ters correctly, together with abilities and information sufficiently extensive to render him useful in almost any situation."
He exemplified, in short, Americans of the type that frequently
went abroad, made their fortunes, and "offer respectable models
for imitation."

Newman, the product of a grammar school or academy, was
also designed to show that "there is less apparent difference between well educated men in Europe and America than is commonly imagined"; and his appearance in the play allowed Humphreys to exploit freely his major comic character, the "Yankey," without giving the impression that the latter was a "typical" American. The Yankee Doolittle, although contributing
nothing to either plot, was the most important character in the
play and the one most carefully analyzed in the author's Preface. Humphreys exhibited him as a specimen of the "inhabitants of the interior parts of New-England, as distinguished by
a peculiar idiom and pronunciation, as well as by a peculiarity
of character" which was "made up of contrarieties":

simplicity and cunning; inquisitive from inexperience and want of knowledge
of the world; believing himself to be perfectly acquainted with whatever he
partially knows; tenacious of prejudices; docile, when rightly managed; when
otherwise treated, independent to obstinacy; easily betrayed into ridiculous
mistakes; incapable of being overawed by external circumstances; suspicious,
vigilant and quick of perception, he is ever ready to parry or repel the attacks
of raillery, by retorts of rustic and sarcastic, if not of original and refined wit
and humor.

Humphreys was more successful in this prefatory characterization of the Yankee than he was in creating the specimen which
he placed before the audience; for Doolittle is so nearly a perfect
example of the conventional stage Yankee that it is difficult to
accept, at its face value, the author's suggestion that he was experimenting with "a new character" who might or might not be
"suited to figure on the stage." As secretary to the president of
the United States, Humphreys must have been at least aware
of Royal Tyler's *The Contrast*, which shared honors with his own
The Widow of Malabar as one of the four American plays produced in Philadelphia in 1790 and to the publication of which
President Washington had subscribed. The similarities be-

tween Humphreys' Newman and Tyler's Manly, as well as the resemblance of Doolittle to Jonathan, suggest the possibility that *The Contrast* was the original source of inspiration for *The Yankey in England*—a source which may easily have faded out of the author's memory during the twenty-four crowded years between the comedy's inception and its completion.

Yet, if Humphreys laid claim to undue originality in his creation of a humorous character type, he failed to exact proper credit for the accuracy with which he represented the character's dialect. After his long residence abroad Humphreys was unusually sensitive to "Yankey peculiarities" in speech, and he apparently took particular care with them while revising his play for production, appending an eight-page "Glossary" of "words used in a peculiar sense, in this Drama; or pronounced with an accent or emphasis in certain districts, different from the modes generally followed by the inhabitants of the United States; including new-coined American, obsolete English, and low words in general." Doolittle spoke a much more consistent dialect than had Jonathan in *The Contrast*, and the young man who played the part achieved "universal admiration" for his assumed "dialect and pronunciation" before an audience of "clergymen, magistrates, selectmen, and other respectable citizens" of Connecticut, all of whom were thoroughly familiar with the speech represented. Some of the humor of the play came from the characteristic Yankee elements in Doolittle's personality and some from the occasional broad and even feculent puns of which he was supposedly unconscious, but much of it was apparently derived from the skilful use of dialect before an intelligently critical audience; and the otherwise undistinguished drama bears witness to Humphreys' success as one of the earliest careful students of the American language.

The publication of *The Yankey in England* seems to have restored, in some measure, Humphreys' old desire to make a show in the world as a man of letters. But he was no longer the man who thought of literary composition as the means to worldly success. He was an honored leader in agriculture and industry and an honorary general in the army, so well known that he was

able to sign his next book merely by his initials and a list of his
distinctions: "LL.D. Fellow of the Royal Society of London;
Honorary member of the Bath and West of England Society;
President of the Society for promoting Agriculture in the State
of Connecticut; and member of many Scientific and Literary
Societies in the U.S. of America." He was past threescore and
was satisfied with his position. For the first time in his literary
life he could relax when he took his pen in hand. Accordingly,
when he prepared *A Discourse on the Agriculture of the State of
Connecticut, and the Means of Making it More Beneficial to the
State*, he allowed himself to range from high, patriotic seriousness to easy, humorous irony—even going as far as to become
facetious over the sacred steady habits of Connecticut and the
fear of innovation. The main body of his address, however, as
befitted the times, was serious; and he urged a co-operative
effort to advance and promote agriculture, both as a way out of
the post-war depression and as a means of counteracting the
current tendency toward emigration. "It is not for me," he
said of the West, "who, first of any man in America, predicted
the rising glory of that region, to express my regrets for the fulfilment of my predictions, at so early a period." But he had no
use for the "barbarous liberty" of the savage, which "still finds
its advocates and admirers"; and he believed that good men
should be convinced that it was to their interest to stay at home.
Accordingly, he preached a doctrine that combined Poor Richard's thrift with Sir Humphrey Davy's agricultural chemistry,
urging good sense and further experimentation and suggesting
that a department of agriculture be instituted in the contemplated "National University." It was a rambling and uneven,
but thoughtful and sincere, address, and it concluded appropri-
ately with an original poem, Humphreys' last: "The Farmers'
Harvest Hymn" beginning "Rise! all who venerate the plough."

This *Discourse* should have been Humphreys' last appearance
as a man of letters, for the succeeding volume was a remarkable
anticlimax. It might have grown out of the author's awareness
of a doubt concerning his actual membership in the Royal

Society and a desire to settle the question by a notable contribution to its discoveries. The result was *Letters from the Hon. David Humphreys, F.R.S. To the Rt. Hon. Sir Joseph Banks, President of the Royal Society, London; Containing Some Account of the Serpent of the Ocean, Frequently Seen in Gloucester Bay.* The author, unfortunately, never succeeded in getting a real glimpse of this great wonder of the month of August, 1817, but he busied himself getting affidavits of the "facts": the monster was as big around as a flour barrel, sixty to a hundred or more feet in length, with a movement like a "caterpiller, but infinitely more rapid." There were also rumors of a companion female serpent, and by the end of September Humphreys was able to report that a three-foot specimen of the breed had crawled upon dry land near Loblolly Cove and had been killed among some whortleberry bushes ("on which," his correspondent assured him, "are still some whortleberries"). By November 5 he was reporting on a new one seen on Long Island Sound, and his scientific enthusiasm had reached a high pitch: "An excitement has . . . . been produced for investigating this department of natural history. The spirit of inquiry and research has gone forth. . . . . The field is illimitable; and, if the cultivation shall be encouraged and prosecuted, the fruit will become incalculably abundant." Practical considerations were also aroused: he referred judiciously to the dangers to fishing and shipping, and he estimated the value of one large serpent, stuffed for exhibition purposes, at fifty thousand dollars. Other people were equally impressed. As scientists, a committee from the Linnaean Society of New England dissected the small specimen killed in the whortleberry bushes and published an account of their findings with illustrative plates and affidavits from witnesses who had seen its supposed parent; and Humphreys reported, on November 14, that when he "last left New Haven, Captain Lee of the Revenue Cutter, was taking on board some additional four pound cannon, with the determination of cruising assiduously in search of him." The newspapers were full of the excitement, and Phineas T. Barnum, who had just mem-

orized the alphabet in the interior of Connecticut, may have
spelled out his first unassigned reading lesson from these reports
of great doings on the coast.

But whether Sir Joseph Banks read of them remains a mystery. The Royal Society did not acknowledge Humphreys' report or record its acceptance. In any case it would have made
no difference to the author, for he sent his letters to the press in
the last months of his life and was dead before the little volume
could have crossed the ocean.

V

The most common type of autobiography was once described
by James Russell Lowell as a man's "design for an equestrian
statue of himself." In that sense nearly all Humphreys' writings
were autobiographical. Although he professed to write—as a
gentleman should—only upon subjects of general interest and
public benefit, he rarely took his pen in hand without sketching
himself to a better advantage than his subject. The basic design was set in his first published book—that of a patriotic, high-
minded officer and gentleman. But he elaborated upon it for
thirty-seven years. When he first went abroad he added a representation of the guardian of American honor in Europe who was
quick to give the lie to slander and to meet threats with defiance.
At home again, he revealed himself as the guardian of public
institutions, morals, and manners, and the enricher of provincial
culture. Later he sketched in the diplomat, moving at ease in
the best Old World society and expressing properly restrained
indignation at the revolt of the French masses, while trying to
improve the material condition of the masses in his own country. Still later he broadened the design to include the benevolent industrialist, the patron of arts and agriculture, and,
finally, the scientist. No early sketch ever gave way wholly to a
later one: his improvements were always elaborations on the
original, and in them all appeared just enough homely details,
delicate personal allusions, to show that the hero was human.

The statue has been carved according to the design. Every

student who reads of the Connecticut Wits in a modern edition must also read that "perhaps the most attractive of the entire group was David Humphreys." Yet it seems hardly possible that any man could have illustrated more perfectly the most unattractive characteristic of American writers during the period following the Revolution—their top-heavy pretentiousness. A more ruthless critic than Lowell has remarked that a good writer achieves dignity by imitating an iceberg, which keeps seven-eighths of its substance beneath the surface. Such a thing was never dreamed of in the philosophy of Humphreys or his American contemporaries. Their country was already beginning to hurtle toward its place in the world, and they had to keep up with it, for their United States contained no cultural eddies into which an educated, well-informed, and energetic man might retire while his literary talent settled at its proper balance and its excrescences fell off or melted away. The times and circumstances encouraged belletristic activity that was seven-eighths, if not wholly, superficial in its results. For a poet to suspend the motion of his human blood in an uncertain effort to attain Wordsworthian harmony and depth was uneconomical, unpatriotic, unthinkable. While men like Hamilton and Jefferson were making the laws of the new country, men like Humphreys felt that they should be equally energetic about making its songs. Their minds were often concerned, primarily, with other things. But it hardly mattered. Most of their readers were even more concerned with other things and were not inclined to look beneath the surface, if the author's intentions appeared good and the surface was sufficiently "American."

The work of David Humphreys offers a remarkable illustration of this characteristic superficiality, because his own superficiality was so honest and wholehearted. The young man who, as a student, turned toward rhetoric instead of scholarship continued to take appearances for realities throughout his life. While so many of his contemporaries were growing in stature, he was blowing himself up with pretensions and thinking (for was not his name *Numps?*) that he was growing too. These pretensions dominate his writings, and the character of his age was such that no one paused long enough, or took the trouble, to puncture them. He was one of his country's foremost writers until he was sixty years old, and he remained so in his own mind until the day of his death. His verse and his prose reveal the beginnings of that great American "Front" which may still be so widely seen in literature and in life. And they also reveal that this front, whatever it may accomplish in life, cannot support a very admirable or very enduring literature.

CHAPTER IX

CITIZEN JOEL BARLOW

I

JOEL BARLOW'S change of residence from America to Europe was the result of accident. His long delay before settling upon a profession left him, at the age of thirty-two, still without an "interest" in the world; and as an unoccupied lawyer he had had nothing to lose by contributing his services to the Susquehanna Company and so entering, through the poor man's door, the edifice of high finance and extravagant speculation. By November, 1787, he had become an agent for the Ohio Company, which exhibited sufficient confidence in him, during the following spring, to make him a member of a committee to examine the reports of other agents. When the Rev. Manasseh Cutler, the genius of the company, joined forces with Colonel William Duer to form the Scioto Association, he took Barlow with him into the new enterprise and had him appointed European agent as a substitute for Royal Flint, who was prevented by a sudden illness from going abroad. The poet-lawyer landed in France on June 24, 1788. He lacked the experience, business judgment, and specific instructions necessary to the performance of his task; yet when the bubble burst he was one of the few important members of the company whose character remained undamaged by the succeeding investigation. Unable to return home immediately, he interested himself in English and French politics during the winter of 1791–92 and was rewarded with honorary citizenship in the French Republic. While his new interests and activities were stabilizing his opinions and forming his mature character, his practical talents were also developing, for by 1796 he had accumulated a fortune large enough to free him from the driving necessity of earning a living and to enable him to look forward to a future spent in the leisurely practice and patronage of arts and letters.

The nature of his successful business activities was a mystery even to the United States Senate, which, late in 1795, recognized his abilities by making him minister to Algiers; but, whatever they were, they had given him the experience required by the complex negotiations which he successfully carried out. Upon his return to Paris in the summer of 1797, he devoted himself primarily to commerce and literature and at the same time revealed his temperamental kinship to Thomas Jefferson by writing letters of long-range political wisdom to his countrymen, studying new systems of education, and taking an active interest in various scientific gadgets and improved methods of agriculture. Robert Fulton became a member of his household; and Barlow, perhaps remembering the experiments of his schoolmate, David Bushnell, was unfailing in his encouragement of his young friend's attempt to perfect the submarine. His intellectual curiosity was insatiable. He read widely in poetry, history, economics, and religion, and in moral, social, and political philosophy. His long periods of residence in England, France, Germany, and Africa, superimposed upon his rural New England background, gave him a cosmopolitan outlook which few of his contemporaries, of any nationality, possessed. He became, more truly than any other American, a citizen of the world.

He was never quite happy in Europe. But business affairs, political and intellectual interests, his wife's health, and his own dread of stormy weather on the Atlantic all kept him abroad for seventeen years. He spent two additional years traveling in his native land, renewing old friendships, and building the home in Washington which, upon the advice of his classical-minded friends, he named "Kalorama." His library was perhaps the most erudite in America, his collection of paintings, furniture, and French china one of the best, and his cellar one of the finest. As a distinguished and influential private citizen, he directed his mind toward schemes for world peace and plans for a great

national university. Had the United States Congress been free
from factional disputes over foreign affairs, his proposed institution, with Noah Webster as research professor of philology,
might have been established as the first university in the world
to concern itself equally with the advancement and the exten-
sion of learning, and the influence of the Johns Hopkins University might have been anticipated by two generations. But
Barlow was not allowed to profit by the approaching "era of
good feeling" or to enjoy for more than four years his "beautiful
view" from the hill above Rock Creek. President Madison per-
suaded him, despite solemn premonitions, to serve as minister
plenipotentiary to Napoleon; and he sailed for France, spent a
disappointing year in vain pursuit of "the Corsican," and died
on the bitter retreat from Moscow. His road was the longest of
any of the Connecticut Wits, and he was the only one of them to
die before he had followed it to its proper end.

II

When Barlow sailed for Europe in the summer of 1788 there
was no man in America better fitted to receive and be influenced
by the new ideas that were stirring in England and France at
that time. His disposition had always been buoyant, and, by a
series of fortuitous circumstances, his mind had remained flexible and inquiring. He had passed through the curriculum of
Yale College, through the examination of a committee of Connecticut Congregational ministers, and through a spirited battle
over the federal Constitution without having his opinions settled in any orthodox groove, philosophical, religious, or political.
The requirements of his ambitious philosophical poem had, of
course, forced him to subscribe for a time to a formal intellectual
belief in certain universal, immutable qualities in human nature; but even this belief had recently broken down when he discovered that the humanitarian speculations in Beccaria's little
duodecimo weighed more heavily in his mind than all the authority of Blackstone's folios. The result of balancing Beccaria
against Blackstone, Burlamaqui, and Montesquieu while preparing for his bar examination had given an enduring bias to his

thought. Having been taught by the Scottish philosophers to distrust reasoning as a guiding power in life and being unwilling to accept their own "common sense," he began to lean toward sentiment for guidance. His youthful determination to love mankind if it killed him was changing from an expression of enthusiasm into a rational principle. He had other biases that were to become important. He had a belief in progress which, he had been flattered to discover, he shared with the respectable Dr. Richard Price; and, although he discussed progress as God's plan, he was becoming inclined almost wholly toward emphasizing man's efforts. He had also the characteristic American tendency, widespread after the Revolution, to overestimate the effect of political institutions on human character.

With such leanings he was well fitted to make a place for himself in the intellectual society of a Europe which, within the following year, was to see the birth of utilitarianism as a philosophy, hear Dr. Price's sermon "On the Love of Our Country" and the reverberations that followed, and feel the impact of the French Revolution. Furthermore, the fact that Barlow was one of Price's few American correspondents gave him a point of contact with the circles in London comparable to those into which Thomas Jefferson, then the American minister to France, was introducing him in Paris. But for a while he had no time for indulging his literary interests. He had to direct his attentions to men of business who might assist the scheme for settling the Scioto country. The year 1789 of all the years in his life, he wrote his wife on New Year's day, had "been the most tedious, the most filled with anxiety and distress." But payments for the land were beginning to come in, the first shipload of settlers was preparing to leave France, and several members of wealthy families, noblemen, and members of the National Assembly were buying land—and by the first of February he felt "in the highest train of success" and in a position to bring his wife abroad to join him. Though his business was not yet finished, he began to have the leisure and disposition to take part in the noncommercial activities about him; and he prepared the formal congratulatory address which he and eleven other Americans presented to the National Assembly on July 10. He was flattered by the "thunderclaps of applause" with which it was received and by the order that it be published; and the reception apparently stimulated his desire "to chin up to the level of the politics of Europe" and reawakened his old literary ambitions, for he immediately sent a copy to America to be published for the edification of his fellow-citizens.

The presentation of the address had been of sufficient importance to keep him from meeting his wife upon her arrival in London, but she joined him in France in time to be with him during his next year of anxiety and distress. For Barlow had never been fully aware of the purely speculative nature of the company by which he was employed, and he was puzzled and worried by the long delay in settling the "colons" he had sent over. He was sure of the rectitude of his own behavior and was trying to hold his end of the enterprise together while awaiting trustworthy news from his associates. By the spring of 1791 he was afraid that the whole affair would be subject to an investigation by the United States government and in early May was making his plans to go to England before returning to America during the summer. It took him longer than he anticipated, however, to "wind off his little affairs in France"; and, after being delayed beyond the season of calm sailing, the Barlows settled down for the winter in London. There Joel looked after his business in a leisurely manner and devoted his spare time to the renovation of society, both by writing and through high converse with Tom Paine, Mary Wollstonecraft (for whom both he and his wife developed a deep and affectionate regard), and a growing circle of politically minded friends.

It was altogether natural that Barlow should have spent his first leisure in literary composition of some sort. He thought of himself primarily as a man of letters rather than as a man of business or a member of any of the professions he had so briefly followed, and he was received in England as "the American poet." Furthermore, coming from the land of the middle-class competence which Timothy Dwight so greatly admired, he had been deeply shocked by the social conditions in Europe and, from disgust at the cynicism of English "democratic" elections, had turned with admiration toward the French Revolution. Yet, as an experienced American who had gone through both a revolution and its reaction, he felt that he had a more temperate and just idea of liberty than almost any European. He had something to say, some advice to give, to the public abroad; and during the last months of 1791 he had for the first time the opportunity to say it. The result was his *Advice to the Privileged Orders, in the Several States of Europe, Resulting from the Necessity and Propriety of a General Revolution in the Principle of Government*, the first part of which was published in London by Joseph Johnson on February 4, 1792.

Privately, he was apologetic about his scheme for the "Renovation of Society." He wrote Abraham Baldwin, on October 17, 1791, that, since he was "obliged to stay in Europe" that winter, he had come to the conclusion that "a little exertion of this kind may do such a phlegmatic, irritable, lazy, uneasy fellow as I am more good than harm." Yet he was also driven by strong feelings, for he exclaimed in the same letter: "I have such a flood of indignation and such a store of argument accumulated in my guts on this subject, that I can hold in no longer; and I think the nurslings of abuses may be stung more to the quick than they have yet been by all the discussions to which the French revolution has given occasion." His indignation was aroused partly by his observations of the social conditions in Europe and partly by the attitude of his personal friends toward Edmund Burke. Barlow had come abroad with a feeling of closer intellectual sympathy toward Richard Price than toward any other Englishman, and Burke's *Reflections on the Revolution in France* aroused his antagonism as much by its attacks on Price's Old Jewry sermon as by its insensitive expressions of contempt for the "swinish multitude." Two of his best new friends—Mary Wollstonecraft and Tom Paine—had already issued public replies to Burke; and his close associates (many of them members of the Revolution Society) were probably engaged in the damning of Edmund Burke in almost every sitting-room the Barlows visited. Thus the atmosphere in which the *Advice* was composed was less "just" and "temperate" than the author's ideas of liberty, and the atmosphere affected the final tone of the book.

The difficulties in determining just how Barlow accumulated the major "arguments" he used in his *Advice* may be illustrated by a characteristic comment found in one of his later notebooks. He had been reading Gibbon's *Essay on the Study of Literature* and made an elaborate note, after which he gave the page reference and added: ". . . . he does not say anything like this, but a reflection of his led me to this." Barlow had indulged in his own train of meditations ever since his school days. But in spite of this propensity it remains possible to find traces in his work of those external "reflections" that stabilized the bias of his mind and provided him with the basic ideas or theories out of which his individual train of argument grew. Like William Godwin, who was settling down at the same time to write out his own scheme for the renovation of society, Barlow followed in the footsteps of Helvetius and Rousseau in taking a "more comprehensive" view of the effect of political institutions than that taken by Tom Paine; but, unlike Godwin, Barlow did not reason logically from a clearly defined, consistent view of human nature. Although his view appeared to be more broadly philosophical than Paine's, his purpose was really almost as polemical, and consequently his argument was more often determined by the persuasiveness of his rhetorical inspiration than by the logical development of a particular point of view. Yet among the inconsistencies of Barlow's *Advice* there seems to be adequate evidence that since coming abroad he had taken at least his first lessons from the *philosophes*.

One of these lessons is revealed in Barlow's dabbling with the doctrine of necessity (which he might have received earlier, from a more respectable source, had he been one of the Yale students to study Edwards' *On the Will*). The title-page of his treatise insisted upon the *necessity* of a general revolution in the principles of government; and Barlow had further emphasized that idea in the "Introduction," which opened with the statement that the French Revolution had been accomplished "be-

yond . . . . the power of retraction at home" and closed with the
statement that he was "taking it for granted . . . . that a general revolution is at hand, whose progress is *irresistible*." Barlow was extremely cautious about subscribing without qualifications to this doctrine, but his tentative use of it gives a clue to
the psychology that lay back of his chapters on "The Feudal
System," "The Church," and "The Military System." The
necessitarianism of the French philosophers (and of Joseph
Priestley, whom Barlow also read), like that of Jonathan Edwards, was based upon the theory that action was determined
by the will, which, in turn, was always governed by motives.
With regard to motives, however, they differed from the Calvinists, holding that man was by nature neither good nor bad—
that his character was formed by the inevitable effect of environment, according to a psychological theory which they often
compared with the theory of gravitation and described as the
primary law of man's nature. This psychological theory, as it
had been expressed in simple terms by Barlow's friend Volney
in a work which Barlow himself was to translate, held that

the secret power that animates the universe . . . . gave [to man] the faculty of
perception. By this faculty, every action injurious to his life gives him a sensation of pain and evil, and every favorable action a sensation of pleasure and
good. By these impressions, sometimes led to avoid what is offensive to his
senses, and sometimes attracted towards the objects that sooth and gratify
them, man has been necessitated to love and preserve his existence. Self-love,
the desire of happiness, and an aversion to pain, are the essential and primary
laws that nature herself imposed on man, that the ruling power, whatever it
be, has established to govern him; and these laws, like those of motion in the
physical world, are the simple and prolific principle of everything that takes
place in the moral world.

Thus education, in the broadest sense of the word, was to many
of these philosophers the only requisite to man's infinite improvement: give him the opportunity to exercise his faculty of
perception, and he would, by the necessity of his nature, choose
good. An argument might arouse the perceptions of the literate
and thoughtful: hence the *Advice to the Privileged Orders*. But
as for the greater part of mankind Barlow wrote:

It depends not on me, or Mr. Burke, or any other writer, or description of
writers, to determine the question, whether a change of government shall take

place, and extend through Europe. It depends on a much more important class of men, the class that cannot write; and in a great measure, on those who cannot read. It is to be decided by men who reason better without books, than we do with all the books in the world.

Such men had to have their perceptions aroused by examples and illustrations: hence the importance of the French Revolution to Europe.

This psychology, or theory of human nature, was a commonplace in the western Europe of Barlow's time. It could be found not only in the writings of the journalist Volney but, with various modifications, in the works of his better-known predecessors: Diderot, Holbach, Helvetius, Rousseau, and Condorcet, and among some of the English followers of David Hartley. Barlow's use of one corollary of this psychology suggests, however, that he was indebted to one particular *philosophe*, the Baron d'Holbach, whose *Le Système de la nature* had been published in 1770 in a volume attributed to the deceased Jean Baptiste de Mirabaud. Although Barlow claimed a certain amount of originality in this part of his work, he gave Holbach's answer, with relatively the same amount of emphasis, to the question: Why, if man's nature makes him necessarily choose good, does he in fact so persistently choose evil? Holbach had traced "the true source of moral evil" to society, in which "authority" upheld "the prejudices and errors which it judges necessary to the assurance and maintenance of its power" and so corrupted the people through the habitual misdirection of their passions.

In short, habit strongly attaches us to our irrational opinions; to our dangerous inclinations; to our blind passion for useless or dangerous objects. Here then is the reason why the most part of mankind find themselves necessarily determined to evil. Here then is the reason why the passions inherent in our nature, and necessary to our conservation, become the instruments of our destruction, and those of the society which they ought to conserve.

Barlow agreed. A "habit of thinking" artificially inculcated in man, he held, caused him to accept the irrational "feudal" organization of society, the dominance of priests, and the existence of a military caste—and the corruption inherent in this authoritative organization of church and state crept downward to perpetuate the habits that kept men opposed to their own best interests. But Barlow did not accept the complete materialism that caused Holbach to deny any distinction between physical and moral man and define habit as "the nature of man modified." The graduate of Yale College merely admitted that "this *habit of thinking* has so much of nature in it, it is so undistinguishable from the indelible marks of the man, that it is . . . . the only point of contact by which men communicate as moral associates." Or, as he expressed the idea again in his chapter on "The Administration of Justice": "It is almost impossible to decide, among moral propensities, which of them belong to nature, and which are the offspring of habit; how many of our vices are chargable on the permanent qualities of man, and how many result from the mutable energies of state."

The reservations with which Barlow adopted the materialistic attitude toward evil may have represented a survival of the ideas used in *The Vision of Columbus*. They may simply indicate a willingness to avoid controversy upon a point irrelevant to his main purpose. Such casual admissions as "mankind are by nature religious" and "honor, like religion, is an original, indelible sentiment of the mind" cast no real light on the question. In either case these theoretical reservations did not affect the practical course of his reasoning along the line of thought for which he claimed originality: a constructive application of the theory of habits that hitherto, he thought, had been used merely to explain the existence of evil. To Barlow a habit of thinking was "a perfectly safe foundation for any system that we may choose to build upon it." It had been used to support "all the arbitrary systems of the world," but it could be used likewise to support "systems of equal liberty and national happiness." As proof he cited "the United States of America," where, he fondly declared,

the science of liberty is universally understood, felt, and practiced, as much by the simple as the wise, the weak as the strong. Their deep-rooted and inveterate habit of thinking is, that *all men are equal in their rights*, that *it is impossible to make them otherwise:* and this being their undisturbed belief, they have no conception how any man in his senses can entertain any other.

"This point once settled," he added, "everything is settled." Such confident assertions pervade the first three chapters of his book. "Banish the mysticism of inequality," he said in his discussion of "The Feudal System," "and you banish almost all the evil attendant on human nature." His comments upon "The Church" are restricted almost entirely to an attack upon it as an institution established by law, but his grounds of objection are the vicious habits of thinking that it promotes. Accordingly, "the difficulty is not that the *church* is corrupted by men; it is, that *men* are corrupted by the church"; and he concluded by holding up the United States as an example of a country in which "the science of liberty and happiness" is promoted by the absence of an established church. In his chapter on "The Military System" he was explicit in saying: "Only admit the original, unalterable truth, *that all men are equal in their rights*, and the foundation of every thing is laid."

Such dogmatic assurance might appear on the surface to be no more than an attempt at self-hypnotism; but beneath it lay a way of thinking that few of the enemies of the equalitarian doctrine (and not many of its later friends) have been able to understand. Barlow did not believe, any more than his friend Thomas Jefferson did, that the equality of man was a physical or scientific "truth" susceptible of proof by "experience direct and positive." Rather it belonged in the category of moral or ethical truths that were "as perceptible when first presented to the mind, as an age or a world of experience could make them." This perception, as even such different philosophers as Rousseau and Holbach agreed, depended less upon observation and reasoning power than upon the natural gravitation of uncorrupted man toward his own happiness. But Barlow was not yet sure whether this movement was dictated by an internal "sense," by an inclination of the sentiments, or by the materialists' "fundamental law of nature." Holbach and Volney, the complete materialists, adhered to the last and upon it based their highly rhetorical appeals for men to yield themselves to the "System of Nature" rather than to the artificial system of contemporary society. For all his apparent assurance, however, Barlow was not willing to go so far. Accordingly, he looked upon such theoretical "truths" as no more than practical hypotheses, holding that the importance of the French Revolution lay in the fact that it was an "experiment" which would "solve a question of the first magnitude in human affairs: Whether *Theory* and *Practice*, which always agree together in things of slighter moment, are really to remain eternal enemies in the highest concerns of men?" Yet his attitude, though it bordered upon the experimental, was not that of the disinterested scientist. It was that of an inventor who wanted to make a cherished idea work. His confident assertions were sledgehammer blows, shaping the physical model of his bright idea according to an established technique. Aristotle's "teaching—*That some are born to command, and others to be commanded*"—had remained true in practice for centuries because of men's "*habit of thinking*"; Barlow wanted to see the new teaching of the French National Assembly—"That *men are born and always continue free and equal in respect to their rights*"—made equally true by a new habit of thinking. He said:

Abstractly considered, there can be no doubt of the unchangeable truth of the Assembly's declaration; and they have taken the right method to make it a *practical* truth, by publishing it to the world for discussion. A general belief *that it is a truth*, makes it once practical, confirms it in one nation, and extends it to others.

The way of thinking illustrated in the *Advice to the Privileged Orders* was typical of the ingenious, gadget-minded humanitarians who were not original thinkers but were able to transform abstract theories into practical devices for the establishment of modern political democracy.

The *Advice to the Privileged Orders* also illustrates the typical indifference of such men to philosophical consistency when it did not serve their humanitarian purposes. In the first paragraph of his chapter on "The Administration of Justice" Barlow took an almost whimsical attitude toward the beliefs he had presented so vigorously in the preceding chapters:

It would be a curious speculation, and perhaps as useful as curious, to consider how far the moral nature of man is affected by the organization of society; and to what degree his predominant qualities depend on the nature of the government under which he lives. The adage, *That men are every where the same*, though not wholly false, would doubtless be found to be true only in a limited sense. I love to indulge the belief, that it is true so far as to ensure permanency to institutions that are good; but not so far as to discourage us from attempting to reform those that are bad.

This confession of his own willingness to base his beliefs upon the indulgence of his feelings explains why he could be so paradoxical in his final chapter. Observation had taught him that men who were apparently attracted by vicious inequalities found nothing attractive in the principles of justice established by the legal system. Centuries of law, backed by all the authority of the state, had not succeeded in changing men's habits of thinking to the extent of abolishing thieves and smugglers. Accordingly, he reversed his contention that society did and could change the nature of man in conformity to its demands and argued that society did not and could not change the nature of man sufficiently to meet certain of its demands.

Innate knowledge, which had been treated as an unimportant possibility in the first three chapters of the *Advice*, became an important point of departure in the fourth. "The great outlines of morality are extremely simple and easy to be understood," Barlow affirmed; "they may be said to be written on the heart of man antecedent to his associating with his fellow-creatures." But when man enters society "he is called to encounter problems which the elementary tables of his heart will not always enable him to solve." This was not a voluntary encounter, because the social compact was "but a *fiction*" upon which no rigid discipline should be founded. Consequently, it was the duty of society to instruct its members concerning its demands upon them. Every person born into society, according to Barlow, had a "*birth-right*" to the knowledge necessary for his existence in it. "To withhold this instruction therefore," he concluded, "would be, not merely the omission of a duty, but the commission of a crime; and society in this case would sin against the man, before the man could sin against society."

This common "crime" represented the failure of society to change the nature of man sufficiently to meet its demands. But

Barlow did not attribute the failure entirely to criminal negligence. Such a change would be impossible, even with the best and most universal instruction, in society as it was then constituted. Evils more tangible than any "habits of thinking" stood in the way of change. The most important, and most vulnerable, of these was poverty—the "root of the tree" of crime at which government should strike by "distributive justice" rather than strike at the "branches," or criminal acts, by "vindictive justice." Accordingly, he drew up a program of social justice based upon a more equable distribution of the "common stock of the community," which he described as consisting "first, in *knowledge*, or the improvement which men have made in the means of acquiring a support; and secondly, in the *contributions* which it is necessary should be collected from individuals, and applied to the maintenance of tranquility in the State." The program bound society, first,

to distribute knowledge to every person according to his wants, to enable him to be useful and happy; so far as to dispose him to take an active interest in the welfare of the state. *Secondly*, where the faculties of the individual are naturally defective, so that he remains unable to provide for himself, she is bound still to support and render him happy. It is her duty in all cases to induce every human creature, by rational motives, to place his happiness in the tranquillity of the public, and in the security of individual peace and property. But *thirdly*, in cases where these precautions shall fail of their effect, she is driven indeed to the last extremity,—she is to use the rod of correction.

Since Barlow introduced this passage with a statement that "the property exclusively belonging to individuals can only be the surplusage remaining in their hands, after deducting what is necessary to the real wants of society," his program is curiously similar to the formula "to each according to his needs, and from each according to his ability"—and chastisement for those who will not subordinate themselves to the state. His optimistic philosophy, however, stood between his humanitarian impulses and any radical proposal for sharing the wealth. "Society at present," he believed, "has the means of rendering all its members happy in every respect, except the removal of bodily disease"; for the world could support many times the existing population "even on its present system of cultivation" without recourse to the infinite possibilities of technological improvements and discoveries. So little of the potential wealth of the world existed in "goods exclusively appropriated to individuals" that men whose faculties were not defective needed the equipment to tap this wealth rather than a share in that which already existed. Barlow had a humanitarian sympathy with the downtrodden but too much optimism and imagination to become a communist.

The combination of humanitarian feeling and high philosophical imagination revealed in Barlow's program of social justice is characteristic of the entire *Advice to the Privileged Orders*. When he looked down on mankind from the heights of philosophy, he saw "beings so nearly equal in power and capacity"—and with so many different abilities, subject to such different schemes of classification—that the principle of equality seemed a workable hypothesis worthy of a practical test. When his sympathies drew his point of view to the level of the oppressed among mankind, he looked up bitterly at "those Draconian codes of criminal jurisprudence which enshrine the idol property in a bloody sanctuary, and teach the modern European, that his life is of less value than the shoes on his feet." From each point of view he found fault with the contemporary social organization; and the obligation to help "renovate" it was stronger than any obligation he might feel toward intellectual consistency. His mind was inquiring rather than systematic; he had never received the severe logical training that William Godwin, for example, had experienced in his early studies of Jonathan Edwards; and the atmosphere in which he wrote was one of enthusiasm and reform. As a speculative philosopher, he thought in the terms of Beccaria, whose "compassionate little treatise" (as Barlow called it in a footnote to his chapter on justice) taught that "no advantage in moral policy can be lasting, which is not founded on the indelible sentiments of the heart of man." Thus he found the source of evil sometimes in the mind of man as it was formed by society; sometimes in society which made demands upon man that the natural disposition of his mind did not enable him to meet. But in either case man was the victim and society the offender; and Barlow's object consistently was the renovation of the latter in order that its members might attain a sort of *potential* "state of nature," which he thought of sometimes in the psychological sense expounded by Rousseau but most often as the future state of wholesome happiness set up as an ideal by Holbach and Volney.

Since Barlow was primarily concerned with the "general revolution in the principle of government" which was going on at the time, much of the *Advice* was devoted to specific comment on political matters; and this comment reveals that the author, in his effort "to chin up to the level of the politics of Europe," had ranged widely in the literature of his subject. He indignantly cited Burke's *Reflections on the Revolution in France, A Letter to a Member of the National Assembly*, and *An Appeal from the Old to the New Whigs;* and he was particularly sarcastic about the "puny whinings" of Dr. Edward Tatham's *Letters to the Right Hon. Edmund Burke on Politics*. He referred to Price's Old Jewry sermon "On the Love of Our Country," which had excited Burke; but he did not mention Mary Wollstonecraft's reply to the *Reflections* in *A Vindication of the Rights of Men*, which he undoubtedly had read. He was liberal in his praise of Paine's *The Rights of Man*, however, and often echoed it in phraseology, sometimes amplifying Paine's ideas in a way that suggests a deliberate attempt to correct his friend's too summary treatment of them. For material used in his attack upon the established church he drew upon Joseph Priestley's *A History of the Corruptions of Christianity* and the recently published works of Boulanger, which also included a number of studies actually composed by the Baron d'Holbach. His earlier reading of Blackstone, Locke, Montesquieu, and Burlamaqui formed a substantial background of erudition, to which he made no direct reference except in a summary of the classical objections to a large republic expressed by "Montesquieu, Voltaire, and many other respectable authorities"—objections that he answered with the forthright denial given by Madison in the tenth number of the *Federalist*. His comments on Beccaria's *Dei delitti e delle pene*, however, indicate that he had probably reviewed that treatise, in its original language, after coming to Europe; and, although he did not mention Rousseau by name, the *Advice* contains a sufficient number of occasional parallels to the *Social Contract* to indicate that Barlow had read that book, even though he did not accept its argument. The amount of miscellaneous, out-of-the-way information scattered through the volume suggests that he was making extensive use of contemporary periodicals and of such scholarly works as Thomas M. Cunningham's *The History of Our Customs, Aids, Subsidies, National Debts and Taxes*, cited in the second part of the *Advice*. In any case he took a historical as well as a controversial view of his subject. A quotation from Cicero's *De divinatione* shows that he was at least conscious of the Romans, and a reference to Gabriel H. Gaillard's elaborate, somewhat sociological, *Histoire de Charlemagne* reveals his interest in the Middle Ages.

The *Advice to the Privileged Orders* was a fairly learned work, and it had outgrown, in substance, the polemical purpose which inspired it and set its tone. But Barlow compensated for the breadth of his prose work by the narrowness of a poem printed five and a half weeks later. *The Conspiracy of Kings: A Poem Addressed to the Inhabitants of Europe from Another Quarter of the World* was a somewhat affected, consciously "literary" satire, modeled on Juvenal and Pope and directed against the "crested reptiles" of royalty who had joined in military coalition against the French Republic. In it he indulged extravagantly in the sitting-room sport of damning Edmund Burke with such epithets as "degenerate slave" and "sordid sov'reign of the lettered world" and expressed his confidence in mankind's ultimate victory over the forces of evil he had attacked in the *Advice*. Four lines presented a curious conception of the state of nature which combined the notion of Paradise with that of perfectibility:

> Hail man, exalted title! first and best,
> On God's own image by his hand imprest,
> To which at last the reas'ning race is driven,
> And seeks anew what first it gain'd from heaven.

But this was a poetic conceit, not an indication that Barlow was thinking seriously in such theological terms. Indeed, the

poem as a whole, with its extravagant epithets, its personifica-
tion, and its extensive symbolism, was hardly serious in any
true sense. It was a decorative summary of the opinions expressed in the *Advice* made with a certain amount of rhetorical
artifice but without any transforming imagination or any new
vigor of argument—so artificial, in fact, that Barlow introduced
into it several lines from Humphreys' portion of the *Anarchiad*
without realizing that he had done so.

Neither of these works was especially popular, although the
five hundred copies of the first edition of the *Advice* were sold in
time for a second printing in June. *The Conspiracy of Kings* was
not immediately reprinted, unless it appeared in broadside
form. Yet they made Barlow well known among the London
revolutionists, and he became temporarily active in their councils. With the coming of spring and the possibility of travel,
however, he turned back to business. Although he possessed
doubtful claims to numerous acres of land in America, he was
hard pressed for cash; and in spite of his susceptibility to seasickness he took the cheapest passage across the Straits of
Dover. The business was mysterious. It was probably a scheme
to dispose of surplus supplies, collected in English ports, in
France. Barlow's first task was to deal with an intermediary
whom he finally located at the émigré headquarters in Coblenz
and by whom he was referred to the Marquis de Lafayette, then
in command of one of the French armies, for further negotiations. Austrian troops and inclement weather prevented him
from reaching France for more than three weeks, and, although
Lafayette sent him immediately to a minister in Paris, the
Marquis's own delay in reaching Paris made it impossible to
complete the arrangements before the fall of the Girondist
ministry brought the whole effort to nothing. Barlow had
again failed, but he apparently had discovered the proper method of grasping opportunity by the forelock: several times during each of the next four years he announced his intention of
returning to America; on every occasion "unexpected" commercial affairs kept him abroad; and at the end of the period he

possessed a fortune of approximately $120,000, two-thirds of it in securities of the French government, which probably represented reward for business services rather than the investment of funds acquired outside the country.

The experiences of the spring and early summer of 1792 also had a direct effect on his literary career. During his trip through Germany he wrote his wife that he found himself "more than ever affected with the fortune of that dear deluded race of mortals that we call our fellow creatures"; and after his experiences with the Austrians he was greatly annoyed by "the cursed tyrannies of men" and enthusiastic over "the land of Liberty." Even when he began to anticipate the failure of his business he did not regret the trip which had led him to so "much information." The conflicts between the king and the people that he witnessed during June left him, unlike Lafayette, on the side of the people, convinced that sooner or later they would have "wit enough to settle the matter according to the laws of nature, which admit no king." It was probably after his return to England, early in July, with such ideas in his head that he set about editing Trumbull's revolutionary poem, *M'Fingal* with notes bringing some of the possible implications of the satire up to date and with a Preface ascribing to the poet an intention "to ridicule monarchy—to expose the absurd arguments and shallow subterfuges which are uniformly used, wherever it is attempted to be supported by reasoning." The ridicule directed against the English nation really fell upon "the *government*, not the people," he declared, adding that "every honest man is put into good humour with himself, the moment he makes the distinction." Barlow may also have taken his mind off his unsuccessful business at this time by completing the first volume of a translation of Brissot de Warville's *New Travels in the United States of America*, which has been attributed to him. Published in Dublin in 1792, it was accompanied by a "Translator's Preface" which, like the Preface to *M'Fingal*, was written in the character of an anonymous Englishman who was strongly pro-American and critical of the English government. A new edition, corrected, with a second volume, *The Commerce of America with Europe*, was issued in London by J. S. Jordan, the publisher of *M'Fingal*, in 1794.

Although Trumbull's poem and Brissot's *Travels* both had a certain propaganda value at this time, Barlow was not content with such comparatively passive efforts at reform. When the imprisonment of Louis XVI, on August 10, necessitated the calling of a National Convention to revise the inapplicable constitution of 1791, Barlow saw an opportunity to be of immediate, practical service to mankind. Accordingly, he hastily prepared *A Letter to the National Convention of France on the Defects in the Constitution of 1791 and the Extent of the Amendments Which Ought To Be Applied*, which was dated September 16, 1792, presented to the convention by Paine during the same month, and published in time for the author to send a copy to Jefferson on October 1. The pamphlet was better organized and more coherent than the *Advice to the Privileged Orders:* it was directed to a specific audience for a specific purpose; and it avoided, except incidentally, the philosophical speculations that carried Barlow beyond his depth in the earlier work. It was an aggressively republican document, based on a complete acceptance of the French Revolution, which he had described in the *Advice* as "an operation designed for the benefit of the people that "originated in the people, and was conducted by the people." Subscribing fully to the recent progress of events, he ignored his praise of Louis XVI in *The Vision of Columbus* and laid down as a starting principle the "doctrine, which no experience can shake, and reason must confirm, *that kings can do no good.*" That the people represented the right and the king the wrong in a fundamental conflict of interests was axiomatic in the *Letter:* the National Convention owed its existence to this assumption, and, had Barlow not shared it, his recommendations would never have reached that body. The fitness of a people to govern themselves was a completely irrelevant question. Government meant restraint, and people needed restraint in inverse proportion to their virtue—if by virtue one meant "those moral habits by which men are disposed to mutual justice and benevolence." And Barlow wrote with expressed confidence "that any people, whether virtuous or vicious, wise or ignorant, numerous or few, rich or poor, are the best judges of their own wants relative to the restraint of laws, and would always supply those wants better than they could be supplied by others." He believed:

A republic of beavers or monkies could not be benefitted by receiving their laws from men, any more than men could be in being governed by them. If the Algerines or the Hindoos were to shake off the yoke of despotism, and adopt ideas of equal liberty, they would that moment be in a condition to frame a better government for themselves, than could be framed for them by the most learned statesmen in the world. If the great Mr. Locke, with all his wisdom and goodness, were to attempt the task, he would probably succeed as ill as he did in his constitution for the colony of South Carolina.

"The sure and only characteristic of a good law is," he concluded, *"that it be the perfect expression of the will of the nation;* its excellence is precisely in proportion to the universality and freedom of consent."

The French had already indicated their state of moral progress by the steps they had taken to overthrow the monarchy and disestablish the church and by the action of the National Assembly in "laying down the great fundamental principle that all men are equal in their rights." Barlow urged them, in general, to complete the steps being taken against the king and the establishment and, in particular, to insure the exercise of equality by correcting thirteen specific defects in the constitution of 1791. He was on the winning side, as he undoubtedly realized in advance, with his general recommendations; but of his more detailed proposals only two were incorporated into the constitution of 1793: representation was based upon population alone, and elections were made annual. Three "defects" in the earlier document were retained: citizenship was to be lost by naturalization in another country, representatives were not held responsible to their constituents, and provision was made for a national guard. Of the remaining eight, three (the abolition of lotteries, the limitation of salaries, and the establishment of schools) were left to legislative action, and five were reflected, if not wholly accepted, in the new body of laws. The age of en-

franchisement was reduced to twenty-one though not to twenty
or below, imprisonment for debt was no longer specifically permitted although it was not abolished, capital punishment was
abolished for private transgressions alone, the right to seize
colonies was renounced but not made retroactive, and the process of constitutional amendment was considerably simplified.
Since the legislature did, in practice, limit salaries and, almost
immediately, provide for schools, the *Letter to the National Convention* may be considered a statesmanlike document. Barlow
had either influential arguments or a keen sense of direction, and
no one has ever been able to say which of the two represents the
real quality of a statesman.

The letter was favorably received by the Convention, and
the author was made an honorary citizen of France. Barlow
looked upon himself as influential. He wrote Jefferson, who had
been urging him to come home and exercise his talents on a
democratic history of the United States, that he "should have
sailed for America before now" but that it appeared he "might
do some good by staying." Thus unusually confident cheerfulness about his European affairs may have been an emotion provoked by the composition of the just published pamphlet which
accompanied the letter—a feeling of that "vital flow" between
the past and the present which later inspired Marcel Proust to
literary activity. For it is a curious fact that *A Letter to the
National Convention* contains no important ideas that were not
acquired by Barlow before he left his native land. The belief
that government should be in the people, for the people, and by
the people was as thoroughly American in Barlow's day as it
was when Abraham Lincoln expressed it in similar language two
generations later. The notion that a king can do no good had
been the popular justification for the Declaration of Independence. An established church had been forbidden by the American Constitution, and Barlow's own experience with the semblance of establishment in Connecticut had been an unrelieved
irritation. His denial of the authority of legal classics, his scorn
of the concept of unchangeable common law, and his humanitarian feeling that society sinned against the individual more

often than the individual against society all dated from the time in Hartford when Beccaria outweighed Blackstone and led him to submit a dissertation against imprisonment for debt as evidence of his qualification for admission to the bar. He occasionally appealed to the "analogy of nature" in the manner of the materialistic moralists and flattered the Convention that its constitution might "anticipate the moral regeneration of society"; but the ideas of the *philosophes* had no important part in his argument. The pamphlet represented a momentary escape from the Europe in which he had not been happy. During more than four years of residence he had spent less than twelve months with the wife to whom he was wholly devoted, and those months were filled with a consciousness of failure in his practical business. But new political developments in France had summoned up, without his conscious effort, the remembrance of things past; and the new occasion and the old ideas had combined to form a literary work that was satisfying in itself and efficacious in its promise. Barlow was acquiring a confidence that rested upon the assurance of the past, as well as upon a hope for the future. If there was any precise point at which his career made a definite change, it was when the composition of *A Letter to the National Convention*, anticipating the change in his material state, gave him an assurance that he had affected but had never really possessed before.

Shortly after being made a citizen of France, Barlow was selected, with John Frost, to deliver an address from the London Constitutional Society to the National Convention. He read the message before the bar of the Convention on November 28, 1792, and a week later left Paris for Savoy with a commission appointed to organize the former duchy into a department of republican France. The Savoyards, as a people, aroused his admiration; and, while his companions were devoting their time to political organization, he busied himself with a letter to the kindred people of Piedmont, urging them to follow their neighbors' example by establishing a republic and affiliating themselves with France. *A Letter Addressed to the People of Piedmont, on the Advantages of the French Revolution and the*

Necessity of Adopting Its Principles in Italy was not published in English until 1795, but French and Italian translations were broadcast immediately. Written from the same point of view as the *Letter to the National Convention*, it stressed the ability of the Piedmontese to effect a revolution and the practical advantages of such an action. It defended the French against charges of atheism and the violation of private property and attempted to explain the "unfortunately true" charge of "cruelty and murder" on the grounds that habits of behavior established under the monarchy had filled the country with traitors. The vengeance finally forced upon the people, he admitted, "has been ill directed, and has fallen on innocent heads." His major argument for a republican revolution was that it would promote peace, since "no person would have any interest in extending or contracting the territorial limits of a state"; and, although he promised a military invasion of Piedmont during the following spring, he assured the poeple that it would be a defensive campaign waged against their rulers and designed to assure their own liberties. The letter was written almost five years before Barlow began to realize how easily a defensive war could become a war of conquest. The reaction against war which followed the American Revolution was still, to his mind, the inevitable result of republican principles. He saw the French already arguing like Americans about the desirability of admitting new territory into their union, and so he addressed the people of Piedmont, as he had the National Convention, with the confident assurance of one who saw new events falling into familiar patterns.

But with all his confidence Barlow did no particular good by staying in France. The Piedmontese did not respond to his *Letter*, nor did the Savoyards reciprocate his admiration sufficiently to elect him to the National Convention, although he was the "organization" candidate for the office. Ironically, however, the remembrance of things past that encouraged him to turn politician brought him the literary fame he no longer greatly desired. The rural scenery of Savoy had made him feel at home for the first time since he left Connecticut; and, when the inn at Chambéry also presented him with an unexpected dish of hasty pudding, the associations between present events and past experiences became so strong that he burst forth into the most spontaneous verse he had yet written. Although *The Hasty Pudding* might be described as an overflow of whimsicality rather than of powerful feeling, the poem reflects a Wordsworthian experience. While writing it, Barlow was lightening the heavy and weary weight of a world which, despite his optimism, was not altogether intelligible to him. He was calling up, through the power of association, the common pleasures of his boyish days and finding in them a release from boredom and loneliness and worry concerning the outcome of the March elections. The result was a mock heroic comparable to Edward Phillips' *Cyder* and was to prove the most popular of all Barlow's poems. He apparently thought of it as a casual production suitable for private rather than for public circulation, but a copy sent to America was printed in the *New York Weekly Magazine* in January, 1796, and it was published as a small volume in New Haven almost immediately. At least four other editions appeared in the course of the same year and three in 1797, and almost every magazine and literary newspaper in the United States pirated it during the same period—even though its author, at that time, was becoming politically obnoxious to most American publishers. The man who had remained in Europe in order to help renovate mankind succeeded merely in becoming the poet of cornmeal mush, and to most students of American literature he is little more than that at the present day.

Yet, in the midst of his practical concern over politics and his occasional escape into verse, Barlow was continuing to meditate his theoretical scheme for improving the whole of Europe. He had completed the fifth chapter of his *Advice to the Privileged Orders*, dealing with "Revenue and Public Expenditure," before leaving London in November, 1792; but he became so notorious during the winter that his publisher, Joseph Johnson, apparently found it impolitic to issue a work composed after the royal proclamation against seditious publications. The manuscript was at one time reported seized by the British government; but, if so, it was probably returned to the author's wife, who took it with her to Paris in June. There, in the intervals between his business trips to various parts of the Continent, Barlow reviewed his argument and finally gave it to the public through the English Press, in September, as *Part II* of the *Advice*. Though primarily an attack upon indirect taxation and the funding of public debts, it was, in its general line of thought, the most radical of all Barlow's writings. For in no other work did the American author fall so completely into the French materialistic tradition of Holbach and Volney. Following their lead, he clearly defined the ideal state of "nature," about which he had been less explicit in the earlier chapters:

> I say *naturally*, not in contradistinction to the *social* state, but in contradistinction to the *unnatural* state, in which government, founded on conquest or accident, has hitherto placed mankind. A natural state of society, or a nation organized as human reason would dictate, for the purpose of supplying the greatest quantity of our physical wants, with the corresponding improvement of our moral faculties, has never yet been thoroughly tried.

Furthermore, he exhibited none of his earlier hesitancy in following their behavioristic theory that the moral nature of man was formed by the conditioning received from his social environment. "The true object of the social compact," he declared, "is to improve our moral faculties, as well as to supply our physical wants." Even when he occasionally referred to the "moral sense," he seemed to think of it as something established in man by society; and when he revived his constructive application of his theory of habits, he did so with an assurance that disregarded any possible need for an appeal to innate ideas of morality:

> I am not preaching a moral lecture on the use of riches, or the duty of charity; I am endeavouring to point out the means by which the necessity for such lectures may be superceded. A duty that runs contrary to habit, is hard to be enforced, either by persuasion or by law. Rectify our habits, and our duties will rarely be omitted.
>
> Good men in all civilized nations, have taken unwearied pains, and given themselves real grief of heart, in censuring the vices and recommending the duties of mankind, relative to the use and abuse of property. Their labours have doubtless done some good; for we may readily conceive that the quantity of misery in the world is not so great as it might have been without them. But

these men have not penetrated to the root of the evil; or rather, they have overlooked it; and the remedies they have proposed have always been partial, unpromising, and without success. They lay the blame to the natural propensities of the human heart, and call upon individuals for reformation. Whereas, the fault lies not so deep, nor is the cure to be looked for from individuals, even with respect to themselves. Habit is the ape of nature; it assumes her appearance, and palms its vices upon her. And as the universal habit with respect to the subject now in question has arisen out of unnatural and degrading systems of government, a reformation can be expected, only from referring back to nature for a change of those systems; and there is no doubt but this remedy will be effectual.

Barlow's intellectual procedure at this time was curious: while addressing the French from a point of view developed before he left America, he was addressing the world from another point of view cultivated after his arrival in France.

Not all the material in the second part of the *Advice*, of course, was derived from the French philosophers. Most of its substance was technical, and Barlow drew upon such technical sources as Cunningham's *History of Taxes*, Sir John Sinclair's *The History of the Public Revenue of the British Empire*, Jacques Necker's *De l'administration des finances de la France*, and Adam Smith's *Wealth of Nations*. He paid to Paine's *Rights of Man* his customary tribute of agreement and admiration and to the works of Burke and Tatham his usual condemnation and abuse. He quoted Cardinal Richelieu's *Political Testament* as evidence of the cynical attitude held by tax-hungry rulers toward the people, and he drew illustrations of the antisocial effects of annuities from Louis Sebastian Mercier's *Tableau de Paris*. But Barlow was making his particular arguments within the general framework of an extremely radical system of thought, and, as a consequence, he slipped into radically new speculations of his own. He summarized his old attitude toward commerce that he had expressed in *The Vision of Columbus:*

Chivalry and hierarchy taught us to believe that all men who did not pay homage to the same monarch, or use the same mode of worship with ourselves, were our natural enemies, and ought to be extirpated. The spirit of commerce has brought us acquainted with those people; we find them to be like other men, and that they are really useful to us in supplying our wants. As their existence and their prosperity are found to be advantageous to us in a commercial point of view, we cease to regard them as enemies; and refuse to go and kill them, unless we are hired to do it.

"But," he added, under the influence of his new theory of the moral nature of man in contemporary society,

as commerce may deal in human slaughter as well as in other things, when ever the government will offer us more money for destroying our neighbours than we can get by other business, we are ready to make enemies of our best friends, and to go to war, as we go to market, on a calculation of profit.

Having renounced innate ideas of morality and brooding over the effects of getting and spending upon men's habits of thought, Barlow speculated further that

perhaps in a more improved state of society, the time will come, when a different system may be introduced, when it shall be found more congenial to the social nature of man to exclude the idea of separate property, and with that the numerous evils which seem to be entailed upon it.

He had committed his imagination to a system of philosophy, and the commitment led him logically to the idea of communism he had avoided a year earlier. But, he announced, it was not his "intention in this work to enter upon that enquiry."

It may be that the disassociation of his attempts at particular, political reform from his more broadly speculative enterprises allowed him to go too far into philosophical speculation for his own comfort—especially while witnessing the government's efforts to change the "habits of thinking" in the Vendée. At any rate, he did not finish the three additional chapters on "The Means of Subsistence"; "Literature, Sciences and Arts"; and "War and Peace" that he had planned. Although a third part of the *Advice* was advertised for "speedy publication" in 1795, Barlow wrote John Fellows in May of that year that other occupations had prevented him from writing the remaining three chapters. A small fragment of chapter vi survives in manuscript, and that, apparently, is all that he ever composed. Henceforth his political writings were to be entirely occasional, directed toward immediate, practical ends.

Barlow's other occupations, however, did not prevent him from taking an active interest in literature. After a winter in Paris he spent the spring of 1794 in Hamburg, where he became friendly with Professor Christoph Daniel Ebeling (by whom he had already been consulted concerning his geography and history of the United States) and formed an acquaintance with the elderly Klopstock and other German writers. From there he wrote Ezra Stiles:

It is to be regretted, that the difference of language has placed such a barrier as it has between us and the German literature. We have been content to borrow from them their improvements in science, without being able to relish the beauties of their writers. These are more numerous, and perhaps more excellent, than those of any other modern nation. We have for some reason or other, neglected to cultivate their language, or translate their works.

Barlow's respect for German literature, however, was based mostly on hearsay; and, although he was one of the first Americans to reveal any interest in Immanuel Kant, he really paid little attention to German philosophy or poetry. One of his greatest literary concerns at this time (stimulated perhaps by his protective interest in *The Age of Reason*) was with writings directed against institutional Christianity. In the letter to Fellows, written from Hamburg in May, 1795, he went as far as to say:

I rejoice at the progress of Good Sense over the damnable imposture of Christian mummery. I had no doubt of the effect of Paine's *Age of Reason*. It must be cavilled at awhile, but it must prevail. Though things as good have often been said, they never were said in so good a way. I am glad to see a Translation, and so good a one, of Boulanger's *Christianisme dévoilé.* . . . . I wish Mr. Johnson would go on, and give us the next volume, the History of that famous Mountebank, called St. Paul.

Barlow's violent, republican anticlericalism, like that of many of his contemporaries, was uncritical: it did not matter whether the attack upon "mummery" was based upon Paine's deism or the atheism of Holbach (the actual author of the works attributed to Boulanger). But for the moment at least the influence of the latter seems to have been dominant; for, although he had given up that line of speculation in his attempts to renovate society, he appears to have been strongly attracted by the materialistic philosophy of history developed by the real Nicholas Boulanger in *L'Antiquité dévoilée* and *Recherches sur l'origine du despotisme oriental.*

By this time Barlow had written Abraham Baldwin that he was "done with poetry" and was thinking more seriously than ever of devoting himself to historical writing. He had not given up the project of a republican history of the United States that Jefferson had urged upon him, but he was gradually coming to the conclusion that a history of the French Revolution would be a more worthy immediate enterprise. His literary plans, however, were interrupted. The Barbary corsairs had long been a source of irritation to the United States government, and the number of American citizens in the slavepens of Algiers had grown embarrassing. The dey was known to be willing to negotiate a treaty for their release; but he was temperamental in his diplomacy and subject to many whims, the influence of palace favorites, and pressure from European maritime powers who were not eager to see the Mediterranean opened to American commerce. The negotiations required a considerable amount of experience in international trading and finance, the enforcement of an agreement demanded a rare combination of delicacy and firmness, and the whole business depended upon at least the tacit co-operation of the French government. Since David Humphreys, who had general supervision of Mediterranean affairs, was not in the good graces of the French, Barlow was called upon by the American government to serve as special minister to the Algerian ruler. Accordingly, he spent the autumn of 1795 getting advice, selecting an enormous number of presents of all sorts, and practicing a few polite phrases in Turkish; and in December he left France for Africa. His mission was successful, but it proved both tedious and dangerous, for he had to remain in the plague-ridden Algerian capital until July, 1797, where his major amusements were riding horseback, cultivating a luxuriant set of black mustaches, and meditating oriental corruption and American red tape.

In the midst of his troubles and boredom, however, he was considering the future and taking stock of his abilities. In April, 1797, he sent to his wife his estimate of their respective "characters" with particular reference to their "taste," "imagination," and "judgment":

> Le goût chez nous deux est infiniment semblable; chose qui a beaucoup contribué en bonheur de notre union. Le jugement est à tous égards de ton côté, et l'imagination du mien. Mon imagination n'est pas brillante, mais elle est plus vaste et plus prompte que la tienne. C'est à elle que je dois le peu de réputation que j'ai acquise dans le monde littéraire. Mon goût, sans être parfait, m'a dirigé assez heureusement dans le stile surtout en prose. Le jugement m'a toujours manqué plus ou moins, tant en sujets de littérature que dans le monde matériel et social.

The result was a decision to make a "slight change" in the works he was meditating: "Au lieu de philosophie politique en grand, je suiverai la philosophie domestique et sociale en petit"; but despite this promise he continued to think of his history, and soon after his release from the six-week quarantine in Marseilles he began a formal outline of the project. He looked upon it as a continuation of Dr. William Robertson's *History of Charles V* and expected to begin with a treatment of the "progress of society" subsequent to the period covered by Robertson's famous work. The surviving notes are of interest because they show that, although Barlow's disillusionment over the French Revolution apparently began with the Vendée massacres in 1794, he had by no means given up his faith in the basic principles of the movement. He planned to include a statement of his faith and his hope in the Introduction:

> I will not pretend to say that the present struggle or the Revolution now under consideration, will succeed in that direct and complete manner as could be wished; or whether this and other nations will be immediately benefitted by it. But could I know that it would not succeed, I would nevertheless retain the opinion that the object of amelioration is still attainable, and that revolution in favor of representative democracy ought to be encouraged. It would still be my opinion that the fault was not in the inherent nature of the operation, but in the manner of conducting it. The mistakes that may have been committed ought to be clearly pointed out, the causes of the failure detailed in a most candid and critical examination; so that other nations, or a future generation here, need not be unnecessarily deterred from a like attempt, whenever they shall feel themselves able to avoid the errors and seize the advantages held up to view in this example.

Having returned to Paris only a few days after the Directory's coup d'état, he was able to grasp its significance and face the possibility that the Revolution "should fail in its intended object; and, instead of establishing a peaceable and rational republic, should lead through long and bloody wars to a monarchy of more extravagant despotism than that from which it rose." Under such circumstances, he thought, a history that distinguished between "causes permanent" and causes "incidental" would be of especial value in preventing a reaction against both the ideal and the result of the great social "experiment."

But the work never progressed beyond the stage of miscellaneous reading and a preliminary outline. Barlow may have become too despondent over the march of events, the appearance of Necker's *De la Révolution françois* may have deprived the subject of its freshness, or he simply may have found the difficulties insuperable. In any case he received little encouragement in the project. Jefferson, in particular, kept urging him to return to America and write his history of the United States. Annually Barlow announced his intention of returning home; and annually the pressure of business or the condition of his wife's health made him change his mind. His only published writings, during the next few years, were letters of occasional advice to or concerning his countrymen. The first of these may have been an anonymous pamphlet, published in Paris early in 1798, entitled *The Second Warning, or Strictures on the Speech Delivered by John Adams, President of the United-States of America, at the Opening of the Congress of Said States in November Last*. A vehement mixture of ironic prose and bad verse, its style is unlike that of any of Barlow's acknowledged works; but it is apparently the pamphlet sent by Barlow to Lemuel Hopkins in April, 1799, and its reputed authorship (together with the report of an outspoken private letter about the President) was probably responsible for Adams' often quoted comment that "Tom Paine is not a more worthless fellow." Certainly he was vehemently opposed to Adams' foreign policy. On March 1, 1798, he wrote "roundly" to Abraham Baldwin concerning the mistakes of the American government; and seven months later, after hearing that Washington had been nominated commander-in-chief of the American armies in anticipa-

tion of possible war with France, he addressed a long communication to the former president, assuring him of the good
intentions of the French Directory and urging him to use his influence in favor of negotiations. The former reached the press
before the end of the year, either through the dishonesty of the
bearer or through the indiscretion of Matthew Lyon (who received a confidential copy from Baldwin) and was excitedly
misinterpreted by the Federalists; the latter was forwarded to
President Adams, who interpreted Barlow's naïve assertions
concerning the good faith of the Directory as "unequivocal
symptoms of blackness of heart." Barlow, of course, had known
nothing of the corruption in high places that American official
representatives had met in France; and, as a punishment for his
innocence, he found his well-meant effort at amateur diplomacy
branded as treason. His letter to John Fellows, written at the
height of his anticlerical zeal, also reached the newspapers in
1799, and he was called an atheist as well. By the end of the
century his American reputation was at its nadir. Those personal friends who were also democrats remained steadfast, but to
such old associates as John Trumbull and Timothy Dwight he
was irrevocably lost.

Yet Barlow continued, with firmness if not with spontaneity,
in his essays to do good. On March 4 and December 20, 1799,
he addressed two *Letters from Paris, to the Citizens of the United
States of America, on the System of Policy Hitherto Pursued by
Their Governments Relative to Their Commercial Intercourse with
England and France*, which were published in London under
that title in 1800 and in Philadelphia and New York under
different titles in 1800 and 1801. In the first of these he explained the limitations of his private letter to Baldwin but repeated his attacks upon American policy. The United States,
he thought, had been particularly foolish in renouncing its opportunity, as a debtor nation, to force a settlement of disputes
by threatening "the sequestration of private property as a
compensation for public wrongs" instead of war. He also took
occasion to give some advice concerning internal affairs, urging
a policy of improvements and finance designed to achieve a

unity of interest during a period of future expansion and especially objecting to the funding system as "one of the most memorable pieces of imbecility and impudence that ever was imposed upon a nation." The letter as a whole, however, was more temperate than such language suggests; and the author's defense of himself offers, in both tone and substance, a significant revelation of the state of mind to which he had come after nearly a decade of active republicanism:

> With respect to men, I am of no party; with respect to principle, I am a republican in theory and practice; notwithstanding the disgrace into which that principle seems to be falling in America. I consider it as my unalienable right, as well as my indispensable duty, to render a service to you wherever I find occasion. And when such service has led me to notice what I thought wrong in the administration of your government; I have always done it; and in such a manner as I thought would be most likely to lead to a correction of the abuse. And I shall not relinquish this right, nor neglect this duty, whoever may be the men, and whatever the party, to whom you may choose to delegate your powers.

He was firm and even defiant in his allegiance to his principles, but he had lost his early enthusiasm and was becoming disillusioned and a little tired. The disillusionment and weariness may also be seen in the fact that his arguments were based entirely upon the same shrewd estimate of the power of human self-interest that characterized Alexander Hamilton and his followers. His different conclusions grew merely from the different value he placed upon the human beings who formed a nation. A financial policy designed to give the rich and well-born an interest in the government, Barlow believed, would alienate the struggling frontiersmen; and to him the future of the New World depended primarily upon the common people and the new regions they brought into the Union.

The second letter, while urging that all laws and treaties be made with a view to the future and the "perfectibility of human society," was even more practical in its renunciation of speculative schemes and its dependence upon discoveries tested by experience. Barlow specifically denied the practicability of the "plan for perpetual peace" originated by Henry IV and "afterwards embellished with the nervous eloquence of J. J.

Rousseau"; and he admitted that the experiment of the French Republic had been, so far, a failure. The secrets of success were the two great principles upon which the American constitutions had been founded—*"representative democracy*, and the *federalizing of states."* The latter made possible the indefinite expansion of a republic beyond the limits set for it by earlier political theory, while the former, he implied, was serving as insurance against the evils implicit in the "revolutionary" governments of France and the other republics of Europe which "as yet" had not had "much experience of the representative principle." The letter was a reasoned attempt to maintain the republican ideal at a time when the United States seemed to be drifting, in its financial policy and political sympathies, toward the English form of government. The two letters, as they went through various editions, were accompanied by other documents dealing with more occasional problems. The appeal to Washington, which Barlow feared might appear in an unauthorized "imperfect form," usually appeared as an appendix to the first letter. A "Memoir on Certain Principles of Public Maritime Law," urging absolute freedom of the seas, ordinarily followed the second, which was also accompanied, sometimes, by a letter "To Citizen——, Member of the French Government" signed by Barlow and his business associate, Fulwar Skipwith. Barlow addressed other appeals for better understanding to the French, publishing them anonymously in the Paris newspapers, until the election of Jefferson made his unofficial mediations no longer necessary.

With these letters Barlow brought his decade of political activity to a close. After the triumph of Napoleon his opinions went unheeded in France, and after the election of Jefferson they were unneeded in America. His native land had vindicated his faith, but his adopted country had betrayed his hopes. There was no occasion for a weary man to take the field again in behalf of republicanism. "I wish to live in the error if it is one," he wrote in 1806, "and die in it. I am too old to examine reasons for discarding a system from which I have never yet deviated." He had gone to France without realizing the significance of the American Revolution he had served. There his effort to "chin up to the level of the politics of Europe" had given him a perspective on the politics of his own country. For a while he had wavered between the fascinating speculations of the *philosophes* and the ideas he had absorbed without realizing it before leaving home. Practical problems had drawn him away from speculations, and the march of events had directed his hopes and expectations back across the Atlantic. Ten years had made him a wiser man but had left him too weary, and without occasion, to make use of his wisdom in any memorable way.

III

When Barlow, in 1795, released *The Hasty Pudding* for publication, he said that he was "through" with poetry. He had published a new and corrected edition of *The Vision of Columbus* in Paris two years before and, having decided, sensibly, that his best talent was for writing prose, apparently resolved to let his poetic reputation rest upon his youthful work. But when he returned to Paris from Algiers in September, 1797, he found a new stimulus to a fancy that could express itself most freely in verse. For young Robert Fulton had just arrived in the French capital with his head full of projects and his baggage full of curiosities. Mechanical problems had the same fascination for Fulton that social and philosophical problems had for Barlow; and the older man, who was beginning to jot down in his notebook new formulas for cement, gunpowder, and the problem of squaring the circle, found in the younger a kindred spirit. He adopted him as a protégé and a member of his household, helped him financially and with his influence, and eventually induced him to collaborate in a literary venture which, though never completed, renewed the middle-aged writer's interest in verse.

Fulton had come abroad ten years before for the purpose of studying painting under Benjamin West, and he intended to support himself in Paris by painting portraits and by exhibiting the first panorama ever to be unrolled for the admiration of Frenchmen. His primary reason for leaving England, however,

had been his disappointment over the failure of the British
government to become interested in his plan for a submarine
torpedo boat. Barlow assisted him in financing his invention
and in getting official witnesses for his demonstrations (which
included staying under water for an hour and successfully blowing up a small vessel) and until the end of his life insisted upon
the efficacy of the submarine as a means for restricting England's
domination of the seas. But, as a citizen of two republics that
were both actively concerned with internal improvements, he
was most excited by the notions Fulton had expressed the year
before in his *Treatise on the Improvement of Canal Navigation.*
The two men were active in the exchange of ideas; and, while
they were converting each other to the practicability of steam-
boats and the perfectibility of man, they also discussed the
problems of inland transportation and its possible contribution
to the improvement of society. Out of these conversations
grew a plan for collaborating on *The Canal: A Poem on the
Application of Physical Science to Political Economy in Four
Books.* Fulton was to furnish the "philosophy" and Barlow the
"poetry": one, the ideas and geological notes; the other, the
versification and the historical and mythological commentary.
By January 1, 1802, only half the first book had actually been
written; but Barlow was still interested in it as late as 1806, and
the project, though unproductive in itself, was apparently responsible for his return to verse-making.

The Canal was to be modeled to a considerable extent upon
Erasmus Darwin's *The Botanic Garden,* which was also a scientific poem in heroic couplets with many scientific, historical,
and mythological notes. Incidentally, it also had celebrated at
some length James Brindley's contributions to the development
of canals and contained a number of suggestions which Barlow
determined to use. He read it carefully. But in his newly
kindled enthusiasm he also read, perhaps more widely than ever
before, in other poets. Darwin, of course, directed his attention
to Ovid and Lucretius, and he read and took notes upon them
both. He read Cowper's translation of Homer, Dryden's Virgil,
and West's Pindar and took notes on them. He re-read James

Thomson's *Liberty*, scrutinized the works of his friend William Haley, made careful notes of words and phrases from Southey's *Joan of Arc* and the two-volume edition of his *Minor Poems*, and at least planned to obtain a copy of Coleridge's *Poems*. He made a note to purchase the thirteenth, concluding volume of Robert Anderson's *A Complete Edition of the Poets of Great Britain* (containing Creech's translation of Lucretius) and Timothy Dwight's *The Conquest of Canäan*. From every possible source he collected similes, examples of poetic diction, and rare or unusual words, especially words with a scientific flavor. His notebooks for this period are often confusing in dates and obscure in meaning, but one thing they make perfectly clear: no middle-aged man ever set about courting the Muses more systematically, or in a more unpromising manner.

Barlow, except in occasional wedding verses addressed to his wife, had lost the impulses of a poet and had become a scholar. He was doing research in methods of verse-making just as he was doing research in the background for *The Canal* and for the new version of *The Vision of Columbus* he was beginning to contemplate. He looked up the *Encyclopaedia Britannica*'s "fanciful article" on rivers, Jedidiah Morse's account of the Hudson in his *American Geography*, and John Gillies' description of the canal of Athos in his *History of Ancient Greece*. Anticipating the nineteenth-century notion of a fundamental conflict between science and religion, he began to wonder whether a knowledge of astronomy and physics would not have prevented the development of ideas of God and religion. Accordingly, he turned to the *Encyclopédie* for its articles on such words as "théiste," "athées," and "athéisme"; and the names of Toland, Bayle, Hobbes, and Spinoza began to appear in his notebooks. He read Descartes critically, noting the "fallacy" in his argument for a First Cause and giving the customary materialistic answer to it: "The fact is matter is naturally and necessarily always in motion." Yet he found a "strong vein of reasoning," even though he did not follow it completely, in Robert Boyle's *Disquisition Concerning the Final Causes of Natural Things*. He was also reading widely in the historians and completing his own collection of works by various French philosophical scientists. The most extensive researches into which he had been led by *The Botanic Garden*, however, were in mythology—the allegorical interpretations of the wisdom of the ancients that were to form the decorations for *The Canal*. Barlow would hardly have sympathized with Darwin's use of the Prometheus story as an allegory against the consumption of intoxicating liquors, the vulture representing cirrhosis; but he did intend to follow the doctor's general method of introducing philosophical comments in the guise of old stories. Francis Bacon's interpretations of the myths formed a great storehouse of suggestions, but he seems to have leaned more heavily upon the "system" of Charles François Dupuis in his *Origine de tous les cultes*. According to this seven-volume predecessor of *The Golden Bough*, Barlow discovered, the story of Manco Capac might be interpreted as a sun-myth; and according to a more arbitrary, truly Darwinian system he thought that the story of Jupiter and Semele might be used to represent the effect of "any great truth unfolded to mankind." He found other suggestions, of course, in Lucretius, in Volney's *Ruins*, in Guérin du Rocher's *Histoire véritable des tems fabuleux*, in Manilius' *Astronomicon*, in Jacob Bryant's *Analysis of Ancient Mythology*, and perhaps in the *Zend-Avesta*, which he planned to buy in either a French or an English translation.

All these mythological researches proved of little use, since he and Fulton never seemed able, at the same time, to find enough leisure to work seriously at their poem. His other reading, however, went into the revision of *The Vision of Columbus*, upon which he was able to work alone, for, despite the resolution he had expressed in 1795, Barlow could hardly have been comfortable over letting his reputation as a philosophical poet rest upon a youthful work which paid high tribute to Louis XVI, took an orthodox view of human history, and was excessively cautious in dealing even with such "new" ideas as those of the Scottish philosophers. While correcting it for publication in 1793 he must have become aware that the poem demanded drastic changes if it were to reflect his mature opinions.

The first five books, dealing with the geography and history of America, required few revisions except for stylistic purposes or for occasional indications of the author's point of view. Barlow's guiding principle in most of these stylistic changes seems to have been Darwin's distinction between the language of poetry and that of prose in the first interlude in "The Loves of the Plants":

Poetry admits of but few words expressive of very abstracted ideas, whereas Prose abounds with them. And as our ideas derived from visible objects are more distinct than those derived from the objects of our other senses, the words expressive of these ideas belonging to vision make up the principal part of poetic language. That is, the Poet writes principally to the eye. The Prosewriter uses more abstracted terms.

Lord Kames had preached the same unfortunate gospel, but Barlow, unlike his more systematic friend Timothy Dwight, had failed to absorb it thoroughly. Accordingly, as he cast a more critical eye over his early work, he found that he had referred to such abstract matters as the "resistless" pride of the oak, the "curse" that tigers exercised upon mankind, and the "extended" quality of a plain. This would never do for a man of his erudition; and so he made the pride of the oak "umbrageous," the tigers "fang" mankind, and the plain more vividly "woodgreen." Furthermore, he had made Chesapeake Bay, the formal plan of Philadelphia, and the city of Norfolk all indiscriminately "beauteous"; whereas they should be properly visualized as "multifluvian," "checker'd," and "sea-nursed." It is a nice question whether these revisions were merely bad or worse than the originals; but the poet certainly out-Darwined his master when he made the bed of the Potomac "earth disparting" instead of "lordly," the weather "brumal" rather than "inclement," and the rising suns "infulminate the stormful sky" above the Andes. Not all his verbal changes, of course, were governed by a consideration of the visual sense. He satisfied his self-conscious scientific inclinations by borrowing such adjectives as "azotic" and "embryon" from Darwin; and the inexplicable fascination of tautology caused him, while reading Southey, to make a note of "commingling" and use it frequently. He deliberately introduced a few coinages, such as "coloniarch" and "cosmogyral," as desirable additions to the English language and brought over "colon," "trist," and a number of others from the French. In all, he made hundreds of such revisions. Most of them, from his point of view, were logical; and most of them, to the modern reader at least, were bad. He undoubtedly thought that he was being thoroughly up to date in his conception of poetry; but he was not sensitive enough to appreciate the revolution in diction accomplished by Cowper and soon to be completed by Wordsworth, and so he chose to imitate the least enduring qualities of contemporary verse.

The Vision of Columbus, however, could not be made representative of the mature Barlow by a revision of individual lines. The author had decided to give it a new title, introduce additional material, re-write several portions altogether, and make it in some respects an entirely new poem. Although he continued to refer to it as a "philosophical" work, he gave the new version an epic title, the *Columbiad*, and apparently thought of it as a modern poem that should be compared with the ancient *Iliad* and *Aeneid*. By his poem, he convinced himself, he could "benefit mankind" just as he had planned to do by writing a history; for earlier poets and historians had been alike in that "almost universally, from Homer down to Gibbon," they had "led astray the moral sense of man" and had "injured the cause of humanity almost in proportion to the fame" they had acquired. This judgment was based upon the theory of habits he had adopted from Holbach and expressed in his *Advice to the Privileged Orders:* these two classes of writers for ages had conditioned men's minds to "false notions of honor and erroneous systems of policy." The "advance of society" could not have been accomplished entirely by having "history well written and poetry well conceived," he admitted; but "such would have been the tendency," for, Barlow insisted, "the public mind, as well as the individual mind, receives its propensities; it is equally the creature of habit. Nations are educated, like a single child. They only require a longer time and a greater number of teachers." He decided, as Walt Whitman was to do fifty years later,

that his poetry would be a corrective to feudalism and superstition, guiding men's habits of thinking toward democratic
ideals and scientific truths.

Despite the new psychological theories that lay back of his
purpose, however, Barlow's attempt to improve mankind fell
into the conventional pattern of such epic poets as the Archbishop Fénelon and Timothy Dwight: the most extensive addition to his poem consisted of a portrayal of ideal manners designed to encourage emulation. He added an entire book, expanding his treatment of the American Revolution, giving a
bolder characterization of American heroes, and drawing a
sharper contrast between the Americans and the British. His
new treatment of the war became the most epic-like section
of the poem. In representing Columbus' mentor, he had exchanged the Miltonic "Angel" for the more allegorical "Hesper";
and he allowed this supernatural genius of the West, like the
gods of Homer, to engage in heroic conflict with the spirit
"Frost" while Washington crossed the Delaware. Washington
himself became a more clearly defined heroic figure; and the impressions created by the entire section were heightened by a
more realistic description of modern war, in which cannon
thundered, smoke rolled, bayonets flashed, naval vessels grap-
pled and sank, and a citadel was mined and blown to blackened
ruins. Barlow declared in his Preface that part of the "real object" of his poem was "to discountenance the deleterious passion for violence and war," and he used this excuse to justify
his dramatic violation of history with the mined citadel at
Yorktown. Yet he was also anxious to demonstrate that the
roaring, smoky, mass conflicts of modern engagements offered
some advantages in description over the single conflicts of the
ancient epics. Accordingly, his military action was epic action,
and his heroes were epic heroes, although the qualities he
stressed were courage and determination rather than individual
aggressiveness.

The touch of epic ambition which caused Barlow to expand
his treatment of the American Revolution, however, was not
sustained. The most striking and revealing revisions of *The
Vision of Columbus* into the *Columbiad* were in its character as a

"philosophic" poem. The speculative eighth book of the earlier work was revised in the light of modern science and French philosophy and almost entirely changed. Barlow had been closely associated in business with William Playfair and may have learned from him of the obscure paper on the *Theory of the Earth* which James Hutton had published in 1785 and expanded into two difficult volumes ten years later. He could not have seen the popular *Illustrations of the Huttonian Theory of the Earth*, which William's older brother, John Playfair, was to publish in 1802. But, whether he received his knowledge directly or by hearsay, Barlow seems to have had a sufficient grasp of the principles of modern geology to make his account of the creation much more up to date than even the one given by Erasmus Darwin in *The Temple of Nature*. This account, which Barlow substituted for the biblical version used in *The Vision of Columbus*, formed one of the most vivid sections of the new poem. Lucretian in its imaginative quality, it reflected Barlow's extensive interest in the sciences of astronomy and physics, as well as in geology; and it laid an effectively conceived, scientific foundation for the new theory of man with which Barlow replaced the notions borrowed from the Scottish philosophers for the earlier poem.

The system of philosophy Barlow adopted for the *Columbiad* was that used in his more speculative, less practical political writings. It was, of course, optimistically progressive; and, as in *The Vision of Columbus*, the progress was in accord with a predetermined plan. In the later poem, however, the plan was Nature's rather than God's. "Her sons decide not," according to the doctrines of French necessitarianism, "how the march must end." But within this broad pattern of necessity man had control over his immediate course of action. As Barlow looked over his youthful explanation of the cause of human troubles, he found that he no longer shared Pope's theory of the individual "ruling passion" or the Scottish philosophers' distrust in human reason. He now believed with Holbach that the errors "twined" with man's knowledge before the dawn of history were responsible for his misery. "Fear, the first passion of his helpless state," had been responsible for the worst of his early errors, for, according to the "system" of Dupuis, fear begot superstition:

> Beat by the storm, refresht by gentle rain,
> By sunbeams cheer'd or founder'd in the main,
> He bows to every force he can't control,
> Indows them all with intellect and soul.

And out of superstition grew all the social evils of mankind:

> Hence rose his gods, that mystic monstrous lore
> Of blood-stain'd altars and of priestly power,
> Hence blind credulity on all dark things,
> False morals hence, and hence the yoke of kings.

Man's first deification of celestial bodies and natural phenomena gave the original wrong bias to his mind and enabled his "pliant faith" to extend "From heavenly hosts to heaven-anointed men"—priests and kings who deliberately united fraud with knowledge in order to debase and enslave their fellow-man. Barlow devoted a large section of this book of the *Columbiad* to a survey of the myths and religions of the Mediterranean region and of the Orient, illustrating the course of human error, as Volney had done in his *Ruins*, by material gained from his extensive reading. It was a sad and discouraging picture of fraud perpetuating a violation of the system of nature which had given man the perception of pleasures and pains in order to guide his automatic motions toward happiness. "Various and vast the fraudful drama grows," commented Barlow on this "unnatural" vision; "Feigned are the pleasures, as unfelt the woes." Man's tragedy was the result of a loss, in "feudal" society, of his true perceptions.

The situation of the human race, however, was pathetic rather than hopeless. As Barlow gazed upon his fellows through the eyes of Hesper, he wrote with some tenderness:

> Man is an infant still; and slow and late
> Must form and fix his adolescent state,
> Mature his manhood, and at last behold
> His reason ripen and his force unfold.
> From that bright eminence he then shall cast
> A look of wonder on his wanderings past,
> Congratulate himself, and o'er the earth
> Firm the full reign of peace predestined at
> his birth.

Looking at human history against the background of astronomical and geological ages that preceded it, the philosophical poet could contemplate the future without impatience and even see signs of rapid progress during the previous two hundred years. He no longer felt that man's hope depended upon some internal sense: it depended, instead, upon the overthrow of error by scientific investigation and the formation of new, more trustworthy habits of thinking. Copernicus represented one great milestone in the progress of thought, for he had broken "the delusive dreams of ancient lore" and opened the way for Kepler, Newton, Galileo, and Herschel. Descartes, in spite of his own mistakes, had overthrown many old errors and so represented another milestone. But Francis Bacon was the greatest of all, for he not only had bade men forego all their "unproved systems" and informed "them what to learn, and how to know" but had stripped the Grecian myths of their mysteries and revealed their errors. To Barlow, writing in an atmosphere of revolt against superstitions, surrounded by the works of Dupuis, Bryant, Guérin, Boulanger, and Volney, *The Wisdom of the Ancients* was as important a book as *The Advancement of Learning*. Both were attacks upon superstition, and, to the enlightened Connecticut Yankee, "Moral Science" appeared to be suffering more seriously than physical science from the errors of the past. But, with his new foundations of knowledge and his improved methods of acquiring and communicating it, man's future prospects were bright. He was at last able to "scrutinize" all systems and

> their truths unfold,
> Prove well the recent, well revise the old,
> Reject all mystery, and define with force
> The point he aims at in his laboring course.

The modern methods of physical science could be applied to the science of morals and governments. Already the American experiment had demonstrated the advantages of placing civil power in a group of confederated states, and it was within the realms of rational probability that such a federal system might be extended throughout the world.

As Hesper revealed his hopes for the human race, Columbus, of course, wanted a prevision of their fulfilment. Thus the concluding book of the *Columbiad* became Barlow's own vision of the future. It was not the facile, conventional vision he had presented in his earlier poem, for the mature Barlow had learned things concerning wayward humanity that had been undreamed of in the philosophy of his youth. He approached the vision with a review of the state of man as he was, attributing to Columbus the solemn, sympathetic "reveries" that were undoubtedly his own:

> He felt the infinitude of thoughts that pass
> And guide and govern that enormous mass.
> The cares that agitate, the creeds that blind,
> The woes that waste the many-mastered kind,
> The distance great that still remains to trace
> Ere sober sense can harmonize the race,
> Held him suspense, imprest with reverence meek,
> And choked his utterance as he wish'd to speak.

Yet the philosophic faith with which Hesper responded to Columbus' unexpressed thought was also Barlow's:

> The paths they here pursue,
> Wide as they seem unfolding to thy view,
> Show but a point in that long circling course
> Which cures their weakness and confirms their force,
> Lends that experience which alone can close
> The scenes of strife, and give the world repose.
> Yet here thou seest the same progressive plan
> That draws for mutual succour man to man,
> From twain to tribe, from tribe to realm dilates,
> In federal union groups a hundred states,
> Thro all their turns with gradual scale ascends
> Their powers, their passions and their interest blends;
> While growing arts their social virtues spread,
> Enlarge their compacts and unlock their trade;
> Till each remotest clan, by commerce join'd,
> Links in the chain that binds all human kind,
> Their bloody banners sink in darkness furl'd,
> And one white flag of peace triumphant walks the world.

The cynicism he had expressed concerning commerce only a few years before had disappeared. Give men the opportunity to exchange ideas along with their goods, he believed, and "enlighten'd interest" no less than their "moral sense" would lead them to peace and mutual understanding.

This brave new world which Columbus was allowed to see was, physically, very much like the one he had seen in the earlier poem. Intellectually, however, it was different. Barlow had become more clearly utilitarian in his social philosophy and more completely a rationalist in morals. He placed more emphasis upon "interest" as a force for uniting the world and less upon "sympathy" and "friendship"; and he expressed greater confidence in the ability of men's minds to expand beyond "local" limits and consider the "strength and happiness of all humankind." Instead of "blest Religion" leading the "raptured mind," he saw a rational "Moral Science" conducting the inquisitive, "lively" mind toward its proper goals. Many of the author's changes in this concluding book of his poem were changes in context that enabled him to keep good phrases which were almost meaningless in *The Vision of Columbus* and give them point and significance in the *Columbiad*. The parliament of man represented in the earlier work had signified little more than the beginning of millennial peace. Its representation remained almost entirely unchanged in the later, but it was made to symbolize the yielding of vanities and errors before utility and truth—the beginning of man's real progress rather than the culmination of his human efforts. Barlow merely added to his description of the hall of nations a description of the "figured Genius" of the earth and a comment that beneath his footstool

all destructive things,
The mask of priesthood and the mace of kings,
Lie trampled in the dust; for here at last
Fraud, folly, error all their emblems cast,
Each envoy here unloads his wearied hand
Of some old idol from his native land;
One flings a pagod on the mingled heap,
One lays a crescent, one a cross to sleep;
Swords, sceptres, mitres, crowns and globes and stars,
Codes of false fame and stimulants to wars
Sink in the settling mass; since guile began,
These are the agents of the woes of man.

This scene, with the legislative session that followed, was presented to Columbus as the ultimate fruit of his toil and risk. It was Barlow's own highest vision of the future. As a poet avoiding the use of "abstracted terms," he did not explain exactly what it meant in his general philosophy; but the "abstracted" meaning is not difficult to guess. While putting the finishing touches on these lines he was also making a new translation, "under the immediate inspection of the author," of Volney's *Ruins*, which he published in 1802, five years before the poem. Volney had also envisioned an assembly of people in which all the superstitions of the world were represented, and his assembly had listened to a reading of "The Law of Nature." What happened afterward he did not tell. But Barlow did. The action of the *Columbiad* concludes with humanity's acceptance of the law of nature as Barlow understood it from reading Holbach and Volney and other French philosophers of the eighteenth century.

One of the curious qualities of the *Columbiad* is its omission of any significant consideration of the French Revolution. Writing the later books of the poem after Napoleon's coup d'état in 1799, Barlow ignored the great experiment in Europe which had so excited him a few years before. He removed, of course, the original "romantic" dedication to Louis XVI and rather ungraciously revised all the internal references to that "pride of monarchs." Instead of having "great Bourbon's virtues shine" directly, he merely reported that "every voice" combined to praise them; and instead of attributing Louis's help in the American war to humanitarian impulses and generous feelings, he made him the dupe of "Gallic sages," whose belief in "Equal Rights" caused them to exercise "honest guile" upon the king by stimulating his antagonism toward England and so making him speak "the borrow'd language of the brave." Except for the Jacobinism of his ingratitude, Barlow's political background appeared entirely American. His invocation was to a power which flourished across the Atlantic and was little more than an ideal to Europeans:

Almighty Freedom! give my venturous song
The force, the charm that to thy voice belong;
Tis thine to shape my course, to light my way,
To nerve my country with the patriot lay,
To teach all men where all their interest lies,
How rulers may be just and nations wise:
Strong in thy strength I bend no suppliant knee,
Invoke no miracle, no Muse but thee.

The political principles he advocated were those of the experiment that had succeeded in his native land rather than those of the revolution that had failed in his adopted country:

EQUALITY, your first firm-grounded stand;
Then FREE ELECTION; then your FEDERAL BAND;
This holy Triad should forever shine
The great compendium of all rights divine.

Profoundly affected though he was by the philosophy of France, when he began to look for the light of the world he found it shining from the customs and institutions of the United States.

Barlow also attempted to make the *Columbiad* "American" in its language. As his notes on contemporary English poets show, he had been interested from the beginning of his revision in new words, especially terms that were concrete or scientific. Furthermore, in his epic treatment of the American Revolution he had tried to take advantage of modern military terms, consistently changing such words as "hosts" to "troops" or "files," "squadrons" to "platoons," and "thunders" to "artillery." Even in *The Vision of Columbus* he had looked forward to the achievement of a universal language; and in the new poem, while scoffing at the story of Babel and the notion of an earlier golden age, he retained this expectation. After he had practically finished the *Columbiad*, apparently, he realized that the English language in America was developing in a consistent, rational way which should be encouraged. He may not have realized until his return to the United States that the spelling of such words as "honor" and "music" had become, in some circles at least, a sign of one's political affiliation and that the omission of unnecessary *u*'s and *k*'s indicated a lack of sympathy with

England and the Anglophile policies of the Federalist party.
But, deliberately or not, his own spellings were "democratic,"
and after reading the Preface to Noah Webster's new *Compendious Dictionary* he added a note on orthography to the proof
received from the printer. In this he explained his principles and
practice:

> Our language is constantly and rapidly improving. The unexampled progress of the sciences and arts for the last thirty years has enriched it with a
> great number of new words, which are now become as necessary to the writer
> as the ancient mother tongue. The same progress which leads to further extensions of ideas will still extend the vocabulary; and our neology must and will
> keep pace with the advancement of our knowledge. Hence will follow a closer
> definition and more accurate use of words, with a stricter attention to their
> orthography.

He followed Webster in proposing a compromise between the
"total and immediate reform" which had been suggested by
Franklin and others and the policy of doing nothing. His own
practice he described as the uniform reduction of the Latin
diphthongs *ae* and *oe* to simple vowels, the omission of *u* in the
final syllable of words derived from Latin *-or* nouns, the use
of final *o* for *ough* in such words as "though" and "through,"
the writing of words pronounced with a final *t* with that letter
instead of *ed*, and the omission of the final letter in words ending
with *ck*. He approved Webster's proposals for dropping a final,
silent *e* and the second *s* in such words as "wilderness"; but,
feeling it "not desirable to be the first in so daring an enterprise,
when it is not immediately important," he refrained from practicing these innovations. Barlow was a somewhat cautious reformer in both his orthography and his neology. In some of his
spellings he followed the practice of the English poets if not the
makers of dictionaries, in others he adopted a simplification that
was already characteristically American; and in his diction, to
which some reviewers objected vehemently, he often anticipated
a usage which soon became standard. The extent to which he
was directly influenced by Webster cannot be determined.
Most of the poem seems to have been completed by the end of
1802, and the postscript on orthography was not written until
after the appearance of Webster's dictionary in 1806. Since his

spellings were not sufficiently consistent to indicate a habitual practice, they may represent a last-minute revision of the manuscript in an effort to make it an up-to-date illustration of the progress of language in his native land.

Barlow had normal, though restrained, hopes for the success of the *Columbiad* as a poem; but he made a careful distinction in his Preface between its *"poetic* object" or "fictitious design" and its *"moral* object" or "real design," basing its claim for consideration almost entirely upon the latter. He wrote:

My object is altogether of a moral and political nature. I wish to encourage and strengthen, in the rising generation, a sense of the importance of republican institutions; as being the great foundation of public and private happiness, the necessary aliment of future and permanent meliorations in the condition of human nature.

With all his hopes for benefiting mankind centered in his versified propaganda, he felt, as he told Abraham Bishop, that it was "essential that it should be got into vogue somehow or other." From the beginning he had planned an elaborate edition. While abroad, after one expensive experiment in employing John Vanderlyn, he had commissioned Robert Smirke to do a series of ten paintings at ten guineas each to be engraved as illustrations, and he had carefully discussed with Fulton and with the revolutionary minded artist the details of the first few subjects. Fulton himself had painted the author's portrait for use as a frontispiece and after Barlow's return to America had seen that all the prints, designed for a large quarto, were sealed in a metal container for transportation across the Atlantic. Barlow's own problem was to find a publisher who could come up to his expectations. Eventually he settled upon C. and A. Conrad and Company, of Philadelphia, and Conrad, Lucas and Company, of Baltimore, as publishers, and Fry and Kammerer, of Philadelphia, as printers. The author himself, however, supervised the project in detail, arranging for three grades of paper, from the finest to "coarse," in an effort to reach various levels of the public, and seeing that the type was the finest ever used in an American book. His demands far exceeded the resources of the Conrads, and he was compelled to finance the

edition himself, eventually investing about ten thousand dollars, no more than half of which could be recaptured if every
copy were sold. The result, however, was a volume which even
the *Edinburgh Review* admitted represented "the very summit of
perfection in the mechanical part of book making."

Such pretentiousness was foreign to Barlow's temperament
and embarrassing to his democratic professions. Accordingly,
he took refuge in dissimulation. The work which he dedicated
to his country he presented to Robert Fulton; and although the
two friends were somewhat estranged at the time of publication
he wrote a cordial prefatory letter to the younger man, giving
him credit for having overruled his own desires with respect to
"such expensive and splendid decorations" as the illustrations,
and for having borne their cost. He also implied that the finished book had been brought before the public in a manner Fulton alone had thought proper and confessed to a personal expense of "nothing but that leisurely and exhilarating labor" in
which he always delighted. Among his friends he made no secret
of the facts of his venture, but before the public at large he felt
it necessary to appear so modest and ingenuous that he could
not be suspected of any common desire for literary fame.

The *Columbiad* was published on Christmas Eve, 1807, and
Barlow waited anxiously for news of its reception. His old classmate, Noah Webster, was favorably impressed and wrote, on
April 9, 1808: "I like most of your neology—your new epithets
and terms are mostly well formed—expressive—and a valuable
addition to our language." The reviewers, however, were not so
sympathetic. The first of them, writing in Conrad and Company's own journal, the *American Register*, merely summarized
the poem from its proof sheets without attempting a criticism.
But the writer for the *Philadelphia Portfolio* read it carefully
and, in January, 1809, damned it for its "ludicrous alliteration,"
"bathos," and "petty offenses against the purity of the English
language." This severity, however, roused a "clamour against
the editor" and caused him to satisfy his politically sensitive
readers with a reprint, in May, of a long review from the London
Monthly Magazine which was favorable, although it too ex-

pressed "regret" at the "disposition in American writers for innovating so fast in our common national language." The *Monthly Anthology and Boston Review* was sarcastic about the entire poem. The most important notice it received—a sixteen-page review by Francis Jeffrey in the *Edinburgh Review* for October, 1809—also condemned its language, listing its gaucheries at length and observing that "republican literati seem to make it a point of conscience to have no aristocratical distinctions—even in their vocabulary." Jeffrey's opinion, however, was more just than that of any other reviewer:

As a great national poem, it has enormous—inexpiable—and, in some respects, intolerable faults. But the author's talents are evidently respectable: and severely as we have been obliged to speak of his taste and his diction in a great part of the volume, we have no hesitation in saying that we consider him a giant, in comparison with many of the puling and paltry rhymsters, who disgrace our English literature by their occasional success. As an Epic poet, we do think his case is desperate; but as a philosophical and moral poet, we think he has talents of no ordinary value; and, if he would pay some attention to purity of style, and simplicity of composition, and cherish in himself a certain fastidiousness of taste,—which is not yet to be found, we are afraid, even among the better educated of Americans,—we have no doubt that he might produce something which English poets would envy, and English critics applaud.

Fulton, in a letter of encouragement, made the most of Jeffrey's use of such words as "giant"; but such judicious patronage from a Britisher probably made Barlow as furious as the misunderstandings of his countrymen left him despondent.

For the "moral object" of the *Columbiad* was grossly misinterpreted. After considerable correspondence about the language and orthography of the poem, Noah Webster finally turned his attention to its ideas and on October 13, 1808, wrote a rather bitter letter explaining his inability to review a book which contained such "atheistical tendencies." The attitude of the author's old friend was discouraging, and Barlow may have laid down Webster's letter in order to take up his pen on October 20 and confess to Mrs. Madison that his hope to see his poem "do some good in the world" had "already somewhat abated." An open letter from another old friend, Henri Grégoire, former constitutional bishop of Blois and member of

the National Convention, was even more discouraging. Grégoire, though complimentary to Barlow as a man and to the
Columbiad as a poem, took vigorous exception to the inclusion
of the cross among the symbols of prejudice as a crime that
offended both justice and propriety. Such testimony that Barlow had fallen into atheism, coming from a long and intimate
associate, was widely publicized in the United States. Barlow
replied in an open letter of his own, dated September 13, 1809,
in which he defied his friend and "all the critics of the English
language to point out a passage, if taken in its natural, unavoidable meaning, which militates against the genuine principles,
practices, faith and hope of the christian system, as inculcated
in the gospels and explained by the apostles whose writings ac-
company the gospel in the volume of the New Testament." He
explained the difference between the attitude toward religious
symbols held by "the sect of puritans" to which he still adhered
and that held by the Roman Catholics and, in general, succeeded in convincing Grégoire that by casting unjust reflections
upon the poet's religious beliefs he was doing a disservice to republicanism. The result was a second letter indignantly clearing
Barlow of the charge that he had formally disavowed Christianity while in France. Thus the exchange, while it may have
hurt the reception of the poem, eventually helped Barlow's personal reputation.

The "gentle" treatment of Grégoire, against which some of
the poet's friends protested, proved wise in the long run; but the
exchange of letters put Barlow's honesty to a test which it could
not pass with complete success. His situation was an extraordinarily difficult one. He had spent many years in intense pre-
occupation with the improvement of mankind, had developed a
positive leaning toward materialistic philosophy, and had devoted much time to an extensive study of comparative religions
and the writings of such evangelistic atheists as Holbach. There
can be no reasonable doubt that in his private beliefs he was
more nearly an atheist than such notorious men as Ethan Allen
and Tom Paine. Such subtle revisions in his poem as his substitution of "religious" for "sacrilegious" as an epithet applied

to Robert Boyle indicate the enormous shift in attitude he had experienced since leaving Connecticut. Yet he was meticulously careful, in his published writings, to distinguish between the institution of an established church and Christianity as a religion; and in all his attacks upon the church he rarely failed to pay the highest tribute to Christianity. He undoubtedly believed, with so many of his contemporaries, that until the Age of Reason was established, the Gospels offered the best guide available for human behavior. Realizing how much religion meant to other people, he encouraged religious practices among at least some members of his family and, personally, was unfailing in his devotion to the Christian ideal of "charity." In France his beliefs had been unexceptional. In America, he found, his character, his politics, and his poetry were all likely to be judged with reference to his heterodoxy. The letter to Grégoire, accordingly, was a highly ingenious, and not wholly honest, attempt to appear conventionally religious before the public without deceiving those few friends who shared his private beliefs. He wrote, in one typical passage, that the sect in which he was born and educated had almost no respect for the emblems and ceremonials of religious worship because they had "entirely lost sight of this part of the institutions of Zoroaster, Isis, and Ceres." As a reflection upon Catholicism, his comment was undoubtedly acceptable to his fellow-Congregationalists; but one of his friends, Josiah Meigs, president of the University of Georgia, emphasizing the word "this" as he read, expressed a fear that even in that statement someone might "smell a Rat"—and, as a matter of fact, the *Panoplist* did so in September, 1810. The entire letter is full of this sort of ambiguity, which, practiced as expedient by so many "enlightened" citizens of conservative communities, encouraged the hysterical fear of atheistical plots and scheming Illuminati exhibited by Timothy Dwight and other respectable men who were ordinarily characterized by a sane common sense.

Not all Barlow's fellow-citizens, of course, were so sensitive to his religious beliefs. Meigs, who had understood the letter to Grégoire, wrote that he had "read often and with great delight the splendid and durable Monument of your Genius and Benevolence and real piety"; and the trustees of the University of Georgia, at one meeting, unanimously voted their thanks for a gift copy of the *Columbiad* and an honorary LL.D. for the author. The first edition was too expensive to sell widely, but Barlow had arranged for a second in two small volumes in 1808, and that proved sufficiently popular for a third to be published a year later. These were partially revised in order to correct some of the oversights and inconsistencies in spelling reforms and for the purpose of taking into consideration a few new suggestions made by Webster during his first, favorable reading of the poem. A two-volume London edition was also published in 1809. Although most of the reviews that attempted criticism of any sort continued to be unfavorable, the poem became a fairly popular work—especially in those parts of the country where republicanism remained an active virtue and literary taste remained independent of criticism and instruction. Barlow himself never gave up his hopes for his last important work. It was one of the two books he took with him on his journey into Russia, and he spent some of his time during the last weeks of his life making minor corrections that were incorporated in the Paris, 1813, edition and in that published in Washington in 1825. The poem lived long enough to inspire the epic ambitions of Richard Emmons and Thomas Hedges Genin, but that inspiration can hardly be called fortunate. As the *Edinburgh Review* justly observed, the best parts of the *Columbiad* were "addressed rather to the judgment than to the heart or the imagination"; but, since the Age of Reason failed to arrive, these parts became lost among the belletristic gaucheries with which it abounds.

IV

Barlow left France, in the autumn of 1804, full of disillusionment concerning the adopted country which he had come to think of as "the land of the Corsican." He and his wife had spent the winter in London rather than sail across the Atlantic during the stormy season, but his mind was crowded with thoughts of America and of the new life that would begin when he reached his native shores. He had known for some years that his political principles would make him unwelcome in Connecticut, but of the country at large Jefferson had recently assured him "that federalism is now in its last agonies, and that we want nothing now but for you to come and write its history." "Marshall," the President added, "is engaged in writing a libel on republicanism under the mask of a History of Genl. Washington. The antidote is reserved for you." Barlow decided to spend some months in traveling and visiting old friends and then, following Jefferson's advice, to settle in Washington.

He had many plans. The most immediate was to see the *Columbiad* through the press, and he retained hopes of producing a history of the United States on which he was still working in 1811. But more important was a project about which he had written Jefferson as early as September 15, 1800:

> I see by the testament of General Washington that he contemplated the establishment of a national university at the federal city, as he seems to have left something to the endowment of such an institution. Would it not be possible to take advantage of the veneration which the people have for the memory and opinions of that man to carry into effect a project of this sort? If so, could you not make of it an institution of much more extensive and various utility than any thing of the kind that has hitherto existed?

The idea of improving the state of higher education was one which had interested him for some time. He had visited both of the great universities in England and had made uncomplimentary notes on what he had found there. He had also examined and been dissatisfied with some of the well-known German universities. Of these and of the New England colleges with which he was familiar, he concluded: "There are so many useless things taught and so many useful ones omitted that it is difficult to say whether on the whole they are beneficial or detrimental to society." Oppressed by the feeling that "the present state of knowledge presents us with little more than a confused idea of the immense void of the unknown that lies before us," he believed that the most encouraging educational developments in Europe were the new societies for the advancement of knowledge that had been organized in France since the Revolution, some of which were "highly worthy of imitation." None of the

institutions of any sort that he had examined, however, overcame his fear lest "we lose the principal advantages of the little
that is known for want of proper methods of teaching it to our
children." Accordingly, he proposed an institution with "the
twofold object of collecting and disseminating knowledge."
Practically adapted to American needs, it should engage in pure
research, geographical and industrial exploration, the training
of teachers, and the assistance and supervision of subordinate
institutions.

As Barlow originally sketched his plan, it amounted to little
more than that of an ordinary college operating under the direction of a comprehensive learned society that took all knowledge
to be its province. As the idea matured, however, it became
more nearly like that of a modern university. Even before he
settled upon a house in Washington he drew up a formal
*Prospectus of a National Institution, To Be Established in the
United States*. Its basic idea was that "the advancement of
knowledge by associations of scientific men, and the dissemina-
tion of its rudiments by the instruction of youth," would aid
each other by being brought together instead of being kept
apart as had been customary—or, as he put it in more succinct
language, "this Institution should combine the two great objects, *research* and *instruction*." Dated January 24, 1806, his
prospectus expressed the hope that a bill providing such an institution would be enacted during the current session of Congress; but party feeling was strong, the times were uncertain,
and the plan was too ambitious for hasty consideration. For the
institution that Barlow wanted would have included a military
and perhaps a naval academy, a school of mines, schools of
civil, hydraulic, and mechanical engineering, an assortment of
trade schools, medical and veterinary schools, a school for training teachers, and an unusually broad curriculum of liberal arts.
Concerning the last he made comparatively few definite suggestions in his prospectus, but he wrote at length concerning the
desirability of a more general and careful study of political science; and his proposal, in a letter, to make Noah Webster a professor of philology shows that his scheme was extensive enough

to include scholarship in linguistics and the subsidy of a comprehensive dictionary. In addition, the university was to supervise the Mint, a patent office, the national library and archives, and various museums of arts and sciences. Of course, Barlow was an amateur in learning, thinking in the general terms common to the philosophical, unspecialized minds of his day. But he was an experienced amateur. He had his own private collection of paintings, curiosities, and useful gadgets; he had first-hand knowledge of the difficulties Fulton had encountered in perfecting his inventions; and while defining a few words for Webster's projected dictionary he had gained some perception of the enormous labor which the work would involve. His prospectus was no irresponsible daydream. Rather, it was a deliberately ambitious, forward-looking project, much more advanced than any of the proposals previously submitted by Benjamin Rush, James Sullivan, Samuel H. Smith, Du Pont de Nemours, and others. Barlow thought that the world needed another Bacon, and, in a limited way, he was trying to outline a practical method for the advancement of learning in America.

Had Barlow's scheme been put into effect, the university ideal later exemplified by the Johns Hopkins University would have been realized in the United States seventy years sooner, technical education would have been advanced by a generation, and America would have led the world in systematized advanced studies. But the plan assumed an early retirement of the national debt and so, for the moment, appeared impractical even to sympathetic members of Congress. The bill providing for the establishment of the institution died in a Senate committee, and, as time went on, international tensity diverted men's attention from national self-improvement. It is barely possible, though certainly not so probable as some writers have suggested, that the Smithsonian Institution was an accidental by-product of Barlow's enthusiasm; and several later attempts were made to establish a national university. But the essential idea of combining research with instruction died with Barlow and did not appear again until it was imported from abroad two generations later.

While Barlow was busy with such serious affairs as the publication of the *Columbiad*, the planning of a university, and the improvement of his newly purchased country estate, "Kalorama," he occasionally relaxed by writing verse. During a visit to Connecticut in November, 1805, he renewed his friendship with Elisha Babcock, who was still publishing the *American Mercury*, which he and Barlow had founded in partnership. Babcock apparently asked his old associate for contributions and received a short poem, "War in Europe," which he published on December 12. As the end of the year approached, Barlow also decided to return to his old custom of writing New Year's verse for the paper-carriers. Accordingly, he hastily dashed off a collection of stanzas after the earlier fashion—fluent, humorous, and mildly satiric in their numerous political references. There can be no better illustration of Barlow's failure to realize, in spite of his theoretical awareness of it, the strength and bitterness of party feeling in the America to which he had returned. The lines may have arrived in Hartford too late for the occasion. They were, in any case, too mild for Babcock to use in that or in any later issue of his paper. The poet was more successful in meeting the spirit of the times in later issues, sending poems in 1807, 1809, and 1810 which were remarkable in America for their detailed comment upon European affairs. The verses were both anti-British and anti-war, thus according with the democratic politics of the paper and with the policy which caused Babcock to reprint the "excellent moral stanzas" of Southey's "The Battle of Blenheim." They were also sufficiently vigorous to rival the New Year's addresses issued by the Federalist *Courant;* but they did not descend to bitter, local personalities. The "wicked wit" was proving to his former friends in Hartford that he could be witty without exhibiting the irresponsibility which had characterized some of his earlier writings of this type.

In the meantime Barlow wrote another poem that he took more seriously than his occasional offerings to the post-boy. Since he had first become interested in politics he had been aware of the importance of the West to the future of the United States, and he had greeted the Louisiana Purchase with enthusiasm, expressing concern only with respect to the possible spread of slavery in the new territory. The expedition of Lewis and Clark into the unknown country aroused his intense interest. He urged his English publisher to reprint Lewis' report as soon as it should be issued in America and celebrated the great adventure in a poem "On the Discoveries of Captain Lewis," which he inclosed in a letter to Jefferson on January 12, 1807. A Shenstonian bit of only thirty-two lines, the poem might hardly be worth attention were it not for the fact that the author himself evidently thought of it as one of his more important works and insisted upon its inclusion among the selections that were to form his "collected works." Beneath the easy fluency and fanciful compliments of the poem, indeed, lay two of Barlow's fondest hopes: the peaceful union of his country and the development of its internal resources. The Potomac, the Ohio, and the Missouri rivers stretched almost across the continent, and the new river (which Barlow thought should be called the "Lewis" rather than the Columbia) would supplement them, so that

> These four brother floods, like a garland of flowers,
> Shall entwine all our states in a band,
> Conform and confederate their wide spreading powers,
> And their wealth and their wisdom expand.

Thus the states, united by nature as well as by politics, would grow in peace until, by the force of their example, they should "settle the storms of the world."

But despite his occasional outbursts in verse Barlow had no real intention of coming again before the world in the character of a poet. Fulton's marriage to a young Englishwoman of fortune instead of to Barlow's sister-in-law, Clara Baldwin (who lived at "Kalorama"), had compelled him to give up any hopes he might have retained for further close association with the inventor and for the completion of *The Canal;* and except for the history he had no other literary plans. Yet, as an important citizen of the nation's capital, a member of various scientific and philosophical societies, and a director of the Bank of Washington, he could not avoid some literary duties. He was called upon

to deliver the annual Fourth of July address before the "Democratic citizens of the District of Columbia" in 1809; and, although Jefferson wondered what he could say "on so hackneyed
a subject," the retired president admitted that his friend had
"risen out of it with lustre." The *Oration* is Barlow's smoothest,
most highly polished prose work. In it he directed attention to
the future rather than to the past, insisting that the novel situation of America

calls for deep reflection on the propensities of human nature, an accurate
acquaintance with the history of human actions; and what is perhaps the most
difficult to attain, a wise discrimination among the maxims of wisdom, or what
are such in other times or nations, to determine which of them are applicable
and which would be detrimental to the end we have in view.

Holding that the situation called for "new theories," he himself
spoke with constant reference to the theory of habits he had acquired in France, distinguishing between "moral nature undis-
guised" and "moral nature disguised by habits materially different from ours." "Nations are educated like individual in-
fants," he declared, as he had in a note to the *Columbiad*; and he
found much to be done in America, for, he said,

our habits of thinking and even of reasoning, it must be confessed, are still
borrowed from feudal principles and monarchical establishments. As a nation
we are not up to our circumstances. Our principles in the abstract, as wrought
into our state and federal constitutions, are in general worthy of the highest
praise; they do honor to the human intellect. But the practical tone and tension of our minds do not well correspond with those principles. We are like a
person conversing in a foreign language, whose idiom is not yet familiar to him.

As he summed up his own notions of popular education, as opposed to those of the "aristocratical subjects of a European
monarchy," he declared:

It is not intended that every citizen should be a judge or a general or a
legislator. But every citizen is a voter; it is essential to your institutions that
he should be a voter; and if he has not the instruction necessary to enable him
to discriminate between the characters of men, to withstand the intrigues of
the wicked and to perceive what is right, he immediately becomes a tool for
knaves to work with; he becomes both an object and an instrument of corruption; his right of voting becomes an injury to himself and a nuisance to society.

There was no blindly irrational faith in "the people" in his
address. If Barlow had heard Alexander Hamilton's famous re-

mark: "Your people, sir, is a great beast," he might have replied: "And my people, sir, will remain a great beast until their habits of thinking are conditioned to their humanity." Some day, he thought, the job might be done.

Part of his optimism was based on the expectation that the United States would soon be out of debt and that surplus funds might be used for education—"if no extraordinary call for money to repel foreign aggression should intervene." He admitted the necessity of a defense, by force, against the "unjust governments of Europe," since it was "not in the nature of their organization" for them to allow "justice" or the "liberty of the seas" by "compact." To such men as Humphreys and the Federalists generally the situation called for a big navy. Jefferson had tried to avoid it by the embargo. Barlow, fearing the destructive expense of a navy comparable to England's and having witnessed the effects of the embargo, had another solution: he suggested that the United States solve its problems of defense by building up a submarine attack. "It might," he announced optimistically, "rid the seas of all the buccaneers both great and small that now infest them; it might free mankind from the scourge of naval wars, one of the greatest calamities they now suffer, and to which I can see no other end." The suggestion, he realized, was visionary, and so he concluded his oration with a note of apology:

I should not have introduced it in this place were it not for its immediate connexion with the means of commencing and prosecuting those vast interior improvements which the state of our nation so imperiously demands; which the heroes of our revolution, the sages of our early councils, the genius of civilization, and the cause of suffering humanity have placed within our power and confided to our charge.

The difference in cost between a battleship and one of Fulton's "plunging boats," multiplied by the number of units in the British navy, he thought, would accomplish the same results that would have been reached had the cost of the Revolution been spent on canals, roads, bridges, and schools: "it would make a garden of the United States, and people it with a race of men worthy to enjoy it."

Barlow was also called upon, during this same year, to express himself formally upon Tom Paine, and the result was another short piece of prose which he planned to have included in his "collected works." Paine had died on June 8, 1809, and James Cheetham, editor of a New York newspaper, immediately planned a biography, writing to Barlow for information in a way that indicated a disposition to play up the more scandalous aspects of Paine's career. Barlow was not anxious to place himself upon record concerning his old associate, for he realized that public opinion was strongly against the author of *The Age of Reason* and believed that the time was not yet ripe for a judicious estimate of his character. Consequently, he wrote Cheetham a private letter advising against the biography but giving an extremely generous and charitable estimate of Paine's character and achievements in case his advice should not be followed. He asked particularly that his letter be neither published nor copied. Two and a half months later, however, a North Carolina admirer of the *Columbiad* published an open letter in the *Raleigh Register* inquiring why Paine had not been mentioned in the poem which called the roll of almost all the other Revolutionary patriots. This time Barlow faced the issue squarely and gave to the newspaper a carefully considered reply, dated October 18, 1809:

Your very flattering letter of the 1st inst. has recalled to mind a subject which has before given me some uneasiness. I have regretted that I could not, as I thought, with propriety notice as you would wish the character of Thomas Paine: I knew him well, and no man has a higher opinion of the merit of his labors in the cause of liberty, in this country and throughout the world—But he was unjust to himself. His private life disgraced his public character. Certain immoralities, and low and vulgar habits, which are apt to follow in the train of almost habitual drunkenness, rendered him a disgusting object for many of the latter years of his life, though his mental faculties retained much of their former lustre.

People who knew only his writings necessarily held one opinion of him, and those who knew only the man held another, Barlow continued,

while those who have known him as I have done, among the most illustrious and most contemptible of human beings, must be afflicted at the contrast, and grieve that they cannot snatch him from among the last, and fix him in that place alone where his good genius ought to have preserved him.

Perhaps these reasons will not be satisfactory to you. They are scarcely so to me—But in the history of the United States, on which I am at present occupied, he will find his place. It is his most proper place where strict and ample justice must be done him, as one of the most able and efficient defenders of our rights—one of the surest guides that led us to independence and peace.

Since the history was not completed, Paine did not achieve his "place" in it; and when Barlow suspected that this would be the case he began to worry about his public statement and instructed Fulton to preserve the more charitable letter to Cheetham as his final commentary on the man who had done so much for him and for the two countries of which he was a citizen.

During these years Barlow was happy and contented upon his fine estate above Rock Creek, and he professed to be living a life of complete retirement. Yet a person so well informed upon European affairs, so acutely interested in politics, and so intimate with the leaders of the party in power could hardly have avoided participation in the business that was going on around him. He probably advised the new president, Madison, even more freely than he had advised Jefferson. In any case, Madison shared his friend's distrust of the English, and Barlow shared the President's disgust with his secretary of state, Robert Smith, who was constantly engaged in sabotaging the government's pro-French policy. Smith resigned under criticism in the spring of 1811 and undertook a public defense of himself in a pamphlet, *Robert Smith's Address to the People of the United States*, which misrepresented the relationship between himself and Madison and invited criticism of the President. Barlow was indignant. He immediately wrote a *Review of Robert Smith's Address*, which answered statements made in the pamphlet, made some personal criticism of its author, and discussed the problems of American foreign relations in a way that defended the Non-intercourse Act and partially justified France's actions with respect to American commerce. The *Review* was not a literary work, and Barlow was willing to keep it anonymous. It was originally published in the *National Intelligencer*, but arrangements were made for a Philadelphia edition of five thousand copies in pamphlet form in July, 1811, and it was reprinted in London during the same year. Barlow wrote Fulton concerning the Philadelphia arrangements but added a warning: "It must not be known who wrote it. *Mind that.*"

The need for secrecy was, at the moment, pressing. Barlow had just been induced by Madison and his new secretary of state, James Monroe, to undertake a delicate mission as minister plenipotentiary from the United States to Napoleon; and under the circumstances his *Review* was a serious indiscretion. On the one hand, it was a personal attack upon a political figure who had the support of a Senate bloc sufficiently powerful to have forced his appointment upon an unwilling president; on the other, while generally favorable to France, it was in some particulars severely critical of that country's handling of certain problems that he was going abroad to solve. France had given diplomatic evidence of a theoretical change in attitude toward the United States, and Barlow was being sent to arrange a closer accord between theory and practice and to estimate and collect indemnities for damage previously done to American commerce. Profoundly distrustful of Napoleon and extremely pessimistic about gaining "justice" by "compact" with any European government, the new minister was not hopeful. Although he wrote Fulton from Hampton Roads on August 2, 1811, expressing optimism concerning the voyage, he added: "But my heart is heavy. I have left my country, possibly and why not probably forever. . . . . I go with an ardent wish, but without much hope of doing good,—and with the full intention, tho with a feeble hope of living to return." A fear that he would not return from "the land of the Corsican" had apparently been in his mind since he had agreed to undertake the mission, for he arranged with Fulton to publish a two-volume edition of his collected works and found time to correct his major political writings and minor poems for that purpose. Fulton expressed a determination to do justice to his friend's genius in the publication, but Barlow was anxious to have the arrangements made before he sailed and expressed regret that Fulton had not found time to do so. His instructions concerning the selections to be used and their order of arrangement were specific, however, and he sailed with a feeling of confidence that if his fears proved justified he had left behind his memorial.

After his arrival in Paris in September Barlow spent more than a year in negotiations without achieving any formal success. He became friendly with the French minister of foreign affairs, the Duke of Bassano, and was on good terms with the empress; but Napoleon, planning his Russian campaign and holding the world in suspense, ignored the American minister. Barlow, an experienced man of business, became impatient with the red tape and lack of "sense" exhibited "on both sides of the Atlantic"; yet he received so many incidental concessions, marks of friendship, and favors for his countrymen in France that he lost his pessimism and "got to be pretty confident of success and great success." Finally, on October 11, 1812, the Duke of Bassano wrote from Vilna that the Emperor was willing to complete the negotiations in person at that city; and on the twenty-sixth Barlow set off posthaste across Europe, traveling day and night through a "majesty of mud," toward the completion of his labors. Before he reached Vilna the mud was frozen and his water bottle was solid with ice within the freezing carriage. The country outside was a picture of devastation, with dead horses, broken wagons, and dead men everywhere. Vilna itself was overcrowded and undersupplied, and the natives—the peasants in the country and the Jews in the city—reflected a "state of society" more "degraded" than anything he had ever seen outside Algiers. And there, gathered with other foreign diplomats, he and his nephew Thomas waited, hearing story after vivid story about the horrors of "this glorious Russian war."

Soon they learned that there was no hope of a French victory, and early in December all foreigners were evacuated from Vilna. In a temperature at thirteen degrees below zero, Barlow and his friend General Waltersdorff, the Danish minister, "out ran the rest" to Warsaw; but Napoleon, fearing assassination at the hands of his own troops, according to the diplomatic gossip, passed them in the night. Soldiers of the French and allied armies were dropping dead by the thousands with "sickness, famine and frost." Barlow's mission had failed, and he himself was ill from hardship and exposure. Nevertheless, he left Warsaw on the eighteenth and got as far as the Polish village of Zarnowiec before his nephew and friends became alarmed and stopped for medical assistance—which came too late. He died on Christmas Eve, five years after his poetic vision of international peace had been given to the world.

At some time during those last few horrible weeks Barlow had found time to compose a poem. His "Advice to a Raven in Russia" was neither a calculated piece of literature ambition nor a philosophical attempt to improve the state of humanity. It was a spontaneous outburst of bitterness directed against a military dictator who had come to represent the scourge of humanity. In comparison to his words on Napoleon, Barlow's attack upon Edmund Burke and the conspiring kings was merely playful. He had hoped that men might be induced to become rational; Napoleon had forced them to become soldiers. He had hoped that they might be made perfect; Napoleon had made them corpses. He had dreamed of a world blanketed in peace; Napoleon had covered it with carrion. A raven might be sent forth anywhere, from India to the West Indies, from Spain to Russia, and the scavenger could find food supplied by Napoleon's ambition. This was the outcome of the glorious experiment of the French Revolution. This was the result of the "necessary" improvement of society. No wonder the enthusiastic advocate of the rights of man was bitter. Fulton did not carry out his promise to do justice to his friend's genius by the publication of his works, but if they ever should be printed in a collected edition the "Advice to a Raven" should be the unauthorized concluding selection. No other member of the group of Connecticut Wits succeeded in producing a poem so memorable or so moving in its bitter irony.

V

Of all the graduates of Yale College whose paths led them into the wide world open to Americans after the Revolution, Joel

Barlow's was the most intricate and interesting. The Redding farm boy who eventually made a fortune in trade tried his hand at a half-dozen professions and gained experience under every variety of Western civilization. The youngster who began his education in Moor's Indian School completed it under the French Encyclopedists. The youth who trembled before his father-in-law grew up to negotiate firmly with Napoleon. The lad who convinced his mother that Hanover, New Hampshire, was too far from home died and was buried in Poland. No other American of his generation viewed so many aspects of life, in so many countries, with so curious and so thoughtful an eye. During all these varied, complicated experiences he achieved and preserved the consistent character of a man who was flexible in mind, firm in principles, and determined in his hope for the welfare of his fellows. He was more often a philosophic spectator of the great events of his time than an active participant in them, but he was too active in a minor way and too close to the major actors ever to achieve detachment or that philosophic indifference which thrives in an ivory tower. His writings, accordingly, reflect the age in which he lived more liberally and broadly than those of more practical men, yet at the same time preserve the vitality of the dreams and hopes and fancies that affected Jefferson and Madison and other men of that type.

Barlow was not, of course, a great writer or even a very good poet; but in these days when most literary reputations, except the greatest, are preserved in anthologies a judicious selection of his writings would give him a better character than he has had. The peculiar value of his literary work as a whole, however, lies in the fact that as a poet, describing visions his associates among the politicians had to conceal lest they be called fools, he revealed so many springs of action which, through the successes of more practical men, formed the institutions and affirmations that are among our most precious heritages from the eighteenth century. The sources tapped by Barlow and his contemporaries in their search for a knowledge of what would be good for mankind were various and often inconsistent with one another. Barlow himself drew upon three: a belief in an internal sense, common to all men, by which they perceived the most important abstract truths; a trust in impulsive humanitarian sentiment; and, finally, an acceptance of deterministic materialism which denied everything except the perceptions of the external senses and the fundamental law of motion. He never wholly and irrevocably renounced any one in favor of another, but the last, derived from Holbach and the Encyclopedists, dominated his mature mind and his major literary works. All of these supported his democratic political philosophy, but long and extensive observation convinced him that if men possessed an internal common sense it was frequently undeveloped and useless and that humanitarian sentiment was by no means universal. His materialism was the mainspring of his democratic optimism.

All three of these springs of action have survived, and optimistic affirmations of democracy are still supported by more or less shy expressions of confidence in the common sense of the masses or, more rarely, by expressions of sentimental humanitarianism. But philosophical materialism and the behavioristic social psychology which Barlow accepted as a corollary to it have become the twentieth century's greatest threat to the existence of democracy. As the basis of the modern business of advertising, this psychology threatens the fundamental democratic liberty of individual expression through the press, and as the chief weapon of the totalitarian state it threatens the very existence of those nations which practice the democratic method of government. While the world has grown steadily more materialistic in its working philosophy, the materialistic fountain of democratic faith has dried up.

A review of the sources of Barlow's faith shows why this is so. The eighteenth-century theorists who adopted materialism as the basis of moral and social philosophy drew with very little discrimination upon the scientific discoveries of their age and borrowed, by analogy with Newtonian physics, the principle of attraction and repulsion as "the fundamental law of the moral world." Naming these forces respectively "pleasure" and "pain," they reasoned, by a logical fallacy, that a man who was free to move "naturally" would be necessarily attracted by that which was good for him and repelled by that which was harmful.

Thus, although humanity had been abused through the ages by the long accumulation of bad habits begun in the infancy of the race, if man could be freed from his old mistakes the whole force of nature would be opposed to any attempt to press new errors upon him. That any single man or any bureau of propaganda could be stronger than "nature" would have been, to them, inconceivable. Barlow's most sincere hope was that his writings would "do good" in their political and moral effect—that they would help preserve and spread those republican principles in which he had lived and in which, as he wrote an acquaintance, he expected to die, whether they represented truth or error. They will hardly accomplish that result in exactly the way he intended; but they should help make clear that if those principles are to be preserved it will not be done by retracing the intellectual course of our ancestors. In a more materialistic age intuitionalism and sentiment are even less adequate sources of democratic faith than they were in the eighteenth century. What the democratic world needs is to find an additional source of confidence, in accord with the dominant temper of the present time, which avoids the errors of analogy and logic upon which Joel Barlow rested so comfortably.

CHAPTER X

PRESIDENT TIMOTHY DWIGHT

I

ALTHOUGH he had professed not to "court the appointment," the election of Timothy Dwight to the presidency of Yale College, in 1795, placed him upon the summit of his ambition. Henceforth he wanted nothing except a long life in which to practice the virtue he called "complacency" —the benevolent helpfulness of a superior person. His duties as president included instructing the Senior class in mental and moral philosophy, rhetoric and oratory, and the fundamentals of religion; and, after the corporation had sought in vain for a professor of theology, he took upon himself the responsibilities of that office, delivering his lectures in a series of Sunday-evening sermons which extended over four years and was repeated for each college generation. Although he was prevented from making any immediate change in the college laws, particularly from abolishing the fagging system for Freshmen, he gradually substituted moral suasion and a standard of "gentlemanly" behavior for discipline by fines and the enforcement of traditional rules. "His government," as one student described it, "was paternal, yet in the highest degree energetic." The students, on the whole, were pleased by his reforms and impressed by his learning and condescension. The enrolment grew, and for a few years the number of tutors had to be increased almost annually. The curriculum was greatly strengthened and the range of instruction extended. A professorship of chemistry and natural history was established, an instructor in Hebrew was appointed, a professor of law and another of languages and ecclesiastical history were added, and, finally, a school of medicine was organized and chartered. From the beginning Dwight was energetic about increasing the material resources of the college, and, in general, his administration proved the most successful Yale had ever experienced.

His successes were not accomplished without annoying difficulties. He had acquired such tolerance in the peaceful surroundings at Greenfield that he would administer communion to halfway covenant congregations, but his old reputation for bigotry pursued him. James Ogden, the brother-in-law of one of his uncles, attacked him vigorously with charges of prejudice against Episcopalians; the democrats were so aroused by the political bias of his first commencements that they publicly announced their intention of staying away from future exercises; and his initial success in getting a grant of funds from the state legislature was achieved at the expense of antagonizing numerous members of that body. Yet Dwight towered above his detractors. He had developed a robust constitution which he preserved by spending his vacation out of doors, traveling by horse and buggy throughout New England and upper New York; and his great energy remained unimpaired until shortly before his death. His powers of observation were acute, and his memory, carefully cultivated because of his bad eyesight, was a constant source of astonishment to his acquaintances. His stately bearing and clear, strong voice were signs of authority. Gradually his complacency settled over Connecticut like a mantle. The democratic press, anxious to destroy an influence it could not ignore, named him "Pope" Dwight. A vulgar pamphleteer tried to condemn the pretentiousness of an opponent's political speech by writing:

> He printed it with copy-right,
> And felt as big as Doctor Dwight.

But the President of Yale remained, as far as any eye could see, unaffected by the cries raised against him. He spread his benevolence abroad by his activity in organizing or operating the Connecticut Missionary Society, the Andover Theological Semi-

nary, the American Board of Commissioners for Foreign Missions, and numerous other religious, scientific, and literary enterprises; and at home he was suspected, at least, of dominating
the councils of the Federalist party, which ruled Connecticut
until the year following his death on January 11, 1817. Except
for occasional sermons published by request, the condition of
his eyesight kept him from literary composition until his students, beginning with the Senior class of 1802, began to worry
about the loss to posterity of so much wisdom and volunteered
to act as amanuenses for his dictation. With their assistance
and that of a series of secretaries employed by the corporation in
1805, he dictated a four-volume account of his *Travels, in New-
England and New-York* and seven volumes of sermons which
were published after his death. During the last years of his life
he also engaged in a considerable amount of miscellaneous literary activity. He seems to have had time and energy for almost
everything; and, while the presidency of Yale continued to
satisfy his formal ambition, the office itself acquired an importance which no one else had anticipated.

There were few external signs of change in Dwight during
most of these twenty-two years at Yale. His life followed the
pattern he held up to the Senior class in his first baccalaureate
sermon:

. . . . Let me advise you to aim, when you commence business, at *distinguished character*. Be not satisfied with merely escaping blame, or mingling
with the mass. Determine to excell; not from the envious wish to look down
on others; but from the generous love of excellence; and from the evangelical
desire of doing good. Let sloth, ignorance, and insignificance, jog quietly on in
the downward track, so congenial to their character. Lift *your* eyes to the hills
of science, dignity, and virtue, and consider the rocks and the steeps, as
obstacles placed there merely to be gloriously overcome. Halt not, on account
of any suspected deficiency in your talents. Toil is the great instrument of
excelling; application the chief source of human distinction.

He let two generations of students go by and preached the sermon again to the class of 1805. Nine years later, however, when
he had completed the pattern and achieved his aim, he decided
to instruct the Seniors with a sermon devoted entirely to the
"Love of Distinction." His attitude had changed. "There is no

pleasure to be found in distinction," he told them in the beginning; and in the conclusion he warned them against the "supreme danger" of following "passion" rather than "conscience." All passion, he had discovered, led to thorns on earth and woes in the world to come. "But among all the passions which mislead, endanger, and harass the mind," he added, "none is more hostile to its peace, none more blind, none more delirious than the love of distinction." That he was speaking from experience was revealed during his last illness when he confessed to a life excessively covetous of reputation and influence. He had so lived that one of his former students began a memorial oration: "The light of Yale is extinguished. The vital force is fled." But his later wisdom might have preferred the words of another, who described him after a longer retrospect as a "Yankee, Christian gentleman—nothing more—nothing less."

II

When the President of Yale faced the concluding fluid years of the eighteenth century, he had already defined his own attitude toward society and placed it upon record in his sermon on *The True Means of Establishing Public Happiness*. He stood for stability in a changing world, and one of his duties, ex officio, was to point out the threats to stability that developed during the year preceding each of his public baccalaureate sermons. The first of these, "On Duties Connected with a Professional Life," was one of particular advice to his first graduating class, but he took occasion to warn them generally:

The present age is, emphatically, and to a degree of frenzy, the age of innovation. Beardless boys, treading on the threshold of science, pert coxcombs, the mere retailers of a few scientific terms, obtained, and understood, as parrots obtain and understand the language which they utter, will inform you, and have the impudence to inform mankind, that the present is the only enlightened age of man; that the world has slumbered in chains of ignorance and prejudice, for six thousand years; that light has just begun to dawn upon the earth; and that true philosophy never condescended to bless mankind until the present age.

The new ideas and the optimistic attitude which had attracted Barlow repelled Dwight; and one passage in the sermon, indeed, might have been a scornful answer to the *Advice to the Privileged Orders:*

In this age of innovation, visionary philosophers have retailed abundantly their reveries, on political subjects, as well as others. They have discovered, that men are naturally wise and good, prone to submit to good government, and pleased to have their passions and appetites restrained; and that all the errors and iniquities of our species are derived merely from the oppression of the privileged and the great. From these principles, adopted in defiance of every fact, they have drawn consequences repugnant to every reason, and fraught with every folly, danger, and mischief. *You* will find all men substantially alike, and all naturally ignorant, and wicked. You will find every man pleased, not merely to be free, but to tyrannize; and to indulge without restraint, and without degree, both appetite and passion; and to be impatient of every law, which in any degree restrains either. The most arrant tyranny, of which you will ever hear, is the tyranny of a mob; and the most dangerous domination, that of a Jacobin Society. All men, when assembled in multitudes, are more unreasonable, more unjust, more tyrannical, and every way more wicked, than when they are separate; because they dare to be so.

The opposition of the two leading Connecticut Wits, with respect to the most important social events of their time, was being vigorously defined.

Their opposition, however, was not nearly so complete as the vigor of Dwight's language might indicate. In an age which placed so heavy an emphasis upon environment that even its greatest scientific worker in problems of heredity—Lamarck— could not escape it, few people would deny the power of habit which Barlow optimistically affirmed in his *Advice*. Dwight certainly did not do so, for he told his audience with assurance: "Whatever you find in man, better than I have asserted, is the result of human discipline, or of divine grace." Agreeing that men could be made better by human discipline, both Dwight and Barlow could have joined, with approximately an equal amount of exaggeration, in the refrain from *Greenfield Hill:* "Habits alone yield good below." Both held reservations concerning the philosophy expressed in that line of verse: Dwight, as a formal article of faith, insisted upon the power of "divine grace"; Barlow, as a "fancy" which he "loved to indulge," maintained the possibility of an inherent knowledge of good. But they agreed that the mass of men were mostly creatures of habit. Furthermore, their two conceptions of the "nature" of man, however divergent they may have been in theory, were not strongly opposed in their practical implications. Dwight, the Calvinist, of course thought of man as being naturally bad, whereas Barlow, the materialist, looked upon him as being neither good nor bad by nature, although he had been corrupted by his environment. Each thought that the state of humanity was pretty good in America; and neither, during the last years of the century, fancied its condition anywhere else in the world. The verbal and emotional vehemence of their opposition was by no means a necessary result of their ideas concerning the effect of society upon the individual or of their conception of the nature of the individual.

The vehemence of their opposition was, more than anything else, a product of the difference in the imaginative qualities of two men who were profoundly affected by the events of the age in which they lived. As a youth Barlow had been able to see visions, and in his middle age he had begun to rationalize his dreams, treating them as reasonable hypotheses, which he hoped might be proved true by bold social experiment. When Dwight was forced to contemplate such fancies, however, he was overcome by the same sort of imaginative shyness that upset him whenever he tried to visualize the strange civilization of a faraway land. He was never able to look upon anything far removed from experience and revelation without getting excited. Ten years after his first baccalaureate sermon he was to tell a class of students that "hypotheses" were "miserable things employed for wicked purposes, by miserable men" and recall his fear of "a few years" before that they might "revive again." The hypotheses of the revolutionary philosophers, especially of those who were French, agitated him far beyond the limits of his customary good sense and caused him to rage against philosophy itself as an aberration of the mind which held out "a general license to every passion and appetite."

The occasion of this public charge against philosophy was the second commencement after his accession to the presidency of Yale, at which he preached, and expanded for immediate publication, two discourses on *The Nature and Danger of Infidel Philosophy*. In these sermons he professed to deal only with those speculations that were opposed to Christianity, although he made clear his equal contempt for "much other philosophy, which busies itself with government, medicine, and various other subjects, which is equally vain and deceitful." He admitted no clear line of distinction between a man's religious beliefs and his social behavior. On the contrary, he insisted:

> So evident is the want of morals on the part of Infidels, in this country, generally, that to say—"A man is an Infidel"—is understood, of course, as a declaration that he is a plainly immoral man. On the contrary, to say—"A man is a true or real Christian"—is universally understood as a declaration, that he is a man distinguishedly virtuous. This phraseology has its origin in the experience, and common-sense, of mankind, and may be fairly assumed as complete evidence of the sentiment alleged.

Before coming to this conclusion he had attempted a survey of the beliefs of almost all ancient philosophers and a summary of the defects, ranging from sodomy to hypocrisy, in their moral characters, and had made a comparison between some of their worst beliefs and those of certain modern deists and infidels. Dwight had little firsthand knowledge of the men whom he discussed. Shaftesbury, Bolingbroke, Hume, and Voltaire were all old objects of attack with borrowed arguments, and most of his new remarks were based upon reading in such secondary sources as Adam Smith's *Letter to Mr. Strahan* on the death of Hume and Bishop George Horne's *Letter* in reply. Joseph Priestley's *Observations on the Increase of Infidelity* encouraged his attitude toward Hume and Voltaire, and supplied him with some new French enemies of true religion—D'Alembert, Rousseau, and, especially, Volney; and he called again the roll of "bad names" listed in John Leland's *A View of the Principal Deistical Writers* and Philip Skelton's *Deism Revealed*. His dragnet was impressive for its thoroughness, if not for its discrimination; and it undoubtedly left his readers with the notion that, although "philosophy at large" might be "not only undeserving of censure, but deserving of the highest praise," it had best be avoided lest they be spoiled by its predominantly vain deceit.

Soon after Dwight had completed his collection of infidel philosophers for the expanded, published version of his sermons, he came across the first of two books which were to set him—in common with many other conservative New Englanders—on the verge of hysteria. This was Professor John Robison's *Proofs of a Conspiracy against the Religions and Governments of Europe, Carried on in Secret Meetings of Free Masons, Illuminati, and Reading Societies*, which had appeared in London in 1797 and was reprinted in Philadelphia the next year. Dwight could do no more, at the time, than introduce a footnote reference to it in his own account of the dangers of infidel philosophy, but he read the book with conviction. About the same time the *British Critic* for August, 1797, reached him with its excited review of another book of the same kind, the Abbé Barruel's *Memoirs, Illustrating the History of Jacobinism*, which was being published in four volumes in London. This work was also soon to be published in America, the first two volumes being printed in Hartford in 1799. Dwight apparently obtained a copy of at least the first volume, dealing with "The Antichristian Conspiracy," and found it even more circumstantial and convincing than Robison's book. The two works professed to expose the existence of a widespread secret organization, started by disbanded Jesuits and carried on by philosophers and Free Masons, which had as its purpose the complete overthrow of Christianity, monarchy, and the established structure of society. Spread over the entire continent of Europe and creeping into Great Britain and America, this "Illuminism" brought together, in one evangelical movement, atheism, republicanism, free love, and communism—every threat to the established institutions of church, state, home, and property. Barruel, in particular, identified the atheistic movement with the French philosophers whose names were already anathema to the orthodox of New England: Voltaire, D'Alembert, and Diderot (with Frederick II of Prussia) were the "chiefs of the conspiracy," which included, among other men of letters, Rousseau, Boulanger, and "a fiend called Condorcet." Group meetings were held in the Hôtel d'Holbach. All the men who were to be distrusted by right-thinking people, all threats against security, all that was evil in the intellectual world, were united and made assailable under a single name. Jedidiah Morse began the assault in a fast-day sermon preached in Boston on May 9, 1798, and within a few months scores of other Federalist, Congregational New Englanders joined in.

Dwight raised his own voice in the hue and cry after Illuminism in a sermon on *The Duty of Americans at the Present Crisis*, which he preached at the request of the citizens of New Haven on the Fourth of July, 1798. He had supplemented the revelations of Robison and Barruel with Helen Maria Williams' vivid account of the Terror, in her letters describing *A Residence in France during the Years 1792, 1793, 1794, and 1795* (which had just been republished in New York); and he was thoroughly convinced of direct connections between the conspiracy, the events of the French Revolution, and the later actions of the Directory. His sermon was based on the parallel between the accounts of the Jacobins and the prophecy in Revelation concerning the pouring-out of the sixth vial and the gathering at Armageddon. Primarily, it was an attempt by a flood of oratory to disassociate the idea of liberty from everything French, to identify it with the practice of religion, and, so, to represent the conspiracy against religion as a threat to everything that the Fourth of July anniversary stood for in America. "Without religion," he declared in the spirit of John Winthrop, "we may possibly retain the freedom of savages, bears, and wolves; but not the freedom of New England. If our religion were gone, our state of society would perish with it; and nothing would be left, which would be worth defending." The duty of Americans was to resist the rising tide of evil by a meticulous practice of morality and an observance of pious institutions. Ringing through this somewhat conventional clerical advice, however, came the suggestion of martial music: Dwight clearly implied that a "defensive" war against France—already under way upon the high seas—in the names of "liberty" and "religion" would not be unjustifiable.

The sermon aroused the anger of Connecticut democrats, and

the intemperate character of the undergraduate orations at the 1798 commencement provoked antagonism toward the college. The United States was in the midst of its first intense factional dispute over foreign affairs, party feeling ran high, and partisans on both sides were willing to believe almost anything. The Yale Phi Beta Kappa society was charged with Illuminism because its meetings were secret. James Cosens Ogden produced *A View of the New-England Illuminati*, in which he charged that Calvinistic clubs were holding secret political meetings and that Connecticut had "become almost totally an ecclesiastical state, ruled by the *President* of the *College*, as a *Monarch*." Dwight's younger brother described a Jacobin as a bloodthirsty villain who would find his greatest delight in murdering his mother. In comparison with such insane charges and countercharges, Dwight's own oratory appeared restrained; and as the conflict became more intense he seems to have made a genuine effort to avoid trouble. His baccalaureate sermon for 1799, "Life a Race," was a model of pulpit eloquence which was supposed to be politically innocuous. Yet his opinions were too strong to be concealed; and even in this he included, among his characters of men who strove unwisely to be great, a representation of the philosopher:

To be learned is the great object of his ambition; and to enjoy the sweets of knowledge the commanding dictate of his relish for pleasure. In his study he dwells: in his books he passes his life. *To think* appears to him the only proper end of human existence; while *to do* is not even entered on the register of his duties. The greatest distinction between men, and brutes, he perceives to be the intellect; and concludes, therefore, that difference in intellect is the only ground of distinction between men. With him an unlearned man passes only for a brute of higher class; a connecting link between apes and real men. From the summit of sublime demonstrations, and the pinnacle of philosophical greatness, he looks down with scorn and pity on the grovelling beings, who creep over the plain below; and is ready to wonder, why such humble creatures were brought into existence; and, still more, why they were endued with the faculties of thought and speech. If it were possible for a proud man to be thankful, he would, at times, feel grateful emotions, that Providence has assigned him to a higher station; and not destined him to a character and to employments, totally unworthy of a rational being. In the mean time, he knows not that the whole end of thinking is action; and the whole use of science, in its most extended researches, the advancement of human happiness; that, when it terminates not in this end, it is gold buried in the earth; useless, because it is not employed in the business of life. He has not discovered, that science is a means, and not an end. He does not discern, that a mind, richly fraught with knowledge, and existing only to think, is a watch, furnished indeed with wheels, and pinions, but without a spring to set it in motion, a balance to regulate it, or a hand to mark its circuits: a pretty object to the eye of curiosity, but of no use to its maker. He mistrusts not, that the clown, who faithfully follows the plough, or wields the hoe and the spade, is a better member of society than himself; nor dreams, that the two mites of such a man will be accepted as a gift to God, while his own abundance will be slighted and forgotten. The whole end of his life, so far as his fellow-creatures are concerned, is to excite admiration; and, so far as himself is concerned, to gratify the love of knowing. To his fellow-men his existence, among them, is as uninteresting, as to the inhabitants of another planet; for he feels no obligation to wish their happiness, and makes no effort to promote it. His talents, though formed for the noblest ends, and furnishing means of distinguished usefulness, are all closeted in his mind, or wasted over his books. After his death, his whole history may be written in this short epitaph:

Here lies a learned Man.

He refrained from presenting his philosopher as Jacobinical, vicious, or immoral; but he was not able to represent him as being, in any way, useful or good. Dwight was still thinking, of course, of the men he had mentioned by name in his earlier sermons, for he continued to devote most of his time, as an instructor, to hearing recitations on John Locke and William Paley.

Such restraint was possible for Dwight in Sabbath sermons in which, as a rule, he pointedly avoided outright politics. He was also able to restrain himself in *A Discourse, Delivered at New-Haven, February 22, 1800, on the Character of George Washington, Esq.*, being content with one philosophical reference in his eulogy of the man he considered one of the four great leaders of history: "Perhaps there never was a mind, on which theoretical speculations had less influence, and the decisions of common sense more." But when he was called upon in 1801 to deliver the New Year's sermon in the First Church in New Haven the occasion called for a more direct recognition of the evils that threatened the world. Like most of his colleagues on the first Sunday of the nineteenth century, he prepared *A Discourse on Some Events of the Last Century*, dealing with the "progress of knowledge" and the revivals of religion during the preceding hundred years. He congratulated his country upon remaining "far behind" Europe in "the speculative sciences" and described the "philosophists" (in a term of distinction borrowed from the *British Critic*) as "scoffers, walking after their own lusts, and alluring others, through the same lusts, to follow them; promising them liberty, as their reward, and yet being themselves, and making their disciples, the lowest and most wretched of all slaves, the slaves of corruption." "*Philosophical pride*, and *the love of sinning in security and peace*," he concluded, "are, therefore the two great causes of Infidelity, according to the scriptures." He gave his hearers an elaborate warning against infidel writings:

The terms employed in them are so wholly abstract, and the phraseology so mysterious and perplexed, that the reader, engaged by the ingenuity of the writer, is lost in a mist of doubtful expressions and unsettled sentiments. His faith is constantly solicited to gravely described dreams; and his eye is required to fix on the form of a cloud, varying its shape through every moment of his inspection. From the highway of common sense he is invited into bye paths where indeed nothing worthy of his curiosity is ever seen. Whatever he reads is uttered with the gravity and confidence of superiour wisdom, and an imposing air of mystery, and with continual hints of something immensely important, in due time to be revealed. Thus he wanders on, a dupe to artfully excited expectation, and loses himself in "a wilderness, where there is no way." He is not informed, but allured; not convinced, but perplexed; yet he is often, perhaps usually, by his own curiosity, pride, and self-consistency, and by the doubt and ridicule artfully thrown in against Revelation, so thoroughly estranged from truth and virtue as never to return. To ruin in this way are surely led most readers, of a particular class, and that a numerous one; readers, pleased with reasoning extended to a certain degree, and conducted with a due mixture of brilliancy; readers, fond of novelty and esteeming singularity of thought a proof of superiour understanding.

This, however, has been but one, and that a very partial object of their reliance. Their writings have assumed every form, and treated every subject of thought. From the lofty philosophical discourse it has descended through all the intervening gradations to the newspaper paragraph; from the sermon to the catechism; from regular history to the anecdote; from the epic poem to the song; and from the formal satire to the jest of the buffoon. Efforts in vast numbers have also been made to diffuse Infidelity in a remark, unexpectedly found in a discourse, when a totally different subject was under consideration, in a note, subjoined to a paper on criticism or politics, in a hint, in a book of travels; or a stroke, in a letter of civility. In these and the like cases the reader was intended to be taken by surprise, and to yield his judgment before he was aware, that he was called to judge. The number and variety of the efforts have also been increased beyond example; have poured from innumerable presses, and from all civilized countries; have been sold at the lowest prices, and given gratuitously; and have been circulated with vast industry, and by innumerable hands, throughout christendom. The intention of this amazing multitude of exertions has plainly been to astonish and discourage their adversaries, to amaze and overwhelm their readers, and to persuade, insensibly, the mass of mankind, that the world was converted to Infidelity.

Dwight's attitude had changed enormously since the publication of *The Triumph of Infidelity* thirteen years before. His standard of fidelity was no longer strict Calvinistic doctrine. Even the violent anti-Catholicism of the poem gave way to a more discriminating treatment of the Roman church and the admission, in a footnote to the published sermon, that even a Catholic might be a true Christian. Infidelity had come to be a secret, insidious, calculated opposition to all churches and all forms of Christianity and to the social organization which supported them—not a matter of theological differences, but a republican network designed to catch the unwary and through them overthrow the very foundations of society. Dwight did not go so far as some of his contemporaries who saw signs of atheism in the growing tendency to speak of human "beings" rather than human "creatures." But he did announce (before Jefferson came into office) that it was "an insult to *God*, to *speak evil*, without cause, *against the Rulers of your people*"; he found evidence of infidelity in any attempt to introduce French notions of liberty (which, he never grew tired of pointing out, "*was not the liberty of New England*") into America; and he assured the citizens of New Haven that all the literature produced in Germany, "from the philosophy of Kant to the plays of Kotzebue," appeared "to be formed to diffuse loose principles, and to unhinge the morals and religion of the scriptures."

The change in Dwight's standards of fidelity, which was so noticeable in his New Year's sermon, left its mark on all the rest of his literary works. His doctrinism had been softened by the mellow years at Greenfield Hill, but he did not achieve any extensive tolerance of sectarian differences until the fear of republican infidelity forced him to take a really broad view of conservative Christianity. The President of Yale, like many another leader before and since, discovered that in a seriously threatened defensive army unity of spirit is of infinitely more importance than conformity in particulars. Henceforth, he began to earn his reputation for an "ardent wish and endeavour . . . . to narrow the grounds of distinction, between different classes of christians, and to unite them all, in the great work, of doing good to man, rendering honour to God, and, seeking eternal life." Within a few years the former "would-be Luther" of the Edwardean faith was to find it a matter of jest in the classroom that he had "been called an Arminian for saying there are means of grace" and was to express scorn that "some Calvinists get as far from Arminians as possible even though it should lead them into absurdities." In various incidental ways he assisted in the removal of certain eccentricities in the practice of religion. In 1801 he finished the revision of Barlow's edition of Watts's *Psalms* which he had undertaken at the request of the general association of Connecticut—not, as has been so often stated, with the idea of eliminating any flavor of republicanism (for all the American references were retained) but for the purposes of adding metrical variety and removing Barlow's unnecessary deviations from the paraphrase which was commonly used in most other parts of America. He encouraged the union of Presbyterian and Congregational churches in Connecticut. He assisted in the establishment of a magazine designed to support true religion without regard to minor differences in doctrine. He became more friendly toward the Episcopalians, who were soon to stand shoulder to shoulder with the Connecticut Congregationalists in opposition to the rising tide of democracy. And it was in this frame of mind—fearful of a dangerous infidel movement, antagonistic toward all speculative fancies, anxious to gain support for the forces of morality, and indifferent to minor sectarian differences—that he undertook the long and tedious labor of putting into final form the system of theology he had preached several times at Greenfield and at Yale.

III

The series of sermons which made up Dwight's *Theology: Explained and Defended* were supposedly preached twice at Greenfield and then again to each generation of Yale undergraduates. According to Dwight's sons, who published them in five volumes in 1818–19, they were "written out at the close of 1809"; but it seems probable that they were merely completed at that time— that one of the major duties of the amanuensis employed by the corporation when Dwight accepted the permanent appointment of professor of theology was to take notes on the series delivered during the following four years, receive corrections, and make a clean copy for publication. In any case they represent sermons that were composed, in their final form, no earlier than 1805, although they had been preached four or five times before. The date of their final form is important, for Dwight had been repeating them from memory (assisted at the most by very brief outlines) during a period when his attitude toward controversial divinity was gradually changing and his emotions were being subjected to different influences. They were originally composed by an evangelical New Light theologian who was determined to bring a wayward congregation back to the fold of Edwardean orthodoxy. They were prepared for publication by a public figure who had strong reasons for wanting as much unity as possible in the acceptance of religious doctrines. That they went through some changes is indicated by the fact that the one hundred and seventy-three sermons, as arranged for publication, will not fit into the school calendar to which they had to conform and by the report that the undergraduate series actually preached consisted of only one hundred and sixty discourses. The probable changes are of more interest than the finished sermons, for, while they made no important contribution to the history of theology, they do provide an extraordinarily good illustration of the way in which a highly systematized body of doctrines, conscientiously held, might become adapted to different times and manners. Some of Dwight's modifications of the New Light theology of his youth were probably conscious and deliberate; others undoubtedly represent a change by unconscious rationalization in the process of "remembering" points he had made previously.

The adaptability of Dwight's system of theology was, to a

very considerable extent, the result of his manner of composing and delivering his sermons. From the beginning of his career in the "desk" he believed that a preacher should appeal to the "heart" and to the plainest understanding; and he adopted the extemporaneous method of delivery which George Whitefield had popularized in America, keeping in sympathy with his congregation and governing his discourse by their response rather than by the logic of the study. The condition of his eyesight, making written composition difficult and the use of notes embarrassing, impelled him to carry over this method even into these carefully systematized discourses that were, in comparison with his other sermons, formal almost to the point of being old-fashioned in their organization. As a result, the argumentative body of his sermons, or his "proof" of the doctrine deduced from his text, was usually characterized by boldness and simplicity rather than by close and meticulous reasoning. Other preachers, of course, could and did write out finespun arguments and memorize them for delivery; but Dwight did not approve of their method in theory and was physically discouraged from adopting it in practice. Furthermore, he seems to have taken a certain artistic delight, even in these doctrinal sermons, in working up from a plain exposition of the text through a striking series of arguments to a vivid and often highly figurative application.

The simplicity of Dwight's arguments made them easily subject to both deliberate and unconscious revisions. The nature of his "proof," of course, varied according to the demands of the doctrine and the established opinions of his audience, sometimes being argumentative and occasionally merely illustrative. In argument his customary method was to offer proof from three sources: authority (almost exclusively that of the Scriptures), reason or logic, and experience. The first hardly varied, perhaps, from the first delivery of one of these sermons to the last, for there can be no doubt of Dwight's exact knowledge of the Bible or of his reverence for its authority, and he probably preserved a good recollection or a written record of the texts supporting the one from which he preached. The others, however, might change from one delivery to the next, for, whatever logic

Dwight may have used during the most aggressive of his New Divinity days, his reasoning was never elaborately or carefully syllogistic in his published sermons. He vigorously, and regularly, denounced what he called "metaphysical preaching" and consciously extended his own "reasonings through a few steps only," never going further than a plain audience could readily follow. Often he merely balanced one proposition against another, making use of what he represented, in his second sermon on "The Decrees of God," as a "general axiom, that every proposition, or *its converse, is true*." But Dwight was not a good logician of any sort. He habitually phrased his "converse" propositions so carelessly that he introduced into them irrelevant elements that affected his judgment. For example, in the published *Theology* he summarized two propositions—the one commonly attributed to Nathanael Emmons and the conventional one—concerning the nature of the soul:

According to the latter of these schemes, the soul of man is one; created at one time; and continuing the same, as to its substance and nature, throughout eternity: according to the other, the soul, for the time being, is the idea, or exercise, existing at that time; commencing its existence with the existence of the idea, and perishing with it.

Just how he would have summarized Emmons' doctrine in the eighties, when they were both "would-be Luthers" of the New Divinity, is a matter of pure, and vain, speculation. But he could hardly have concluded with an emphatic "perishing with it" until after he had seen Bishop Horne's analysis of Hume's atheism, while gathering material for the sermon on *The Nature and Danger of Infidel Philosophy*. It was a supposed resemblance between Emmons and Hume that affected his judgment to the point of making him totally "unable to comprehend" one of the most striking doctrines developed by the theological movement with which he was allied in his youth.

Arguments from "experience" were even more subject to revision as Dwight's attitudes changed and were even more influential in the modification of his theological opinions. He expressed his belief in the superiority of experience over reason in his sermon on "the Unity of God," when he observed "that, when we appeal to Reason as a guide in subjects of Theology, its true character, as such a guide, can be estimated only by the decisions, which it has actually made. . . . . We are, therefore, to look only at what Reason has actually done, to learn what it can be expected to do." What reason had "actually done," he knew by observation, had been to lead the ancient philosophers into polytheism and the moderns into atheism. So, while preaching on the "Decrees of God," he could dismiss the necessity for finespun reasoning upon the difficult question of moral agency by saying that "the metaphysical nature of Moral Agency, both in God and his creatures, is a subject, perhaps as tenuous, as difficult to be fastened upon, and as easily evanescent from the mind, as any, which we attempt to examine." He affirmed the doctrine of predestination as "proved" by the Scriptures and engaged in some troubled reasoning upon it. Yet when he came to answer one of the most persistent and difficult objections to it—that it discouraged all human effort toward reformation—he appealed primarily to the proof of contrary experience:

> In my apprehension, it is never true, that the attempts of the man concerned, toward the attainment of salvation, make no difference as to the event. On the contrary it is clear, that of those who are saved, few, very few, indeed, can be found, who have not made such attempts; nor is there any satisfactory reason to believe, that those, who make them with persevering earnestness and zeal ultimately fail.

Although "the decree of God" extended to farming and scholarship "as absolutely, as to our salvation," he argued, experience proved that a man would fail in those professions unless he exercised toil and study. Seeing "no reason, why the same language should not be used, with the same propriety and force, concerning our secular, as concerning our spiritual, business," he implied that a man might "be pronounced, and justly, a fool or a madman" for refusing to use such means of grace as prayer. His grandfather Edwards, whose doctrines he professed, would have been more vigorous than those contemporaries who "sometimes" called him an Arminian. Dwight found the whole subject of moral agency distressing, and the sermons on the "Decrees of God" were not very satisfactory. But they do show how one of the great doctrines of his system could become modified by this "experimental" method of "proof."

The best illustration of what happened when Dwight argued from experience, however, can be seen in matters of less theological and more practical moment. In his fourth sermon on the Fifth Commandment, dealing with the "Duty of Rulers," for example, he maintained the proposition that the foundation of all government is "the Will of God" by attacking the contrary theory of the social compact with an appeal to the experience of an American audience:

> The absurdities of this doctrine are endless. He, who knows any thing of the nature of savages, knows perfectly, that *no savage was ever capable of forming such a design;* and that civilized life is indispensably necessary to the very perception of the things, pre-supposed by this doctrine, and absolutely pre-requisite to the very existence of such an assembly [as would be necessary to create a "body politic"]. Every one, acquainted at all with savages, knows equally well, that, if they were capable of all this comprehension, *nothing, short of omnipotence, could persuade them to embrace such a scheme of conduct.* There is nothing, which a savage hates more, than the restraints of civilized life; nothing, which he despises more, than the civilized character, its refinements, its improvements, nay, its very enjoyments. To have formed such an assembly, or even to have proposed such a system, men must have already been long governed, and civilized.

Dwight might have used such an argument earlier, but it would not have been so strong twenty years before when he had looked with favor on the frontier regions and dealt with savages as the subject of romantic verse. Since then, however, as his *Travels* show, his attitude had changed as a result of two reactions: first, finding notions of the noble savage in the speculative philosophers he distrusted, he reviewed his knowledge of the Indian with particular attention to his more degraded characteristics; and, second, having observed the way in which democracy flourished upon the frontier, he had come to look upon the pioneers of Vermont with a skeptical eye which particularly noted the Indian characteristics they possessed. His "experimental" knowledge of all the people of the forest had changed from what it had been in his youth; and so his proof of the historical absurdity of the social compact, drawn from experience, was more vigorous than it could have been before.

Another reason why Dwight was able to adapt his Edwardean system of theology to his own age was that from a long habit of extemporaneous speaking he was not sufficiently self-critical to remove from his sermons all traces of the new ideas he had once held and later renounced. He had, for example, completely rejected the Scottish philosophers in whom he had been interested during his tutorship. He had made the contrary systems of Locke and Paley the basis of his presidential instruction; he had redefined the term "common sense" before he left Greenfield; and when he used the term in his *Theology* he usually indicated clearly that he was using it in its nontechnical, popular signification. Occasionally, however, he slipped back into a use of the phrase that Thomas Reid would have accepted or into the statement of an idea that Dugald Stewart would have approved. In his sermon "The Soul Not Material" he found occasion to remark that his doctrine presented "one remarkable instance of the agreement of the Scriptures with Common sense" and illustrated his statement by observing: "All nations have united in the opinion, that the human soul is an immaterial being, wholly distinct from the Body." It was not a reasoned opinion, for he did not intend to claim that "a savage could correctly define, or explain, his views of it." Nor was it the result of Revelation, for he used the opinion of the American Indians (whom he regularly used as horrible examples of men lacking Revelation) as an instance of it. He was obviously thinking, without being critically aware of the fact, in terms of the internal sense, common to all men, which he had once accepted and later denied. Similarly, in the following sermon, he held that the soul was not a "chain of ideas and exercises" because such an idea was "directly contrary to the natural conceptions of mankind, and therefore false"; and he spoke of these natural conceptions as products of a *"mode of thinking . . . . constituted by God himself*, and inwrought in our very nature." Stewart might have used the passage as an illustration of what he meant by his phrase, "the fundamental laws of belief," which he adopted as a substitute for Reid's "common sense." Born methodizer though he might be, Dwight was often a very loose thinker.

This characteristic looseness of thought was perhaps the secret of his ability to affirm, on the one hand, some of the most difficult doctrines of his grandfather Edwards and, on the other, to make them acceptable to an age that would not have followed the ingenious reasoning of Samuel Hopkins or Nathanael Emmons. Dwight had none of the mysticism of Jonathan Edwards. His sermons are almost completely free from references to personal religious experience, and his friends often commented on his remarkable reticence, or "modesty," concerning his individual "assurance." In his third sermon on the "Evidences of Regeneration," indeed, he expressed the "opinion, that God, for wise and good reasons, administers his Spiritual Providence in such a manner, as to leave his children destitute of the Faith of Assurance, for their own Good." Yet in these sermons he made a distinction between the "Natural" and the "Evangelical" affections and preached that the only real evidences of regeneration came from something like the sixth, supernatural sense affirmed by Edwards. In describing its activity, however, Dwight did not use Edwards' strongly personal term "delight"; his was "relish"—the same word he adopted when, under the influence of Lord Kames, he had attempted to describe the activity of the internal sense of "taste." No one, of course, can do more than guess concerning such matters; but it seems as though Dwight, unable to understand from personal experience this element in his grandfather's theology, could follow it in his own system only by thinking in terms of the Scottish "common sense" limited to a peculiar class of mankind. The same shadow of a rejected idea may also have fallen across his second sermon on the "Decrees of God," in which he insisted that men were "intuitively conscious" or "irresistibly sensible" of their own free agency; and a reflection of the Scottish insistence upon the limits of human reason can be seen in Dwight's statement that if this intuitive consciousness appears to contradict the doctrine of predestination it is because "we are unable to discern the nature of their mutual connexion." Hopkins and Emmons, with their metaphysical arguments concerning the benevolence of God, might allow him to be the author of sin; but Dwight denied that God was the "efficient" cause of "the sinful volitions of mankind" and condemned their theology as "verging . . . . towards a *Pantheism*" differing only slightly from "that of *Spinosa*." As he made clear in his sermon on "Man," he looked upon a human being as the possessor of a finite "frame," created from the dust of the ground, yet "fitted to give ['warnings'] of approaching or commencing evil"—able, in other words, to "discern the nature of moral good and evil." Exactly what this "fitting" was he never explained. Sometimes he appeared to think of it as the intellectual "conscience"; sometimes as a nonintellectual "disposition." There is no reason to suppose that he was clear about it in his own mind; and the occasional appearance of the Scottish notion elsewhere in his sermons suggests that here again the "moral sense" of Kames and Beattie and Reid crept into the Edwardean system through the gap left by Dwight's indifference to metaphysics.

As a result of Dwight's method of reasoning, his use of proof from experience, and a characteristic looseness of thinking—all determined in part by his method of composing and delivering his sermons—the Edwardean theology was partially relieved of its original strictness and pruned of its later refinements while being systematized for Yale undergraduates. Yet its broad outlines were unchanged. Dwight preached the total depravity of man, whose chief end was to glorify God without respect to selfish interests and whose eternal fate was foreknown. With regard to the ordinances of the church, he stood firmly against baptism for children of unbelievers, just as though he had never communed with halfway covenanters; and he insisted upon the same qualifications for communicants that Edwards had fought for at Northampton. It is extraordinary that he could have made the system of Jonathan Edwards so acceptable to the early nineteenth century, yet change it so little. But the most remarkable quality Dwight possessed as a theologian was his ability to hold on to old-fashioned orthodoxy with one hand while he kept the other on the pulse of a new age. He could lead a new idea into the Calvinistic scheme with an ingenuity that none of his contemporaries could match.

Perhaps the best illustration of this facility was his treatment of the utilitarianism he found in Paley's *Moral Philosophy* and saw becoming more and more acceptable to the world at large. In his last sermon on the text "It is more blessed to give, than to receive" Dwight preached the doctrine that "Virtue is founded in Utility," accepting the definition of "Utility" (though without using the phrase) as the greatest happiness for the greatest number. Specifically denying that it was "founded in the Will of God," he appeared to be denying both Edwards' conception of "the Nature of True Virtue" and President Clap's second obligation to virtue in his essay on the same subject. But there were two peculiar characteristics of the utilitarianism taught by the President of Yale. In the first place, he had preached in his sermon on "The Chief End of Man" that in "a conformity of heart, and of effort," to the directions of God "consists all the worth, and all the happiness of Rational creatures." In the second, he argued that man did not know enough to pass judgment upon the aggregate good of his actions and therefore had to subordinate himself to the wisdom of God as it was revealed in the Scriptures. Thus, in theory at least, the "utilitarian" standard of ethics set up by Timothy Dwight amounted to about the same thing as President Clap's "conformity to the moral excellence of God"; and in each case the guide for the unregenerate majority of mankind was the same—the rules of conduct laid down in the Bible. He pointed out the difference between his theory and that of other utilitarians in his sermon, "Utility the Foundation of Virtue":

The great objection to this doctrine arises from a misapprehension of the subject. It is this: that *if Virtue is founded in Utility, then Utility becomes the Measure of virtue, and, of course, the Rule of all our moral conduct.* This is the error of *Godwin:* and, in an indefinite degree, of *Paley,* and several other writers. Were we omniscient, and able to discern the true nature of all the effects of our conduct; this consequence must undoubtedly be admitted. To the eye of God it is the real rule. It will not, I trust, be denied, that he has chosen, and required, that to be done by his Intelligent creatures, which is most useful; or, in other words, most productive of good to the universe, and of glory to himself; rather than that which is less so. But, to us, Utility, as judged by ourselves, cannot be a proper rule of moral conduct. *The real use-fulness of our conduct, or its usefulness upon the whole, lies in the nature of all its effects, considered as one aggregate.* But nothing is more evident, than that few, very few indeed, of these, can ever be known to us by our own foresight. If the information, given us by the Scriptures concerning this subject, were to be lost; we should be surprised to see how small was the number of cases, in which this knowledge was attainable, even in a moderate degree; and how much uncertainty attended even these. As, therefore, we are unable to discern with truth, or probability, the real usefulness of our conduct; it is impossible, that our moral actions should be safely guided by this rule.

Later, in a sermon on "Mischiefs and Preventives of Lying," he referred to the "unhappy influence" of Paley's confusion between utility "the Foundation of Virtue" and utility "the Criterion of Virtue"; and he strongly insisted upon the necessity for such a distinction before his classes which recited from Paley's book.

The extent of Dwight's ingenuity in conducting utilitarian ethics into the Edwardean system and there smothering it can be seen in a sermon on the "Consistency of Benevolence with Providing Peculiarly for Our Own," in which he used the doctrine of utility in a violent attack upon William Godwin. Arguing from the general proposition that any conduct which "would frustrate the great end of benevolence by lessening human happiness . . . . cannot be our duty," he reasoned that the greatest good could be accomplished only by a division of labor that brought man's duties within the limits of his comprehension and effective activity. "One man, for example," he said, taking his illustration from an early version of the production line, "to whom the whole business of making so simple a thing, as a *pin*, was allotted, could hardly finish twenty in a day. Ten men, dividing the several parts of the business among them, can easily finish more than forty-eight thousand." Furthermore, he continued, for the sake of its greatest efficiency, the "division of human industry should be Voluntary." Hence God "divided the business of mankind" into little parts by "separating them into families," the members of which, through the influence of "Natural affection," became voluntary performers of their duties. "These observations" and others showing the importance of the family, Dwight exclaimed, "clearly show the folly of Godwin's system of human perfectibility," for:

This wretched apostle of Atheism, with a weakness exceeded only by his audacity, has undertaken, in form, to show himself wiser than his Maker. For this purpose, he has boldly declared marriage to be an unjust monopoly; and the institution of families to be the means of preventing the happiness and the perfection of man. Of this perfection a promiscuous concubinage, and a community of labours, and of property, are, in his opinion, essential constituents. Nor has the whole concurring experience of mankind, invariably opposed to his doctrine, been sufficient to awaken him from his dreaming speculations to sober thought, and the exercise of common sense. This system, if it may be called such; this crude gathering together of ideas into a mob; he professedly founds on the doctrine of disinterested good-will: and *these* he professes to be the genuine consequences of this glorious principle. Were they indeed its consequences, every good man would be struck with amazement and horror: for they would undoubtedly annihilate all the comfort, peace, and hopes, of mankind. That Benevolence, which is the only virtue, would prove the most fruitful and efficacious cause of absolute destruction to all human good: and its glorious character, instead of being the voluntary cause of happiness, would be exchanged for that, of being only, and fatally, the voluntary cause of misery.

Utility might be the foundation of all virtue; but Dwight would have disagreed with the moral system formed by any utilitarian, for each would have made Godwin's mistake of undertaking "to show himself wiser than his Maker" by setting up his own fallible notions of utility as its criterion.

These sermons reveal Dwight's mind in its most characteristic activity—acutely perceiving new ideas and methodically and ingeniously adapting them to his own inability to imagine anything better than he had experienced in person or had read about in the Scriptures. During the greater part of his early life he had kept his religious and his social beliefs fairly well separated. His *Theology* marked the final union of the two. His system of belief had become modified by his reactions to what he considered the terrible state of society and in turn had absorbed and smothered some of the ideas produced in that society. There was some justice in the title, "Pope" Dwight, given him by his enemies. Henceforth his religious and social philosophies were closely identified; and although he continued to boast that he had never preached a political sermon on the Sabbath in his life, he began in his theological sermons to make Calvinism a bulwark against the rising tide of democracy.

The sermon in which Dwight most clearly pointed out the political implications of his doctrines, by answering such arguments as those advanced by Barlow in his *Advice to the Privileged Orders*, was one consisting entirely of "Remarks" upon the depravity of man. Having proved in a preceding discourse that the depravity of man was derived from Adam, he believed he had also made it evident that "the corruption of Man is not the result of any given form of Government, nor of any given character in Rulers." That the rulers of mankind, by keeping them poor and ignorant, had "contributed in a very great and guilty degree to the increase of their corruption," he admitted; but he insisted that example, temptation, and precept had been more influential than oppression in extending corruption and that in these respects philosophers had been notoriously worse than rulers. Furthermore, he found little to choose between two forms of government in their contributions to "the depravation of mankind":

Monarchies have produced this effect by immense patronage; by the operations of despotic power, demanding and effectuating a slavish dependence, and a base sacrifice of principle, in their subjects; by splendour, luxury, war, and a general dissoluteness of manners. *Republican governments*, although in certain circumstances more favourable to virtue, have yet, at times been equally pernicious by furnishing opportunities, and strong temptations, for the sacrifice of integrity at elections, for caballing, bribery, faction, private ambition, bold contentions for place and power, and that civil discord, which is naturally accompanied by the prostration of Morality and Religion.

Experience proved that subjects of good rulers were often as corrupt as those of bad and that well-informed and free men could be as depraved as the ignorant and oppressed. Even when rulers had the least influence possible over their subjects, as in the case of the American Indians, men were no less vicious.

In the state of society existing among these people, men are as independent, and as little influenced by power, authority, and governmental example, as men, living together, can be. Here, neither kings, nor nobles, nor priests, have any other weight, or control, than that, which springs of course from the mere gathering together of human beings. Yet no man, who knows anything of the morals of these people, can hesitate to acknowledge them corrupt, in a degree enormous and dreadful. Fraud, falsehood, lewdness, drunkenness, treachery, malice, cruelty, and murder, acted out in the most deplorable manner, are strong and dreadful features of the savage character. Here, then, the vice exists anterior to artificial society, and in the state, nearest that, which is called ,'*The State of Nature.*" What is true of the *American savages* is true of all others; and universally furnishes undeniable proof of the fearful depravity, originally inherent in Man, and wholly independent of the causes alleged. . . . .

Wherever virtue distinguished a nation (as, Dwight admitted, it distinguished the "Republics" of Switzerland, Holland, Massachusetts, and Connecticut), it could be attributed to the prevalence of "mediocrity of life" and the influence of the Protestant clergy—not to the necessary influence of the form of government. Dwight found no evidence in experience that men were better without government than with it or necessarily better under one form than under another. Thus, to him it was completely "evident from these discourses, that the scheme of Human Perfectibility is without any foundation."

Most of the theorists whom Dwight opposed in this sermon—and certainly Joel Barlow—would have admitted the truth of these factual observations, arguing instead that error entered the minds of men ages before they reached the state of civilization represented by American Indians, that "republicanism" to them meant something different from the government of Athens or Rome, and that the perfecting of mankind was to be a long and difficult process. They had new hypotheses concerning social reform and wanted to see a new social experiment. Dwight realized something of the sort and in attempting an advance rebuttal revealed, with unusual clarity, the cavity of imagination in which his conservatism was so firmly wedged:

To such persons, as insist, that the melioration suggested has failed, because the means used were imperfectly fitted to accomplish the end; I answer: If the end were possible; it is reasonable to believe, that amid so great a variety, extent, and continuance, of these means, directed to this end by the highest human wisdom, some one system would have succeeded. As these have all failed; it cannot be rationally doubted, that all others will fail. Those particularly, which are now offered as substitutes, promise not even the remotest degree of success; and are, on the other hand, fraught with the most portentous threatenings of absolute ruin. To these things I will add, that the authors of them, on whom their efficacy ought first to be proved, are farther removed from virtue, than mankind in general. Until their own character, therefore, is materially changed for the better, they may be unanswerably addressed with the forcible Jewish proverb, *Physician, heal thyself.*

Even though he hated the word, Dwight could always see the value of a hypothesis which had been proved true in the past or of a new one if it were sufficiently restricted to a minor improvement in a clearly defined field of knowledge; but a major hypothesis affecting the whole of society so completely dazzled his eyes that he regularly turned them away and, instead, contemplated the defects in the character of the man who presented it.

Timothy Dwight, in many ways, represented the universal type of conservative, possessing most of the virtues and faults of his kind. That he should have appeared prominently in the midst of the strains and stress of the late eighteenth century is in no way remarkable. Nor is it of any great significance that he brought the old doctrine of human depravity to bear against the excesses of democracy. Such use of it had been a part of the New England tradition since the wilderness Zion had been established on the shores of Massachusetts Bay. The political element in his sermons is notable because it made the Edwardean system useful in an age to which it was foreign and so preserved it long after it might have faded from the unreceptive minds of succeeding generations. He not only made Calvinism acceptable to many of his contemporaries but made it seem expedient to those who shared his temperament and fears. His was not the voice of a dominant group crying down an antinomian minority. While Unitarianism was overrunning eastern Massachusetts, Methodism was sweeping the frontier, Quakerism was flourishing in Pennsylvania, and the latitudinarian doctrines of the Episcopalians were spreading in New York and along the southern seaboard, Dwight preached the total depravity of man and the absolute decrees of God and caused his hearers to cling tenaciously to his teaching. The spirit of the age dignified man, and most of the religious sects conformed, finding human beings either essentially good or at least free to wish efficaciously for goodness. Among people who avoided formal religious affiliations a benevolent deism flourished; and even the materialists, who made no distinction between the moral and physical nature of man, looked upon him as the master of his fate and the captain of his soul. Dwight denied the natural dignity of man and made the present and future dignitaries of Connecticut accept the denial.

He succeeded by convincing them, through the authority of his person and the force of his oratory, that his theological premises offered the soundest support for the social and political conclusions they had already reached as a result of temperament, training, or interest. To a people disturbed and worried by the threat of republicanism Dwight held up visions of fantastic speculations, violent changes in manners, and violations of home and property. Look, he ordered them, at the "moral and political science"—or "*science falsely so called*"—that "considers man as originally a virtuous being; accidentally, and in some small degrees, warped from the path of rectitude, and always ready to return to it again":

On this fundamental folly were founded all those vain, empty, miserable systems of policy, which, in a portentous succession, deluged Republican *France* in misery and ruin. In the treatises, laws, and measures, brought into being in that nation, during its late wonderful struggle to become free, the people were uniformly declared to be good; honest; virtuous; influenced only by the purest motives; and aiming only at the best ends. These very people, at the time, were employed in little else, except unceasing plunder, uniform treachery, the violation of all laws, the utterance of all falsehood, the murder of their King, Nobles, and Clergy, and the boundless butchery of each other. In a state of immorality, in a prostration of all principle, at which even this sinful world stood aghast, this despicable flattery was continually reiterated; and the miserable objects of it very naturally concluded, that, as they were praised *while* they were doing these things, they were praised *for* doing them. Of course they were fixed in this conduct beyond recall. Every malignant passion was let loose, the reins were thrown upon the neck of every sordid appetite; the people became a collection of wild beasts; and the country a den of ravage and slaughter.

If philosophy and vain deceit fixed man in such conduct, then the "sound and true policy," which, Dwight insisted, "will always consider Man as he is," should take the contrary view set forth in the general heading of these "Remarks": "*The fundamental principle of moral and political science, so far as man is concerned, is his Depravity.*" If this "first great fact in the science of Man" were accepted, sound policy could "treat him accordingly":

Its measures will be universally calculated for depraved beings; and it will, therefore, never hesitate to establish every necessary restraint. Whatever is good in man it will regard as the result of wise, careful, efficacious discipline, realized and blessed by God. Such discipline, therefore, it will regularly establish, protect, and encourage. Honest, well disposed, and orderly citizens it will protect; the violation of private rights, and the disturbers of public peace, it will punish. Nor will its restraints and punishments stop, until they have gained in some measure their end.

The young representatives of the élite of Connecticut listened and treasured their teacher's words. His appeal to their "heart" was enormous. For he taught a doctrine sanctified by tradition and showed them that by adopting it they could take strong measures to protect their own interests and feel virtuous while doing so. Both Calvinism and Federalism survived longer in Connecticut than in any other state in the Union.

IV

The same lack of creative imagination that prevented Dwight from getting a clear view of foreign civilization, speculative philosophy, and republican politics made his *Travels, in New-England and New-York* one of the best American books of its kind. The man who had viewed the prospect from Greenfield Hill with such contentment spent his academic vacations from 1796 until near the end of his life traveling through the country he loved so well. As a tutor in Yale he had been one of several poets who looked forward to the rising glory of America; as president he decided that the glory of New England at least had already risen and was threatening to pass away. Realizing how rapidly the country was changing, he wanted to catch it as it was—to seize "the form, and colours, of the moment" and preserve the picture for posterity. He took a notebook with him on his trips and kept rather elaborate notes, attempting when he got home to set down his most important observations while they were still fresh. The strain upon his eyes, for a while, became too great; but, when the Senior class of 1802 volunteered to write for him, he employed its members and those of the three succeeding classes in making a first draft of the book. Later, with the help of his professional amanuenses, he renewed his labors, added further observations, and sometime after the spring of 1815 finished the account, which was published posthumously in four volumes of over five hundred pages each. Two motives drove him to its composition: first, an abiding and energetic curiosity concerning the facts of the New England countryside, its inhabitants, and their institutions, manners, and morals; and, second, a profound irritation at the ignorant and wilful misrepresentations of his beloved land by foreign travelers and journalists. No one else, he feared, was likely to tell the truth of things as they were in New England, for no one else had seen them so thoroughly and intimately. He and the members of his party were reputed to be the first people ever to visit Provincetown merely out of curiosity; and he finished his book with the confidence that descriptions of such rural pilgrimages would provide a novel contrast to the conventional accounts of European travelers, who devoted an excessive amount of attention to the cities where they could see "acted" plays.

The work was organized in the form of a series of journeys to various destinations in New England and New York and concluded with almost an entire volume of observations on particular subjects ranging from the mythology of the Iroquois to the future prospects of the United States. Although Dwight adopted the convention of addressing his reports to an imaginary English correspondent, he confessed that he intended them primarily for American readers, whom he apparently believed more susceptible to instruction by having their mistaken impressions attributed to a foreigner than by direct correction. The accounts of the country as a whole and of the many towns were often highly statistical, but even in his tables of figures concerning populations and prices Dwight reveals the love of details and facts which keeps his *Travels* alive long after such an attempt at imaginative verse as *The Conquest of Canäan* has become practically unreadable. Everything about New England was worthy of note. The new burial ground at New Haven was, to Dwight, a wonder; the manufacturing village of Humphreys-ville a matter of romance. He looked upon the brick city of Hartford as a monument to the wisdom of its selectmen and took an everlasting delight in the neatness of the New England homes that faced the highway or clustered around a trim village green. If he heard a strange story that bordered upon folklore, he investigated and reported upon his investigations; and he also noted that the finest oysters could be bought in New Haven for a dollar a bushel. He put down his observations con-cerning the phenomenon which may have formed the basis of the legend used by Hawthorne in "The Great Carbuncle"; and he explained the practical reason why American vehicles took the right side of the road when passing one another instead of following the English custom of taking the left. Almost nothing was too ordinary or too out of the way for the record.

He devoted so much space to descriptions of natural scenery that he felt obliged to apologize for it in his Preface, giving as excuse his own pleasure, the fact that the "very fine" scenery of New England had never before been adequately described, and the delight landscapes aroused in both lighter and graver minds. No American poet, he particularly regretted, had ever done jus-tice to the autumn brilliance which no English poet had ever been able to enjoy; and he tried to preserve the White Moun-tains in October in his own prose:

Of course, the darkness of the evergreens was finely illumined by the bril-liant yellow of the birch, the beech, and the cherry, and the more brilliant orange, and crimson of the maple. The effect of this universal diffusion of gay and splendid light was to render the preponderating deep green more solemn. The mind encircled by this scenery, irresistibly remembered, that the light was the light of decay; autumnal and melancholy. The dark was the gloom of evening, approximating to night. Over the whole, the azure of the sky cast a deep, misty blue; blending, toward the summits, every other hue; and predominating over all.

In the stiffened style of a man grown too important to relax into purposeless description, Dwight was making an effort to enable others to see what he really saw and to share the ministerial emotions aroused in him by the view. And he kept making it, constantly, even when the emotions were as "unutterable" as the "exquisite but violent" pleasure with which he looked upon Niagara.

Dwight was hardly less interested in the antiquities of New England—partly because of the antiquarian impulse that caused him to make his first systematic investigations of the countryside and partly because he found in the influence of the past one of the anchors of security about which he became so concerned in the 1790's. He was unusually frank about motives of the latter sort, while commenting upon the strong feelings with which he looked upon Plymouth Rock. No New Englander could avoid gazing upon it, he said, with emotions different from those "excited by other places of equal, or even superiour importance." And he added:

> For myself I cannot wish this trait in the human character obliterated. In a higher state of being, where truth is universally as well as cordially embraced, and virtue controls without a rival, this prejudice, if it must be called by that name, will probably become useless, and may, therefore, be safely discarded. But in our present condition every attachment, which is innocent, has its use, and contributes both to fix and to soften man. The fierce, and the roving, spirit of our race, are alike dangerous; and where a ruling principle of a higher nature cannot be certainly established, nor its efficacy safely relied on, a wise man will press into the public service every harmless emotion, every useful tendency of the human heart, and secure to himself, and to the world, the benefits, which, experience assures him, will be derived from its influence. Nor will he foolishly lessen the attachment to country, nor discourage its desirable exertions, by coldly scrutinizing its metaphysical nature, doubting its propriety, or stigmatizing it with the names of prejudice and weakness.

It would be a foolish admiral, Dwight observed, who, on the eve of battle, would tell his men that enthusiasm for their country was nonsense; and so, no fool himself, he frequently used parts of his book to press into what he considered the public service various attachments that might encourage stability in his own crucial times.

This attitude of mind lay back of one paragraph in the *Travels* which has since become the most notorious passage in all Dwight's writings:

> It is however to be observed, that a considerable number even of these people [i.e., pioneers or "foresters"] become sober, industrious citizens, merely

by the acquisition of property. The love of property to a certain degree seems indispensable to the existence of sound morals. I have never had a servant, in whom I could confide, except such as were desirous to earn, and preserve, money. The conveniences, and the character, attendant on the possession of property, fix even these restless men at times, when they find themselves really able to accumulate it; and persuade them to a course of regular industry. . . . . The secure possession of property demands, every moment, the hedge of law; and reconciles a man, originally lawless, to the restraints of government . . . . and [prompts him] perhaps to become in the end a religious man.

No one who heard Dwight's characterization of the man of wealth in the baccalaureate sermon, "Life a Race," which he preached in 1799, 1806, and 1812, could have misunderstood his meaning in this passage; nor could many of his students who had heard him on the servant problem, in one of his favorite classroom digressions. He was making the same shrewd observation that George Bernard Shaw made when he had Henry Doolittle reject a fortune because it would bring with it "middle class morality." To Dwight, morals properly should be founded upon "virtue" and established by training and authority. But in dealing with an unregenerate shiftlessness which could not experience virtue, had never received correct training, and would not subject itself to authority, something else was necessary. The love of property, in comparison with the shiftless passions, was a relatively harmless attachment which might well be put to use, in "the public service," to "fix and to soften" such people as domestic servants, common laborers, and pioneers.

Dwight made this attitude clear elsewhere in his *Travels*. "Savages," he said for example, "can be successfully changed into civilized men only in two modes." The first, by conversion to Christianity, was the manner most to be desired.

Christianity, by establishing a sense of duty to God, always conveys with it motives, capable of prompting the soul to any thing which it commands; such as the attainment of mental peace, the approbation of God, the esteem of good men, safety from perdition, and a title to eternal life. Even Indians under its influence have in many cases exhibited fair specimens of virtuous and commendable conduct.

If, however, Indians were "to be civilized without the immediate influence of christianity," they must be changed from sloths, sots, and vagabonds by degrees, and the other mode of civilizing them must be used:

> The only passion, which can be immediately substituted for the Indian love of glory, is that, which has been substituted in every civilized nation: viz. *the love of property*. Wherever this can be established, Indians may be civilized: wherever it cannot, they will still remain Indians. The belief, that our exertions will promote our benefit, and our consequence, will ever stimulate us to exertion. Without this belief, the great body of mankind will not exert themselves at all.

Dwight saw no hope for improving Indians in this manner until they were removed from the neighborhood of the white settlements and established in reservations of their own. Rhode Islanders, on the other hand, might be civilized by this mode at home:

> It is not impossible, perhaps not improbable, that the energy awakened in this State by the diffusion of manufactures, may be productive of some beneficial consequences both to learning and religion. . . . . The wealth of the inhabitants is visibly increasing with rapidity; and will probably continue to increase through an indefinite period. Wealth, wherever it is spread, generates of course the desire of character; and this passion regularly stimulates mankind to the use of those means, by which it may be gratified. . . . . Should this be the course of events in Rhode-Island it is hardly possible, that the character of the inhabitants at large should not be essentially meliorated.

According to a publisher's note, "the prediction of the writer" had "to a considerable extent been fulfilled" between 1800 and 1821. If such a mode of reform could work for the rogues to the east, why should it not be equally effective for those to the west? Dwight was not dealing with ideals. He was writing as a practical man who had been taught by experience that morality flourished best among the middle-class holders of small properties in a state like Connecticut.

Dwight's attitude toward the foresters or pioneers was colored, of course, by the fact that he knew many of them when they represented a dissatisfied minority in the land of steady habits. They were not, in his view, engaged in heroic efforts to build a civilization in the wilderness. They were escaping from a civilization for which they were not fitted.

> These men cannot live in regular society. They are too idle; too talkative; too passionate; too prodigal; and too shiftless; to acquire either property or

character. They are impatient of the restraints of law, religion, and morality; grumble about the taxes, by which Rulers, Ministers, and School-masters supported; and complain incessantly, as well as bitterly, of the extortions of mechanics, farmers, merchants, and physicians; to whom they are always indebted. At the same time, they are usually possessed, in their own view, of uncommon wisdom; understand medical science, politics, and religion, better than those, who have studied them through life; and, although they manage their own concerns worse than any other men, feel perfectly satisfied, that they could manage those of the nation far better than the agents, to whom they are committed by the public. After displaying their own talents, and worth; after censuring the weakeness, and wickedness, of their superiours; after exposing the injustice of the community in neglecting to invest persons of such merit with public offices; in many an eloquent harangue, uttered by many a kitchen fire, in every blacksmith's shop, and in every corner of the streets; and finding all their efforts vain; they become at length discouraged: and under the pressure of poverty, the fear of a gaol, and the consciousness of public contempt, leave their native places, and betake themselves to the wilderness.

They were, in short, socially inefficient nonconformists, republicans in politics, Separatists (at best) in religion, and willing victims of quackery in medicine—encouragers of everything to which Dwight stood opposed. Had their political influence not been felt in national affairs, Dwight might have ignored them or even looked upon them through rose-colored spectacles. But Vermont became a democratic stronghold in New England in 1804, and Dwight inevitably looked at its citizens with as much suspicion as he directed against French philosophers. Nevertheless, Vermont's four or six electoral votes were a small matter in comparison with Virginia's twenty-four or -five; and the President of Yale concluded that, on the whole, the frontier region provided a valuable service for the rest of New England:

In mercy . . . . to the sober, industrious, and well-disposed, inhabitants, Providence has opened up in the vast Western wilderness a retreat, sufficiently alluring to draw them [the "restless"] away from the land of their nativity. We have many troubles even now: but we should have many more, if this body of foresters had remained at home.

Had he lived when the western states held greater political power, he might have been less willing to attribute the frontier to the "mercy" of Providence.

But Dwight was less disturbed by frontier democracy than he was by the sort of republicanism he attributed to the influence of speculative ideas, and his antagonism toward foreigners in general and philosophers in particular runs through the *Travels*. Although he admitted that "a frank, open-hearted, worthy man, from Great Britain, who has the liberality to lay aside his national peculiarities, is as agreeable a companion, as I wish to converse with," he was extremely sensitive to "the English disease of finding fault with the language of Americans," to the tendency of all foreigners to generalize from insufficient evidence, and to their willingness to treat all the United States as a single geographical unit. He was active in the defense of his country against foreign criticism and devoted four entire chapters to a page-by-page rebuttal of mistakes made in Volney's *View of the Climate and Soil of the United States*, Isaac Weld's *Travels in North America*, La Rochefoucauld's *Travels through the United States of North America*, and John Lambert's *Travels through Lower Canada and the United States*. Volney, of course, came in for the most severe criticism, for he not only was more inclined toward generalizations but also revealed atheistical principles. By this time generalization, abstraction, atheism, and Jacobinism had all become entwined in Dwight's mind in opposition to his hardheaded factual devotion to the "truth of things as they are." His most emphatic criticism of "the philosophy of the French school" described it, in italics, as *"a system of abstract declarations, which violated common sense, delivered in an abstract style, equally violating all just taste, and sober criticism."* Its language, he said, "like the signs of the unknown quantities in Algebra, is without meaning, until you arrive at the result, and the application: and it is never designed to come to a result, nor to admit of an application."

Yet, for all his insistence upon an inability to understand the French philosophers, Dwight revealed in the *Travels* a better comprehension of the intellectual currents to which he was opposed than he had shown in his *Theology* or in any of his earlier writings. Hitherto he had thought of "infidel philosophy" as being almost entirely a sort of deism, holding, as its greatest heresy, that man was essentially good. He had named the names of materialists, but he had paid no great attention to their ideas. At last, however, he recognized fully the heresy of philosophers who held that "man . . . . sprang, like a mushroom, out of the earth by a chemical process; and the powers of thinking, choice, and motivity, were merely the result of elective affinities." He continued to attack Herbert and Hume, but he began to stress the power for evil of Holbach, as well as Voltaire: "From the Système de la Nature, and the Philosophical Dictionary, down to the Political Justice of Godwin, and the Age of Reason, the whole mass of pollution was emptied on this country." And their influence, outside of New England, he believed to have been great.

Dwight had come to look upon deism and French philosophy, however, as symptoms of a universal disease that affected people who had never been contaminated by *Political Justice* or *The Age of Reason*. In a single paragraph he diagnosed his age and, like a child passing the village pesthouse, held his nose against possible contagion:

The idolatry of the ancient heathen nations was the worship of calves and cats, of blocks and stones. The idolatry of the present day, still more stupid and unmeaning, is the worship of Abstract Terms. To the astonishment of every sober man, France has exhibited the spectacle of 25,000,000 of the human race, prostrating themselves with religious reverence before the word, *Reason*. Had the weakest of these worshippers formed a definition of this term, and by applying it to any thing, to which it was ever applied, given it a meaning; he must have been a mere zoophyte to have continued his homage for a moment. A multitude of the Americans have paid their devotions to the word, Liberty. This word has a real and important meaning; but in the minds, and mouths, of most men appears to have no meaning at all. That, which it signifies, is by mankind at large respected, and loved; but they *worship* only the abstract term. A few years since, I should have been hardly induced to believe, that multitudes of my countrymen could so idolize this bare word, as to sacrifice at its shrine the very thing, which it denotes.

Thus he found a common characteristic in the orator practicing the "Boston style" in Faneuil Hall on the fifth of March and the checked-shirt-and-leather-apron men along the wharves, the Sage of Monticello and the grammarless denizen of the log cabin, and the shades of Ethan Allen and Sam Adams. No specific definition of "liberty" would have permitted them to stand together; they agreed only in their willingness to bow down before an abstraction. They formed a threatening group just beyond the periphery of Dwight's imagination, and he took a more determined stand than ever upon "the truth of things as they are" in his effort to resist them.

This intensification of a temperamental unwillingness to speculate affected every part of the *Travels*. Dwight not only made his observations meticulously factual but restrained his imagination on occasions when he might properly have been expected to exercise it. He was an unusually well-informed man, who made an effort to keep abreast with scientific thought and was particularly concerned with stimulating scientific studies at Yale. His book reflected a constant interest in geological theories; and, although he did not abandon the main outline of biblical history, he revealed in the classroom a willingness to accept the Mosaic account of the creation as a literary rather than a strictly scientific document. His appreciation of Edward Jenner's experiments with the cowpox was immediate, and he hailed their results as one of the great achievements of the eighteenth century. He delighted in performing "experiments" for himself and on every occasion spoke out strongly against quackery and empiricism in medicine. He could not, of course, have been expected to have any well-formed conception of modern scientific method, but he should have been as sensitive as Joel Barlow was to the contemporary gropings toward it. Yet his conception of a proper "experiment" was one he recorded in an effort to show that animal rather than vegetable putrefaction was the cause of "autumnal diseases":

A number of years since, I put a quantity of ground-pepper into a tumbler of water; and, a few days afterwards found a thin skum spread over the surface. Within a few days more, I perceived, on examining this scum again, I found not the least appearance of life. After another short period, the scum was replenished with living beings again; and, after another became totally destitute of them. This alternate process continued, until the water became so fetid, as to forbid a further examination. The conclusion, which I drew from these facts, was, that the first race of animalcules, having laid their eggs, died; and were succeeded in a short time by a second; and these by a third.

Then, after a few observations concerning the resemblance of this scum to that found on stagnant pools, he ventured an application of his "scientific" observations:

Whatever instrumentality vegetable putrefaction may have; I am inclined to suspect, for several reasons, that animalculine putrefaction is the immediate cause of those diseases, whatever they are, which are justly attributed to standing waters. It will, I believe, be found universally, that no such disease is ever derived from any standing waters, which are not to a considerable extent covered with a scum: and perhaps most, if not all, of these, which have this covering, will be found unhealthy.

All this represented, to Dwight, firm intellectual ground—observed facts and plain reasoning upon them. His application could be changed from a suspicion to a certainty by a universal observation of what he believed to be true, and by no other method. To him the scientific way was that of pure Baconian induction, utilizing the broadest possible observation and the simplest possible reasoning.

Of course, Dwight's enthusiasm for Jenner's work was probably determined by the fact that his famous grandfather had died of an inoculation and he himself had suffered permanently from the ill effects of that method of avoiding smallpox. Furthermore, even the most objective observer would not have derived from Jenner the idea of a properly controlled experiment. Yet Dwight readily accepted the highly imaginative hypothesis upon which Jenner worked: that a minor disease of the lower animals could be transferred to human beings in order to make them immune to a major disease which affected them alone. He could speak with awe and admiration of the discovery, but he looked upon it as the result of Providence rather than of a method adaptable by all men. Scorning imaginative hypotheses as he did in philosophy and in social and political theory, he could not have appreciated their value as a part of the standard methodology of scientific procedure. In his own experiment he kept his feet on the ground, investigating the simplest alternative to the accepted theory, interpreting his observations according to the simplest analogies, and making the simplest possible application of them. If universal observation failed to confirm his suggestions, the next simplest explanation might be put to the test of experience. Eventually, by this "sure" process, someone might have hypothesized microbes and mosquitoes, but, more probably, mankind would have remained shaken by malaria until the millennial dawn.

If Dwight's unimaginative fear of the imagination had allowed him, on occasions, to appreciate its possible contribution to the advancement of knowledge, he still would have chosen the step-by-step process as the only method of progress compatible with security. When he devoted the last section of his *Travels* to "Prospects of the United States," abandoning, after Waterloo, his pessimistic views of the state of the world, he seemed to take satisfaction in the slowness of human improvement.

Almost all our institutions, perhaps all, which deserve to be permanent, have with as much regularity as seems compatible with the present state of mankind, been in the course of improvement. Manners, laws, learning, and in some respect religion, may be justly considered as being *now* progressive. The mechanical, manufacturing, and liberal arts, literature, and science, are at the present time advanced, upon the whole, beyond any preceding attainments. . . . . We are also learning, though it must be confessed by slower degrees, that we are not so much wiser, and better, than the rest of mankind, as many of our people have heretofore believed, or at least professed to believe. Persons of this cast are beginning to suspect, that modesty is one excellence of the human character, and a proof of other excellencies; and that boasting furnishes fewer, and smaller, claims to respect than they have been accustomed to imagine. This melioration of our character will undoubtedly make a slow progress; yet I believe it is really progressive.

He constantly discounted brilliance and stressed the importance of hard work. "Genius, in the abstract," he said in his first volume, "is a mere capacity for exertion"; and in the last: "Genius may be generally and accurately defined to be *the power of making mental efforts.*" When discussing education, he laid down two fundamental principles: "The admission of truth, the comprehension of good sense, requires the toil of sober, vigorous thought. The admission of fiction, and of philosophical as truly as poetical fiction, demands nothing, but the lucious indulgence of fancy." Thus he opposed novel-reading by girls not only because of the dangers involved in judging a flesh-and-blood suitor by Sir Charles Grandison but because a mind and taste "fascinated by mental luxury" would "reject the dictates of sober truth, and sound understanding, and from self-indulgence, by habit rendered indispensable, imbibe the wretched doctrines created by the philosophists of the present day."

Yet only a relatively small portion of the *Travels* was devoted to such theorizing, and even Dwight's theorizing was often more shrewd and, in its hard-headed attention to facts, more valuable than the fanciful speculations of his contemporaries. When he dismissed the dramas of Aeschylus, Sophocles, Euripides, Corneille "and his splendid train of followers," Shakespeare "and his," Schiller, and Kotzebue with the statement that "among all their productions there is scarcely one which an Apostle would even read," he was writing from a point of view highly colored by prejudice against a foreign civilization which encouraged the immoral theater and the scandalous behavior of actors. But, when he discussed the reasons why America was inferior to Great Britain in its literature, he kept his mind fairly steadily upon things as they were. Having marshaled an array of facts against the climatic theories of genius and having dismissed the notion that literary genius was an arbitrary gift of God, he cited all the customary explanations of American deficiency: the energetic demands of American life, the scarcity of libraries, the easy access to English writings, the absence of a long and respected literary tradition, and the lack of literary patronage in the form of university fellowships or easy clerical livings. All these things, as many of Dwight's contemporaries had already observed, prevented American authors from obtaining any "tolerable reward for their labours" and so restricted the business of authorship. But in the midst of them Dwight offered one hard observation that goes further than any theory toward explaining his own literary career and the careers of his friends: "No American has within my knowledge been willing to inhabit a garret, for the sake of becoming an author." The reasons for their unwillingness may have varied with every individual, and it might be possible to follow trains of speculative causation forever. But the observation, which Dwight alone has recorded, is one of the major facts in the literary history of early America: hundreds of young men felt the charm of what Trumbull called the "flowery road to fame," and hundreds of others amused their leisure hours with quill and paper, but not one of them exhibited a willingness to sacrifice and to sweat in order to write a living line.

The frequent hardheaded observations of cultural as well as physical facts give Dwight's *Travels* a value above that of mere description, interesting though the latter usually is. He was concerned with the state of language, learning, morals, religion, and manufactures in New England and with the personal characteristics of its inhabitants. These were his formal classifications of subjects particularly treated, but he by no means confined his treatment of them to the sections set aside for that purpose. His interest ranged everywhere, and if he lacked creative imagination he possessed an abundance of probing curiosity. His view of what he found was sometimes jaundiced and often rosy; but on the whole, while Barlow was incorporating into the *Columbiad* the dream which he and many other Americans shared, Dwight was successfully getting into his *Travels* the reality with which he and many others were content.

V

While Dwight was engaged in dictating, revising, and completing his monumental *Theology* and *Travels*, he was indulging in a large amount of miscellaneous literary activity, most of it supplementary to these two major works. Eight of his occasional sermons and one address were published during these years, and he left written out for posthumous publication, in addition to his system of theology, between one hundred and thirty and one hundred and fifty additional sermons. He contributed to religious and scientific periodicals, and toward the end of his life he revived "The Friend" in a series of six papers that were to be used in a periodical he hoped to establish. After the close of the war with England, when the era of good feeling allowed him to relax in his defense of society, he turned again to verse and four days before his death stitched the finished manuscript of a fifteen-hundred-line poem entitled "The Trial," which was "a contest between *genius* and *common sense*, in which *truth* acts as *umpire*." About half of this material is identifiable and available. Slightly more than a third of the miscellaneous sermons were published in New Haven and Edinburgh in 1828, together

with a few already in print, and more were promised if the first
two volumes were successful—which apparently did not prove
to be the case, for no more appeared, although some of them are
still extant in manuscript. Most of the contributions to periodicals were anonymous, and many of Dwight's minor journalistic
efforts may now be buried beyond recognition. The most important journalism of his later life, however, probably consists of
the eighteen "Lectures on the Evidences of Divine Revelation,"
which he thought too incomplete for a book but published in the
Boston *Panoplist and Missionary Magazine* between June, 1810,
and December, 1813; a dissertation on "The Manner in Which
the Scriptures Are To Be Understood," which appeared in the
same periodical for May and June, 1816; several articles in the
Memoirs of the Connecticut Academy of Arts and Sciences; and a
long answer, in pamphlet form, to the *Quarterly*'s review of
Charles Jared Ingersoll's *Inchiquin the Jesuit's Letters*. His
poem and his last attempt at the periodical essay apparently
are lost.

The first five of the occasional sermons have little interest
other than that of the circumstances which provoked them.
Two were funeral addresses, conventional in form and plain in
style, published more in honor of the subjects than of the
preacher, although the second (on Governor Jonathan Trumbull) gives an excellent picture of Dwight's ideal statesman
whose public character was disfigured by "not a single visionary
measure." Two extolled eleemosynary institutions and reflected
Dwight's growing concern for charitable and missionary activities. The first, preached at the opening of the Andover Theological Seminary in 1808, revealed both his disturbance over the
unlearned clergy in Baptist and Separate churches and his increasing belief that the last vial of Revelation was being poured
out and a "wonderful Era in the affairs of men" was approaching; and the second, on three "Female Charitable Societies" in
New Haven, was widely used for the purpose of encouraging the
sort of activities that were supposed to foreshadow the new era.
The remaining discourse, *A Sermon on Duelling*, became the
most famous of the lot. Although Dwight prefaced it with a

declaration that it did "not intentionally apply to any facts or persons," it was first preached in New Haven on September 9, 1804, two months after Burr had killed Hamilton, and was repeated before an acutely interested New York audience in January. More vivid and rhetorical than the sermon on the same subject in the *Theology*, it was undoubtedly occasional in its inspiration and owed much of its effect to Dwight's horror at the recklessness of his own cousin.

These sermons, like those in the two-volume posthumous collection, were much less formal than those in the *Theology*, highly illustrative, and designed to appeal more to the heart than to the head. Dwight was never the type of "cold Preacher," who, as he told the students entering Andover, "naturally makes a frozen audience." He never uttered "the truths of the Gospel" with a "wind-and-weather indifference." On the contrary, his inability to be "cold and dull" called forth one of the few criticisms that his former student, Gardner Spring, allowed himself to utter in an almost worshipful memorial address before the New York alumni of Yale College:

> If as a preacher, he had a fault, it was that he was too familiar with the decorations of human eloquence—too often suffered his pen to rove amid scenes of enchantment—too often pleased the taste and imagination of his audience at the expense of probing their consciences, and therefore sometimes failed in the pungency of his discourses.

The series of baccalaureate sermons included in this collection and the discourse "On the Parental Character of God" preached in 1809 illustrate this characteristic. But, on the whole, Dwight followed the advice on preaching that he gave his students in his first baccalaureate: he drew his illustrations from familiar sources and rarely attempted to astonish his congregations with his learning. If any of his hearers found his description of revelation as "a window in that dark mansion, which you now inhabit, opening to the regions of immortality" too florid and not the "chaste, manly, energetic style" he recommended, Dwight might have recognized a legitimate difference in taste. His success proved that his taste generally corresponded with that of most of his audiences. In any case his manner was his own; and, as he told his students, "a borrowed coat never sate well on any man . . . . every man's manner is a good one, and for himself the best."

The rhetorical coat was often a good one for Dwight, and it was fortunate that he wore it naturally instead of a more severely logical garment. He took pride in the revivals of religion that occurred in Yale during the early years of his presidency, and again in 1811 and 1815; but he might have found it difficult to justify his character as a revivalist without violating his system of theology or his antagonism toward finespun reasoning. When he preached on that subject, however, he could "naturally" emphasize the satisfaction aroused by a revival rather than its use. Since every outburst of religious feeling "partially" shared the character of the millennium, he held: "Every such revival is therefore a solid foundation of joy to all the rational creatures of God." The metaphysics of Calvinistic revivalism went deeper than Dwight liked to dive; but his ordinary method of preaching enabled him to avoid metaphysics by stirring the souls of his congregation to an appreciation of the joys of the millennium without disturbing their minds. Similarly, in a separately published *Sermon, Delivered in Boston, September 16, 1813, before the American Board of Commissioners for Foreign Missions*, he could issue a call to Protestant nations to begin the mighty work of foreign missions on the grounds of propriety rather than of use. "The present is the proper time for this glorious undertaking," he insisted.

It is the proper time, as it is marked out by the Spirit of prophecy. Almost all judicious commentaters have agreed, that the Millennium, in the full and perfect sense, will begin at a period, not far from the year 2000. . . . . But, should we fasten upon the year 2000, as the period in which there shall be a complete accomplishment of the predictions concerning this wonderful event, how evidently it is necessary, that all the measures, by which it is to be accomplished, should be now formed, and immediately begin to operate.

The impulse of some New Light preachers toward revivalist sermons seems to have been an emotional product of the doctrines of election and reprobation that made evangelical preaching illogical: in the presence of the awful goodness of God, it did not become a saint to be cocksure of his regeneration, and the indif-

ference of a sinner was an offense unto God and unto all men
who appreciated his power and excellence. So, from a deep feeling of propriety, they occasionally preached of Hell and viewed
the results with satisfaction—unless they made too many converts. If the number of repentant sinners became suspiciously
large or their repentance excessively enthusiastic, the preacher
might become embarrassed (as Jonathan Edwards was) by a
conflict between his oratorical effectiveness and his theological
tenets. Dwight felt no such embarrassment. Feeling the propriety of revivals of religion and of the good works of mission-
aries, he advocated them on the grounds of propriety, drawing
rhetorical illustrations of their correspondence to the state of
things during the coming millennium and avoiding any logic
that might have introduced difficult questions of cause and
effect. Had he cultivated a different style of preaching he might
have been forced to make some new adjustments in either his
theology or his activities.

The increasing tendency to dwell upon the approaching millennium was the most curious development in Dwight's later
writings. His grandfather Edwards, of course, had thought that
the thousand years of peace might begin in the year 2000, and
the Rev. Joseph Bellamy, Edwards' disciple, had published a
book on that subject in 1758. The idea was a familiar one to
Dwight, and he had used it in some of his earlier writings. But
when David Austin began his agitated warnings of its approach
during the latter years of the eighteenth century, Dwight remained unimpressed. "Mr. Austin was perfectly rational," he
told his students some years later, "upon every subject except
the Millennium." Yet even then he was beginning to change his
mind.

Perhaps the most important reason for the change was the
cumulative intensity of his conviction that he was one of the
few sane men in a world gone mad. The threat of a war with
France in July, 1798, had caused him to brood on Armageddon,
even though he felt the conflict justified. But when the United
States, on June 18, 1812, declared war on England and so joined
forces with the Anti-Christ, he thought "It is done" and began

to expect the voices and lightnings and thunders and the hail-stones of the weight of a talent. Connecticut, of course, remained secure in her steady habits. Governor Roger Griswold, with the support of his council, refused a request to call out the state militia to assist in "Mr. Madison's war," arguing that it was illegal to do so since the country had not been invaded. While he was still persisting in this refusal Dwight preached one of his most remarkable sermons: *A Discourse, in Two Parts, Delivered July 23, 1812, on the Public Fast, in the Chapel of Yale College*. Taking as his text "Watchman, what of the night?" and "The dawn cometh," he surveyed the ominous state of the world, attributing the ill-boding events of the period to the rise of deism, the activities of the Bavarian Illuminati, and the spread of French infidelity. Were it not for the rhetorical character of so many of his other sermons, his words might be taken as evidence of hysteria. For example, he exclaimed:

The spirit of Infidelity has the heart of a wolf, the fangs of a tyger, and the talons of a vulture. Blood is its proper nourishment: and it scents its prey with the nerves of a hound, and cowers over a field of death on the sooty pinions of a fiend. Unlike all other animals of prey, it feeds upon its own kind; and, when glutted with the blood of others, turns back upon those, who have been its coadjutors, and who, if either its disposition, or its measures, would admit of friendship, would have been its friends.

Bad as the French Revolution was, the militaristic expansion afterward was even worse. The domination of the French infidels made conditions in their own country seem but "a prelude to the funeral of this great world."

Under the names of contributions, war-takes, and other claims, professedly claims of the nation, they *gathered the riches of the whole people as a nest, and as one gathered eggs that are left: and there was none, that moved the wing, or opened the mouth, or peeped.* With this singular mass of wealth in their possession, they raised armies, in different years amounting to 5, 7, 9, and 12 hundred thousand men: the strongest and most formidable body, which was ever assembled upon this globe. This incomprehensible multitude they emptied out upon every neighbouring state. The lava did not run in a stream, as in the eruptions of the natural world. It flowed down all the sides of the immeasurable crater at once: and like an ocean, rolled its waves of fire over the whole face of the world, within its reach. Nothing withstood its power.

The work of destruction was still going on, while America remained the only republic "on the face of the earth; and that,
merely because the giant was unable to wade through the bil-
lows of the Atlantic."

In the United States there was still some hope. A revival of
religion had begun during the last years of the century, the
African slave trade had been abolished, the practice of vaccina-
tion had spread, and missionary and Bible societies were becoming numerous. But the good was being threatened by the
"dreadful evil" of "party-spirit"—"*a smoke in the nostrils of
Jehovah; an abomination, which he cannot away with.*" Somehow
Dwight held this party spirit responsible for the war, which, he
said, many Americans believed unnecessary and unjust, for
which the country was not prepared, and by which the government was inviting invasion. His greatest fear, however, was
that the war might bring on a formal alliance between his country and France; and, although he declared that on this subject
his feelings were "inexpressible," he expressed them:

To ally America to France, is to chain living health and beauty, to a corpse
dissolving with the plague. The evils, which we have already suffered from
this impure and monstrous connexion, are terrible omens of the destruction,
which we are to expect from a connexion still more intimate. The horrors of
war, compared with it, are mere amusement. The touch of France is pollution. Her embrace is death.

Thirty days later the General Assembly of Connecticut met
in special session to consider the action of the governor with
respect to the federal demands for militia, and on the Sunday
before they gathered Dwight preached another public sermon,
on the same text, in the Yale Chapel. He began by referring to
the belief expressed in the earlier discourse that the people of
America were "placed, in prophecy, under those symbolical predictions in the Apocalypse, which are denominated by *the seven
vials;* particularly under the concluding operations of the sixth,
or the commencing operations of the seventh." Since the discussion had "excited a considerable interest in the minds of this
audience," he announced, he had determined to continue it with
the distinct understanding that no party would be arraigned

and no public measure censured during the course of his observations. Yet in answer to a question concerning the "immediate
duty" of Americans in the present crisis, he replied: "It is our
indispensable duty to abstain from any intimate connexion with
the Romish Empire"—especially from an alliance with France,
"the only Romish power, with which we are in any danger of
being connected." The number of people opposed to such an
alliance, he believed, was "daily increasing: and will, probably,
soon include a great part of our people." Another, more difficult, duty was to refrain from party politics, which was occupying the minds of Americans to such an extent that they
were in danger of losing their souls and ruining their country:

To a party no people were ever more attached, or more true. But where
shall we find the same attachment to the common good? *Tell it not in Gath;
publish it not in the streets of Askelon;* that the inhabitants of all lands, except
the American States, love the country, which gave them birth; that the Lap-
lander clings to his frosts and snows; and believes that Paradise once smiled
beneath them; that the Icelander pines, and sickens, and dies, with melancholy, however pleasant in other respects may be his circumstances, if de-
tained for any length of time from his own burning mountains and desolate
wastes; . . . . and that an American, to whom climate and soil, arts and commerce, learning and freedom, religion and laws, have endeared his country,
by showering upon it their best blessings, regards it as a land of strangers, or a
residence of parties.

Some members of his audience listened and moved on to Hartford, where, as members of the Federalist legislature, they
pleased Dwight by their nonpartisan devotion to the common
good in upholding the governor's refusal to contribute militia to
the army, resolving that the war itself was "unnecessary" and
viewing with alarmed reprobation any tendency toward an
alliance with France.

Thus Dwight, by this time the most forceful public figure in
the state, in the name of "the common good" as opposed to
"party-politics," declared his independence of the federal government of the United States and helped lay the ground for that
finely nonpartisan Hartford Convention of which his younger
brother served as secretary. He was not, of course, alone. Sympathy with England was widespread in New England, where
many newspapers gleefully announced British victories abroad

and clergymen preached against France while the English were burning the Capitol. For the President of Yale, however, this attitude marked the final restriction of his gradually narrowing point of view. His imagination, which had always balked at crossing the Atlantic, could now hardly cross the Hudson and remain under control. He had wrapped himself in the cloak of his virtue until he could see only darkness. But, since he believed that "our night . . . . may not commence, until the Sun of that day shall set in thick darkness, which will be terminated only by the last morning of this guilty world," he felt that the intervening millennium *must* be near at hand.

Yet, as time went on and no earthquake shook the world, Dwight abandoned his apocalyptic hobbyhorse and found that republicanism and French infidelity were not the only subjects worthy of his opposition. He sympathized with the English against Napoleon, but he had the not uncommon experience of finding it difficult to remain comfortably on their side. The difficulty was brought into the open in January, 1814, by an article in the *Quarterly Review* on *Inchiquin the Jesuit's Letters during a Late Residence in the United States of America*. The letters had been written by Charles J. Ingersoll, of Philadelphia, who had tried to correct the unflattering pictures of America given in most travel-books by writing in the guise of a distinguished foreigner who had been favorably impressed by the United States. The *Quarterly*, in a review commonly attributed to Robert Southey, made an attempt to give a "correct" view of the United States by pointing out the faults which the "Jesuit" had overlooked; and Dwight, acutely aware of the contumely he had suffered because of his friendship toward England, was enraged at such a tactless blow at Anglo-American relations. The man responsible (Dwight could not believe it a gentleman of Southey's reputation) was no better, and deserved no better treatment, than the president of the United States. Dwight had not read the *Letters* and did not want to read any such "silly book" by any such "silly man" as the republican former congressman. But the United States had been attacked in the peculiarly stupid way that Dwight had been brooding about while writing his own *Travels*, and he set about defending, not a fellow-author and the son of an old schoolmate, but his country and, incidentally, his own unpublished work. The defense was addressed to George Canning, publisher of the *Quarterly*, but it dealt vigorously with Francis Jeffrey and the *Edinburgh Review* as well and so formed an American prose counterpart to certain sections of Byron's *English Bards and Scotch Reviewers*.

Dwight was generous in opening praise for Great Britain. He declared that the existing war, in his opinion, was "unnatural, impolitic on our part, causeless, and unjust."

The *British* nation . . . . had for many years been employed, in defending what was left of the liberty, and safety, of the human race; the protestant religion; and the remains of literature, arts, science, civilization, and happiness; from the jaws of the *Corsican Cyclop*. . . . . The human race are your debtors: and to you, under God, it is owing in a great measure, that the inhabitants of this country are in possession of their own liberty and independence. . . . . [The English] have done more to define, and perpetuate, liberty; to form a wise, upright, and stable government; to improve agriculture, arts, and manufactures; to extend learning, and science; and to advance the interests of morality, and religion; than any other nation, ancient or modern.

But the English possessed, to an exaggerated degree, every fault they found in Americans, as well as a number that were peculiarly their own. If the American treatment of the Indians was "scandalous," it was not so "infamous" as the English behavior toward the Hindus—"and the name of *Harrison* will go down to posterity with less infamy, than those of *Clive*, and *Sykes*." If the wording of the New Jersey constitution inadvertently permitted women to vote and a case of woman suffrage had been known in the United States, that was not nearly so reprehensible as the relative situations of Old Sarum and Birmingham. And of the fifty thousand London "Females, who," according to Colquhoun's *Police of London*, "support themselves chiefly, or wholly, by prostitution" Dwight declared firmly: "This is worse, Sir, than voting." The contemptible and abhorred institution of the camp meeting had been derived directly from England; southern planters, on the whole, were splendid men in comparison with the slave-holding plantation owners of the British Indies; and, admirable though the English Sunday school was, it bore witness to a necessity for educating the poor which did not exist in the United States. Even in language English usage was worse than American and responsible for "ten times" as much neologizing.

Wherever a contrast existed between the two countries, it was to the advantage of the United States. The middle-class competence of New England was much to be desired above the extremes of poverty and wealth in Britain; and, even though Connecticut and Vermont had dishonorable, pollution-diffusing laws permitting civil divorce, the morality in all the New England states was superior to that of the dissolute nobility of the British Isles. The worst general characteristics he found in the English, however, were their bad manners, smugness, and stupidity:

> We know, that you are a great nation, and have achieved distinguished glory in many ways, and those of supreme importance. But we do not think, that you have any knack at making friends. You form too high an estimate of your own importance to suffer you to be agreeable to others; loftily claim the respect, which other nations solicit; and receive it as a tribute, where other nations receive it as a proof of civility.

One of the few occasions that Dwight had heard of on which an Englishman had the grace to praise American food occurred when an inn-keeper, annoyed by his guest's bad manners, had ordered his beefsteak sprinkled with sulphur and heard it pronounced "delicious." "*Frenchmen*," Dwight concluded, voicing the observation that had provoked his annoyance, "known to possess scarcely a twentieth part of your honesty, and inferiour to you in every respectable attribute, beside civility, will secure many friends, where you make only enemies."

Yet if Dwight was trying to improve international relations, he was going about it by exhibiting the same characteristics he had condemned in Englishmen. The man whose notions of controversy had been formed by the Queen Anne wits, the New Light theologians, and the newspaper editors of the Jeffersonian period was hardly the person to preach civility in argument. He exhibited no more temperance with respect to the Scottish reviews than he had on the subject of French infidelity. "The *Edinburgh Review* sometimes exhibits superiour talents," he admitted in his Introduction; "but, on the whole," he added, "it is a nuisance to the world." And of the two distinguished periodicals, he said:

> Amid all the base reflections, cast upon the people of the United States, for their destitution of understanding, and worth, in these dirty-minded effusions of spite and ribaldry, there is not one, half so humiliating, as the fact, that the *Edinburgh and Quarterly Reviews are republished in this country.*

He took delight in Byron's treatment of Jeffrey, quoting from the review of *Hours of Idleness* and from the "cauterizing verses" of the reviewer in *English Bards and Scotch Reviewers* and following the quotations up with the favorable remarks on Byron in 1813. Byron perhaps had encouraged Dwight to adopt the tone he used in his own attack, for in explaining the *Edinburgh*'s change of attitude he wrote:

> The Noble Poet had brandished his cat-o'-nine-tails with such force and dexterity, that this descendant of the ancient family [Lord Monboddo's apes] feels the tingling to the present time. Rely upon it, Sir, there was never one of this breed, who could be operated upon, to any valuable puprose, in any other manner.

If the *Remarks on the Review of Inchiquin's Letters* served no other purpose, it provided one hundred and seventy-six pages of evidence that Dwight's opposition to the English war was not the result of Anglophilia.

This outburst of illiberal patriotism, however, did not lead Dwight into any expression of enthusiasm for the republican leaders of his own country. He said in one place:

> Mr. *Jefferson* and Mr. *Madison* are, we will suppose, weak men. To the former, indeed, you allow a plausible address, and considerable talents: and it must be acknowledged, that he possesses, in no contemptible degree, the talent, which is styled cunning. As to talents of any other nature, I will leave him to display and his friends to admit them. Place both these Magistrates as low as you please.

Later he added:

> Except for the Missions of *Pike, Lewis, and Clark,* to explore the *Mississippi,* there is not a single measure originated by either, during the fourteen years of their reign, which has reflected the least credit upon their character, or produced the least benefit to the United States. . . . . . Mr. *Jefferson,* though possessed of considerable ingenuity, and a good deal of cunning, is absolutely destitute of wisdom, as well as of principle; of that sound, practical good sense,

which alone has ever been of any use to mankind in the management of either their public or their private affairs. Of Mr. *Madison* it is enough to say, that, without the cunning of his Master, he has humbly trodden in his steps. If the art of governing consisted in originating, or defending, abstract propositions, or general principles, Mr. *Madison* would not have been without his share of reputation among rulers. But as it actually consists in the exercise of practical good sense and skill in the business of man, directed, as well as prompted, by a public, and not a party, spirit; no niche will ever be furnished for his reception among respectable men of this character.

Still, they have been useful instructors to the *American* people. Mr. *Jefferson* has taught us, that Infidelity is an unprofitable guide, in the management of national interests. Mr. *Madison*, as well as his Master, has strongly exhibited the visionary nature of theoretical specuations in the public concerns of mankind. From both, also, have we learned, that far other moral dispositions, than such as are possessed by these gentlemen, are necessary in the Ruler, who is to do good to his country.

The best he could think to say of either of the American presidents was that they were not so bad or so low as some of the kings of the country with which the United States was then at war.

These *Remarks* undoubtedly enabled Dwight to relieve himself of some of the intemperate feelings that otherwise might have spoiled the *Travels*, which he began to revise and put in final form a year later. His other journalistic writings of the time were also, in one way or another, supplementary to his more durable work. *A Statistical Account of the City of New Haven*, which he contributed to the first volume of the *Memoirs of the Connecticut Academy of Arts and Sciences* and published in pamphlet form in 1811, consisted of material later incorporated in the *Travels*. The series of "Lectures on the Evidences of Divine Revelation" contained comparatively little, aside from illustrative material, which was not worked, in abbreviated form, into the *Theology*; and his article on "The Manner in Which the Scriptures Are To Be Understood" merely developed at some length the idea he had expressed at Greenfield and had preached consistently ever since: that the Bible was not the product of human literary genius but a revelation to men of plain understanding, who put down the knowledge revealed to them in plain language for plain people. His "Observations on Language," contributed to the Academy *Memoirs* for 1816, developed the idea that appeared constantly in his *Theology*, *Travels*, and other writings: "that all nations will uniformly have such words, as express those ideas, which they wish to communicate" and will retain no others for any length of time. Within the limits of biblical authority and Lockean epistemology it revealed a good deal of acuteness in perception; but it is chiefly remarkable for the great display of linguistic learning by which Dwight may have wanted to show that the erudition of Yale College was equal to that of the independent scholar, Noah Webster, whose contributions were the mainstay of Connecticut's first learned journal. Dwight's final contribution, a letter "On Light" published the same year, was the most interesting, for it consisted of original observations, growing out of his own eye disease, which he thought might "elucidate, in a degree, the nature of light." His description of the very bright "lucid appearances, sometimes fixed, and sometimes moving," which at times crowded his field of vision was vivid, and the hints of a lifelong battle against headache and the fear of blindness were moving; but the scientific conclusions were not very impressive. He apparently thought in terms of Newton's corpuscular theory of light, and his "experiments" with arousing images by pressing his fingers against the closed eyelids merely "proved" that light consisted of particles of matter pressing with different degrees of weight or velocity against the optic nerve.

The last public literary appearance Dwight made was as chairman of a committee instructed by the General Association in June, 1816, to prepare *An Address to the Emigrants from Connecticut, and from New England Generally, in the New Settlements of the United States*. In this, addressed mainly to the settlers in Ohio, Dwight showed no signs of the attitude toward pioneers that appeared in his *Travels*. Nor did he, after the successful conclusion of the Napoleonic wars, give any indication that the revelations of St. John the Divine were still occupying his thoughts. The *Address*, naturally, urged the emigrants to make provision for churches and schools, to hold to the gospel as a check upon human depravity, and to keep the Sabbath and avoid the use of spirituous liquors. But there was no passive appeal to the "propriety" of such actions in view of the approaching millennium. On the contrary, it placed an active, stirring emphasis upon the present as a prelude to an indefinite future of vital, human effort.

> How high and momentous are the destinies of your settlements, and of that immense wilderness which lies beyond! You must increase. The states and territories to which you have emigrated are capable of sustaining an immense population. A vast tide is rolling on day and night from the Atlantic states to the west. A new state is peopled, with almost as much facility, as a township was settled a century ago.
>
> Within less than fifty years past, the population of the United States has doubled twice. Should it increase according to the same ration, for a hundred years to come, it will amount to more than a *hundred and twenty millions*, and still there will be room for more! Let it be remembered, that this mighty mass of rational and immortal beings will consist of the grand-children and great grand-children of the present generation; that millions and millions of them will be your descendants; that they will imbibe from you their moral and religious principles; that their characters will be moulded in your institutions, and receive the impression of your virtues and your vices.
>
> Yes, brethren and friends, you are *peculiarly* acting for posterity. The institutions which you establish may bear your image and superscription for centuries to come. They may remain the imperishable monuments of your wisdom and piety, or the sad memorials of your folly and sin. . . . . The early habits of a people are like the first roads in a new country, which it is extremely inconvenient and difficult to alter, after the inhabitants have long been accustomed to them, and have built their houses and shaped their farms by them. Or, to vary the figure, early habits, in new settlements, are so many deep and broad channels, in which the thoughts of succeeding generations, on all important subjects, naturally run; and from which it is not easy to divert them.

After two decades of reaction to an intense, frightening social pressure which caused him to narrow his vision more and more to things of which he was sure, Dwight at last found a release and lifted up his eyes to the future, recapturing the vision of the rising glory of America that he had once seen in the optimistic days after the first war against England.

Dwight probably composed the concluding chapters of his *Travels* under the influence of this new spirit; and it was under its influence, also, that he felt able to turn back to belles-lettres, composing the Spenserian stanzas of the debate between Genius and Common Sense during his evening walks and dictating them upon his return home very much as he had composed and dic-

tated *Greenfield Hill* thirty years before. The poem and the revival of "The Friend" both came during a second period of
recuperation from disappointment and bitterness. He was older,
of course, and already suffering from the cancer which brought
his life to an end on January 11, 1817. But his greater maturity
and more flexible command of language might have enabled him
to write a philosophical poem which, though not profound,
would be the first thoroughly readable work of its kind in
America. Some day it may yet come to light and, perhaps, give
Dwight a better place than he has yet received in American
literature.

VI

Prolific though Dwight was during his later years, the extent
of his influence cannot be measured in his writings. Nor were his
political counsels wisely expedient enough to be enduring. Publicly, he was sufficiently powerful to be cordially hated; but his
most impressive power was exerted in the classroom. Thirteen
hundred and one students passed through his classes during his
presidency at Yale, and the number tutored and taught at
Greenfield Academy brought the total of his charges up to an
estimated two thousand. He was not a severe instructor, but
graduate after graduate of Yale bore testimony in later life to
the permanent impression the great Dr. Dwight made upon
him. Students matured under his instruction and, as one of
them said, "had their principles, literary, political, moral, and
religious, settled for life." Carefully preserved notebooks covering all his Senior courses show how the boys hung on every
word, noted down, and made neat records of the most incidental
wisdom he uttered in the classroom. One of his students actually published, in 1833, a volume of notes on his decision on Senior
debates and seriously proposed further volumes of class notes—
not on lectures, for Dwight never lectured formally except in the
course of theology, but upon his comments upon the textbooks
and the recitations from them. Though his students held him in
such respect that they always rose when he entered the room
and remained standing until he was seated, Dwight was much

less formal in class than in public, commenting easily and shrewdly upon the lesson with illustrative remarks drawn from Shakespeare, Richardson, Fielding, the English poets, and the everyday details of life, often in homely language and with quiet humor. Many of his boys, in turn, passed on his influence to their own students, for Yale was the mother of colleges in those days; and the institutionalized impact of Dwight's personality has been felt by thousands alive today who attended one of the "New England type colleges" before most of them became so respectable that they began to cater primarily to the well-to-do.

He also became a name by which the sterner virtues were preserved. His *Theology* was commonly treated with enormous respect, though few contemporary journals reviewed it—possibly because editors were unwilling to be critical of so worth while an influence. His miscellaneous *Sermons* were published as quickly in Scotland as in his native state; and when an anonymous English nonconformist wanted to make an effective attack upon the theater, in 1824, he fathered it upon the "late President of Yale," publishing *An Essay on the Stage* with Dwight's name and all his degrees upon the title-page and describing it as a reprint from an imaginary Middletown edition. The politicians and the common people alone remained unimpressed, and Connecticut was captured by the democrats in the 1818 elections.

Dwight's way through the world was a consistent and, on the whole, a strait and narrow one. He was early converted to "the truth of things as they are"; and, although he came to scoff at William Wollaston's notion that conformity to such truth was the basis of morality, he continued to hold that it was the basis of all right thinking. If he deviated for a while into the notion that things could be seen as they were by any other lights than the divine glow of revelation or the commonplace lamp of experience, he soon settled more firmly than ever into the orthodox teaching of his undergraduate days and spent much of his life denouncing intellectual will-o'-the-wisps. Temperamentally devoid of any great constructive imagination, he was given little opportunity, by the march of contemporary events, to develop it or little encouragement to have faith in other men's imaginings. Disturbed, frightened, placed on the defensive, he became convinced that "slow" and "sure" were synonymous terms. But his very lack of creative imagination caused him to indulge in fantasies. He saw the apocalyptic beast and heard things that go bump in the night where there was nothing but social change in the mask of anarchy and rumbling challenges to human intelligence and understanding. In an age when men's imaginings were running far ahead of their performances, Dwight's particular genius for exertion and for attention to facts was gravely needed—and in minor ways he exerted it constructively. But broader issues usually aroused him only to violent reaction; and most of his public utterances, during the last two decades of his life, survive as nothing more than vivid reminders that no man can flounder more wildly than the one who hangs his clothes on a hickory limb and refuses to go near the rising tide which engulfs him.

EPILOGUE

Blazed Trails

EPILOGUE

BLAZED TRAILS

THE most remarkable characteristic of American civilization in the days of the Connecticut Wits was its decentralization—physical, intellectual, and literary. Its energy was centrifugal. Young men of similar social backgrounds, cast in the same educational mold, moved by a common ambition, were thrown almost beyond the range of communication with one another before they reached the ends of their careers. Their country contained no single metropolis which served as a physical point of attraction, no national system of coherent intellectual training, no widespread reading public with well-defined standards of appreciation. Even the common denominator of political belief achieved during the period was soon threatened by the new hopes and fears aroused by the French Revolution. Men were impelled to wander abroad rather than to congregate and cohere.

The Wits all wanted to be poets—great poets, in most cases—and with their impulse to wander they were able to find, even in their restricted cultural environment, many formative notions that were later to provoke memorable verse. While Wordsworth was still a schoolboy, Dwight was trying to unify a long poem by drawing upon the theories of contemporary psychology, and Barlow was planning a philosophical poem celebrating his own age. Humphreys had been trying to make the lively image the mainstay of his verse for thirteen years before Keats was born. And later, in a different environment, Barlow anticipated Shelley by two decades in his efforts to exploit the ideas of the French atheists, the discoveries of science, and the speculations of the mythologists as material for poetry which would reform the world. It is conventional to speak of them as being behind the times in a vain attempt to re-create the age of Queen Anne in the literature of America; but, actually, of their more important works only the two long poems by Trumbull, the collaborations of the "wicked wits," and the satire by Dwight went back to the time of Swift and Pope—just as the poems of Churchill and the *Rolliad* group were going back in England at the same time, and as *English Bards and Scotch Reviewers* and the *Georgiad* were later to go back so brilliantly. Although their vision was not very clear, they were looking forward toward the greater poetry of England and marking out some of the more exciting paths to be followed by their own countrymen. Two generations before "transcendentalism" became a term of reproach and then of respect, they were revolting against the intellectual system of John Locke by asserting that every man had recourse to knowledge beyond the limits of his "understanding"; and one of them was versifying a plea for the "natural life" a full half-century before Whitman individualized the "System of Nature" in his "Song of the Open Road."

They were blazing new trails, but their pioneer efforts were obscured and brought to nothing by their peculiar inability to make even their newness stimulating and attractive. Their failure may be attributed, in part, to qualities inherent in their provincial environment. Perhaps the most paradoxical of these was the familiarity of Americans in general with the great literature of England and their limited acquaintance with minor writers. They thought of poetry in terms of *Paradise Lost* and *An Essay on Man* and expected their own poets to invite comparison with Milton and Pope or, at least, with Thomson. An ambitious provincial writer had to be pretentious in order to attract any attention at all, and the attention he received was usually a superficial sort that hardly encouraged a strict standard of composition or intelligent self-criticism. Most American readers were eager for a great national poet but not interested in a merely good one—or able to recognize one if he appeared. Such writers as the Connecticut Wits, accordingly, were constantly overreaching themselves on one hand while also keeping an excessively cautious grasp upon the methods of expression that had been tried and found good by the great English poets. As a result, they usually fell flat somewhere between the extremes of ambition and imitation.

The fault was not wholly—or even largely—the public's. The Wits were products of their environment, and not one of them possessed the inner store of energy and alertness, the genius, to burst through the restrictions to which they were born. Pretentiousness came naturally to them. Their industry was directed toward quantity rather than quality: if they sweat at all, it was over mass production, not in casting to write a living line, for literature was a means to an end or an ornament upon an active life, not a life in itself; and, as Dwight observed, they would not live in garrets in order to become authors. Nor had they any conception of how much the florid style in verse had wilted during the course of the eighteenth century. The most frequently imitated passages in Milton were still fresh and new to them in their inexperienced youth, and Trumbull alone among them seems to have been able to penetrate the surface and appreciate the genuine craftsmanship of Pope. As a consequence, they reversed Pope's formula for true wit by attempting to express new thoughts in a way so often used that it had almost worn out. They poured new, and often still fermenting, wine into old bottles and were inclined toward self-pity when the overexpectant public found the liquor sour.

Even their later countrymen, who were most anxious for a national literature and might have understood what they were saying, looked upon their work with reprobation or indifference. When Emerson found the material for his earliest revolt against the "understanding" in the intuitionalism of the Scottish "common sense," he found it in the Harvard curriculum and not in Trumbull or Dwight or Barlow; and, whether Whitman found the "System of Nature" in Volney or in some other source, he certainly did not get his ideas from the *Columbiad*. The failure of the Connecticut Wits to have any great influence upon American literature, however, is not remarkable. The early literary history of America has an appearance of continuity usually because the writers of one generation reflected the ideas of those Europeans who influenced their successors, not because their own influence was direct and immediate. Consequently, the importance of a study of the Connecticut Wits, in the literary history of the United States, lies in its revelation of the cross-currents and complexities of a period which formed the intellectual climate in which a later, and better, literature developed.

Indeed, the greatest value of the writings by the Connecticut Wits, both in verse and in prose, lies in the illumination they cast upon an age which was to have, socially and aesthetically, an extraordinary influence upon the future. Their story shows how men of different temperaments found sustenance for their dispositions in a limited provincial environment and, broadening their fields of activity with those of their country, absorbed the many cultural influences that prepared the way for a new literature and formed a new national character. Few groups of writers, in any country, have started from a common point of departure and left such comprehensive records of so many interests and such varied activities. Their intellectual horizons were as broad as those of any other Americans in their generation; and there was hardly a profession that one of them did not follow, hardly a place in the Western World that one of them did not visit. They drew ideas from such antipodal sources as Jonathan Edwards and the Baron d'Holbach. They actively practiced almost every form of literature; and their writings were affected by the literature of the Orient and of Palestine, of Greece and Rome, and of such modern nations as England, Italy, France, Spain, and Portugal—and, to a lesser degree, by that of Germany and Peru and by the oral literature of the North American Indians. They were called upon, in some official capacity, to give advice to George Washington, the regent of Brazil, Thomas Jefferson, the Empress Josephine, James Madison, the dey of Algiers, the French National Assembly, and the United States Congress. They went to extremes of conservative federalism and radical republicanism and suffered the extremes of hope and fear over the great events of their time. They made laws, preached sermons, fought battles, treated illness, taught school, pleaded cases, passed judgments, negotiated treaties, manufactured goods, farmed land, bred livestock, speculated in real estate, promoted colonization, edited periodicals, founded missionary societies, kept shop, and directed banks. They ranged from Africa to Russia, from Virginia to the Vermont and Michigan frontiers. Their experiences were, in epitome, those of the new American people; and most of their experiences were reflected, in one way or another, in their writings.

Out of the richness of this experience the three Wits who, for various reasons, kept on writing when they no longer expected to be spare-time Popes or Miltons eventually wrote themselves down as representatives of three common types of humanity. The types may be universal. They are certainly thoroughly American—so timelessly so that one of the greatest difficulties in telling their story has been to keep them in the past where they belong and not allow them to become costumed figures of certain people of more importance in our day than they were in theirs. They had their more important counterparts, of course, in their own times. John Jay and Jefferson and John Adams left a personal impression upon history not unlike that made by Humphreys and Barlow and Dwight upon their writings; but, as men of deeds rather than of words, they did not leave so clear an indication of the intellectual, cultural, and emotional forces at work when the United States, as a nation, was forming itself and beginning to make its place in the world. The period, in America, is more important for the institutions and for the ways of thinking that developed in it than for the literature it produced, and for that reason the most interesting of the writings considered here are those in which Barlow and Dwight attempted to mark out proper ways of life and thought for their countrymen.

Neither accomplished his desire to have the whole nation follow his design for the future; but their extravagant hopes and fantastic fears do mark the extreme boundaries of a political course down which their countrymen have zigzagged ever since.

It is a strange fact that the people who have combined imagination and hardheadedness with such fabulous results in science and industry have never been able to achieve an effective union of the two in politics. It may be that the man with a peculiar genius for watching his step is incapable of seeing as far into the future as the social or political goal must be, or possibly the goal itself is so nebulous that it can hold the attention only of those men who are temperamentally averse to looking closely at the difficulties before them. Or it may be that the confused mass of people, revolting from dreams to immediate realities and back again for generation after generation, force their political leaders to extremes and refuse to be content with the man who can both see a goal and watch his step. Other countries have attempted to reduce imagination to diagrams of the future and to force the confused mass into these patterns, but that is not the way ingrained in the American character by the institutions of our forefathers and the opportunities offered by material circumstances. Yet, when the way becomes difficult, men must have either a map or a trustworthy sense of direction; and those who by heritage and training distrust the former grow desperately to need the latter. The past, seen obscurely through a haze of generalization and artificial interpretation, may be a dangerous source of "wisdom"; but, seen with all the clarity and detail that scholarship can provide, it may be the only point of reference by which a free people can line themselves up toward the future they desire but cannot realize in advance.

The Connecticut Wits, in their mature writings, wanted to blaze trails which future generations would follow. They succeeded merely in marking the limits of a vista along which we can look back. But in doing so they may have achieved the most constant of all their desires—to do good for their country —by helping fix the sense of direction which their countrymen need more than any of their ideas and more than the aesthetic pleasure offered by any literature.

Check List of the Writings of the Connecticut Wits

A CHECK LIST OF THE WRITINGS OF
TRUMBULL, DWIGHT, HUMPHREYS
AND BARLOW

Consisting (I) of first editions of books and of editions other than the first that have been quoted in the preceding text; (II) of first known printings in broadside, in periodicals, and in miscellaneous contemporary publications; and (III) of notes on manuscript collections and on books and articles containing manuscript material—with a note on writings doubtfully or erroneously attributed to the Connecticut Wits.

JOHN TRUMBULL

I

An Essay on the Use and Advantages of the Fine Arts, Delivered at the Public Commencement, in New-Haven. September 12, 1770. New Haven, [1770].

The Progress of Dulness, Part First: Or the Rare Adventures of Tom Brainless. [New Haven], 1772; [New Haven], 1773.[1]

The Progress of Dulness, Part Second: Or an Essay on the Life and Character of Dick Hairbrain. [New Haven], 1773.

The Progress of Dulness, Part Third, and Last: Sometimes Called the Progress of Coquetry, or the Adventures of Miss Harriet Simper. New Haven, 1773.

M'Fingal: A Modern Epic Poem, Canto First, or The Town Meeting. Philadelphia, 1775 [1776].

M'Fingal: A Modern Epic Poem in Four Cantos. Hartford, 1782.

Biographical Sketch of the Character of Governor Trumbull. [Hartford, 1809].

The Poetical Works of John Trumbull, LL.D. 2 vols. Hartford, 1820.

II

Broadsides: *An Elegy on the Death of Mr. Buckingham St. John, Tutor of Yale College, Who Was Drowned in His Passage from New Haven to Norwalk,*

---

[1] Whenever an edition other than the first is quoted in this study, that edition is indicated by a second place and date in the check list. All titles mentioned in the text but not in the check list are of items published in collected works and, unless otherwise noted, are quoted from the first collection in which they appear.

May the 5th, 1771 [New Haven(?), 1771]. *The News-Carrier's Address to His Customers* ("In England, where the poets scribble") [Hartford, 1783]. New Year's verses from the *Freeman's Chronicle* ("The rising year, with glory bright") [Springfield, 1784]. *Address of the Carrier of the Connecticut Courant to His Patrons* ("The carrier of the weekly news") [Hartford, 1824].

Original publications in periodicals: the *Boston Chronicle*, "The Meddler," September 4, 1769—January 15, 1770. The *Connecticut Journal and New-Haven Post-Boy*, "The Correspondent," February 25–July 6, 1770; "To My Good Catechist," February 5, 1773; "The Correspondent," February 12–September 3, 1773. The *Massachusetts Spy*, "An Elegy on the Times," September 22, 29, 1774. The *Connecticut Courant*, "By Thomas Gage . . . . Proclamation," August 7, 14, 1775 (also issued as an eight-page pamphlet: *A New Proclamation!* [Hartford, 1775]); a letter supporting a copyright proposal(?), January 7, 1783; verse letter, signed "William Wimble," October 9, 1786, and undeterminable parts in later contributions of the "wicked wits." The *New Haven Gazette and the Connecticut Magazine*, parts of "American Antiquities" and related verse, October 26, 1786—February 21, 1788. The *American Museum*, "The Speech of Proteus to Aristaeus," "The Downfall of Babylon," "The Prophecy of Balaam," July, 1787; "Ambition—An Elegy" ("On the Vanity of Youthful Expectations"), August, 1787. The *Columbian Magazine*, "The Wedding: An Epithalamium," June, 1789. The *New York Evening Post*, a letter to Samuel Converse, May 17, 1826.

Miscellaneous contemporary publications: a treatise on versification(?) in Noah Webster's *A Grammatical Institute of the English Language, Part II* (Hartford, 1785). Contributions to Joel Barlow's *Doctor Watts's Imitation of the Psalms of David, Corrected and Enlarged* (Hartford, 1785). Parts of the "Prologue" and "Epilogue" to *The Widow of Malabar* in *The Miscellaneous Works of Colonel Humphreys* (New York, 1790).

III

The "Tyler Papers" in the Cornell University Library contain the most important collection of Trumbull manuscripts, including (1) the following poems, printed for the first time in Alexander Cowie's *John Trumbull*: "Come, Blessed Saviour, quickly come," "From a Pastoral," "Introduction to a Satirical Poem," "Poetical Inspiration," "And as When Adam Met His Eve," "Mount 'Fancy's Horse,'" "On the Philanthropy of the Author of *Tristram Shandy*," "Join Too the Hooting Owl," "Elegy on B. St. John" (first version), "Epistle Addressed to Mr. I. J.," "To a Lady on Returning Her Thimble," "On the Marriage of Two Special Friends of the Author," "On Some Ladies Joining to Hiss Mr. Q——'s Oration," and "Dear Friend, This Verse"; (2) four unpublished poems: "First Lines of a Translation of the Beginning of the Poem of Silius Italicus on the Punic War," "So Some Fair Tower," "While You, My Friend, to Flow'ry Meads Resort," and "Funeral Oration"; (3) the "Speculative Essays on Various Subjects"; and (4) a number of critical essays, including "On a Passage in L. Kaims," "Critical Reflections," "On Satirical Productions," and an "Extract to James A. Hillhouse," from which extensive quotations are given in Cowie's "John Trumbull as a Critic of Poetry," *New England Quarterly*, XI (December, 1938), 773-93.

The "Woodbridge Papers" in the Burton Historical Collection of the Detroit Public Library also contain important Trumbull manuscripts, including (1) two poems published in Cowie's biography: "An Epitaph on Phineas White" and "Epistle to Mr. H——"; (2) the following unpublished poems: "The Village Merchant . . . . in the Manner of Goldsmith," "Elegy on the Death of a Sheriff, Being a Parody on Gray's Elegy . . . . ," "Imitative Translation of Part of Boileau's 9th Satire," a fragment of about eighty lines beginning "The Muse now mourns in sad, repentant verse," "Epitaph To Be Inscribed on the Marriage Bed of Miss S—— W——," an exchange of trivial verses with Elisha Babcock, and one other trivial poem crossed out; (3) a manuscript of the "Epithalamium" entitled "Epithalamion Stephani et Hannee" and a transcript of an item in the *Detroit Gazette* for October 3, 1823, supposedly taken from the *Portland* (Maine) *Statesman* and including about seventy lines beginning "To thee dear Nancy, thee my sweeting"; (4) the four chapters of his novel with a brief sketch of a continuation ("The Mathematical Metaphysician") and an essay on a coquette; and (5) several letters, the most important being addressed to Joseph Howe, September 9, 1773.

Of the fourteen Trumbull letters listed in Cowie's bibliography, the most valuable are those to Oliver Wolcott, in the "Wolcott Papers" in the library of the Connecticut Historical Society; the 1772 letter to Silas Deane, in the possession of the Rev. Anson P. Stokes and partly printed by Cowie; and that to the Marquis de Chastellux in the 1820 *Poetical Works*. An interesting additional letter has been printed by Katharine A. Conley, "A Letter of John Trumbull," *New England Quarterly*, XI (June, 1938), 372–74.

The Yale University Library contains another manuscript of the "Epithalamium" and two short notes by Trumbull.

TIMOTHY DWIGHT

I

A Dissertation on the History, Eloquence, and Poetry of the Bible. New Haven, 1772.

A Valedictory Address to the Young Gentlemen Who Commenced Bachelor of Arts at Yale-College, July 25, 1776. New Haven, [1776].

A Sermon, Preached at Stamford, in Connecticut, upon the General Thanksgiving, December 18th, 1777. Hartford, 1778.

America, or a Poem on the Settlement of the British Colonies, Addressed to the Friends of Freedom and Their Country. New Haven, [178—?].

A Sermon, Preached at Northampton, on the Twenty-eighth of November, 1781, Occasioned by the Capture of the British Army, under the Command of Earl Cornwallis. Hartford, [1781].

The Conquest of Canäan: A Poem in Eleven Books. Hartford, 1785.

The Triumph of Infidelity: A Poem. N.p., 1788.

Virtuous Rulers a National Blessing: A Sermon, Preached at the General Election, May 12th, 1791. Hartford, 1791.

Greenfield Hill: A Poem in Seven Parts. New York, 1794.

A Discourse on the Genuineness and Authenticity of the New-Testament; Delivered at New-Haven, September 10th, 1793, at the Annual Lecture, Appointed by the General Association of Connecticut. New York, 1794.

The True Means of Establishing Public Happiness: A Sermon, Delivered on the 7th of July, 1795, before the Connecticut Society of Cincinnati. New Haven [1795].

A Discourse, Preached at the Funeral of the Reverend Elizur Goodrich. New Haven, [1797].

The Nature, and Danger, of Infidel Philosophy, Exhibited in Two Discourses, Addressed to the Candidates for the Baccalaureate, in Yale College. New Haven, 1798.

The Duty of Americans at the Present Crisis, Illustrated in a Discourse, Preached on the Fourth of July, 1798. New Haven, 1798.

A Discourse, Delivered at New-Haven, February 22, 1800, on the Character of George Washington, Esq. New Haven, 1800.

A Discourse on Some Events of the Last Century. New Haven, 1801.

The Psalms of David, Imitated in the Language of the New Testament . . . . in Which the Psalms Omitted by Dr. Watts Are Versified, Local Passages Are Altered, and a Number of Psalms Are Versified Anew, in Proper Metres. Hartford, 1801.

A Sermon on the Death of Mr. Ebenezer Grant Marsh, Senior-Tutor, and Professor-Elect of Languages and Ecclesiastical History in Yale College. Hartford, 1804.

A Sermon on Duelling. New York, 1805.

A Sermon, Preached at the Opening of the Theological Institution in Andover. Boston, 1808.

A Discourse, Occasioned by the Death of His Excellency Jonathan Trumbull, Esq., Governor of the State of Connecticut. New Haven, 1809.

The Charitable Blessed: A Sermon, Preached in the First Church in New-Haven,
  August 8, 1810. New Haven, 1810.
A Statistical Account of the City of New-Haven. New Haven, 1811.
The Dignity and Excellence of the Gospel, Illustrated in a Discourse. New York,
  1812.
A Discourse, in Two Parts, Delivered July 23, 1812, on the Public Fast, in the
  Chapel of Yale College. New Haven, 1812; Boston, 1813.
A Discourse, in Two Parts, Delivered August 20, 1812, on the National Fast, in
  the Chapel of Yale College. New York, 1812; Boston, 1813.
A Sermon, Delivered in Boston, September 16, 1813, before the American Board
  of Commissioners for Foreign Missions. Boston, 1813.
Remarks on the Review of Inchiquin's Letters, Published in the Quarterly Review;
  Addressed to the Right Honourable George Canning, Esquire. Boston, 1815.
[With others] *An Address, to the Emigrants from Connecticut, and from New*
  England Generally, in the New Settlements in the United States. Hartford,
  1817.
Theology: Explained and Defended, in a Series of Sermons. 5 vols. Middle-
  town, 1818–19.
Travels, in New-England and New-York. 4 vols. New Haven, 1821–22.
Sermons. 2 vols. New Haven, 1828.
Decisions of Questions Discussed by the Senior Class in Yale College, in 1813
  and 1814; from Stenographic Notes, by Theodore Dwight, Jun. New York,
  1833.

II

Original publications in periodicals: The *Connecticut Journal and New-Haven Post-Boy,* "Mankind Pursuing Shadows: Or False Notions of Happiness" (?), August 14, 1770; [possibly some hand in the first series of "The Correspondent," February 25–July 6, 1770; and in the earlier "The Meddler," *Boston Chronicle,* September 4, 1769—January 15, 1770]. The *Boston Magazine,* "Columbia, Columbia, to Glory Arise," December, 1783. The *New Haven Gazette and the Connecticut Magazine,* "The Friend," March 23, 1786—October 4, 1787; a historical account of the Gothic gospel, March 1, 1787; an essay on the judgment of history concerning America, April 12, 1787. The *American Museum,* "Address of the Genius of Columbia, to the Members of the Continental Convention," June, 1787; "On the Doctrine of Chance: Containing Remarks on Ethan Allen's Oracles of Reason" [". . . . supposed to have been written by the rev. mr. Dwight, author of the Conquest of Canaan"], October, 1787; "Address to the Ministers of the Gospel of Every Denomination in the United States," July, 1788; "A Song: Written in 1771" ("Look, lovely maid"), April, 1789; "Reflections on the Second Marriages of Men," December, 1789. The *American Magazine,* "The Seasons Moralized," December, 1787; "A Hymn" (sung by the students at Greenfield in May, 1788), June, 1788. *Gazette of the United States,* "The Critics: A Fable," July 13, 1791. The *Connecticut Courant,* a sermon, March 16, 23, 30, 1795. The *New England Palladium,* "Farmer Johnson's Political Catechism," March 31–May 8, 1801; "Morpheus," November 24, 1801—March 9, 1802. The *Connecticut Evangelical Magazine,* "Brief Account of the Revival of Religion Now

Prevailing in Yale College," July, 1802 [as one of the editors, Dwight may have contributed frequently to this periodical]. The *Panoplist*, "Lectures on the Evidences of Divine Revelation," June, 1810—May, 1812, and June–December, 1813; "On the Manner in Which the Scriptures Are To Be Understood," May and June, 1816; "The Maniac of Gadara: An Irregular Ode," November, 1816. The *Religious Intelligencer*, "Observations on the Present State of Religion in the World," August 10–September 14, 1816. *Memoirs of the Connecticut Academy of Arts and Sciences*, "Observations on Language," No. XXIII (1816); "On Light," No. XXIV (1816).

Miscellaneous contemporary publications: "Epistle from Dr. Dwight to Col. Humphreys," *The Miscellaneous Works of Colonel Humphreys* (New York, 1790). "Message of Mordecai to Esther," *American Poems* (Litchfield, 1793).

III

There is no really important collection of Dwight manuscripts, unless one is included in the papers of Miss Elizabeth B. Dwight, of Philadelphia, about which nothing can be learned. The most extensive is that in the Yale University library, which includes nine sermons, notes on fifty-three others (preached in the Yale Chapel), a small volume somewhat improbably called his "commonplace book," some biographical anecdotes apparently used for the "Memoir" in his *Theology*, David L. Daggett's student notebooks on "Dr. Dwight's Observations of Paley's Moral and Political Philosophy" (1808) and "Miscellaneous Notes from Doct. Dwight's Remarks [on Blair's Lectures on Rhetoric and Oratory]" (1807), Alexander M. Fisher's notes on "Dwight's Remarks on Paley's Philosophy," perhaps a score of letters, and a few bills and miscellaneous items.

The New York Public Library contains Joshua Leavitt's notebook on "Dr. Dwight's Remarks on . . . . Westminster Assembly's Shorter Catechism with Vincent's Explanations," a volume of "Notes from President Dwight's Remarks on Locke's Essay on the Human Understanding," and a valuable letter to Noah Webster which has been printed by Theodore A. Zunder, "Noah Webster and *The Conquest of Canaan*," *American Literature*, I (May, 1929), 200–202.

Individual letters may be found in the "Barlow Papers" in the Harvard College Library, the "Pickering Papers" in the Massachusetts Historical Society Library, the "Wolcott Papers" and elsewhere in the Connecticut Historical Society Library, and in the Boston Public, Pequot, and Henry E. Huntington libraries. Charles E. Cuningham has made an exhaustive search of private and public sources for his biography, *Timothy Dwight* (New York, 1942), and has listed the private owners of manuscript material which he has used and quoted; but the only manuscript of particular literary interest which he discovered was that of a poem celebrating Burgoyne's defeat, in the "McClure Papers" in the Dartmouth College Library.

DAVID HUMPHREYS

I

A Poem Addressed to the Armies of the United States of America. New Haven, 1780; revised and republished, New Haven, 1784.

A Poem on the Happiness of America: Addressed to the Citizens of the United States. London, 1786; Hartford, [178—?].

An Essay on the Life of the Honorable Major-General Israel Putnam. Hartford, 1788.

Poems by Col. David Humphreys, Late Aid-de-Camp to His Excellency General Washington: Second Edition, with Several Additions. Philadelphia, 1789. [The *American Museum*, I, No. I, apparently is to be considered the first edition.]

The Miscellaneous Works of Colonel Humphreys. New York, 1790.

A Poem on Industry, Addressed to the Citizens of the United States of America. Philadelphia, 1794.

Considerations on the Means of Improving the Militia for the Public Defense. Hartford, 1803; New York [in *The Miscellaneous Works*], 1804.

The Miscellaneous Works of David Humphreys, Late Minister Plenipotentiary from the United States of America to the Court of Madrid. New York, 1804.

A Valedictory Discourse, Delivered before the Cincinnati of Connecticut, in Hartford, July 4th, 1804, at the Dissolution of the Society. Boston, 1804.

The Yankey in England: A Drama in Five Acts [n.p., 1816?].

A Discourse on the Agriculture of the State of Connecticut, and the Means of Making It More Beneficial to the State. New Haven, 1816.

Letters from the Hon. David Humphreys, F.R.S., To the Rt. Hon. Sir Joseph Banks, President of the Royal Society, London, Containing Some Account of the Serpent of the Ocean, Frequently Seen in Gloucester Bay. New York, 1817.

The Conduct of General Washington, Respecting the Confinement of Capt. Asgill, Placed in Its True Point of Light. New York, 1859.

II

Original publications in periodicals: The *Connecticut Journal and New-Haven Post-Boy*, "Immortal Pope! thy Son immortal see"(?), November 30, 1770; verse letter, "The Correspondent," No. XXXII (?), July 23, 1773. The *New Haven Gazette and the Connecticut Magazine*, "An Elegy on the Burning of Fairfield" [a "correct copy"—"an imperfect sketch having been frequently printed in America"], June 29, 1786; letter to the Secretary of War, June 29, 1786; a speech before the state legislature on the encouragement of agriculture and manufactures, October 26, 1786; "The Conduct of General Washington, Respecting the Confinement of Capt. Asgill, Placed in Its True Point of Light," November 16, 1786; "The Genius of America," January 25, 1787, and other parts of "American Antiquities" and related verse, October 26, 1786— February 21, 1788; song, "It Rains" (from the French), September 20, 1787. The *Connecticut Courant*, "Mount Vernon: An Ode," October 9, 1786; "The Monkey, Who Shaved Himself and His Friends: A Fable, Addressed to the Honorable William Wimble, Esquire," February 26, 1787, and undeterminable parts in other contributions by the "wicked wits." The *American Museum*, "An Epithalamium," June, 1787; "An Elegy, on Lieutenant De Hart," "An Ode—to Laura," "An Epitaph" (on Alexander Scammel), "Anacreontic," March, 1788.

Miscellaneous contemporary publications: "On a New Variety in the Breeds of Sheep, in a Letter to the Right Hon. Sir Joseph Banks, Bart.," *Philosophical Transactions of the Royal Society* (1813).

III

The most extensive and valuable collection of Humphreys manuscripts is in the Archives of the United States Department of State, and there are some in the Library of Congress, including a few letters in the "Papers of the Continental Congress." Many of these were transcribed with care and published in full by Frank Landon Humphreys in *The Life and Times of David Humphreys* (2 vols.; New York, 1917), together with others from the important collection of James D. Dewell, of New Haven, and from the "Pickering Papers" in the Massachusetts Historical Society Library, the "Dreer Collection" in possession of the Pennsylvania Historical Society, and other sources, including some previously printed in *Dawson's Historical Magazine*. The unusually important letter to Mrs. Nathanael Greene containing information concerning his comedy and the lines on Portugal rejected from "A Poem on Industry" was in his own possession.

The Yale University Library contains about fifteen letters (most of them late) and a Latin dissertation. The 1786 letter to his brother John was first printed in Henry P. Johnston, *Yale and Her Honor-Roll in the Revolution, 1775-1783* (New York, 1888). Various government publications have included Humphreys' official correspondence, especially *Naval Documents Relating to the United States Wars with the Barbary Powers*, Vol. I (Washington, 1939); *Naval Documents Related to the Quasi-war between the United States and France* (3 vols.; Washington, 1935-36), and the early volumes of *American State Papers: Foreign Relations*.

JOEL BARLOW

I

The Prospect of Peace: A Poetical Composition, Delivered in Yale-College, at the Public Examination of the Candidates for the Degree of Bachelor of Arts, July 23, 1778. New Haven, 1778.

A Poem, Spoken at the Public Commencement at Yale College, in New Haven, September 12, 1781. Hartford, 1781.

An Elegy on the Late Honorable Titus Hosmer, Esq., One of the Councellors of the State of Connecticut, a Member of Congress, and Judge of the Maritime Court of Appeals for the United States of America. Hartford, [1782?].

Doctor Watts's Imitation of the Psalms of David, Corrected and Enlarged, by Joel Barlow, to Which Is Added a Collection of Hymns. Hartford, 1785.

A Translation of Sundry Psalms Which Were Omitted in Dr. Watts's Version, to Which Is Added a Number of Hymns. Hartford, 1785.

An Oration, Delivered at the North Church in Hartford at the Meeting of the Connecticut Society of the Cincinnati. Hartford, 1787.

The Vision of Columbus: A Poem in Nine Books. Hartford, 1787.

[With William Playfair] *Prospectus pour l'établissement sur les rivières d'Ohio et de Scioto, en Amérique.* Paris, [1789].

[With others] *Addresse des citoyens des Etats-Unis de l'Amérique, prononcée devant l'Assemblée nationale, par M. William Henry Vernon, dans la séance de samedi au soir, le 10 juillet 1790.* Paris, 1790.

Advice to the Privileged Orders in the Several States of Europe, Resulting from the Necessity and Propriety of a General Revolution in the Principle of Government. Part I. London, 1792; New York, 1792.

The Conspiracy of Kings: A Poem Addressed to the Inhabitants of Europe from Another Quarter of the World. London, 1792; Paris, 1793.

A Letter to the National Convention of France, on the Defects in the Constitution, and the Extent of the Amendments Which Ought To Be Applied. London, 1792; New York, n.d.

[Trans. and ed.] Brissot de Warville, *New Travels in the United States.* 2 vols. London, 1794. [Vol. I originally issued in Dublin, 1792; Vol. II also published as *The Commerce of America with Europe* (New York, 1795).]

[Ed.] John Trumbull, *M'Fingal: A Modern Epic Poem.* London, 1792.

Advice to the Privileged Orders. . . . . Part II. Paris, 1793.

A Letter, Addressed to the People of Piedmont, on the Advantages of the French Revolution and the Necessity of Adopting Its Principles in Italy. . . . . Translated from the French by the Author. London, 1795; New York, 1795.

The Hasty Pudding: A Poem in Three Cantos. Written in Chambéry, in Savoy, January, 1793. New Haven, 1796.

The Second Warning, or Strictures on the Speech Delivered by John Adams, President of the United States of America at the Opening of the Congress of Said States in November Last. Paris, 1798.

Letters from Paris, to the Citizens of the United States of America, on the System of Policy Hitherto Pursued by Their Government Relative to Their Commercial Intercourse with England and France. London, 1800. [Letter I originally

issued in Philadelphia, 1799; various editions also include: "To Citizen
——, Member of the French Government," signed by Fulwar Skipwith and
Barlow; "Memoir on Certain Principles of Public Maritime Law"; and a
letter to Washington, dated Paris, October 2, 1798.] New Haven, 1806.

[Trans.] *Volney's Ruins, or Meditations on the Revolution of Empires.* New
York, [1802?]; Boston, 1835.

Prospectus for a National Institution, To Be Established in the United States.
Washington, 1806.

The Columbiad: A Poem. Philadelphia, 1807.

Oration delivered at Washington, July Fourth, 1809, at the Request of the Demo-
cratic Citizens of the District of Columbia. Washington, 1809.

Letter to Henry Gregoire, Bishop, Senator, Compte of the Empire, and Member of
the Institute of France, in Reply to His Letter on the Columbiad. Washington,
1809.

Review of Robert Smith's Address. Philadelphia, 1811; London, 1811.

II

Broadsides: *Burlesque chapter of Chronicles* [New Haven, 1777]. New
Year's verses for the carrier of the *American Mercury* ("In the days when old
Jupiter held the prime station" [New Haven, 1785]; "I'm come, my friends, as
Post-Boys use" [New Haven, 1786]).

Original publications in periodicals: The *American Mercury,* editorial
and miscellaneous prose notes, July 12, 1784—November 7, 1785; "War
in Europe" (verse), December 12, 1805; New Year's verses (probably
first printed as broadsides no longer extant), January 8, 1807, January 12,
1809, January 4, 1810; letter to Abraham Baldwin (said to have been first
published as an unauthorized broadside in Fairhaven), November 8, 1798.
The *Connecticut Courant,* announcement of plans for an edition of the Psalms,
August 8, 1784; defense of Barlow and Babcock almanac against charges of
plagiarism, November 16, 1784; undeterminable parts in the contributions of
the "wicked wits," beginning October 23, 1786. The *New Haven Gazette and*
the Connecticut Magazine, parts of "American Antiquities" and related verse,
October 26, 1786—February 21, 1788. *New York Weekly Magazine,* "The
Hasty Pudding," January, 1796, pp. 41–49. The *Connecticut Journal and*
New-Haven Post-Boy, letter of May 23, 1795, to John Fellows (unauthorized),
August 28, 1799. The *North Carolina Register,* letter dated October 18, 1809,
in response to an inquiry from John Montgomery.

Miscellaneous contemporary publications: Selections from the unpublished
"The Vision of Columbus" in Noah Webster, *A Grammatical Institute of the*
English Language, Part III (Hartford, 1785). United States Department of
State, *Message from the President of the U. States, Transmitting Copies and Ex-*
tracts from the Correspondence of the Secretary of State, and the Minister Plenipo-
tentiary of the United States at Paris, May 26, 1812 (Washington, 1812).
Letter on Paine in the Appendix of James Cheetham, *Life of Thomas Paine*
(New York, 1809).

III

The most valuable collection of Barlow manuscripts is the "Barlow Papers," originally collected by Lemuel G. Olmstead and now on deposit in the

Harvard College Library. These papers include numerous letters to Ruth (Baldwin) Barlow, written both before and after their marriage, correspondence with Robert Fulton, Abraham Baldwin, Noah Webster, Alexander Wolcott, Oliver Wolcott, Jr., Josiah Meigs, and numerous others; the "atheistic" letter to John Fellows, dated Hamburg, May 23, 1795; a manuscript diary of Barlow's first trip to England; his notes and outline for the history of the French Revolution and a fragmentary continuation of the *Advice to the Privileged Orders;* notes on reading and financial matters and on the Algerian mission; "A Dissertation Read at Fairfield, April 1786, on Examination for Admission to the Bar"; a copy of his undated "Premium Offered for the Best Essay on the Means for Rendering the Fine Arts the Most Beneficial to Political Liberty"; Thomas Barlow's letters on the Russian journey, and Joel's letters to Clara Baldwin; the original "plan" for *The Vision of Columbus;* and a number of poems, together with several poems addressed to Barlow and copies of other verses, including at least one group of stanzas by Theodore Dwight. The collection also contains Barlow's notes for the order of printing the edition of his *Works,* which Fulton was supposed to publish, and corrected copies of the writings (with the exception of the *Columbiad*) supposed to be included. These manuscripts formed the basis of Charles B. Todd's *The Life and Letters of Joel Barlow,* and numerous extracts, more accurately transcribed, appear in Theodore A. Zunder's *The Early Days of Joel Barlow* and M. Ray Adams' "Joel Barlow, Political Romanticist," *American Literature,* IX (May, 1937), 113–52. Other letters from this collection have been printed by William C. Lane, "Letters of Christoph Daniel Ebeling," *Proceedings of the American Antiquarian Society,* XXXV (new ser.; October, 1925), 272–451, and in the *Proceedings of the Massachusetts Historical Society,* VIII (2d ser.), 267–76. The poems have been printed as follows: all the wedding verses with the exception of a single stanza, the epigram on the French Revolution, and parts of the poem on Burgoyne's defeat in *The Life and Letters:* "Go Rose my Chloe's bosom grace," verses about a lost horse, a fragment on Cyrus the Great, the complete poem on Burgoyne, a poem addressed to Doctor Prime, "To a Friend at Cambridge," "To Betsy," and "To Mr. Abraham Baldwin" in *The Early Days of Joel Barlow;* and a mock-epic fragment, "The sun who sails secure in ether," in Zunder's "A New Barlow Poem," *American Literature,* XI (May, 1939), 206–9.

The Pequot Library of Southport, Connecticut, contains a considerable number of Barlow letters which have been used and quoted by Zunder and Adams; and two copies, in Barlow's hand, of the unfinished poem, *The Canal,* from which Adams has printed a few lines.

The Library of Congress contains numerous Barlow manuscripts, the most valuable being those in the "Henley-Smith Papers," which include the letters written to his wife during the Russian expedition and two poems: "On the Discoveries of Captain Lewis" (inclosed in a letter to Jefferson, suggesting that the name of the Columbia River be changed to Lewis) and the "Advice to a Raven in Russia." The latter poem and extracts from the letters have been printed in Leon Howard's "Joel Barlow and Napoleon," *Huntington Library Quarterly,* II (October, 1938), 37–51. An emended version of the poem was printed by Olmstead in the *Erie* (Pennsylvania) *Chronicle* for

October 10, 1843, and used by Duyckinck in his *Cyclopaedia of American Literature*. The "Jefferson Papers" contain a number of letters from Barlow and some financial notes; the "Washington Papers," a letter of introduction and a certified copy of the published letter of October 2, 1798; and there are other manuscripts of less importance. Some of Barlow's official correspondence has been published in *Naval Documents Relating to the United States Wars with the Barbary Powers*, Vol. I (Washington, 1939).

The Aldis Collection in the Yale University Library contains a printer's copy of the *Columbiad* (partly made up of revised pages of the Paris, 1793, edition of *The Vision of Columbus* and partly manuscript), which has bound in it a letter to Abraham Bishop concerning the problems of publication and a letter to Elisha Babcock inclosing the unused New Year's verses for January 1, 1806. The Library also contains a number of letters and miscellaneous items.

Other manuscript collections are: the New York Historical Society manuscript of *The Vision of Columbus;* a number of letters in the "Wolcott Papers" in the library of the Connecticut Historical Society, including those published by Theodore A. Zunder, "Six Letters of Joel Barlow to Oliver Wolcott," *New England Quarterly*, II (July, 1929), 475–89; several letters in the New York Public Library; and an interesting letter to William Haley and a copy of a declaration relative to the Algerian mission in the Henry E. Huntington Library. Some Barlow material also appeared in print for the first time in the following: William P. and Julia P. Cutler, *Life, Journals, and Correspondence of Rev. Manasseh Cutler* (2 vols.; Cincinnati, 1888) [from a manuscript collection presented by John M. Newton to the Historical and Philosophical Society of Ohio]; Victor C. Miller, *Joel Barlow: Revolutionist, London, 1791–92* (Hamburg, 1932); Beckles Willson, *America's Ambassadors to France (1777–1927)* (New York, 1925); Alice C. Sutcliffe, "Fulton's Invention of the Steamboat, Mainly as Recorded in His Original Manuscripts Never Before Published . . . . ," *Century*, LXXVIII (September and October, 1909), 752–72 and 809–34; Theodore A. Zunder, "Notes on the Friendship of Joel Barlow and Tom Paine," *American Book Collector*, VI (March, 1935), 96–99; "Joel Barlow and Seasickness," *Yale Journal of Biology and Medicine*, I (July, 1929), 385–90; Dixon Wecter, "Joel Barlow and the Sugar Beets," *Colorado Magazine*, XVIII (September, 1941), 179–81.

Many Barlow manuscripts exist in duplicate; and excessive claims of importance are made for those in the private possession of descendants of Tom Barlow in the following, otherwise valuable, articles by Ezra K. Maxfield: "The Tom Barlow Manuscript of the *Columbiad*," *New England Quarterly*, XI (December, 1938), 834–42; "A Newly Discovered Letter from Joel Barlow to His Wife, from Algiers," *American Literature*, IX (January, 1938), 442–49; "To the Editors of *American Literature*," *ibid.*, X (November, 1938), 351–52. See M. Ray Adams, "On the 'Newly Discovered Letter' of Joel Barlow," *American Literature*, X (May, 1938), 224–27.

NOTE ON WRITINGS DOUBTFULLY OR ERRONEOUSLY ATTRIBUTED TO TRUMBULL, DWIGHT, HUMPHREYS AND BARLOW

So many items in the preceding check list were published anonymously that the evidences of authorship are not always conclusive; and, although the list follows the balance of probability, it has seemed desirable to mark certain doubtful titles with the query (?). The following additional works, sometimes attributed to the Connecticut Wits, have been rejected for the reasons indicated: (1) *Thomas Gage's Proclamation Versified* ([New York, 1775] broadside) has been attributed to Trumbull, apparently by confusion with his real burlesque of the same subject; Victor H. Palsits more convincingly ascribes it to Freneau. (2) *The Double Conspiracy, or Treason Discovered but Not Punished* ([Hartford], 1783) has been assigned to Trumbull on the inadequate and unconvincing grounds of typographical similarity to *M'Fingal* and the (merely satiric) style of its "Epilogue." (3) *Observations on the Peculiar Case of the Whig Merchants Indebted to Great Britain at the Commencement of the Late War* (New York, 1785) is included in the Trumbull check list in the *Proceedings of the Massachusetts Antiquarian Society*, XLIV (new ser.; October, 1934), 235, without evidence of his authorship; and no such evidence seems available. (4) *An Essay on the Stage* (London, 1824) was, according to the title-page, reprinted from a Middletown edition "By Timothy Dwight, S.T.D., L.L.D., Late President of Yale College" and was accepted as authentic in Dexter's *Biographical Sketches* and then rejected in the list of "Errata" included in the succeeding volume; stylistically unlike Dwight's work, it contains a long quotation from a funeral sermon preached by Robert Hall ten months after Dwight's death and is certainly spurious. (5) James K. Paulding's *The United States and England* (New York, 1815) has been attributed to Dwight by Library of Congress catalogue cards, evidently by confusion with his own attack upon the same article in the *Quarterly Review*. (6) *The Glory of America, or Peace Triumphant over War* (Philadelphia, 1783) has been attributed to Humphreys and accepted as authentic by Frank L. Humphreys in his rather uncritical bibliography; it is characterized by none of the rhetorical or other peculiarities that marked Humphreys' work at that time and was probably ascribed to him because of the appearance of the name D. Humphreys (the Philadelphia printer) on the title-page. (7) *Strictures on Bishop Watson's "Apology for the Bible"* (New York, 1796) is listed as Barlow's in most library catalogues, included in Florence S. Hellman's manuscript (Library of Congress), "Joel Barlow, 1754–1812: A Bibliographical List," and accepted by M. Ray Adams and other scholars; yet there seems no reason to doubt the statement on the title-page that it was by "a citizen of New York," who, according to the preface, sent the work to the printer a few pages at a time and may have been either John Fellows or any of the group of freethinkers who surrounded him at the time. (8) *The History of England from 1765 to . . . . 1795* (5 vols.; London, 1795), ascribed to Barlow in the *British Museum Catalogue of Printed Books*, is a continuation of Smollett's continuation of Hume's history as "Parson's Genuine Pocket Edition of Hume's History" and could hardly have been the work of Barlow at the time he was so completely engaged in French politics and business affairs, although he may have lent his name to it. This work, however, has not been available for examination.

Bibliographical Notes

BIBLIOGRAPHICAL NOTES

CHAPTER I

Any student of the history of Yale College must be primarily indebted to Franklin B. Dexter, whose *Biographical Sketches of the Graduates of Yale College with Annals of the College History* (6 vols.; New York, 1885–1911; New Haven, 1912) provides the skeleton and much of the substance for any study of the institution and whose editions of *The Literary Diary of Ezra Stiles* (3 vols.; New York, 1901) and *Extracts from the Itineraries and Other Miscellanies of Ezra Stiles* (New Haven, 1916), supplemented by Isabel M. Calder's *Letters and Papers of Ezra Stiles* (New Haven, 1933), make available the most valuable contemporary comment relative to the college during the late eighteenth century. Dexter's *Documentary History of Yale University* (New Haven, 1916) has also been useful in clarifying some of the obscurities in the later records, and his early *Sketch of the History of Yale University* (New York, 1887) and numerous later articles have helped place in perspective the source material made available in the above volumes. Ebenezer Baldwin's *Annals of Yale College, from Its Foundations to the Year 1831* (New Haven, 1838) has been useful for the same purpose. The essays in *Yale College: A Sketch of Its History*, edited by William L. Kingsley (2 vols.; New York, 1879), although uneven in quality, have all been of some use, especially with reference to the religious constitution of the college and to the literary societies and the dramatic interests of the students; and Anson P. Stokes's *Memorials of Eminent Yale Men* (2 vols.; New Haven, 1914) contains material supplementary to that in Dexter's *Biographical Sketches*. In addition to the college annals and Stiles's papers, the most valuable contemporary sources of information have been: the correspondence of David Avery and David McClure (class of 1769) with Dr. Eleazar Wheelock, liberally quoted in E. H. Gillette, "Yale College One Hundred Years Ago," *Hours at Home*, X (February, 1870), 328–36; the manuscript diary of Elijah Backus for 1777, photostat in the Yale University Library, partly printed in the *Connecticut Quarterly* for October, 1895; the autobiographical sketch, "James Kent," reprinted in the *New York Genealogical and Biographical Record*, IV (January, 1873), 1–7; the material in Henry P. Johnston's *Yale and Her Honor-Roll in the Revolution, 1775–1783* (New York, 1888); John Trumbull's prefatory "Memoir" in his *Poetical Works* (2 vols.; Hartford, 1820), which, like his *The Progress of Dulness*, has to be used with some care; the "Memoir" based on the author's notes in

Timothy Dwight's *Theology: Explained and Defended* (5 vols.; Middletown, 1818–19); the manuscript "Barlow Papers" in the Harvard College Library; the documents in Emily E. F. Ford's *Notes on the Life of Noah Webster*, edited by E. E. F. Skeel (2 vols.; New York, 1912); and the contemporary files of the *Connecticut Journal and New-Haven Post-Boy* and the *Connecticut Courant*. Useful background information is contained in President Thomas Clap's *Annals of Yale-College* (New Haven, 1766), *A Brief History and Vindication of the Doctrines Received and Established in the Churches of New-England* (Boston, 1757), and *The Religious Constitution of Colleges* (New London, 1754), used with Dexter's "Thomas Clap and His Writings," *Papers of the New Haven Colony Historical Society*, V (1894), 247–74; in the *History of the City of New Haven*, edited by Edward E. Atwater (New York, 1887); and in Chauncy Goodrich, "Invasion of New Haven by the British Troops, July 5, 1779," *Papers of the New Haven Historical Society*, II (1877), 31–92.

The discussion of the Yale curriculum is based upon a careful weighing of evidence which is not wholly satisfactory. None of the histories of the college is very illuminating on this subject; nor is G. Stanley Hall, "On the History of American College Textbooks and Teaching in Logic, Ethics, Psychology, and Allied Subjects," *Proceedings of the American Antiquarian Society*, IX (new ser.; April, 1893), 137–74; and John C. Schwab's broadside, *A Partial List of the Text-Books Read in Yale College in the Eighteenth Century* (n.p., n.d.), does not always agree in substance with his pamphlet, "The Yale College Curriculum, 1701–1901," reprinted from the *Educational Review* for June, 1901. Ezra Stiles's well-known list was not made until the end of this period. The information given by Schwab has been checked by references to the course of study found in the contemporary material listed above, and in a few doubtful cases the weight of evidence has been settled by the existence in the library of numerous duplicates, which may have been purchased for use as textbooks by the poorer students. Problems of discipline as revealed in the college and other contemporary records, on the other hand, have been admirably surveyed. Alexander Cowie's *John Trumbull* (Chapel Hill, N.C., 1936), and *Educational Problems at Yale College in the Eighteenth Century* ("Tercentenary Pamphlets," Vol. LV [New Haven, 1936]), have given an excellent account of this aspect of college life during the early part of the period; Theodore A. Zunder's *The Early Days of Joel Barlow* (New Haven, 1934), has made an extensive use of the records for the latter part; and Harry R. Warfel's *Noah Webster, Schoolmaster to America* (New York, 1936), has given an interesting survey of the college during the time of Barlow's residence.

The basic source of information concerning the library has been the facsimile reprint of Thomas Clap's *A Catalogue of the Library of Yale-College in New-Haven* (London, 1743), supplemented by later catalogues. The *Catalogue of Books in the Library of Yale College in New Haven, January, 1808* (New Haven, 1808) gives some information about editions; but more are identified in Daniel C. Gilman, "Bishop Berkeley's Gifts to Yale College," *Papers of the New Haven Colony Historical Society*, I (1865), 147–70, and in "Bishop Berkeley's Gift of Books in 1733," *Yale University Library Gazette*, VIII (July, 1933), 1–26. The library itself now has many duplicates of volumes contained in the original collection. The account of the outside literary interests of the students is based upon occasional allusions in diaries, correspondence, and memoirs but mostly upon internal evidence found in the early writings of the Connecticut Wits, checked against book advertisements and allusions in newspapers.

The following specific texts have been quoted: James Beattie, *Essay on the Nature and Immutability of Truth in Opposition to Sophistry and Scepticism* (Edinburgh, 1771); Thomas Clap, *An Essay on the Nature and Foundation of Moral Virtue* (New Haven, 1765); Henry Home, Lord Kames, *Elements of Criticism* (3 vols.; Edinburgh, 1762); Benjamin Martin, *The Philosophical Grammar* (London, 1738); John Ward, *System of Oratory* (2 vols.; London, 1759); and William Wollaston, *The Religion of Nature Delineated* (London, 1759).

CHAPTER II

The biographical facts concerning Trumbull's early life have been thoroughly covered in Alexander Cowie's *John Trumbull*, from which this deviates in only a few minor matters of chronology that required more careful attention because of a different plan of approach. Mr. Cowie's kindness and generosity also made possible a study of the available unpublished material in the Trumbull bibliography, although, for various reasons, quotations from manuscript material other than that of the Burton Historical Collection of the Detroit Public Library and in the Connecticut Historical Society are restricted to selections from extracts already printed in his biography and in his two articles, "John Trumbull as Revolutionist," *American Literature*, III (November, 1931), 287–95, and "John Trumbull as a Critic of Poetry," *New England Quarterly*, XI (December, 1938), 773–93, and in Moses C. Tyler's *The Literary History of the American Revolution* (2 vols.; New York, 1897). Other valuable sources of information have been Trumbull's own "Memoir" and the various treatments of Yale College listed in the notes for chapter i; the "Wolcott Papers" in the Connecticut Historical Society; Samuel G. Goodrich, *Recollections of a Lifetime* (2 vols.; New York, 1857); the detailed notes in Benson J. Lossing's edition of *M'Fingal* (New York, 1864); James H. Trumbull, *The Origin of M'Fingal* (Morrisania, N.Y., 1868) (cf. the *Historical Magazine*, III [2d ser.; January, 1868], 1–10); Frank L. Humphreys, *The Life and Times of David Humphreys* (2 vols.; New York, 1917); and Lennox Grey, "John Adams and John Trumbull in the 'Boston Cycle,'" *New England Quarterly*, IV (July, 1931), 509–14. All the secondary information about Trumbull's activity as an essayist and propagandist, however, has been checked against the files of the *Boston Chronicle*, the *Connecticut Journal and New-Haven Post-Boy*, and the *Connecticut Courant*. Cowie's bibliography of Trumbull's writings through 1775 has been invaluable, for it is more comprehensive and, apparently, more trustworthy than the Trumbull check list in the *Proceedings of the American Antiquarian Society*, XLIV (new ser.; October, 1934), 231–33.

CHAPTER III

Of the many short biographies of Dwight the most valuable with reference to his early life are: the "Memoir" in his *Theology;* the anonymous "Biographical Notice of the Rev. Timothy Dwight," *Analectic Magazine*, April,

1817; Calvin Chapin, *A Sermon . . . . at the Funeral of the Rev. Timothy Dwight* (New Haven, 1817); Benjamin Silliman, *A Sketch of the Life and Character of President Dwight* (New Haven, 1817); and Gardner Spring, *An Oration . . . . in Commemoration of . . . . Timothy Dwight* (New York, 1817). Notices in Benjamin W. Dwight's *Descendants of John Dwight of Dedham* (2 vols.; New York, 1874), William B. Sprague's *Annals of the American Pulpit*, Dexter's *Biographical Sketches*, Stokes's *Memorials*, and the *Dictionary of American Biography* have also been useful. Comments in the various writings of Ezra Stiles, though highly prejudiced, are revealing and important; and, in fact, most of the works mentioned in the notes for the first chapter have been drawn upon for this. Files of the *American Magazine* and the *American Museum* have been used to supplement those of Connecticut newspapers, and Theodore A. Zunder's "Noah Webster and *The Conquest of Canaan*," *American Literature*, I (May, 1929), 200–202, contains important information concerning Dwight's relationship to the former periodical and concerning the composition of his epic. Although there are few available manuscripts bearing upon Dwight's early career, a small amount of unpublished material in the Yale University and New York Public libraries has been of value.

Specific texts not quoted in earlier chapters are: Andrew Ramsay's "A Discourse upon Epic Poetry," prefatory to the Littlebury and Boyer translation of Archbishop Fénelon's *The Adventures of Telemachus* (2 vols.; London, 1721), and Thomas Hunter, *Reflections Critical and Moral on the Letters of the Late Earl of Chesterfield* (London, 1776).

Charles E. Cuningham's *Timothy Dwight, 1752–1817: A Biography* appeared after this was written, but the statements made in this text have been checked against the information he has derived from new manuscript sources.

CHAPTER IV

The most valuable source of information concerning Humphreys is the original material published in Frank L. Humphreys' uncritical and somewhat erratic biography, *The Life and Times of David Humphreys* (2 vols.; New York, 1917), although Frederick Humphreys' *The Humphreys Family in America* (New York, 1883), Dexter's *Biographical Sketches*, Johnson's *Yale and Her Honor-Roll*, Stanley Williams' article in the *Dictionary of American Biography*, Zunder's *The Early Days of Joel Barlow*, Stiles's *Literary Diary*, and Edward B. Coe's article on "The Literary Societies" in Kingsley's *Yale College* have all been useful. Further information has been derived from correspondence by and about Humphreys in the manuscript "Papers of the Continental Congress" in the Library of Congress and in the different editions of *The Writings of George Washington* by W. C. Ford, Jared Sparks, and John C. Fitzpatrick, and from *The Diaries of George Washington*, edited by Fitzpatrick (4 vols.; Boston, 1925).

CHAPTER V

The most meticulous biographical work on Joel Barlow is Theodore A. Zunder's *The Early Days of Joel Barlow*, which includes numerous transcripts of manuscripts that are accurate, except for occasional slips apparently caused by working from photostats. Charles B. Todd's *Life and Letters of Joel Barlow* (New York, 1886) contains more manuscript material but is far less accurate. For all the unpublished material included in the "Barlow Papers" in the Harvard College Library, however, this chapter makes use of the originals. The following have also been useful: Dexter's *Biographical Sketches;* Stokes's *Memorials;* Stiles's *Literary Diary;* Humphreys' *The Life and Times of David Dumphreys;* Ford's *Notes on the Life of Noah Webster;* Johnston's *Yale and Her Honor-Roll;* Moses C. Tyler's *Three Men of Letters* (New York, 1895); Moses Hill's *Genealogy of the Hill Family from 1632, Including a Biographical Sketch of Joel Barlow* (Norwalk, 1879); C. B. Todd's *The History of Redding, Connecticut* (New York, 1906); William E. Grumman's *The Revolutionary Soldiers of Redding, Connecticut, and the Record of Their Services* (Hartford, 1904); J. T. Headley's *The Chaplains and Clergy of the Revolution* (New York, 1864); Charles K. Bolton's *The Elizabeth Whitman Mystery* (Peabody, Mass., 1912); Caroline H. Dall's *The Romance of the Association, or One Last Glimpse of Charlotte Temple and Eliza Wharton* (Cambridge, 1875); Zunder's "Six Letters of Joel Barlow to Oliver Wolcott," *New England Quarterly,* II (July, 1929), 745–89, and "A New Barlow Poem," *American Literature,* XI (May, 1939), 206–9; Elihu H. Smith's anonymous "Account of Mr. Joel Barlow, an American Poet," *Monthly Magazine and British Register,* VI (1798), 250–51; and the files of the *American Mercury.*

Editions of other works quoted are: Cesare, Marchese de Beccaria-Bonesena, *An Essay on Crimes and Punishments* (Charlestown, S.C., 1777); William Blackstone, *Commentaries on the Laws of England* (4 vols.; Oxford, 1765); Jean J. Burlamaqui, *The Principles of Natural and Politic Law,* trans. Thomas Nugent (2 vols.; Cambridge, Mass., 1807); Garcilasso de la Vega, *The Royal Commentaries of Peru,* trans. Sir Paul Rycault (London, 1688); Henry Home, Lord Kames, *Sketches of the History of Man* (4 vols.; Edinburgh, 1774); Richard Price, *Observations on the Importance of the American Revolution, and the Means of Making It a Benefit to the World* (Boston, 1784); William Robertson, *The History of America* (2 vols.; London, 1777); Voltaire, *Essay on Epic Poetry,* ed. Florence D. White (Albany, 1915).

CHAPTER VI

The standard source of information about the activities of the Wits at this time is Luther G. Riggs's edition of the *Anarchiad* (New Haven, 1861); but that is incomplete in its factual account and inadequate in its estimate of the complexity of motives affecting the Hartford poets. The complicated relationship of state and federal finance, land speculation, and rival claims of militia and Continental soldiers has never been adequately studied. The treatment here makes use of details derived from contemporary newspapers and the following secondary sources and records: Charles Miner, *History of Wyoming* (Philadelphia, 1845); A. B. Hulbert, *The Records of the Original Proceedings of the Ohio Company* ("Marietta College Historical Collections," Vols. I–II [Marietta, 1917]); Albert S. Bolles, *The Financial History of the United States from 1774 to 1789* (New York, 1892); William G. Sumner, *The Financier and Finances of the American Revolution* (2 vols.; New York, 1891); Henry Bronson, "A Historical Account of Connecticut Currency, Continental Money, and the Finances of the Revolution," *Papers of the New Haven Colony Historical Society*, I (1865), 171 ff. (paged 1–191); *Records of the Connecticut State Society of the Cincinnati, 1783–1804* (Hartford, 1916); *Memoirs of the Massachusetts Society of the Cincinnati*, ed. Frank Smith (Boston, 1931).

The most detailed accounts of the popular uprisings and of the impression they made in Connecticut are to be found in the weekly newspaper reports and in George R. Minot's *The History of the Insurrections, in Massachusetts, in the Year MDCCLXXXVI, and the Rebellion Consequent Thereon* (Worcester, 1788); but Josiah G. Holland's *History of Western Massachusetts* (Springfield, 1855) has been valuable for its general survey, and some use has been made of Andrew M. Davis' "The Shays Rebellion: A Political Aftermath," *Proceedings of the American Antiquarian Society*, XVIII (April, 1911), 57–79, and John Noble, "A Few Notes on Shays' Rebellion," *Proceedings of the American Antiquarian Society*, XV (new ser.; October, 1902), 200–232. Identifications of individuals satirized are made on the basis of information derived from an extensive search of local histories; such standard reference works as Dexter's *Biographical Sketches*, Sprague's *Annals of the American Pulpit*, the *Dictionary of American Biography*, *Appleton's Cyclopaedia of American Biography*, the *National Cyclopaedia of American Biography;* and various miscellaneous works, including Benson J. Lossing, *The Pictorial Field Book of the Revolution* (2 vols.; New York, 1851), Bernard C. Steiner, "Connecticut's Ratification of the Federal Constitution," *Proceedings of the American Antiquarian Society*, XXV (April, 1915), 70–127, J. C. Hamilton, *History of the Republic* (7 vols.; Philadelphia, 1868), Thomas C. Cochran, *New York in the Confederation* (Philadelphia, 1932), Alexander C. Flick (ed.), *History of the State of New York* (10 vols.; New York, 1933–37), D. S. Alexander, *A Political History of the State of New York*, Vol. I (New York, 1906), E. W. Spalding, *New York in the Critical Period 1783–1789* (New York, 1932). R. J. Purcell's *Connecticut in Transition 1755–1818* (Washington, 1918), has been especially valuable for general background, as has William D. Love's *The Colonial History of Hartford* (Hartford, 1914), and, for some details, the same author's "The Navigation of the Connecticut River," *Proceedings of the American Antiquarian Society*, XV (new ser.; April, 1903), 385–441.

The most comprehensive treatments of the later wits are Marcia E. Bailey's *A Lesser Hartford Wit, Dr. Elihu Hubbard Smith, 1771–1798* ("University of Maine Studies," Ser. II, No. 11 [1928]) and Karl P. Harrington's *Richard Alsop* (Middletown, 1939). There is no satisfactory biography of Theodore Dwight; and Mason F. Cogswell does not even appear in the *Dictionary of American Biography*. The most detailed summary of Hopkins' career in print is Walter P. Steiner's "Dr. Lemuel Hopkins, One of the Celebrated Hartford Wits and a Forgotten, Distinguished American Student of Tuberculosis," *Johns Hopkins Hospital Bulletin*, XXI (January, 1910), 16–27, which should be supplemented by Howard W. Haggard's "The First Published Attack on Perkinism: An Anonymous Eighteenth Century Poetical Satire," *Yale Journal of Biology and Medicine*, IX (December, 1936), 137–53. John Trumbull's annotated copy of *The Echo, with Other Poems* (New York, 1807) and the

Hopkins manuscripts in the "Wolcott Papers" in the Connecticut Historical Society Library have been useful sources of information, as have the "Dwight Papers" and the "Cogswell Papers" in the New York Public Library and various Dwight and Cogswell manuscripts in the Yale University Library. The basic source for the brief summary given here, however, is the files of the *Connecticut Courant* and the *American Mercury*. Information concerning Trumbull's later career is found in the material listed in Section III of the Trumbull check list. Use has also been made of Leonard Chester's *Federalism Triumphant in the Steady Habits of Connecticut Alone, or, The Turnpike Road to a Fortune: A Comic Opera or Political Farce in Six Acts* [n.p., 1802].

CHAPTER VII

Most of the sources of information for this chapter have been given in the notes for chapter iii, but they should be supplemented by the later Timothy Dwight's *A Discourse in Commemoration of the Rev. Timothy Dwight . . . . Delivered on the Occasion of the One Hundred Fiftieth Anniversary of the Church at Greenfield Hill* (Southport, 1876); and particular attention should be called to the change in attitude reflected in Dwight's 1795 letter to Jonathan Ingersoll (quoted in Eben E. Beardsley, *The History of the Episcopal Church in Connecticut* [2 vols.; New York, 1865], II, 212) from the point of view somewhat acridly reported upon by Ezra Stiles in the early years of his pastorate and verified by the tenor of Jonathan Edwards' ordination sermon, *The Faithful Manifestation of Truth . . . .* (New Haven, [1783]). The identification of characters in *The Triumph of Infidelity* has been suggested with some guidance from Leonard Chester's malicious series of articles, "The Triumph of Infidelity Resuscitated," in the *American Mercury* from January 27 to April 7, 1803. Cuningham gives a full account of Dwight's personal and educational activities during this period.

CHAPTER VIII

Humphreys' later career is covered fairly thoroughly in Frank L. Humphreys' biography, and many details concerning his literary activities are given in the prefaces and appendixes of his own published works. Additional material is found in the following: the *Diaries* and *Writings* of Washington; Thomas Clark Pollock, *The Philadelphia Theatre in the Eighteenth Century* (Philadelphia, 1933); William G. Brooks, "Nathaniel Cutting's Journal of an Embassy to Algiers in 1793, under Col. David Humphreys," *Historical Magazine*, IV (September–December, 1860), 262–65, 296–98, 359–63; the collections of state papers noted in Section III of the Humphreys check list; and in the various collections of Barlow manuscripts. R. T. Gould gives a comprehensive account of the sea-serpent affair in *The Case for the Sea-Serpent* (London, 1930), based on the *Report of a Committee of the Linnaean Society* (Boston, 1817) and other contemporary reports, exclusive of Humphreys'. The manuscript of Trumbull's letter is in the Connecticut Historical Society Library, and the report on the salaries paid at Humphreysville is in Timothy Dwight's *Travels*.

CHAPTER IX

Four studies (in addition to Todd's *Life and Letters*) based upon original material deal with Barlow's later life: A. B. Hulbert's Introduction to *The Records of the Original Proceedings of the Ohio Company* contains what appears to be the best and most judicious survey of Barlow's part in the Scioto affair, though some additional information is contained in two earlier articles by the same author, "Andrew Craigie and the Scioto Associates," *Proceedings of the American Antiquarian Society*, XXIII (new ser.; October, 1913), 222–36, and "The Methods and Operations of the Scioto Group of Speculators," *Mississippi Valley Historical Review*, I (March, 1915), 502–15, and II (June, 1915), 56–73; and the account given in the *Life and Correspondence of Rev. Manasseh Cutler, LL.D.* (2 vols.; Cincinnati, 1888) should be taken into consideration. Victor C. Miller, *Joel Barlow: Revolutionist, London, 1791–92* (Hamburg, 1932), makes extensive use of official documents in English archives for the years indicated but comes to questionable conclusions. M. Ray Adams, "Joel Barlow, Political Romanticist," *American Literature*, IX (May, 1927), 113–52, is an excellent treatment of his life and writings during his first residence abroad. Leon Howard, "Joel Barlow and Napoleon," *Huntington Library Quarterly*, II (October, 1938), 37–51, supplements Todd on the Russian journey.

Original material listed in Section III of the Barlow check list, however, contains much information not used in the above studies and has been the major source of biographical detail, and especially for Barlow's reading and intellectual interests. The following also include various facts and opinions, sometimes conflicting, about Barlow: the several editions of Washington's *Writings*, and those of Jefferson, John Adams, and Madison; the *Historical Index to the Pickering Papers, Collections of the Massachusetts Historical Society*, Vol. VIII (6th ser.; Boston, 1896); Gouverneur Morris, *A Diary of the French Revolution* (2 vols.; Boston, 1939); Albert J. Beveridge, *The Life of John Marshall* (4 vols.; Boston, 1919); Francis Wharton, *State Trials of the United States during the Administrations of Washington and Adams* (Philadelphia, 1849); Alexander Stephens, *Memoirs of John Horne Tooke* (London, 1813); John G. Alger, *Glimpses of the French Revolution* (London, 1894); C. K. Paul, *William Godwin, His Friends and Contemporaries* (London, 1876); Thomas C. Rickman, *Life of Thomas Paine* (London, 1819); Moncure D. Conway, *The Life of Thomas Paine* (2 vols.; New York, 1892); Paine's Preface to *The Age of Reason, Part II* (London, 1795); *The Life and Times of David Humphreys*; "Letters of Abijah Biglow, Member of Congress, to His Wife, 1810–1815," *Proceedings of the American Antiquarian Society*, XL (new ser.; October, 1930), 305–406; and most of the contemporary periodicals consulted. Zunder's "Notes on the Friendship of Joel Barlow and Tom Paine," *American Book Collector*, VI (March, 1935), 96–99, should be supplemented by the letters on Paine noted in the check list; and his "Joel Barlow and George Washington," *Modern Language Notes*, XLIV (April, 1929), 254–56, by the Washington letter printed in facsimile in the *Catalogue of the American Art Association*, for March 11–12, 1936. For the relationship with Fulton see J. F. Reigart,

Life of Robert Fulton (Philadelphia, 1856); R. H. Thurston, *Robert Fulton* (New York, 1891); William B. Parsons, *Robert Fulton and the Submarine* (New York, 1922); Alice C. Sutcliffe, "Fulton's Invention of the Steamboat," *Century*, LXXVIII (September and October, 1909), 752–72 and 809–34. Cf. Fulton's own *Torpedo War and Submarine Explosions* (New York, 1810).

The difficulty in dealing with the intellectual influences upon Barlow during this period is mainly one of elimination and redaction, and perhaps no one can write with any degree of authority on that subject unless he has not only a thorough acquaintance with Barlow but a specialized knowledge of eighteenth-century French and English thought and a close knowledge of the individual members of intellectual circles in England, France, and—to some extent—Germany during the 1790's. Internal evidence that Barlow's closest affiliation was with the Baron d'Holbach (whose writings he knew as the compositions of Mirabaud and Boulanger) seems to be borne out by the notebooks and letters in the "Barlow Papers"; but the extent of direct indebtedness, as opposed to indirect influences through other Encyclopedists and such contemporaries as Condorcet and Volney, cannot be determined. Rousseau, of course, offered the greatest difficulty in elimination; but Barlow denied the main thesis of the *Contrat social* while possibly borrowing some commonplaces from it, and in his discussion of inequality he seems to have leaned upon the anonymous *Code de la nature, ou le véritable esprit de ses loix, de tout tems négligé ou méconnu* (Paris, 1755) rather than the *Discours sur l'origine et les fondements de l'inégalité parmi les hommes*. The former work (attributed to "Morelly" by Édouard Dolléans in his Paris, 1910, reprint), indeed, probably should have been considered in some detail with reference to Barlow's dalliance with the idea of communism and "distributive justice." In his proposals concerning education Barlow is much closer to Condorcet's *Rapport et projet de décret sur l'organisation générale de l'instruction publique* (which was presented to the National Assembly in April, 1792) than to *Émile*. Most of the investigation along these lines has had to be in the writings of authors mentioned in the text, but the following secondary sources have been particularly useful: Charles W. Hendel, *Jean-Jacques Rousseau, Moralist* (2 vols.; London, 1934); Harald Höffding, *Jean-Jacques Rousseau and His Philosophy*, trans. Richards and Saidla (New Haven, 1930); Ernest Hunter Wright, *The Meaning of Rousseau* (London, 1929); John Morley, *Diderot and the Encyclopaedists* (2 vols.; London, 1923); W. H. Wickwar, *Baron d'Holbach: A Prelude to the French Revolution* (London, 1935); F. K. Brown, *The Life of William Godwin* (London, 1926). F. de La Fontainerie has provided a convenient translation and edition of the writings of La Chalotais, Turgot, Diderot, and Condorcet and his *French Liberalism and Education in the Eighteenth Century* (New York, 1932), and Allen O. Hansen a survey of proposals for national education in America before Barlow in his *Liberalism and American Education in the Eighteenth Century* (New York, 1926). The *Encyclopédie* was used with Mouchon's *Table analytique et raisonnée* (2 vols.; Paris, 1780). Quotations in the text are from the Philadelphia, 1808, reprint of an anonymous translation of Holbach's *System of Nature, or the Laws of the Moral and Physical World* (2 vols.) and from Volney's *The Ruins, or a Survey of the*

Revolutions of Empires with *The Law of Nature, or Principles of Morality Deduced from the Physical Constitution of Mankind and the Universe* (London, 1857).

Grégoire's *Critical Observations on the Poem of Mr. Joel Barlow, The Columbiad* was printed in a pamphlet (Washington, 1809) and widely copied in periodicals; and Barlow's response called forth a second, conciliatory letter, which first appeared in the *National Intelligencer* for July 12, 1810. The suspicions of the *Panoplist* concerning Barlow are revealed in its "Remarks" on this correspondence in September, 1810, and in its belated review of the poem (December, 1813).

CHAPTER X

Purcell's *Connecticut in Transition* has been most valuable for a general survey of this period, and G. H. Hollister's *The History of Connecticut* (2 vols.; New Haven, 1855) for details concerning the state's attitude toward the war with England. Vernon Stauffer, *New England and the Bavarian Illuminati* ("Columbia University Studies in History, Economics and Public Law," Vol. LXXXII, No. I [New York, 1918]), gives a thoroughly detailed account of the excitement over "infidel plots," which is also treated in James K. Morse, *Jedidiah Morse: A Champion of New England Orthodoxy* (New York, 1939). Dwight was stimulated by the following: John Robison, *Proofs of a Conspiracy against All the Religions and Governments of Europe, Carried on in Secret Meetings of Free Masons, Illuminati, and Reading Societies* (Philadelphia, 1798); the Abbé Barruel, *Memoirs, Illustrating the History of Jacobinism*, trans. Robert Clifford (4 vols.; New York, 1798–99); Helen Maria Williams, *A Residence in France, during the years 1792, 1793, 1794, and 1795; Described in a Series of Letters from an English Lady; With General, and Incidental Remarks on the French Character and Manners* (New York, 1798); and, perhaps, *The Cannibal's Progress, or the Dreadful Horrors of French Invasion, As Displayed by the Republican Officers and Soldiers, in Their Perfidy, Rapacity, Ferociousness and Brutality, Exercised towards the Innocent Inhabitants of Germany*, trans. Anthony Aufrère (Hartford, 1798). Theodore Dwight expressed himself vehemently on two occasions: *An Oration, Spoken at Hartford, in the State of Connecticut, on the Anniversary of American Independence, July 4, 1798* (Hartford, 1798); *An Oration, Delivered at New-Haven on the 7th of July, A.D. 1801, before the Society of the Cincinnati* (Hartford, 1801). James C. Ogden attacked Dwight in *An Appeal to the Candid, upon the Present State of Religion and Politics in Connecticut* [n.p., 1796] and in *A view of the New England Illuminati* (Philadelphia, 1799). Isaac Hillard, speaking for the Separates, joined in the democratic chorus in several pamphlets, including *The Steady Habits of Connecticut, Versified* (Danbury, 1807). The outstanding collection of arguments on the approach of the millennium was David Austin's *The Millennium, or the Thousand Years of Prosperity, Promised to the Church of God, in the Old Testament and in the New, Shortly to Commence, and To Be Carried on to Perfection . . . .* (Elizabeth-Town, 1794).

In addition to the biographical notices mentioned in the notes to chapter iii, the following have been useful sources of information concerning Dwight's scientific interests and educational activities: Nathaniel Chauncey, *An*

Address Delivered before the New England Society of Philadelphia, on the Fourth of May, 1818 (Philadelphia, 1818); Denison Olmstead, "Timothy Dwight as a Teacher," *Barnard's American Journal of Education*, September, 1858; F. B. Dexter, "Student Life at Yale College under the First President Dwight (1795–1817)," *Proceedings of the American Antiquarian Society*, XXVII (new ser.; October, 1917), 318–335. The most valuable sources for details, however, are the *Decisions* and the student notebooks mentioned in Section III of the Dwight check list. The discussion of Dwight's innovations in theology has, on the whole, followed the account given in Williston Walker's *A History of the Congregational Churches in the United States* (New York, 1894); but consideration has been given to Frank H. Foster, "The Eschatology of the New England Divines," *Bibliotheca sacra*, XLIII (April, 1886), 287–303, and a number of reviews of *Theology: Explained and Defended;* and Sprague's *Annals of the American Pulpit* and various works of reference have been used. Cuningham's biography is excellent on Dwight's educational achievements but not on other aspects of his career.

INDEX

INDEX

[References to authors by works and by adjectives derived from their names or from their well-known works are indexed under the author's name. Thus, for example, *Paradise Lost* may be found under "Milton." References by pseudonym are indexed under the proper name followed by the pseudonym quoted in parentheses.]

Aberdeen, University of, 42

Adams, John, 38, 66, 71, 77, 128, 302, 303, 409

Adams, Samuel, 379

Addison, Joseph, 23, 26, 31, 40, 104, 105, 107, 177

Aeschylus, 383

Algiers, dey of, 300, 408

Allen, Ethan, 172, 173, 179, 212, 214, 218, 324, 379

Alsop, Richard, 201

American Magazine, 218

American Mercury, 160, 162, 173, 187, 188, 189, 201, 330

American Museum, 124, 209, 211, 219, 248

American Register, 322

Ames, William, 8, 22, 43, 49

Anarchiad ("American Antiquities"), 61, 180–200, 201, 203, 212, 219, 230, 241, 243–44, 262, 288; background of, 169–80

Anderson, Punderson, 15, 16

Anderson, Robert, 308

Andover Theological Seminary, 343

Arbuthnot, John, 23, 39, 219

Aristotle, 31, 108, 282

Arminianism, 207, 355, 359

Atheism, 308, 323, 324, 366; *see also* Holbach; Volney

Athenian Mercury, 24

Athenian Oracle, 24

Austin, David, 388

Babcock, Elisha, 77, 160, 161, 201, 330

Bacon, Francis, 23, 309, 315, 329, 381

Baldwin, Abraham, 140, 276, 300, 302, 303

Baldwin, Clara, 331

Baldwin, Ebenezer, 16, 19

Baldwin, Ruth; *see* Barlow, Ruth

Banks, Joseph, 267, 268

Barlow, Joel: student at Yale, 6, 20, 21–22, 24, 25, 29, 30, 32–33, 134, 135–36; soldier, 20, 32, 134; student in Hanover, 133; in Hartford, 134–35, 160–65, 169–200; in New Haven, 137–39, 140; in Northampton, 139–40; army chaplain, 140–58; in Algiers, 255, 300–301; in Europe, 271–300, 301–19, 326; in the United States, 272–73, 319–26, 327–36; minister to Napoleon, 273, 336–38

—referred to, 3, 4, 23, 27, 76, 117, 118, 119, 128, 170, 171, 173, 179, 187, 196, 197, 225, 245, 248, 368, 405, 407, 409

—works: burlesque of Chronicles, 21; early unpublished verses, 135–38, 141, 143–44; *The Prospect of Peace*, 136, 142; early newspaper verses, 137, 160; *The Vision of Columbus*, 138, 139–40, 141, 142, 144–59, 161, 162, 163, 164, 165, 198, 255, 256, 280, 290, 297, 306, 308, 309–13, 319; sermon on Arnold, 141; *A Poem, Spoken at the Public Com-*

mencement, 141–42, 152; An Elegy on
. . . . Hosmer, 144; edition of Watts's
Psalms, 160–61, 170, 355; bar dissertation, 163–64; collaboration in "American Antiquities," 187, 196, 197, and
passim; An Oration before the Cincinnati, 200; address to the National Assembly, 274–75; Advice to the Privileged Orders, 276–87, 288, 295–98, 311,
346, 367; The Conspiracy of Kings, 287–
88; editor of M'Fingal, 289; editor of
Brissot's Travels, 289–90; A Letter to
the National Convention, 290–93, 294;
A Letter . . . . to the People of Piedmont,
293–95; The Hasty Pudding, 295, 306;
contemplated history of the United
States, 300, 302, 327, 335; contemplated history of the French Revolution, 300–302; The Second Warning,
302; Letters from Paris, 303–5; The
Canal, 307, 308, 309, 331; the Columbiad, 309–26, 332, 334, 384, 407; translation of Volney's Ruins, 318; Letter to
Henry Gregoire, 324; Prospectus for a
National Institution, 328–29; later
newspaper verses, 330; "On the Discoveries of Captain Lewis," 331; Oration Delivered at Washington, July
Fourth, 1809, 332–33; letters on Paine,
334–35; Review of Robert Smith's Address, 335–36; "Advice to a Raven,"
338

Barlow, Ruth (Baldwin), 134, 141, 150,
274, 275, 289, 293, 296, 300–301, 302,
308, 326

Barlow, Samuel, 138

Barlow, Thomas, 337, 338

Barnum, Phineas T., 267–68

Barruel, abbé, 349

Bassano, duke of, 337

Bayle, Pierre, 308

Beardsley, Ebenezer, 215, 218

Beattie, James, 28, 29, 49–50, 56, 156–57,
229, 364

Beccaria-Bonesana, Cesare, marchese de,
113, 188, 189, 311, 326, 334

Beckwith, George, 65

Bellamy, Joseph, 42, 44, 58, 65, 214, 215,
388

Berkeley, George, 29, 49, 137

Berkeley scholarships, 7, 18

Bishop, Abraham, 321

Blackbourne, John, 23

Blackmore, Richard, 23, 84

Blackstone, William, 162, 163, 273, 286,
293

Blair, Hugh, 109

Blair, Robert, 51

Boehme, Jacob, 213

Boileau-Despréaux, Nicolas, 74

Bolingbroke, Henry St. John, viscount,
59, 213, 348

Boston Chronicle, 40–41

Botsford, Amos, 19

Boulanger, Nicolas, 286, 299, 315, 349

Boyle, Robert, 308, 325

Bradford, William and Thomas, 73

Brazil, prince (regent) of, 259, 408

Brindley, James, 307

Brissot de Warville, Jacques Pierre, 289,
290

British Critic, 349, 353

Brooke, Henry, 65

Browne, Isaac Hawkins, 220

Browne, Sir Thomas, 23

Bryant, Jacob, 309, 315

Buckminster, Joseph, 137, 138

Buffon, G. L. L., comte de, 195

Bulkeley, Ann Frances, 241

Bunyan, John, 39

Burgoyne, John, 76, 143, 144

Burke, Aedanus, 189, 195

Burke, Edmund, 276, 278, 286, 287, 338

Burlamaqui, Jean Jacques, 162, 163, 164,
273, 286

Burr, Aaron, 386

Bushnell, David, 272

Butler, Samuel, 23, 24, 40, 52, 54, 70, 71,
73, 75

Byron, George Gordon, Lord, 205, 393,
395, 406

Camoëns, Luis Vaz de, 146

Campbell, Roy, 406

Canning, George, 393

Carew, Thomas, 136

Carey, Mathew, 124, 125, 159, 211, 219, 248, 250

Cervantes, Miguel de, 23

Charles I (of England), 74

Charles II (of England), 83, 213

Charles IV (of Spain), 255

Chastellux, marquis de, 71, 124, 132, 246

Chaucer, Geoffrey, 23

Chauncy, Charles, 215, 216, 218

Cheetham, James, 334, 335

Chester, Leonard, 181, 184, 203, 216–17

Chesterfield, Philip Stanhope, Lord, 102, 104, 230

Chubb, Thomas, 213

Churchill, Charles, 25, 40, 54, 199, 406

Cicero, 6, 31, 114, 287

Cincinnati, Society of the, 165, 175–76, 182, 183, 189, 191, 195, 197, 200, 234, 247, 261

Clap, Thomas, 6, 7, 9, 10, 14–17, 23, 26, 30, 46, 82, 83, 364

Clark, William, 321, 395

Claudian, 40

Clinton, George, 191, 193, 196

Clive, Robert, 393

Cogswell, Mason W., 201

Coke, Edward, 66

Coleridge, Samuel Taylor, 204, 308

Collins, Anthony, 213

Collins, John, 186

Colquhoun, Patrick, 393

Columbus, Christopher, 146; *see also under* Barlow

Commerce, cultural effects of, 101, 153–54, 256, 297–98, 316

Common sense, Scottish philosophy of, 43, 157–58, 164, 227, 234, 274, 280, 281, 283–84, 298, 309, 313, 315, 339, 340, 346, 361, 362–63; *see also* Beattie; Kames; Reid; Stewart

Communism, 284, 285, 298, 366

Condorcet, marquis de, 279, 349

Connecticut Courant, 70, 77, 170, 176, 179, 181, 182, 185, 187, 189, 191, 192, 196, 201, 202, 205, 330

Connecticut Journal and New-Haven Post-Boy, 41, 60–63, 82, 114, 183

Conrad, C. and A., and Company, 321, 322

Conrad, Lucas, and Company, 321

Copernicus, Nicolaus, 315

Corneille, Pierre, 383

Cornwallis, Charles, 101, 113

Cowley, Abraham, 23, 84

Cowper, William, 88, 229, 231, 238, 307, 311

Crabbe, George, 204

Creech, Thomas, 23, 308

Cumberland, Richard, 30

Cunningham, Thomas, 287, 297

Cutler, Manasseh, 271

Cyrus the Great, 139

Daggett, Naphtali, 7, 10, 16, 17, 19, 21, 22, 30, 93, 134, 235

D'Alembert, J. le Rond, 348, 349

Dalrymple, David, 72

Dana, James, 215, 217

Dante Alighieri, 199

Dartmouth College, 133

Darwin, Erasmus, 307, 309, 310, 313

Dassouci, 74

D'Auberteul, Michel René Hilliard, 195

Davy, Humphrey, 266

Day, Luke, 178, 181

Deane, Silas, 69, 73, 83

De Hart, lieutenant, 117

Deism, 28, 48, 53, 64, 211–12, 213, 214, 348, 370, 378, 379

Démeunier, Jean Nicolas, 195

Denham, John, 23

Descartes, René, 29, 156, 308, 315

Diderot, Denis, 279, 349

Dilworth, Thomas, 223

Donne, John, 25

Dryden, John, 23, 39, 86, 118, 143, 218, 307

Du Bartas, Guillaume de Salluste, 23, 84

Duer, William, 271

Dunning, Tertius, 187, 188

Du Pont de Nemours, Pierre Samuel, 329

Dupuis, Charles François, 309, 314, 315

Dwight, Nathaniel, 201

Dwight, Theodore, 81, 201, 203, 351, 391

Dwight, Timothy: student at Yale, 13, 15, 17–18, 19, 24, 25–30, 32–33, 79, 81–83; tutor, 20, 21, 53, 79–81, 83–97, 98–99; army chaplain, 81, 97, 99, 100; at Northampton, 81, 101–2; at Greenfield, 81, 103–11, 206–38, 354, 399; president of Yale, 207, 342–401

—referred to, 3, 4, 27, 68, 112, 115, 116, 118, 120, 124, 128, 133, 136, 139, 140, 142, 143, 147, 150, 151, 187, 201, 245, 248, 250, 257, 275, 303, 310, 312, 325, 405, 406, 407, 409

—works: possible contributions to "The Meddler" and "The Correspondent," 40, 44, 81–82; other early contributions to newspapers, 82, 208–12; *America*, 83–84, 136; "Song," 84; "The Trial of Faith," 84; "The Message of Mordecai to Esther," 84, 85; *The Conquest of Canäan*, 84, 87–98, 99–100, 108, 109, 110, 139, 155, 161, 199, 208, 232, 237, 308, 372; *A Dissertation*, 85–86, 88, 213; *A Valedictory Address*, 98, 99, 100; *A Sermon, Preached at Stamford*, 100; "Columbia, Columbia," 100, 248; *A Sermon, Preached at Northampton*, 101–2, 104, 142; "The Critics," 103; "Epistle to Col. Humphreys," 104, 224, 248; "The Friend," 104–10, 111, 206, 210, 222, 233, 384, 399; "Address of the Genius of Columbia," 209; *The Triumph of Infidelity*, 212–220, 230, 237, 354; *Greenfield Hill*, 220–30, 237, 346, 399; "A Hymn," 230; "The Seasons Moralized," 230; lost poetic debate between Genius and Common Sense, 230, 384, 398–99; "The Dignity and Excellence of the Gospel," 231–32; *Virtuous Rulers*, 232; *A Discourse on .... the New Testament*, 232–33, 234; *The True Means of Establishing Public Happiness*, 234, 235–37, 345–46; *Travels*, 344, 360, 371–84, 396, 397, 398; *The Nature and Danger of Infidel Philosophy*, 348–49, 358; *The Duty of Americans*, 350–51; *A Discourse .... on Washington*, 352; *A Discourse on .... the Last Century*, 352–54; edition of Watts's Psalms, 355; *Theology*, 355–71,

384, 386, 396, 397, 400; *Sermons* (1828), 375, 384–85, 386, 400; "Lectures on .... Revelation," 385, 396; "The Manner in Which the Scriptures Are To Be Understood," 385, 396; miscellaneous later sermons, 385–86, 387; *A Discourse in Two Parts*, 389–91; *Remarks on the Review of Inchiquin's Letters*, 392–96; *A Statistical Account*, 396; "Observations on Language," 396–97; "On Light," 397; *An Address to the Emigrants*, 397–98; *Notes on Decisions*, 399; *Essay on the Stage* (spurious), 400

Dyer, John, 229

Ebeling, Christoph Daniel, 298

Echo, 183, 201, 204

Edinburgh Review, 322, 323, 326, 393, 394, 395

Education: reforms of, 45–57, 48–49, 55–56; of women, 63–64, 207; national, 266, 327–29, 333

Edwards, Jonathan (the elder), 9, 11, 12, 22, 28, 29, 46, 49, 80, 85, 101, 111, 213, 217, 235, 277, 278, 285, 355, 356, 359, 361, 363, 364, 365, 369, 381, 388, 408

Edwards, Jonathan (the younger), 85, 101, 214–15, 216, 217, 218

Edwards, Pierrepont, 203, 218

Eliot, T. S., 25

Ely, Samuel, 178, 181

Emerson, Ralph Waldo, 407

Emmons, Nathanael, 358, 362, 363

Emmons, Richard, 326

Encyclopaedia Britannica, 308

Encyclopédie, 308

Encyclopédie méthodique, 195

Equality, 258, 280–82, 285, 319

Erasmus, Desiderius, 31

Ercilla, Alonzo de, 146, 147

Euripides, 383

Fellows, John, 298, 299, 303

Fénelon, François, 23, 87, 92, 97, 312; *see also* Ramsay, Andrew

Fielding, Henry, 400

Fitch, Jonathan, 21

Flint, Royal, 271

Fontenelle, Bernard le Bovier de, 24
Franklin, Benjamin, 128, 225, 266, 320
Fraser, James, 309
Frederick II (of Prussia), 349
Freeman's Chronicle, 77
French, Moses, 178
Freneau, Philip, 70, 73, 230
Frontier, 121–22, 224, 261–62, 266, 304,
    330–31, 360, 374–77, 397–98, 409; *see
    also* Western lands
Frost, John, 293
Fry and Kammerer, 321
Fulton, Robert, 272, 306, 307, 309, 321,
    322, 323, 329, 331, 333, 335, 336, 348

Gage, Thomas, 69, 70, 72
Gaillard, Gabriel, 287
Gale, Benjamin, 181
Galileo Galilei, 315
Gama, Vasco da, 146
Garth, Samuel, 23
Gay, John, 23, 24, 39, 65, 229
Genin, Thomas Hedges, 326
George III (of England), 74, 241
Gerry, Elbridge, 196
Gibbon, Edward, 277, 311
Gifford, William, 243, 262, 263
Gillies, John, 308
Godwin, William, 277, 285, 364, 365–66,
    379
Goldsmith, Oliver, 25, 68–69, 223, 224,
    229, 238
Goodman, Thomas, 181
Goodrich, Samuel G., 205
Goodwin, Henry, 186, 187
Gray, Thomas, 25, 51, 52, 86, 117, 130,
    138, 144, 254
Green, Jacob, 65
Greene, Nathanael, 113, 116, 117, 119,
    122, 126, 140, 189, 190
Greene, Mrs. Nathanael, 250
Grégoire, Henri, 323–26
Gresham College, 31
Griswold, Roger, 389

Guérin du Rocher, 309, 315
Guthrie, William, 22

Haley, William, 146, 308
Halfway covenant, 58, 207, 215, 363
Hamilton, Alexander, 194, 251, 269, 304,
    322, 386
Harrison, William Henry, 393
Hartley, David, 279
Harvard College, 57, 69
Hawthorne, Nathaniel, 113, 373
Helvetius, Claude Adrien, 277, 279
Henry, Prince (of Portugal), the Navi-
    gator, 252
Henry IV (of France), 304
Herbert, Edward, of Cherbury, 213, 379
Herrick, Robert, 84
Herschel, William, 315
Hichborn, colonel, 190
Hillhouse, James, 192
Hobbes, Thomas, 308
Holbach, Paul H. D., baron d', 279–80,
    281, 286, 296, 299, 311, 313, 318, 324,
    340, 349, 379, 408
Holmes, John, 22, 71
Homer, 7, 18, 23, 45, 75, 85, 90, 91, 92,
    108, 145, 147, 198, 199, 223, 254, 307,
    311, 312
Hopkins Grammar School, 25, 79
Hopkins, Joseph ("Joseph Copper"), 176,
    177, 181, 183, 185, 188, 189, 192
Hopkins, Lemuel, 3, 160, 169–71, 173,
    179–80, 182, 183, 196, 197, 200–202,
    302
Hopkins, Samuel, 44, 58, 65, 214, 362, 363
Horace, 6, 7, 23, 81, 104, 114, 223, 229
Horne, George, 348, 358
Hosmer, Titus, 144
Howe, Joseph, 20, 21, 53, 67
Hubbard, Sarah, 38
Hughes, John, 23, 24
Humanitarianism, 162–64, 250–51, 253,
    274, 281, 282–83, 284, 285, 289, 292–93,
    318, 340; *see also* Beccaria; Slavery
Hume, David, 29, 49, 59, 102, 156, 213,
    348, 358, 379

Humphreys, David: student at Yale, 18, 19, 22, 24, 25, 31–33, 112, 114–15; at Wethersfield, 65, 112–13; tutor at Philipse Manor, 113; later residence in Connecticut, 113, 131, 169–96; army officer, 113–23; in Europe, 113–23; at Mount Vernon and in Philadelphia, 132, 196, 243–48; minister to Portugal, 241, 249–52; minister to Spain, 241–42, 249–52; later years, 242–43, 255–68

—referred to, 3, 4, 27, 104, 133, 140, 141, 143, 171, 178, 179, 180, 182, 185, 195, 200, 219, 268–70, 288, 300, 333, 405, 409

—works: early writings, 114–15; *Miscellaneous Works* (1804), 115, 255–61; sonnets, 115–16, 258–59; "Elegy on the Burning of Fairfield," 117; "Elegy on Lieutenant De Hart," 117; "An Epitaph," 118; "An Epithalamium," 118; "An Impromptu," 118; "An Ode Addressed to Laura," 118; "A Letter to a Young Lady," 118, 123; "The Shepherd: A Song," 119; *A Poem Addressed to the Armies*, 119–23, 124, 125, 130, 248; "An Epistle to Dr. Dwight," 123, 248; *A Poem, On the Happiness of America*, 125–31, 185, 198, 221, 247, 249, 256; "A Poem on the Future Glory of the United States," 129, 256; "The Conduct of General Washington," 132, 185; "Mount Vernon," 178, 185; collaboration in "American Antiquities," 183, 186, 187, 192, 197, 199, and *passim;* "The Genius of America," 190; "The Monkey Who Shaved Himself," 191; *An Essay on . . . . Putnam*, 243–45, 247, 248; *The Widow of Malabar*, 246–47, 248, 256, 264; *Miscellaneous Works* (1790), 247, 248; *An Oration*, 247, 248, 249; Prologue and Epilogue, 247, 248, 256; *Poems* (1789), 248; *The Yankey in England*, 250, 262–65; *A Poem on Industry*, 250–52, 255, 257, 259; *A Poem on the Love of Country*, 253, 255; *A Poem on the Death of General Washington*, 254; "Thoughts on . . . . a Navy," 259–60; "A Memorial to . . . . the Cincinnati," 261; *A Valedictory Discourse*, 261–62; *A Discourse on the Agriculture*, 266; "The Farmer's Harvest Hymn,"

266; *Letters [on] . . . . the Serpent of the Ocean*, 267–68

Humphreys, John, 131

Hunter, Thomas, 102

Huntington, Enoch, 79

Hutton, James, 313

Hypotheses, 282, 285, 347, 368–89, 391

Indians, 83, 95–96, 121, 148–49, 150, 360, 361, 367, 372, 375–76

Ingersoll, Charles J., 385, 392

Illuminati, the, 325, 349–51, 389

Jay, John, 125, 409

Jefferson, Thomas, 128, 195, 211, 241, 255, 269, 272, 274, 281, 290, 292, 300, 302, 305, 327, 331, 332, 333, 335, 339, 354, 379, 395, 396, 408, 409

Jeffrey, Francis, 323, 393, 395

Jenner, Edward, 380–81

Johns Hopkins University, 273, 329

Johnson, Diodate, 15, 16

Johnson, Joseph, 276, 295, 299

Johnson, Samuel, 64, 72, 104, 117, 244

Jones, Ira, 187, 188

Jones, Samuel, 193, 196

Jonson, Ben, 23, 24

Jordan, J. S., 290

Josephine, empress (of France), 337, 408

Juvenal, 23, 64, 287

Kames, Henry Home, lord, 26–27, 29, 47–49, 55, 56, 86, 91, 92, 95–98, 108, 109, 110, 115, 120, 142, 149, 151, 152, 157, 204, 213, 222, 310, 362, 363

Kant, Immanuel, 299, 354

Keats, John, 405

Kepler, Johannes, 315

Klopstock, Friedrich Gottlieb, 299

Kotzebue, August F. F. von, 254, 383

Lafayette, marquis de, 159, 288, 289

Lamarck, chevalier de, 346

Lamb, John, 223

Lambert, John, 378

Lane, Job, 17

Lansdown, George Granville, lord, 23
Lardner, Nathaniel, 233
La Rochefoucauld-Liancourt, F. A. F., duc de, 248, 255, 378
Laud, William, archbishop, 74, 83
Lear, Tobias, 250
Ledyard, Isaac, 214
Lee, captain, 267
Lee, Richard Henry, 196
Leland, John, 213, 348
Lemierre, Antoine Marin, 246
Lewis, Meriwether, 331, 395
Lincoln, Abraham, 292
Lincoln, Benjamin, 190
Linguet, S. N. H., 195
Littlebury and Boyer, 23, 87
Livingston, John Henry, 217
Locke, John, 8–9, 27, 29, 46, 49, 154, 157, 234, 235, 286, 291, 352, 361, 397, 406
Lockwood, James, 17
Louis I (of Etruria), 255
Louis XVI (of France), 122, 158–59, 241, 290, 309, 318
Lowell, James Russell, 268, 269
Lowth, Robert, 22, 68, 85
Lucian, 7
Lucretius, 307, 308, 313
Lyman, Jonathan, 15
Lyman, Joseph, 19, 217
Lyon, Matthew, 303

Mably, G. Bonnot de, 195
McGillivray, Alexander, 241
Macpherson, James, 71, 199
Madison, James, 273, 286, 335, 336, 339, 389, 392, 395, 396, 408
Madison, Mrs. James, 323
Man, nature of, 46, 154–58, 162–64, 210, 226–27, 231, 278–83, 296–97, 304, 314, 322–23, 346–47, 358, 361, 363, 367–68, 370–71, 374–77; see also Kames; Locke
Manilius, 309
Marmontel, Jean-François, 149
Marshall, John, 132, 327

Martin, Benjamin, 7–8, 49
Mason, George, 196
Mason, John, 227
Mason, William, 68, 220
Massachusetts Centinel, 188
Materialism, 155–56, 213, 214, 280, 281, 293, 296–97, 311, 314, 324, 332–33, 340–41, 347, 378–79
Meigs, Josiah, 176, 177, 179, 180, 182, 186, 325
Memoirs of the Connecticut Academy of Arts and Sciences, 385, 396, 397
Mercier, Louis Sebastien, 297
Middle-class society of America, 126, 127, 223, 257, 275, 368, 376, 394
Millennium, 83, 102, 136, 151, 317, 387–89, 392, 398
Milton, John, 23, 24, 31, 39, 51, 52, 53, 67, 75, 84, 87, 89, 91, 92, 100, 108, 116, 130, 138, 145, 147, 173, 198, 199, 205, 229, 253, 312, 406, 407, 409
Mirabaud, Jean Baptiste de, 279
Mirabeau, H. G. R., comte de, 195
Mitchell, Stephen Mix, 17, 18, 40, 45, 193
Monroe, James, 336
Montaigne, Michel de, 23
Montesquieu, C. L. de S., baron de, 101, 162, 163, 164, 273, 286
Monthly Anthology and Boston Review, 323
Monthly Magazine, 322
Moore, Edward, 65, 229
Moore, Thomas, 204, 205
Morgan, Thomas, 243
Morning Herald, 179
Morris, Robert, 195
Morse, Jedidiah, 227, 308, 350
Motte's Miscellanies, 23, 39, 42, 135
Murray, John, 62, 216, 218

Napoleon Bonaparte, 3, 254, 273, 305, 318, 326, 336, 337, 338, 339, 392, 393, 397
National Intelligencer, 335
Neal, Daniel, 227

Necker, Jacques, 297, 302
New Divinity (New Light), 9, 14, 27–28, 42, 45, 62, 63, 64, 101, 207, 214, 215, 218, 231, 356; see also Bellamy; Jonathan Edwards (elder and younger); Nathanael Emmons; Samuel Hopkins
New-England Palladium, 204
New Haven Gazette and the Connecticut Magazine, 104, 132, 176, 177, 181, 183, 184, 185, 186, 188, 189, 208, 210
New London Gazette, 192
New York Weekly Magazine, 295
Newton, Isaac, 80, 214, 315, 340, 397

Ogden, James C., 343, 351
Oglethorpe, James, 83
Oldham, John, 23
Origen, 216
Otway, Thomas, 23
Ovid, 23, 307
Owen, Daniel, 186

Page (of western Massachusetts), 190
Paine, Thomas, 73, 162, 275, 276, 277, 286, 290, 297, 299, 302, 324, 334–35, 379
Paley, William, 235, 352, 361, 364, 365
Panoplist, 325, 385
Parker (of western Massachusetts), 190
Parnell, Thomas, 84
Parsons, Samuel H., 81, 100, 113, 119, 126, 182, 183, 184, 185, 191, 192
Penn, William, 83
Perfectibility (of man), 164, 228, 260, 278, 287, 304, 307, 317–18, 324, 366, 368; see also Progress; Society, renovation of
Perkins, Elisha, 202
Peters, Samuel, 195, 243
Philadelphia Portfolio, 322
Phillips, Edward, 295
Philosophy (speculative), attacks on, 211, 231, 253, 345–54, 360, 378–80, 382; see also Reason, limitations of; Illuminati
Pike, Zebulon M., 395
Pindar, 86, 307
Plato, 10

Playfair, John, 313
Playfair, William, 313
Plutarch, 244
Pope, Alexander, 23, 24, 25, 39, 45, 50, 51, 64, 68, 82, 83, 84, 90, 92, 93, 99, 103, 104, 114, 130, 135, 138, 145, 153, 154–56, 198, 199, 204, 212, 218, 219, 220, 223, 224, 229, 246, 253, 287, 313, 406, 407, 409
Portugal, prince regent of, 255; see also Brazil, prince of
Price, Richard, 153–54, 162, 274, 276
Priestley, Joseph, 213, 218, 278, 286, 348
Prime, Benjamin Young, 137
Princeton College, 124
Prior, Matthew, 23, 40, 54, 84
Progress: conceptions of, 29–30, 101–2, 131, 142, 149, 151–54, 164, 180, 200, 210, 224, 228–29, 313–18, 352, 382, 398 (see also Millennium; Perfectibility; Society, renovation of); reactions against idea of, 107–8, 209, 230–37; see also "Things as they are"
Proust, Marcel, 292
Putnam, Israel, 113, 116, 119, 126, 243, 244, 245

Quarterly Review, 263, 385, 392, 393, 395
Quintilian, 31

Racine, Jean, 247
Raleigh Register, 334–35
Ramsay, Andrew, 87, 88, 89
Ramsay, David, 243
Reason, limitations of, 42–43, 48–50, 55–56, 60, 155–57, 362; see also Philosophy
Redwood, Martha, 118
Reid, Thomas, 361, 364
Rhetoric, 30–32, 51, 71, 117, 120–22, 124, 126–29, 130–31, 220, 247, 249, 258, 262, 269, 288, 342, 386–87
Richardson, Samuel, 382, 400
Richelieu, cardinal, 297
Robertson, William, 140, 148, 149, 150, 152, 195, 301
Robison, John, 349

Rochester, John Wilmot, earl of, 59

Rogers, Robert, 245

Rolliad, 179, 198, 406

Rousseau, Jean Jacques, 277, 279, 281, 286, 287, 305, 348, 349

Rowe, Nicholas, 23

Rush, Benjamin, 202, 329

Rycault, Paul, 23, 148

St. John, Buckingham, 51, 52

Scammel, Alexander, 118

Scarron, Paul, 74

Schiller, J. C. F. von, 383

Science, interest in, 7–8, 19, 26, 266, 308, 313, 315, 342–43, 380–81, 397; *see also* Hypotheses

Shaftesbury, Anthony Ashley Cooper, earl of, 23, 213, 218, 348

Shakespeare, William, 3, 23, 108, 259, 383, 400

Shattuck, Job, 178, 180, 190

Shaw, George Bernard, 375

Shays, Daniel, 77, 178, 180, 188, 189, 190

Shelley, Percy Bysshe, 405

Shenstone, William, 25, 51–52, 117, 118, 138, 331

Sinclair, John, 297

Skelton, Philip, 348

Skipwith, Fulwar, 305

Slavery, Negro, 44, 223, 251, 331, 390

Smalley, John, 65

Smirke, Robert, 321

Smith, Adam, 297, 348

Smith, David, 183

Smith, Elihu H., 84, 201

Smith, Robert, 335

Smith, Samuel, 329

Smithsonian Institution, 329

Society, renovation of, 164, 275–85, 315; *see also* Millennium; Perfectibility; Progress

Socinus, 213

Sophocles, 383

Southey, Robert, 204, 308, 310, 330, 392

Spenser, Edmund, 23, 24, 40, 115, 116, 229, 230, 259, 398

Spinoza, Baruch, 308, 363

Spring, Gardner, 386

Stadtholder, 241

Steele, Richard, 23, 30, 41; *see also* Addison, Joseph

Sterne, Laurence, 49, 64

Stewart, Dugald, 361

Stiles, Ezra, 15, 16, 22, 28, 30, 99, 116, 119, 165, 206, 213, 214, 215, 218, 219, 234, 299

Stoughton, Israel, 227

Strong, Nehemiah, 19, 30

Sullivan, James, 329

Swift, Jonathan, 23, 25, 39, 40, 43, 44, 45, 50, 51, 53, 54, 64, 77, 78, 135, 176, 188, 219, 406

Sykes, William Henry, 393

Target, Gui Jean Baptiste, 195

Tasso, Torquato, 199

Tatham, Edward, 286, 297

Temple, William, 24

"Things as they are," 111, 221, 230, 378, 380, 383, 385, 400; *see also* Wollaston

Thomson, James, 25, 39, 127, 130, 136, 222, 229, 308, 406

Tillotson, John, 216

Tindal, Matthew, 213

Toland, John, 213, 308

Trumbull, Benjamin, 217

Trumbull, Rev. John, 37

Trumbull, Colonel John, 176

Trumbull, John: student at Yale, 5, 7, 13, 15, 16, 18, 24, 25, 30, 32–33, 37, 48; tutor at Yale, 20, 51–65; treasurer of Yale, 21; in Hartford, 38, 169–96, 202–5; in Wethersfield, 48–51, 55, 114; law student in Boston, 66–73; in Detroit, 205

—referred to, 3, 4, 27, 77–78, 79, 81, 84, 86, 87, 92, 99, 112, 114, 115, 116, 118, 119, 120, 128, 133, 136, 142, 143, 144, 160, 165, 170, 171, 180, 187, 196, 197, 202, 213, 241, 303, 383, 406, 407

—works: early unpublished poems, 39–40; "Epithalamium," 40, 45, 143, 182; "The Meddler," 40–41, 42, 81, 105; "The Correspondent," 41–45, 54, 60–64, 66, 82, 107, 114, 169, 179, 204, 214; "Prospect of the Future Glory of America," 45; translation from the *Georgics*, 45; *Poetical Works*, 45, 76, 205; *Essay on . . . . Fine Arts*, 45–48, 55, 56, 86, 136; "A Critical Dissertation," 48; "Speculative Essays," 48–50, 53, 56, 154, 157; "Epistle," 50; verse letter to Humphreys, 50; "Advice to Ladies," 50, 51; *An Elegy on . . . . St. John*, 51–52; "On the Vanity of Youthful Expectations," 52, 78; fragment of a novel, 53–54, 64–65; *The Progress of Dulness*, 53–60, 65, 66, 69, 76, 204; "To My Good Catechist," 60; "The Owl and the Sparrow" and other miscellaneous verse, 65; "Ode to Sleep," 67; *M'Fingal*, 67, 70–77, 103, 143, 179, 182, 195, 199, 203, 289, 290; biblical paraphrases, 67–68; "An Elegy on the Times," 68–69; epigram, 69; "To a Young Lady," 69; "A New Proclamation," 70; critical essays, 73; "The Genius of America," 76; collaboration in "American Antiquities," 182, 183, 191, and *passim*; unpublished satire, 203; *Biographical Sketch*, 204; later criticism, 204–5; last New Year's verses, 205; Prologue and Epilogue, 246

Trumbull, Governor Jonathan (the elder), 169, 175, 177

Trumbull, Governor Jonathan (the younger), 260, 385

Trumbull, Sarah Hubbard, 38

Tryon, William, 117, 191

Turgot, A. R. J., 153

Turkish Spy, The, 24

Tyler, Royall, 264, 265

Utilitarianism, 274, 317, 364–66

Vanderlyn, John, 312

Vaughan, William, 24

Vega, Garcilasso de la, 24, 148, 150

"Versifier, The," 201

Vincent, Thomas, 22

Virgil, 6, 23, 45, 75, 85, 91, 92, 145, 198, 199, 223, 229, 307, 311

Volney, C. F. C., comte de, 278, 279, 281, 286, 296, 309, 314, 315, 318, 348, 378, 407

Voltaire, F. M. Arouet de, 59, 102, 104, 146–47, 149, 152, 156–57, 213, 286, 348, 349, 379

Wadsworth, James ("Wronghead"), 181, 189, 190, 191, 196, 198, 199

Wadsworth, Jeremiah, 116, 119, 171, 179, 180, 182, 193, 242, 244

Waldo, Albigence, 244, 245

Waller, Edmund, 23

Waltersdorff, general, 337

Ward, John, 31–32, 120–22, 130–31

Washington, George, 20, 113, 114, 118, 121, 122, 123, 124, 125, 126, 128, 132, 141, 159, 177, 182, 186, 189, 190, 192, 195, 196, 202, 242, 243, 244, 250, 254, 255, 259, 260, 302, 303, 305, 312, 327, 352, 408

Watts, Isaac, 8, 24, 38, 39, 135, 160, 161, 170, 355

Webb, Samuel B., 114, 115

Webster, Noah, 20, 76, 93, 110, 138, 160, 161, 179, 180, 204, 218, 219, 273, 320, 322, 323, 326, 328, 329, 397

Weems, Mason, 132, 245

Weld, Isaac, 378

Welles, Jonathan, 30

West, Benjamin, 306

West, Gilbert, 307

West, Stephen, 65

Western lands, 119, 121–22, 127, 171–77, 182, 271, 274, 330–31; *see also* Frontier

Wetenhall, Edward, 6

Wheelock, Eleazar, 18, 133

Whitaker, Nathaniel, 65

White, Ebenezer, 15

White, Phineas, 41

Whitefield, George, 42, 357

Whitman, Elizabeth, 137, 138

Whitman, Walt, 311, 406, 407

Whittelsey, Chauncy, 16, 28

Williams, Helen Maria, 350

Williams, William ("William Wimble"), 175, 176, 177, 181, 182, 183, 184, 185, 188, 189, 191, 192, 199

Winthrop, John, 350

Wolcot, John ("Peter Pindar")

Wolcott, Oliver (the elder), 192

Wolcott, Oliver, Jr., 170, 179, 241

Wolcott, Roger, 24, 84

Wollaston, William, 10–13, 26, 48, 400

Wollebius, Johannes, 8, 22

Wollstonecraft, Mary, 275, 276, 286

Woodhull, Richard, 7, 15

Woolston, Thomas, 213

Wordsworth, William, 4, 204, 249, 269, 295, 311, 405

Wycherley, William, 23

Xenophon, 139

Yale College: referred to, 3–5, 32–33, 51, 52, 115, 119, 154, 218, 219, 234, 257, 273, 280, 338; physical appearance, 5–6, 20; curriculum, 6–13, 22, 73, 235, 242–43, 352; conditions of study at, 14–22; library of, 22–25; intellectual environment of, 25–30; literary societies of, 30–32, 112; *see also under* Barlow; Dwight; Humphreys; Trumbull

Yates, Abraham, 193, 196

Young, Edward, 64, 84

Zend-Avesta, the, 309

Zoilus, 108